THEY FOUGHT FOR
KING AND KAISER

JAMES
AMBROSE BROWN
THEY FOUGHT FOR
KING AND KAISER

SOUTH AFRICANS
IN GERMAN EAST AFRICA
1916

ASHANTI PUBLISHING
(PTY) LIMITED
JOHANNESBURG

Published by Ashanti Publishing (Pty) Ltd
A Division of Ashanti International Films
P.O. Box 10021
Rivonia 2128

ISBN   1 874800 32 4   Standard Edition
        1 874800 33 2   Collector's Edition
        1 874800 34 0   Limited de Luxe Edition

© James Ambrose Brown
© Richard Wood
First published 1991

End-paper photograph of 13-pounder gun on three wheels and a tree-trunk, in the Kilimanjaro column. (From: *The Great War*, issue 107, 2 September 1916)

Book Design: Photoprints, Cape Town
Typeset by Photoprints
Printed by CTP Book Printers, Cape Town

BK2542

On 6 February 1916 South Africa's famous leader Lieutenant-General Jan Christiaan Smuts became Commander-in-Chief of the forces in East Africa. In January 1917 he was formally ordered to hand over his command to Major-General A R Hoskins and left for London. He had crossed the Rufiji River and captured all important towns, the whole of the railway system and all the seaboard. Immense difficulties were left to be faced by his successors.

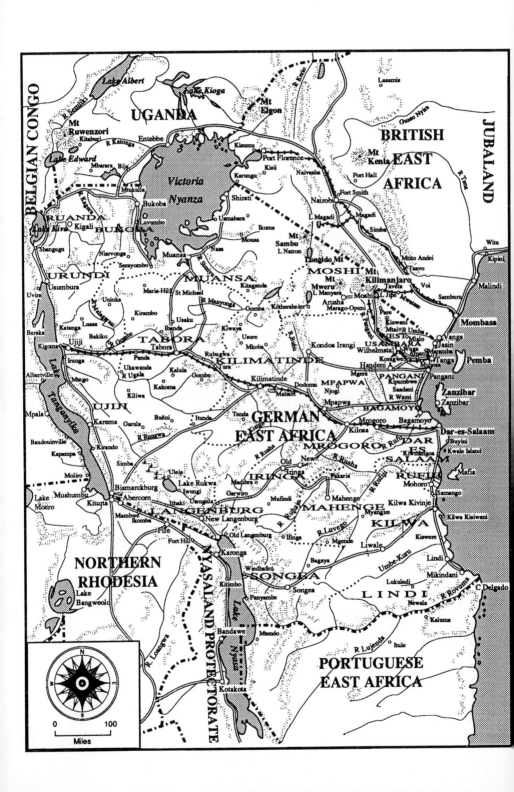

Contents

Foreword

Less than eight decades after its end, the campaign for German East Africa is almost forgotten. The memory of the 1st South African Brigade's immolation at Delville Wood still burns bright, but it is one of those strange twists of history that the epic four-year struggle in German East, conducted over wild and often savagely beautiful terrain by some of the toughest fighting men in Africa – white and black – should have become so obscured by the passage of time.

Possibly it is because of an incredibly short-sighted World War I policy of raising composite units for foreign service – only one of our existing regiments, the 1st Battalion of the South African Cape Corps, bears any East African battle honours on its regimental colours. Possibly it is also because the German East African (GEA) campaign was an ambiguous affair in its days of final resolution.

Yet in terms of human hardship the GEA campaign was every bit as desperate as the 1st Brigade's fighting in France. The casualties speak for themselves. By 1917 over 3 000 Imperial troops had been killed in action; more than 6 000 had died of wounds and disease. Of that toll, almost 2 000 were South Africans. And the war was far from over.

German East Africa should have been a sideshow in the war against the Kaiser. The Germans had been *in situ* for only a few years; their armed forces in 1914 consisted of 300 white soldiers and just over 5 000 black local 'askaris' – and the colony was almost sealed off by a Royal Navy blockade.

But the Germans were not shown the door in short order, primarily because the German military commander was a talented soldier called Colonel Paul von Lettow-Vorbeck. At first sight von Lettow was a typical example of the much-caricatured shaven-headed Prussian *junker;* but it was a misleading impression. A man of high intelligence and flexible mind, he had been honed by the German military training system and had seen action in South West Africa. It would be fair to say that by the time he landed in German East Africa he was one of the most formidable soldiers Africa had ever seen, although few realised it.

Von Lettow scored his first victory within months of the outbreak of war by thrashing a combined British and Indian expeditionary force at the port of Tanga, and followed it up with a series of victories that by the beginning of 1916 had turned German East into a nagging ulcer on the British flank.

The antidote to this troublesome Prussian and his recruit-swollen army lay reasonably near at hand, in the shape of the Union of South Africa, which was now geared up for war and had just conquered South West Africa. And so an army of 20 000 men on horse and foot – volunteers to a man – was raised and sent eastwards to reinforce the troops under General Sir Horace Smith-Dorrien, himself a hero of the Anglo-Boer War.

Many were bushvelders, familiar with rein and rifle since their youngest days; a great many had seen action before – in colonial campaigns, in South West Africa and in the Anglo-Boer War. Among them were soldiers like the ex-Boer guerrilla, Brigadier-General Jaap van Deventer; Colonel Manie Botha, a nephew of Prime Minister Louis Botha; and Colonel Coen Brits, as towering in body as Van Deventer and so loyal to Louis Botha that, when he was ordered to mobilise in 1914, he replied with a later-to-be-famous telegram saying: 'Mobilisation complete. Who must I fight? The English or the Germans?'

Smith-Dorrien was soon taken ill, however, and recalled. In his place was appointed the best the South Africans had to offer: Jan Christiaan Smuts, boy genius turned Boer War general turned politician turned general again.

And so the scene was set. Smuts and von Lettow, so different in appearance and background and temperament, had this one supreme quality in common: they inspired an intense loyalty from those who served under them.

The German East Africa campaign did not end as swiftly and decisively as the one in South West Africa. It went on till the very end of World War I. At the exhausted finish, von Lettow and his remaining ragged askaris laid down their arms and marched into captivity not because they had been vanquished in battle, but because the country they served had surrendered.

By then Smuts (like most of the South Africans) was long gone from the scene, recalled in early 1917 to button on frock coat and cut-throat collar for the greater political battles of the war; in his place was Jaap van Deventer, who had completed the task of neutralising von Lettow and who (rather to his embarrassment) was made a Knight Commander of the Bath for his efforts.

This is the story James Ambrose Brown has set out to tell, and it is a magnificent account, drawing on scores of official and personal records, tracking down almost-forgotten facts and blending rich narrative ingredients with the expert hand of one who, during World War II, saw action himself not so very far from the battles of Smuts and von Lettow.

No respecter of conventional wisdom or time-hallowed military or political icons, Brown's comments will infuriate some readers and cause others to rethink long-held opinions. So be warned: Brown's account is written with a clear, sharp eye, compassion and integrity that leave no room for 'fudging' or prevarication.

The story leaves one staggered by the sheer tenacity and endurance of those who participated. After reading this book no South African will dare say he did not know what his countrymen did in East Africa during World War I.

Willem Steenkamp
Cape Town, 1991

Acknowledgements

The author gratefully acknowledges the assistance, advice and practical help of the following individuals, institutions and publications: The South African Military Historical and Archival Services; Library of the National War Museum; Fort Wynyard Library of the SA Naval Museum; Library of Parliament; Library of the Castle Museum; Library of Rhodes University; Library of the University of Cape Town. The author is especially grateful to Cmdr W M Bisset for research suggestions and material from his personal collection; to Al J Venter for use of his library; to Rt Hon Piet van der Bijl for period documentation; to Ute Seemann for German translation and editing; to Willem Steenkamp for his thought-provoking Foreword; to Mrs Patricia Pilkington-Jordan for use of the personal memoir of Senator Rupert Pilkington-Jordan; and to Dr Frank Mitchell. Acknowledgements to authors and publishers of diaries and letters are made in the Bibliography as is the invaluable material from out-of-print books in German and English on the campaign in German East Africa, including maps from General Collyer's campaign history. Special thanks to Richard Wood for his finely detailed maps. Photographs have been copied from material and from periodicals of the 1914–1918 war and from photo albums kept by families of campaigners, in particular, Mrs B I Holliday who provided rare photographs of No 26 Squadron, the Royal Flying Corps taken by her father Mr H C Trew. Other photographs are from archives of the Imperial War Museum, the *Bundesarchiv* and the published memoirs of General P von Lettow-Vorbeck. To Mrs Naomi Musiker for expertly compiling the index to this book, I express my sincere gratitude.

Prologue

On his way to the jungle battlefields of German East Africa in the late months of 1915, a young English army doctor went ashore in Cape Town. He was struck by posters on the walls of the harbour city of a bearded man in the uniform of a British general. A year later, when he was recovering from malaria after the man-killing march down the Pangani River, he recalled his impression of that poster.

Its caption read: 'John Smuts Wants You!' Who was John Smuts? The face on the poster was that of Jan Christiaan Smuts, and he was calling South Africans to arms to fight in an imperial war. In his classic book on the war in East Africa, *The March on Tanga*, Francis Brett Young wrote that the first time he saw the face in the poster in the flesh was on that brutal march. An electrifying presence. The face of a man who could drive men beyond exhaustion and sickness and not lose their faith in him.

That poster evidently fascinated Brett Young; but did he actually see it with that wording? No one in South Africa called Smuts 'John'. After the battle of Messines Ridge on the Somme in 1917 Smuts did appear in a recruiting poster, by a lithographic artist, A Holland, and printed by the Government Printing Works in Pretoria. It was a crude copy of the official photograph of Smuts as a Lieutenant-General.

It was a poor likeness, making his intelligent, urgent face narrow-eyed and harsh. The caption called for drafts to replace the heavy losses of the South African 1st Brigade in the Somme battles. 'The success of the South African Brigade at Messines Ridge is one of the glories of the war. As a unit their reputation is almost unrivalled.'

It was signed with a facsimile of his signature and the words: 'Wants You'. It expressed the General's hope and trust that sufficient fresh drafts would be sent forward. However, this poster was not printed until after the battle at Messines in June 1917 and Brett Young wrote his book in convalescence in 1916.

Was there an earlier poster with the words 'John Smuts', or was the fever-stricken Brett Young confusing it with the famous British recruiting poster in which Lord Kitchener called the men of England

and the Empire to arms in the autumn of 1914? Who could forget that thrusting finger, the black buffalo moustaches and the compelling eyes of the great British military hero and Minister of War?

'Your Country needs YOU!' It was a challenge that brought men of all ranks of society flocking to join Kitchener's new army. Amateurs who knew nothing of war, they were eager to fill the gaps in the professional ranks of what the German emperor had called a 'contemptible little army'. It had landed in France, a hundred thousand strong in the first days of wild enthusiasm for the challenge of a showdown war between the British and German empires.

That army had been forced to retreat when the French armies were overwhelmed and broken only twenty days after the war began. They had surrendered the great fortress of Namur and had been mauled in their attempts to retake it. The British Expeditionary Force was obliged to fall back, and it did so in a classic rearguard action of marching and fighting. The German advance was stopped.

Smarting from the Kaiser's insult, Kitchener assured the British Cabinet that he would raise an unprecedented force from the nation's eager volunteers. He promised to raise in six months a million trained men in some fifty divisions. Kitchener saw clearly what the public could not even imagine. This war would not be over by Christmas. It was going to last at least four years.

The Virtue of Unquestioned Obedience

The greatest virtue of a soldier in the 1914 war was obedience. Human life was accepted as of a temporary nature. God and King were supreme; too much reasoning was not to be encouraged. The empire was a symbol of all that was most worthy of a man's sacrifice.

In truth, the empire was still a magnificent façade of power that hypnotised both its subjects and its enemies. The map of the world was red from end to end even though, in fact, much of that empire had no idea how it had come about that white men ruled them. Being part of it distilled a kind of glory in the very beer of the average man.

In 1914 that empire was about to be tested in what would be its first evidence of total loyalty to the Crown. Men were committed to this war, 450 million of them, of every race and tribe, by a single declaration of the King Emperor. 'We are at war with Germany.' Banners and patriotic hymns burst forth on every side in a spirit of willing sacrifice impossible to emulate or even describe today.

The response of the empire was amazingly spontaneous. The Motherland called. Her sons, wherever they were, must answer the call that challenged them from posters of Britannia surrounded by her ironclads churning the waves of hostile seas that she was determined to command.

Much had happened since 1914; most of it disastrous. On the Western Front the power of the machine gun, a weapon of under-estimated deadliness, had been used by the Germans with devastating effect against two British offensives. Kitchener's new army was all but destroyed. Page after page in the newspapers listed the names of dead, wounded and missing. Casualties were in figures unimagined.

Elsewhere, British, Australian and New Zealand troops tackling 'the soft underbelly of Europe' through Turkey were suffering appalling losses after landing at the Dardinelles with huge but ineffective naval support. There too, the fighting had become a stalemate of costly bayonet attacks from trenches against machine guns.

Much worse was to come as the combatant nations strove to achieve a decisive victory. By 1916 the total of British, French and German casualties, dead, wounded and missing in the battles of Verdun and the Somme was already over a million and a half. Poison gas had been introduced, and in England voluntary service had been replaced by conscription.

In the deadly slogging match the first idealism had gone out of the war. Lord Kitchener was dead. On his way to Russia on a secret mission the British cruiser *Hampshire* struck a German mine and sank within fifteen minutes. Only a dozen men survived. Kitchener was last seen in the gunroom immediately after the explosion. He was extremely sensitive to cold after years of service in India and Africa and was dragged under by his heavy greatcoat.

Kitchener's Permission

But before he drowned, Kitchener had given reluctant permission for the reinforcement of British East Africa, where the Germans had taken the initiative. Until then, War Office policy had been cautious. The new order was soon to put Smuts in command of a large new army of colonial soldiers.

In South Africa, Smuts's appeals and reputation among his old Boer comrades and the British raised twenty thousand men from the *dorps* and cities to fight a campaign in East Africa in which more than half the European population had no interest; to which they were downright antagonistic. Some even favoured the enemy.

Smuts's call, like Kitchener's, was to redeem the reputation of a British expeditionary army sent to Africa from India. It had been thrashed and humiliated three times, first when attempting a seaborne landing at the steamy Indian Ocean port of Tanga in November, 1915.

The new army was also to support, with fresh men, a full-scale attempt to invade the German colony and eliminate the threat of a smaller German-led army of tribal askaris. Smuts saw the defeat of the largely Indian army at Tanga as a disgrace to British arms, indeed, the greatest disgrace to British arms for a century. It led him to believe that the Indian soldier was not worth his salt.

Only a few months after Tanga a new British commander decided to try his luck by attacking the little fishing village of Jasin just inside German territory. Four companies were surrounded by the enemy and surrendered with nearly five hundred casualties. After this fresh humiliation, Lord Kitchener at the War Office rebuked the commander: 'You are entirely mistaken that offensive operations are necessary . . . concentrate your forces and give up risky expeditions.' A third British commander prepared to try his luck; the Irish Brigadier-General Michael Tighe. On his way from Mombasa to take up his command in Nairobi his train was ambushed, the line was blown up and his carriage was riddled with rifle fire. The enemy had been harrying the railway line to Nairobi for months and were already masters of hit-and-run tactics in the bush.

Tighe waited for reinforcements, pushed the railway line towards the German borders, built up supply dumps and prepared his plans to expel the Germans from their foothold on British territory. Among his new forces were three battalions of South Africans recently arrived and eager for battle. The plan was to encircle the German defenders of a hill called Salaita, defeat them and force them back through the only gap between the mountains at Taveta. Once seized, it would force the Germans to relinquish the foothills of Mount Kilimanjaro.

In the dusty assembly camp at the railhead at Mbuyani the South Africans made preparations. Some had already fought in German South West Africa and tasted victory. Among them were British and Boer veterans of the Boer War. Most were recruits from all parts of the Union: gold miners, farmers, clerks, artisans and professional men of every kind, all equally eager to prove their patriotism.

Black Soldiers as Equals

The operation was entrusted to Brigadier-General Wilfred Malleson. He had under his command two brigades, one part Indian, part British, the other, the 2nd South African Infantry Brigade. The 5th, 6th and 7th Battalions were cock-a-hoop. Though ill-trained, they were convinced that they would quickly deal with the handful of native troops led by Germans. They were psychologically unprepared to meet black soldiers as equals. As a staff officer wrote later, it was an attitude that cost them dear.

As they marched out across the dusty plain on the morning of 12 February 1916, columns of Indians and British soldiers moved in a converging attack; they were in the mood for an easy victory. That same day Smuts and his staff sailed for East Africa. He landed at Mombasa, to be met by General Tighe, who came on board the troopship as soon as it docked at Kilindini. Smuts was informed of the disastrous attack by the forces on Salaita Hill. 'I want to see the place for myself, at once,' Smuts told him.

If he was shocked at the news that his soldiers had broken and run in the face of heavy machine-gun fire and a bayonet charge by askaris, he did not show it. He left that same evening with Brigadier-General J J Collyer, his Chief of Staff. The wood-burning locomotive panted its way from the plantations and dense tropical forest of the coastal region, climbed towards the dry plains to Voi and from there towards the base at Mbuyani on the new military line that Tighe had ordered built towards the frontier during the past months by engineers labouring round the clock to complete it for the big offensive.

Smuts had little sleep that night as the train rattled and swayed across the dark plain, sparks from its funnel illuminating the thick bush and thorn trees on either side. What he heard from Tighe, who in exuberant Irish style and not noticeably crestfallen had rattled on about 'inexperience and lack of training', only confirmed Smuts's opinion of British generalship in Africa.

Collyer, steady, clear-thinking, was not a man to be panicked by bad news. He had made notes of the sorry tale of ineptitude and muddle. 'True, it's a reverse to morale,' he assured Smuts, 'but losses were not severe.'

III News at Home

Smuts did not consider 138 dead and wounded slight. He had arrived in this country to win the war, and this would be ill news indeed at home. It particularly irked him that he must reverse his opinion of Indian troops. The day had been saved by 'a finely fought action by the 130th Baluchis, who took the brunt of a bayonet attack, enabling the South Africans to extricate themselves.' True, they were raw, but it galled him to learn that the Baluchis had collected the abandoned rifles and machine guns and returned them next day.

By the time he reached the terminus at Mbuyani early next morning Smuts knew where to lay the blame: on the almost casual overconfidence of a general with no experience of battle. How Tighe had entrusted this man Malleson with the operation was typical of British staff methods; and it was entirely unacceptable to South Africans with a concern for losses.

Cold-eyed, Smuts went forward from Malleson's headquarters to see for himself. The corpses of most of his dead had been recovered from the tangle of bush, and sixty who could not be accounted for had been buried by the Germans where they fell. Everything had miscarried, even to the removal of the wounded. There were insufficient stretchers, and wounded men had to be dragged in groundsheets by four men to dressing stations two miles back in the bush.

Vultures of the great plain were circling over the fatal hill, which looked innocent enough now, except for the slash of new trenches visible up the slope of the otherwise bald hill. Smuts scanned the position from a mile and a half away. 'My brave boys,' he called them as he saw the dead carried to the cemetery back at their starting point. They were the first of two thousand who would soon lie in this tropical land which he called 'the furthest reach north of our African trek.'

Now the details of the attack began to emerge. The hill itself appeared to one observer as 'a mere kopje, about 1 200 yards by 800 yards in extent, oval in shape and rather steep'. No wonder it had looked easy to the companies of 7th SAI who got within four hundred yards of the hidden Germans before a withering volley of rifle and maxim fire burst from concealed trenches, cutting through the low grass on a rising slope of ground carefully denuded of all bush to make a clear field for the machine guns.

Panic and Confusion

'No one who fell or took cover before that fire even saw where it came from. We had expected to attack the trenches reported to be higher on the hillside . . . the firing came from the foot, and men were falling all round before they knew it.'

J Lindon Bradford, a machine-gunner of the 5th Infantry Regiment, recalled: 'Although I had selected a spot for our gun, we never had an order to fire a shot! I saw two flags, one a German and the other a green flag with a half-moon and a dot,* fluttering in the wind . . .' All was panic and confusion.

The crestfallen troops reformed or straggled back in the full heat of the barren, sun-blasted plain to base camp at Mbuyani: more than a hundred without their rifles, machine-gunners without their maxims, waterbottles empty, all shocked by defeat and by the unexpected reality of death in the field.

They had been told that the action would be walkover against a handful of native troops with German officers. Aerial reconnaissance had reported no movement and some fresh but empty trenches the day before. No one apparently took notice of that as significant.

Malleson ordered a two-brigade advance by six thousand troops with forty-one machine guns and eighteen artillery pieces, including

---

* The insignia of Islam; crescent and star.

naval 4-inch guns and 5-inch howitzers. He expected to brush aside an enemy outpost of some three hundred men – and without artillery. In his excessive confidence and contempt Malleson was sure that the assault would be over before the enemy could bring up reinforcements to counter-attack.

But before the full story of this first fatal encounter of Smuts's new army is told the question has to be asked: What were South Africans doing there on the plains of Serengeti in February 1916? They were four thousand miles from home, and they had taken up arms in a quarrel that most of their white countrymen were against, and the opinions of the blacks were not considered of the least importance. Nothing in the lifetime of the average man is seized on with more eagerness than the chance to put on a uniform and go into the desperate adventure of war. When the warlike instinct is given the blessing of church and state and the sacred banners of national honour, duty, justice and freedom are raised, then the rush of would-be heroes is unstoppable.

But nothing in history is inevitable. Until the moment of catharsis, there must be alternatives. But if the alternatives are contrary to national interests as conceived by politicians and opinion-makers, then the pressures building up will be uncontainable: the boil will burst at a pinprick.

The imperial boil had been festering for a long time.

THE UNION LION TO BRITANNIA: "Here I am. The knot in the tail looks odd, but it
doesn't really matter."
[General Botha's resolution pledging South Africa to loyal support was adopted on Thursday by the House of Assembly, only a small minority of Hertzogites voting against it.]
(The *Cape Times*, 12 September 1914)

CHAPTER

1

Colonial Rivalry in Africa

Europe was in its last frenzy of empire-building. The mystique of empire had endowed the idea of conquest of inferior peoples a kind of holy aura, almost as if the Divine Will approved the aggressor as an instrument of its purpose. Smuts expressed it thus: 'The hundred million barbarians of Africa . . . that vast deadweight of immemorial barbarism and animal savagery' had to be brought to 'the light and blessing of ordered civilisation'.

It was the accepted wisdom of 1895 when he said that. The South Africa that he was born into had been fighting for two centuries to defeat and isolate the indigenous peoples, themselves in many cases invaders and conquerors of weaker peoples.

The nations of continental Europe were in the last stages of carving up the African prize. Already the continent was red, British imperial red, from the Cape to Cairo. The British peoples had celebrated the sixtieth year of Queen Victoria's reign with vast acquisitions by the empire. The kings and queens of Europe had followed her triumphant procession through London. Her subjects of every race and creed had followed her train in splendid uniforms and native costumes.

The empire was regarded as a free association of nations, a triumph of civilisation and all that was best for mankind. In the race for colonies Germany had been a latecomer. She had a few islands in the Pacific, a toehold in China, and in Africa she had Togoland, the Cameroons and South West Africa.

Germany was an authoritarian, recently feudal, military and bureaucratic state with an emperor who was all but an absolute ruler over a hierarchy of princelings and a strutting military caste. Militarism was exalted to a kind of religion. As a German historian noted: 'The Prussian lieutenant stalked through the land like a demi-god . . . militarism permeated the whole of bourgeois life.' Even civilian officials wore uniform.

Over all ruled Kaiser Wilhelm II. He was determined to make Germany a power with a voice in world politics. What colonies he ruled as emperor were held to be ridiculously disproportionate to her

1

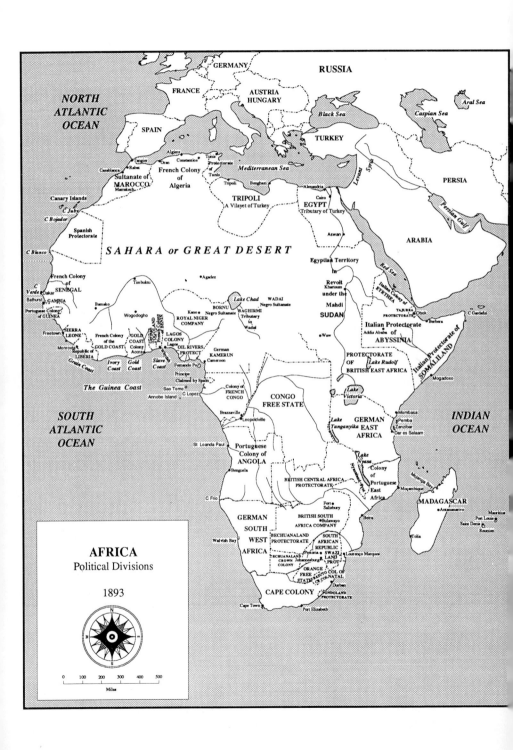

AFRICA
Political Divisions

1893

0 100 200 300 400 500
Miles

size and economic power. The banker and industrialist Walther Rathenau wrote: 'The last hundred years have seen the partition of the world. What a pity we virtually took nothing and gained nothing.' The dreams of colonial zealots were for more and greater colonies in Africa.

It is salutary to recall that during the eighteen-nineties Britain was preparing for the seizure of all South Africa. Jan Smuts had written his violent polemic against Britain in *A Century of Wrong* indicting the 'monstrous evil of British aggression' in her rule over countries 'largely inhabited by peoples who hated her'. He called it 'the ramshackle empire' and urged his 'Brother Africanders' to remember the blood shed by their people and to throw off the tyranny of 'an unjust and hated government seven thousand miles away'.

'History will prove,' he wrote, 'that the allegation of humanity, civilisation and equal rights upon which the British Government bases its actions is nothing but a cloak for that hypocritical spirit of annexation and piracy that has always characterised her actions in dealing with our people.'

Hot words from a young lawyer agitating for the Boer War with the resounding call to arms: 'Freedom shall rise in South Africa as the sun rises from the morning clouds . . . then shall it be from Zambezi to Simon's Bay – AFRICA FOR THE AFRICANDER.'

That he was a Boer imperialist apparently did not occur to him. Annexation was, after all, the spirit of the time, whether one were Boer, Briton or German. It was a period of rancorous squabbling over the corpse of Africa between European powers who had discovered, through their explorers and traders, that this vast continent lay all but helpless for the plucking.

Carving up Africa

A century later, in the climate of a Europe without frontiers and without colonies, it is hard to conceive the diplomatic manoeuvrings, the treaties signed and broken, the brutality and bloodshed that tainted the doings of all the white usurpers who squabbled like vultures among themselves about who ruled what and where one sphere of influence began and another ended.

On the invitation of Prince Bismarck, the European powers with a stake in Africa met in Berlin in 1884-85 to consider the future of Africa. The diplomatists were in session for three months; and having decided on boundaries, they solemnly resolved that it was a sacred duty to preserve the native races of Africa, watch over their interests and promote their material and moral advancements.

Five years later they met again, in Brussels. The European Anti-Slavery Conference declared its emphatic desire to protect the native races of Africa from slavery and oppression.

After this solemn rhetoric the British Government found no objection to the annexation of South West Africa and German East Africa by Germany. Both territories were to be fought for by South African forces within twenty-five years. By then both had been subjugated with the utmost brutality and colonised by German settlers. No one at the table in Brussels, it seems, had expected any objection from the native inhabitants. After all, the invaders would be bringing them out of barbarism into the light of European civilisation.

Hardly was the ink dry on the pens of the Brussels Conference when Germany appointed a commissioner and military commander for South West Africa. With reinforcements from Germany von Francois seized the territory round Windhoek, and two years later the first settlers arrived. In 1893 he stormed the stronghold of Hendrik Witbooi, the Hottentot leader, and began the prolonged campaigns that were to end only in 1905 with the virtual extermination of the Herero people and the appropriation of their land.

Elephants, because of their tusks were hunted extensively for their valuable ivory by natives and Europeans alike in the forests of East Africa. German print of 1890s.

Eyes on South Africa

In South Africa the Boer republics had their own problems, not least of which was the threat of conquest. Both Britain and Germany looked with greedy interest on the new wealth of the hitherto barren and uncultivated Transvaal.

As early as 1873 the German explorer Karl Mauch first kindled the desire for possession. 'Would to God,' he wrote, 'that this fine country might soon become a German colony.' A year or two later Bismarck was urged by zealots 'to send a steady stream of Germans through Delagoa Bay to secure future domination over the Transvaal and so pave the way for a great German Empire in Africa.'

In 1895 – the year of the high moral posture at the Brussels conference – *Die Grenzboten*, an important political journal in Berlin, wrote: 'For us the Boer states signify a great possibility. Their absorption in the British Empire would mean a blocking of our last road towards an independent agricultural colony in a temperate climate.'

Two years later the same paper pointed out that 'our new German colonies appear to be very good starting points for attack.' The *Koloniales Jahrbuch* noted 'the importance of South Africa as a country that can receive an unlimited number of white immigrants. This must rouse us to the greatest exertions to secure there the supremacy of the Teutonic race.' It stressed the Low German origin of the Boers. 'We must, before all, stimulate their hatred of the English.'

When the Germans had built their railway line from Lüderitz Bay harbour to Keetmanshoop on the border of South Africa a German politician stood up in the *Reichstag* to declare: 'If war should break out between us and Great Britain . . . the line would greatly facilitate our attack on the Cape Colony.' None of this went unnoticed in the Transvaal Republic, which did not intend to be swallowed by either Germany or England.

It was in the same fever of colonial grab that the Germans looked at the huge and inviting mass of unnamed territory that is now Tanzania. The man who was resolved to plant the German flag there was Dr Carl Peters. He was President of the Society for German Colonisation. With tireless zeal he persuaded the chiefs of the coast and the hinterland to set their names to treaties.

Transfer of Power

In return for titles and favours these begged the Kaiser for a charter of protection. The nominal ruler was the Sultan of Zanzibar. When he protested, the British silenced him with verbal pressure and the Germans demonstrated with warships. By 1886, the European powers had

Uniforms for the Protective Force in German East Africa

restricted his power to the offshore islands and a narrow strip of coast. They declared the vast hinterland to be 'a German sphere of interest'.

The German East Africa Company had become the effective ruler of sixty thousand square miles of the Sultan of Zanzibar's mainland, and with it the authority to claim all duties levied by the customs previously imposed by the local ruling families.

The Germans installed company officials with an unparalleled insolence and highhandedness that very quickly brought the privileged Swahili and Arab upper classes into a state of revolt. They were the owners of plantations worked by thousands of slaves cultivating sugar, rubber, coconuts and sesame in a flourishing economy in which the slaves were liberated to the extent of being granted land for cultivation, and they could build houses for their families in return for labour and military service.

It was an Islamic society that bitterly resented the German contempt for its customs and religion. A young Englishman wrote: 'Zanzibar is full of Germans. They walk the streets with the air of conquerors, taking any fruit that they want and raping any woman that they see. You can imagine what a state the Arabs are in. Two German sailors have been stabbed.'

The German agents ridiculed the Sultan of Zanzibar's weakened authority and were hastening to replace it as soon as possible by their own. They assumed in their arrogance that the agents of the Company were simply replacing a corrupt system by a superior system.

It was during this 'transfer of power', as it was called, that a young German first came to notice. Emil von Zelewski went from town to town along the coast to inform the governors that the Germans would be taking over the administration of the country and the customs. When he was ordered to present himself four times a day at the

German office to make his report and receive his instructions, the Wali of Pangani refused to co-operate. Zelewski signalled to the warship *Möwe* standing off the harbour, and a hundred marines marched through the town. They interrupted the festal prayers at a mosque on a holy day, took the Wali's personal guard prisoner and, after wrecking his harem in search of him, tore down the prison doors and released the convicts.

The young Zelewski called together the notable men of the town who had not fled and announced: 'If my orders are not obeyed I will send a warship with eight hundred men to destroy the town and send you in chains to Germany.' German documents of the day noted a beneficial effect. 'The quick, confident intervention of the marines seems to have made a lasting impression . . . and tolls were levied without difficulty.'

In an Arab account of the affair the writer Hemedi recorded how 'every morning Zelewski and his twelve soldiers walked about the town. If they saw women they seized them and did what they liked with them. When we asked them why they did so, they said it was a German custom.'

Confusion and Taxes

Soon the coastal towns were in a state of confusion, groaning under a poll tax, a burial tax, an inheritance tax and road tolls. Company officials demanded proof of ownership of land, and where there were no written deeds (which was normal) they confiscated that land.

Outrageous as such behaviour was, it must not be assumed that this was a blameless society. It was certainly one ripe for purgation in some form. It had flourished through the Arab slave trade that had all but depopulated the interior as far inland as the Congo and Lake Tanganyika.

Its most prosperous towns and ports had grown rich on this trade. But with the arousing of the European and American conscience, and the bloodiest war on the American continent, the slave trade was all but abolished by the time of the German seizure.

The navies of Germany and England zealously examined the dhows still trading from small ports on the long tropical shores of the Indian Ocean and its islands. Boarding parties with pistol and cutlass stormed over their decks and burst open the stinking holds. Schoolboy magazines of the period were full of stories about deeds of derring-do under the guns of cruisers.

At this time of general conciliation of colonial neighbours the British were ready to support the Germans in the assertion of their 'legitimate authority'. They threatened the Sultan of Zanzibar when his subjects rose in revolt and used their naval power to back the German claims.

To the inhabitants it was plain that a society that had worked very well in its own way, with its loyalties and alliances and commercial systems under a ruler who was less than authoritarian, was being displaced. The new repressive regime demanded absolute obedience.

Soon the inhabitants of the towns on the coast formed local armies, pooled their weapons and looked for leaders. The chiefs of remote districts who traded with the coast sent thousands of warriors. 'As for these Germans,' they declared, 'we will never become their slaves if we have to fight to the last man.'

Plantations were turned into armed camps where untrained warriors were organised in armies eager to be let loose. The handful of German officials were besieged in their houses by mobs demanding the head of Zelewski. They placed a guard on the house, tore down the company flag and ripped it to shreds.

Meanwhile a German warship ranged the coast and shelled Tanga and other ports to heaps of rubble. When the mobs stormed a company house the cruiser *Leipzig* landed 260 marines, who carried out punitive raids on inland villages and burned, plundered and destroyed them with artillery fire. As they retired to their boats they fired on rioters armed with spears and bows, and killed over a hundred.

Resistance Leaders

So began a resistance that was to last for years and give rise to legendary heroes. The most remarkable and longest resisting of these was Abushiri, son of an Arab father and an Abyssinian mother. His army soon drove out the few German officials, and forts had to be built to resist further attacks.

Captain Hermann von Wissman, a German soldier and explorer, was ordered to recruit six hundred askaris from the British Sudan. The British joined the Germans in a blockade of the coast while the Germans sacked the port of Bagamoyo and marched on Abushiri's fort with three hundred Germans and seven hundred black soldiers.

The German guns quickly demolished the wooden palisades of the fort, and Abushiri's warriors fled. The writer Hemedi was there and recorded the débâcle. 'When our leader saw that we were defeated he was the first to flee . . . I commended myself to God and ran. While we were showered with bullets, men pursued us. The cannon roared like thunder and we were hit as we fled. When we had gone some way we saw that the stockade was on fire, the Europeans were sacking the fort and corpses lay about unheeded.'

One by one the towns fell, devastated by naval gunfire. Leaders were hunted down and hanged.* Most people were ready to submit to German rule. They signed peace treaties and agreed to fly the German flag over their villages. Abushiri was betrayed and in hiding, still hoping to raise a new army, with a price of ten thousand rupees on his head.

He was seized by a treacherous chief and put in chains, then taken to the coast and quickly tried. 'I die a good Muslim,' he declared from the scaffold.

Then there rose another name to strike terror: the Swahili Bwana Heri. To subdue him, Zelewski led a thousand men in an orgy of crop and village burning, leaving scores of settlements in smouldering ruins. Bwana Heri could never be caught. In the words of one German officer: 'Our efforts to surprise him were frustrated because his men had learned of our landings through spies and were waiting for us. They threw themselves against us in small bands and attacked our camps and resting places by day and night . . .'

Bwana Heri might have resisted much longer as a guerrilla fighter, but he made his last stand behind the palisades and earthworks of a fort. For four hours the German guns bombarded the primitive defences. The defenders fought back with accurate and intense gunfire. Between pauses in the firing the fifteen hundred defenders could be heard raising their voices in prayer.

When the Germans at last stormed in they found the place full of dead and dying. Bwana Heri himself had escaped. After another serious defeat he surrendered, and having agreed to accept the Germans as rulers of the coast he was given a post in the administrative hierarchy. So at last the whole coast was subdued.

Machemba was the next resistance leader to emerge. He was the ruler of the Yao people in the south-west. When he was called on to come to the coast and submit he sent the message: 'Since I was born I have not set foot on the coast. Shall I go there now because you call me? If you are strong enough come and get me.' The Germans took him at his word, and after great destruction of crops and villages he submitted.

Lords of the Land

With martial law now imposed everywhere, the natives had to accept and respect the new authority. Captain von Wissman wrote of a grotesque ceremony of abasement imposed on a tribe of the Baga-

---

* In 1989 an illustrated history of German colonialism, *Die Deutschen Kolonien*, by H M Schindler, published photographs of rebels in chains and on the gallows.

moyo district. The people had to bow down before him, covering their heads and breasts with dust as a sign of contrition and humiliation. Von Wissman gave them his pardon and ordered rice and cattle to be distributed. It was ordained that all Africans should greet any passing white man by standing up and saluting 'to demonstrate beyond question that we are the lords of the land'.

That was in 1890, the year when the final boundaries were drawn giving Britain a protectorate over Zanzibar and German Tanganyika. That same year Britain tightened its grip on Nyasaland and Northern Rhodesia.

For the Germans in East Africa submission was almost complete. Only in the remote central highlands there remained a defiant people, the Wahehe, six-foot warriors who had subjugated all their less warlike neighbours and kept them in perpetual bondage.

Captain Emil von Zelewski set out over the mountains with 360 askaris, a field gun and machine guns. He was confident that he would soon make short work of the Wahehes' spears. The Wahehe could follow the progress of the German force with its cumbersome European style of marching and its chanting porters. Their tactics had long been perfected. They would gather in silence round their enemy in the concealing undergrowth, then with appalling suddenness they would burst out on the doomed column, strung out as it was in single file.

In his contempt for his native enemy Zelewski approached the tribal capital with his machine guns still dismantled on his porters' heads and his ammunition boxes screwed shut. When four thousand warriors burst upon him from all sides it was too late to form square. The askaris fired till their ammunition was exhausted, then fought with the bayonet and died where they stood. Zelewski fired till his revolver was empty and went down with a spear in his throat. His askaris were massacred to a man. Only a handful of porters escaped into the bush.

Mkwawa, the Wahehe leader, was a thorn in the German flesh for seven long years of cruel and bitter warfare. He made masterly use of the bush, leading the enemy again and again into ambush. Even when his capital at Iringa fell, he remained uncaptured, rallying the last of tribal resistance.

Fighting over the same ground in 1916 against Smuts's army Colonel von Lettow-Vorbeck wrote that his retreat to Iringa 'brought me to the places where the great chief Kwawa [sic] had defied the Germans in the early days . . . some of the many assembled natives were able to recall for me what they had witnessed of the annihilation of Zelewski's expedition on the spot.'

That was only ten years after Zelewski's skull had been recovered from the obliterating jungle by another soldier, Captain Tom Prince. He was the man destined to pursue Mkwawa to the bitter end. Tom Prince was born a British subject of a German mother. At the site of the Zelewski massacre he held up the skull and swore to avenge him and destroy the Wahehe.

What became of Zelewski's skull is not part of the legend. The skull of the great black guerrilla fighter ended up in a glass case in Germany. When he was trapped in the bush by a German sergeant he refused to surrender and face ignominy. Mkwawa blew out his brains. His skull was taken as a trophy and to prevent its use as a holy relic.

By No Means Over

Such was the time and such were the means of subjugation. It was 1894, and it was still far from ended. No African peoples fought more stubbornly and persistently for their freedom than the tribes and chiefs of the Tanganyika hinterland. It was a country that favoured every kind of resistance by its size and a terrain of mountains and rivers, among the largest in Africa, swamps and dense forest and impenetrable thorn-bush . . . all of it unpenetrated except by jungle trails opening into villages and fields of native cultivation; a land of plenty for its inhabitants.

Resistance continued as bitterly as before as the first trickle of white settlers began to develop estates of coffee, sisal and tobacco on the cool slopes of Kilimanjaro and the Usambara Mountains. Work began at once on a metre-gauge railway through the mountains from the port of Tanga, hacked through the jungle, and its numerous rivers and streams were bridged.

Ten years after the Imperial Government had accepted responsibility for the development of the territory there were still only about two thousand Germans in the entire country: administrators, district officers, researchers, engineers and missionaries.

The Magic Water

At home in Germany there was still some resistance to the whole idea of colonies. The continual uprisings were discouraging the kind of mass immigration that the dreamers had hoped would ease the pressure in the Fatherland of eighty million people in a rapidly industrialising society. In fact, the worst was still to come. Since the Africans had been defeated on their own ground by superior arms they looked to their ancient ways for a superior power.

Since bows and spears were futile against machine guns, power to overcome was sought in the supernatural. Magic would make them invulnerable. A magic water would turn bullets to water. It is a measure of the hatred and frustration felt by peoples powerless against firearms that they were ready to believe this with fanatical trust. The phenomenon appeared first in German East Africa in 1905 in the southern district of Liwale.

Reports from nervous district officers told of tribal medicine men peddling the magic water. Officers of remote military posts heard that their askaris had been told – and readily believed – that when the attack on the fort came, their bullets would be as harmless as raindrops! The prophets of the Maji-Maji Rebellion persuaded their followers that the spirit of a water snake had appeared to them, promising immunity. They were to rush fearlessly on the German rifles with the battlecry: '*Maji! Maji!*' (Swahili for water).

Unknown to the settlers the tribesmen were being worked up into a state of agitation. The storm broke like the African monsoon. A party of Benedictine missionaries was hacked to death near Liwale in the remote south. German garrisons in isolated forts were besieged and without hope of relief as the Maji warriors swarmed across the land, killing Europeans and Arabs with impartial fury.

Settlers in Panic

At this same time the German settlers in the new colony of South West Africa were abandoning their farms in panic as the Nama and Herero peoples rose to reclaim their lands. Between 1904 and 1907 Germany was dealing with uprisings thousands of miles apart and on opposite sides of the continent. It was a bad start, though nothing new in the tale of empire.

In German South West Africa the pastoral Herero rose against the white cattle farmers who had taken over their best grazing and water. German newspapers expressed patriotic horror with illustrations of women clutching their children as farmsteads burned. The French, who had little love for the Germans after suffering defeat at their hands, published dramatised pictures of blond-headed, bearded settlers fighting with clubbed rifles as the assegais pierced them.

The Herero rising suited German colonial policy. Now it had a pretext for teaching the natives a severe lesson. General von Trotha, who was sent to put down the rebellion, reported to the Chief of Staff that he would need 'rivers of blood and money to annihilate the rebellious tribes'.

Among those on his staff was a young adjutant by the name of Paul von Lettow-Vorbeck, who passed on to the troops the notorious extermination order to pursue the remnants of the broken Herero tribe as it fled into the desert. The Chief of the General Staff, Count Schlieffen (famous in history for his plan to invade France through Belgium in 1914) wrote of his approval of von Trotha's 'policy of the sword':

Mount Kibo, seen from the 4 330 m high Kibo camp from the south-east, highest of twin peaks of Kilimanjaro.

'Trotha wants to exterminate the whole nation or drive it out of the country. In this we can only agree with him . . . Once racial war has broken out it can only end with the annihilation of one of the parties.'

A Costly Victory

In South West Africa the black Herero and the yellow-skinned Hottentot Nama lost their land with an estimated sixty to eighty thousand dead. It cost the colonisers nearly three thousand men and seven hundred million marks.

Meanwhile in German East Africa the policy was one of scorched earth. Under the generalship of Count von Götzen an area the size of Germany itself was put to the torch, the crops were burned and the leaders were hanged. Between eighty thousand and a hundred thousand people died, mostly from starvation.

This extreme brutality was exonerated as a panic reaction to the solidarity of the tribes united by the magic potion. The need to stamp out revolt once and for all was the order. By 1907 the Germans could survey a gutted land and rest on their bloodstained laurels, wearied by the strife and longing for the good colonial life. The chiefdoms were abolished and the tribes were administered by *akidas,* or tax-collectors. *Jumbes,* or headmen, who swore loyalty, wore the gold-trimmed toga of authority and held court with a gold-headed staff of office under a certificate embossed with the Imperial Eagle.

13

Colonel Richard Meinertzhagen, Chief Intelligence Officer to Smuts.

British Excesses

Lest at this distance anyone should shudder at the excesses of the German colonists and soldiers, it ought to be remembered that the British
annexations of the same period were hardly less rigorous. It was only
a few years since the scorched earth policy of Lord Roberts and the
horrors of the concentration camps, in which twenty-six thousand Boer
women and children died of disease in the process of establishing the
rule of empire that ended all-effective Boer resistance and set up Lord
Milner as proconsul over a ruined land. Since we have given German
figures let it be remembered that the adult internees of the Bloemfontein camp died at the rate of 383 per thousand and the children at
500 per thousand.

In 1902, in Kenya, a young officer of the King's African Rifles was
given the task of preserving the King's peace among the Kikuyu.
Richard Meinertzhagen expressed his situation as an officer of the
British imperium in these words: 'Here we are, three white men in the
heart of Africa, with twenty nigger soldiers, and fifty nigger police . . .
policing a district inhabited by half a million savages, well-armed, who
have only quite recently come in touch with the white man.' This was
the officer who was to serve General Smuts in 1916 as his Chief Intelli-

gence Officer; a soldier of his time, brilliant and fearless and more intelligent than most generals.

Soon he was engaged in bloody affrays with the Kikuyu. In 1905 and 1908 the Gusii people of Kenya rose in revolt twice against the British encroachment on their lands. Both ended in total defeat by modern weapons. For those who believe that British hands were not stained in blood, reports of the period, little known publicly, tell of many punitive expeditions carried out in the name of pacification.

A British official, B Popham-Lobb, calculated native losses in six operations in Kenya to be 2 426 killed and thrice as many wounded. Again it was rifles and machine guns against spears. To its credit, the British Colonial Office was concerned, but Kenya was far away and the man on the spot pretty well made his own decisions.

It made ugly reading then and it still does. One must not assume that the Gusii, a pastoral and agricultural people numbering about fifty thousand, were peaceful. They had been fighting over cattle, women and territory for centuries before the British cast covetous eyes on their pastures. They rose in arms to throw off the European yoke and return to African ways.

A Fanatic Cult

Rejecting all things European, they embraced a fanatic cult known as Mumboism. This prophesied a golden age once the white men had been evicted. It was a millenarian movement, particularly in revolt against the missionary teachings and the undermining of the native way of life. Its leaders led rituals grounded in ancient, and to the missionaries, disgusting, perversions that raised the people to ecstatic states. This people's land bordered on parts of German East Africa, so it is no coincidence that they too believed in the great snake and the magic water.

The British established their authority in 1908 in this territory of gently rounded hills, a pleasantly cool climate and fertile, rain-drenched valleys, a delightful green oasis that made these highlands so pleasant and fruitful above the semi-desert lowlands and the parched grass and thornlands to the east.*

When the Gusii rose in revolt in 1905 the 3rd King's African Rifles were dispatched with a hundred African police under W Robert Foran. It was a small punitive force reluctantly consented to by Sir Charles Eliot.

Foran has left a vivid description of the action.

---

* In 1905 the European population was 1 700, of whom two hundred were officials. Many were retired officers.

Tribal Massacres

'The tribesmen,' he wrote, 'did not understand the power of modern weapons. They boldly attacked the small force of two hundred askaris with masses of spearmen. Captain Jenkins formed a square and gave battle. He let the attack have a good dose of lead, but this did not halt their determined advance. They ran straight up to the rigid wall of bayonets. Their losses were great. The machine gun was kept in action so long that it became almost red-hot. Before the warriors were repulsed they left several hundred dead and wounded spearmen heaped up outside the square of bayonets. This was not so much a battle as a massacre . . . the lesson was effective. Early next day the leading chiefs came in and surrendered, the tribe being sentenced to pay a heavy fine in cattle and sheep for their past misdeeds.'

Although the Germans have earned odium for their methods, the British (being victors in the Great War and having the sympathy of the rest of the world) were no laggards when it came to scorched-earth tactics.

But little was ever heard. When the Gusii revolted again in 1908 the British colony raised an expeditionary force to put an end to it. Foran, with his police, sent a message to the soldiers to inform them that the chiefs had asked leave to surrender '. . . and were now peacefully returning to their villages with their livestock'.

The fact that an assistant district commissioner had been attacked and wounded with a spear and the tribesmen were massing on the hills in arms, had filled the advancing KAR with determination to settle the matter.

'To my amazement,' wrote Foran, 'the information was ignored.' 'Another medal cheaply won,' remarked a British officer. The King's African Rifles went into punitive action 'burning villages, devastating standing crops, capturing livestock and hunting down the bolting warriors . . . They burned down a great many villages and captured over four thousand cattle.'

On 1 February 1908, a telegram received by the Colonial Office read: 'Result of operations in Kisii [Gusii] to 28 January cattle captured 5,636 sheep and goats 3,281. Kisii reported generally demoralised.'

Churchill's Anger

Winston Churchill, then Colonial Under-Secretary, was dismayed by this report. 'I do not like the tone of these reports. No doubt the clans should be punished, but 160 have now been killed outright . . . it looks like butchery, and if the House of Commons gets hold of it [the information] all our plans in East Africa Protectorate will be under a

16

cloud. Surely it cannot be necessary to go on killing these defenceless people on such an enormous scale.'

Churchill demanded a full report 'upon any causes of discontent' that might have provoked the uprising. With this admonition to 'induce the enemy to submit peacefully' the matter was closed. However, a former governor of the colony, Sir Charles Eliot, noted regretfully that punitive expeditions were often 'needlessly waged by British officers who are hungry for medals'.

No one doubted that the British were there to stay and that the spearing of an assistant district commissioner had been an excuse to destroy the existing order. As it was in German East, so it was in British territories claimed for the Crown, and the natives were awakened to the realities of foreign conquest. Who would have imagined at that time that within a few years Germany and Britain would be fighting for these lands? Meanwhile, in Europe, the conquest was received as the natural order of things. The military minds were quick to note that the tribes that resisted most stoutly would make the best fighting material.

In Tanganyika, a brief period of development and prosperity followed a public outcry in Germany that nearly brought down the government. The charges were maladministration and the well-docu-

Native women in chains (around 1900), building roads.

mented atrocity stories repeated by the liberal opposition. The newly formed Colonial Office took over from the Foreign Office with a mandate to create a humane, efficient ruling class of civil servants dedicated to the welfare of the Africans and the stamping out of the systematic brutality of plantation owners and district officers.

The memory of Carl Peters, founder of the Society for German Colonisation was not soon erased from the liberal German conscience. This early administrator and empire-building adventurer had been dismissed from the colonial service for his brutality. His floggings and hangings fell little short of the atrocities of the Belgian rubber planters of the period, who cut off the hands of workers who failed to bring in enough rubber. His excesses earned him the Swahili title of *Mikono wa Damu*: the man with blood on his hands.

A Liberal Governor

The Germans tried to establish a new kind of administration with the appointment of Albrecht von Rechenburg as Governor of what was now regarded as the most important German colonial possession, a beautiful land, richly endowed with human and natural resources and unlimited potential.

There was to be no more forced labour, no more floggings. New land laws curtailed the rapacity of plantation owners who had taken what they wanted. Rechenburg encouraged African cultivators to grow cash crops with the help of German agronomists. The seven years of peace before the Great War of 1914-1918 saw remarkable developments as the industrious Germans toiled to establish a colonial paradise; not only for the settlers but for the natives also, with a thousand elementary, secondary and vocational schools in which sixty thousand pupils were taught. The work of the bacteriologists Ehrlich and Koch on tropical diseases saved thousands of lives. Ehrlich's .606 serum became a standard therapy for the tropical scourge of sleeping sickness.

'On the basis of its achievements in medicine and agriculture alone,' wrote Charles Miller, the American historian, 'the German presence in East Africa seemed more than justified.' A hundred thousand acres were under sisal; two million coffee trees on the fertile slopes of Kilimanjaro yielded a thousand tons of beans a year; thirty-five thousand acres were under cotton and there were huge plantations of tobacco, cereals and sugar.

The picture emerges of prosperous German farmers in their cool hill bungalows and of settler houses in the German style of timber and stone that in the Usambara Mountains 'might have been a cosy Bavarian hamlet'.

Beautiful Kilima 'Njaro – from Old Moshi. The Swiss-like chalet and the garden of Alpine flowers harmonise perfectly with the snow-clad peak of Kibo, the highest of the twin peaks which constitute the mountain.

Drums of Empire

The Arab ports that had seen only rickety jetties and lateen-rigged dhows from India and Arabia were built as efficient modern ports capable of receiving naval ships. From the port of Tanga the new Northern Railway skirted the Pangani River through virgin forest and over torrent and swamp to reach Taveta in the shadow of vast Kilimanjaro and within a few miles of the border of British East Africa.

The four hundred-mile railway across the middle of the country from Dar es Salaam to Lake Tanganyika gave access to the markets of the Congo, and by 1912 it was more than halfway there. Expectations of prosperity were never so high as the colony prepared for the great Dar es Salaam Exhibition, a trade fair that was designed to show off their achievements to the world.

Over the border in British East Africa there was little to compare with all that. The Uganda Railway ran from Mombasa to Nairobi, a dusty town inhabited by a few hundred Europeans, mostly ranchers, civil servants, police, soldiers and Boers who had trekked north half a century before and again been overtaken by British rule. The King's African Rifles kept any tribal resentments in check on land that had been proclaimed for the Crown and generously parcelled out to settlers.

It is ironic that while the British and German neighbours were bringing order and law to societies that had warred and slaved for centuries, the tribes of Europe were beating their own war-drums before a

19

In the saloon carriage of the Usambara Railway. On the left the married couple Mr and Mrs Prince – she, the daughter of a German owner of large estates, he officer of the Protective Forces and 'pioneer of colonial agriculture' (1912).

continental war on an unimagined scale, a titanic collision of interests that could only end in winner-take-all. A war of rival empires was brewing.

Germany had the largest and most efficient military machine in the world. Her new navy was rapidly expanding to challenge British superiority on the oceans and empire sea lines of trade. Her colonial zealots were beating the drum. Emil Zimmerman, an exuberant advocate of world mastery and empire, was prophesying a German dominion in Africa. From the Atlantic to the Indian Ocean, it was to embrace the entire area of *Mittel-Afrika,* embracing British and German East Africa, Angola, the Cameroons, Nigeria and all West Africa to Cape Verde. This was to produce raw materials for the conquest of world markets by German industry and recruits for an army of a million askaris trained for further African conquest.

An intoxicating vision! A population of fifty million Africans ceaselessly toiling under the supervision of half-a-million Germans. Great towns would spring up in Chad and Tanganyika and the Congo. 'The Chad Express, carrying a freight of German bagmen, would run regularly from Berlin across a prostrate Near East and Egypt southwards.' So wrote the British writer and historian John Buchan, later Governor-General of Canada, in his novel *Greenmantle.*

All these heightened expectations formed the climate of the era and the mood of belligerency of the time. They also created the men of the time who were to leave an indelible impression. In the wilderness of East Africa two men were destined to meet as archetypal adversaries: the Boer politician and soldier Jan Christiaan Smuts, and the German professional soldier Paul Emil von Lettow-Vorbeck. In the fight between them one was to win, yet lose; the other was to lose, yet win.

THE SACRIFICE TO VANITY

THE KAISER: "A magnificent celebration, my people!" [The feature of the attacks during the three days, January 26th, 27th and 28th, in celebration of the Kaiser's birthday, was their expensive uselessness. We estimate the German losses at 20,000.– *Reuter Special War Service*.]
(The *Cape Times*, 16 February 1915)

2

War Awakening

Seven months before the outbreak of war in August 1914 von Lettow was posted to East Africa with the rank of Lieutenant-Colonel. He was the son of a Prussian general, and he looked it with his blunt, almost naked head, scarred face, dominating nose and wide, intelligent eyes. It was the face of a commander, masterful, yet not without a trace of humour.

He was forty-four years old and he had been serving as a soldier since he was nineteen. In 1900, at the age of thirty, he served in China at Kaiachow in defence of German possessions there. A Chinese rebellious movement, known as the Boxers, rose against the European settlers, demanded their expulsion and protested against their grip on foreign trade.

The murder of the German minister, Baron Clemens von Ketteler, was the signal for the siege of all embassies and foreign cantonments.

In his response to the revolt the German Kaiser exhorted his soldiers to give no quarter:

'Take no prisoners! Anybody who falls into your hands must be destroyed. Just as a thousand years ago Attila's Huns gained a reputation for ruthless violence, so let the name of Germans, through your actions in China, acquire a similar reputation that will last a thousand years, so that never again will a Chinaman dare even to look askance at a German.'

Lt-Colonel Paul von Lettow-Vorbeck, Commander of the German troops in East Africa; later promoted General.

The direct order by the King-Emperor no doubt impressed the young officer, who was himself to pass on a notorious order for massacre in Africa when the Herero subjects of Germany rose in revolt. The Kaiser's speech was also to create the fearsome image of the German soldier that stuck to him throughout the war. The word 'Hun' became synonymous with German.

In China, von Lettow saw the British troops in action. He formed a poor impression of their officers' ability to lead and move men in battle. After the German annexation of South West Africa he had a chance to observe Boer forces on commando when he served on the staff of General Louis Botha in a foray against black rebellion.

Contrasting Botha with the clumsiness of the British commanders, he later wrote: 'The excellent qualities of this Low German race that had for many generations made its home on the African veld commanded my respect.' It is possible that this 'detached duty' was a secret mission to assess the Boers' fighting qualities at a time when German ambitions were to call on the Boers to help them establish a German-dominated South Africa.

But it was in 1904 in South West Africa, in hard campaigns against the Herero, that he learned how to fight in bush country with a small force, making headway against a tenacious enemy, with long lines of communication, poor rations and sickness and under constant attack. The enthusiastic young men who left Germany with their rifles garlanded with flowers died like flies.

Von Lettow did not fight in the Maji-Maji risings. He had been appointed to the General Staff. There he studied the German tactics in the bush during that period of tribal revolt.

Lesson of Native Wars

With his experience of the bush in South West Africa von Lettow knew that a thorough knowledge of the native wars would be important, especially in the inevitable conflict between the rival colonial powers in Central Africa. Tactics used by the East African natives were circulated in the field service manuals for use by the colonial troops, the *Schutztruppe*.

The *Schutztruppe* manual noted the tribal warrior's 'mobility and incredible marching powers, coupled with accurate knowledge of the country'. It explained how he avoided direct battle by lying in wait, discharging his firearms and retreating to fresh cover to repeat the process. Having saved casualties and having worn the enemy down he had made him vulnerable to the annihilating spear attack.

Von Lettow noted that to fight, to escape and reform, often in the rear of the advancing enemy, was the essence of their tactics. He studied them closely. They were almost precisely those that he would use himself.

Von Lettow arrived at Dar es Salaam in January 1914. 'I hardly expected the nature of the task that was to confront me in a few months' time. But during the past ten years the universal war had more than once seemed so imminent . . . I knew that the fate of the colonies, as of all other German possessions, would only be decided on the battlefields of Europe . . .' His immediate decision was to put the colony on such a war footing that it would at least share the burden of the homeland and make things difficult for its enemies across the borders.

His plan met with hostility from the new governor and most of the colonists, who were now white-helmeted bwanas, cool in their tropical whites, and ladies reposing on the verandahs of elegant townhouses and new hotels. Dr Heinrich Schnee was a man of peace who wanted only enough time to develop the colony on a new principle of 'the welfare of the natives entrusted to my care'. They were no longer to be regarded as mere tools of 'the more highly developed races'.

Schnee's plan was to create a flourishing colony for the benefit of all, and he hoped to keep it neutral. As long as the British colonies did the same, both could carry on development without disturbance till the question of supremacy was settled in Europe. In the Governor of Kenya he found a like-minded man.

German Liberals Sickened

Schnee's hope was to germanise the territory, not turn its peoples into brutalised work units under the whip. In that he agreed with Professor Bonn of Munich University: 'We wanted to build on African soil a new Germany and create daughter states as you have done in Australia and Canada.' His was the voice of many German liberals sickened by military and colonial excesses in Africa, and he expressed the hope in an address before the Royal Colonial Institute in England in 1914, just before the war broke out

Schnee echoed this liberalism. At once he came in conflict with von Lettow. The Colonel came away from that first meeting, which had turned into a confrontation, determined that he must raise and train a force of volunteer settlers, among whom were retired officers and soldiers, on his own. His Prussian stiff neck made him unpopular with officials, missionaries and the snugly-ensconced settlers just beginning to enjoy the fruits of their efforts.

Von Lettow's Trek

Ten years of peaceful development had wrought marvels, von
Lettow noted, when he set out
by boat, train, on foot, on
horseback and bicycle to reconnoitre the territory that he proposed to defend, with or without the Governor. From
Usambara, in the mountains
near the British border, he went
by rail to the country round Kilimanjaro and Meru Mountain.

Dr Heinrich Schnee, Governor of German
East Africa from 1912. He followed von Lettow into the bush until 1918.

'At Usambara I met an old
friend from our military college
days.' Captain Tom Prince, now
a retired soldier, was a thriving planter eager to join von Lettow's
army.

Together they noted that the Uganda Railway, running from the
British port of Mombasa to Nairobi, was the British colonists' weak
point. Up there at three thousand feet in the clear air of the wooded
mountains, with the green coffee plantations covering the fertile
slopes, the two soldiers estimated that they could raise a force of three
thousand Germans.

'Already we have a Volunteer Rifle Corps,' Prince assured him.
'So far, unfortunately only with sporting rifles . . . it has been impossible to get Dr Schnee to press for military weapons.'

It was still some six months before the declaration of war.

New Moshi was at the terminus of the Usambara Railway. Engineers had blasted and brilliantly exploited the mountain range to get
their narrow-gauge line through from the coast to the vast forested
bulk of snow-capped Kilimanjaro, a gift to Wilhelm II from his grand-
mother Queen Victoria, since Wilhelm had no mountain like it in Tanganyika.

From the terminus, von Lettow went on to Marangu, where he
met the British consul, far from his official headquarters in Dar es
Salaam. Neither von Lettow nor the Consul, Norman King, had any
illusions about why they were there on the border. King was actually
making an assessment of the fighting value of the German settlers in
different regions and sending reports to the War Office.

As von Lettow wrote: 'He was excellently informed on the internal conditions in our colony.' In Dar es Salaam, too, King had been
seen wherever he could pick up information. At a game of bridge at

the officers' mess or the planters' club, meeting people and making enquiries at the post office where German telegrams were handed in for transmission by British telegraph link at Zanzibar.

Askaris Untrained

Von Lettow also met Lieutenant-Commander Schoenfeld (retired), 'the energetic leader who was later to defend the mouth of the Rufiji River against a superior enemy with such stubbornness'. Turning south to Arusha he met some brother soldiers and made his first inspection of a company of askaris. He noted that they were not trained to meet a modern enemy and were armed with the old 1871 pattern rifle, using black powder. Its discharge of a cloud of white smoke had been considered no disadvantage against a native adversary who rushed out of concealment, giving time only for a volley before coming to close quarters.

The askaris had not been trained in musketry, and the machine gun was unknown to them. Von Lettow watched a demonstration of bush war as it had been fought. 'The Meru warriors in full war dress of ostrich feathers remained concealed . . . then at only a few paces' distance fell on the column with loud cries.' In just such a manner, von Lettow reflected, 'Zelewski's expedition had been overwhelmed in a very few minutes.'

The new commander returned to Dar es Salaam. He had noted that the Masai prairie was healthy for human beings and cattle, with room 'for the settlement of hundreds of thousands of Europeans'. He was amazed that a country so capable of cultivation was so uninhabited. Indeed, he believed that East Africa could support a population 'barely less than that of Germany'.

The education and training in agriculture and in manual skills of the natives impressed him, but he noted that the askari companies were few and far between and without communication other than heliographs. He also noted the information from a missionary that 'foreign Arabs and Swahili were appearing in the country and telling the people that the Germans would soon be going, and that the English would take possession of the land'.

That was in June 1914, only two months before the outbreak of war. He knew that the German Staff had prepared a plan for the invasion of France and Belgium. Britain was still a probable enemy, but there was no time to waste. He had to set about planning offensive operations against British East Africa and raising an army.

At the moment there was a protective force of 216 Germans and 2 540 askaris and a police force of 45 Germans and 2 154 askaris. All were scattered about the immense territory and untrained for the war that von Lettow envisaged.

26

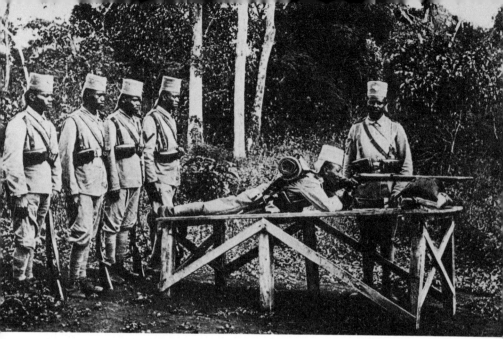

Askaris at shooting drill in 1915.

Germany Mobilises

Early in August he was on the railway station at Kidodi when a telegram came from Governor Schnee: 'Return immediately to Dar es Salaam'. Next day he was told that His Majesty had ordered mobilisation. 'I managed to catch a goods train from Kilossa and so arrived at Dar es Salaam on the 3rd of August.'

He had found a number of retired officers of the *Junker* class, men who lived by what von Lettow called 'the spirit of military life and true discipline'. His own military training had been 'under the guidance of admirable commanders', and he felt capable of adapting his training to the new conditions.

On 4 August the German armies crossed the frontiers of Belgium in an act of undeclared war. The Schlieffen Plan was in operation. Seven armies of about a million and a half men were marching over the frontiers in sweeping advances planned to encircle Paris within a few days.

'The question that immediately forced itself on us,' von Lettow recorded, 'was whether, in the now obviously imminent universal war in which England would almost certainly join, the Colony would remain neutral or not.'

Neutrality was what Dr Schnee and his officials most ardently hoped for. All communication with Germany had now ceased. The supreme military power in the colony was in the hands of the governor. At all costs he wished to avoid a bombardment of the coastal towns where the settlers were appalled by the prospect of losing all their gains as British warships shelled them to rubble. Schnee wished to make some kind of bargain with the British. If they did not attack, he would not open his ports to ships of the German Navy in the Indian Ocean.

Von Lettow argued that 'we could best protect our colony by threatening the enemy in his own territory', and the first task was to collect the forces scattered all over the country and concentrate them in the north near Kilimanjaro. Once he had his forces in threatening array the British would have to react with their own, which would prevent their use in other more vital theatres of operation. It was a vast spoiling exercise that he envisaged. The British would have to expend 'many milliards to try to crush our diminutive forces'.

From the beginning he saw that it could go on for years with the British deploying ever-increasing resources in men and money. And so it turned out. The small, intimidating, eagle-eyed martinet got his way after a British warship sailed into Dar es Salaam harbour on 8 August and blew up the wireless station. That was when all communication with Germany ceased.

Von Lettow Attacks

They were on their own. Within ten days of the outbreak of war von Lettow attacked the British East Africa Police Force garrison at Taveta. The twenty-four police there fired a token volley and fell back in good order on Voi.

'This action,' wrote Charles Miller 'gave von Lettow the distinction of being the first and only German commander of the war to occupy British soil.'

Taveta had fallen easily, but it was to loom large in the minds of British planners as the key to the gateway into German East Africa. It was also the place where the South African infantry would soon litter the bush with their dead and wounded when it came to retaking it on the slopes of Salaita Hill.

The Germans were now well placed to begin a series of raids against the single-line railway from Mombasa to Nairobi, which would tie up the small resources of the British army in patrolling the line night and day. It was an exercise in futility in the vast stretches of the Serengeti plains that wore down morale and achieved nothing except what von Lettow wanted: to bring in British troops in ever-increasing numbers, thus bleeding the British army in Europe.

Meanwhile in Quetta, at the Indian Staff College, Richard Meinertzhagen had been noting in his diary the progress of the great continental powers towards war. The feelings that this volatile man expressed from day to day were a mixture of apprehension, indignation, patriotism and excitement.

A German reconnaissance plane.

A Remarkable Diarist

Meinertzhagen's writing precisely mirrors the mood of the time as they waited for news to reach them in the last days of peace. On 1 August he wrote:

> Europe is heading for disaster and there is going to be a most terrible catastrophe. I feel it coming. Germany, the one power who could stave off a world war, stands by with folded arms, confident in herself, arrogant and perhaps now powerless to check the forces which she has bred and nursed these many years.
> It is not only a dream enjoyed by the Kaiser and his officers, it is a dream consciously desired by the whole of Germany – an intense desire for world domination, and, as a means to this end, a deliberate intention to bring about a world war. We are the real enemy, not France or Russia. Their defeat is only a stepping stone towards our doom, and the real cause of war, should it break out, is naval competition and the jealousy it has engendered between Germany and ourselves . . . [There are] two inherent German diseases – bitter jealousy of Britain and bitter hatred of the French. I doubt whether either of these diseases can be cured except by the blood of millions of human lives and the expenditure of millions in gold.
> [Later] France has mobilised. That will force Germany to do likewise and nothing now can avoid conflict. May God be with my country. There is a general feeling of silent elation at the Staff

College . . . some of my brother officers seem to think it is an occasion for uproarious behaviour.

3 August 1914. Quetta.

Late last night came the news that German troops had invaded France. No news from England, except that everything is calm. The calm before the storm. All shipping is disorganised or racing for harbour, business in London is paralysed.

5 August 1914. Quetta.

I feel absolute confidence in the ultimate result of this war. We shall eventually win because our cause is just. But Germany will fight well and hard and it may be she will not be brought to her knees before next summer. At the Quetta Club this evening occurred a disgraceful scene. The band played 'Rule, Britannia!' and everybody cheered. Fritz, the German waiter, was still on duty, and some young cavalry officers got hold of him with intent to duck him in a trough. I made myself most unpopular by rescuing the unfortunate fellow and did not mince my words . . .

24 August 1914. Bombay.

I reached Bombay and at once reported to General Aitken, from whom I learned that our destination is German East Africa and that I am in charge of his Intelligence Section.

One of the most remarkable aspects of a very remarkable man was Richard Meinertzhagen's almost uncanny prescience. If one did not know that this diary was written from day to day it could almost read as a chronicle in advance of what actually happened. Or should have happened. He foresaw the strategies that should have been employed and the disasters that could have been avoided. The irony was that nobody listened to his advice.

Admirer and Critic

Meinertzhagen became Smuts's Chief of Intelligence, and he was his staunch admirer and severest critic. His diaries present a vivid picture of both the campaign and Smuts as a leader and a man.

Here is his assessment of the situation in East Africa, written in Bombay at the time when von Lettow was beginning to concentrate his forces in the north and get into position to hold the British on the Kilimanjaro front. Von Lettow was building up his forces at Moshi at the very time (13 August) when Meinertzhagen was writing:

I look with misgiving on any attempt to invade German East from the coast . . . much better concentrate opposite Taveta and compel the Germans to concentrate at Moshi. Build a railway across the Serengeti and occupy the Kilimanjaro and Arusha districts. Tanga and the Usambara Railway would then automatically fall into our hands. If necessary, I should not attempt more during the war. Our position would secure British East from invasion and would give us a healthy country for our men.

The Tanga Débâcle

If Meinertzhagen's reasoning had prevailed the British would have been spared at Tanga the most costly débâcle in human lives and morale ever suffered by British arms in Central Africa. It would also have saved the need for the 1916 'March on Tanga' to take it and the suffering of thousands of men and animals attempting to reach the port through the Usambara Mountains and the steaming swampy plains of the Pangani River; a miasma of disease.

Meinertzhagen had served in the King's African Rifles from 1901 to 1905. He knew German East Africa and had contacts there who were already informing him on what lines the Germans were concentrating and giving him their strength. But nobody paid any attention. Although he was the only officer in the invading force who had any knowledge of the interior of East Africa, his assessments were ignored.

Before the force even embarked from Bombay with troopships and a naval escort, and in a mood of dangerous complacency about the opposition, Meinertzhagen wrote with misgiving:

> The troops sent with the force constitute the worst in India, and I tremble to think if we meet with serious opposition. I have seen many of the men and they did not impress me at all, either as men or soldiers. Two battalions have no machine guns, and the senior officers are nearer to fossils than active, energetic leaders of men.

It is not within the scope of this book to recount the disastrous landings at Tanga and the wretched performance of both Indian units and British naval assistance. It is worth noting, however, that some of those in command would soon be in command of South Africans. They would infuriate Smuts by their incompetence, ignorance, hidebound tactics and general assumption that the British gentleman-officer knew it all, although in fact they had not the faintest idea of how to use troops in Africa. Smuts lost no time in getting rid of some of them.

What became a four-year war at an unforgivable cost in lives and money could have been finished in one daring stroke if it had been handled as Meinertzhagen outlined it. A decisive defeat of the still small German force at Taveta would have settled the matter.

So they sailed, the armada of twenty-one ships escorted by a battleship and two cruisers, to disaster.

Their orders were to occupy Tanga, place it in a state of defence and push on with the rest of the force to the healthy highlands near Nairobi and from there turn south to eject the Germans from Kilimanjaro. Having achieved that they would advance towards the Central Railway from Dar es Salaam.

It all looked very good in the senior officers' mess. The force, having reached Mombasa after a wearisome voyage at nine knots across the Indian Ocean, left there for the beaches of Tanga confident that the plan made in London would work well. No resistance was expected from the enemy, and indeed the War Office had not even envisaged a campaign in East Africa.

In the event, eight thousand men with sixteen machine guns, a mountain battery and the six-inch guns of the destroyer *Fox*, were beaten by von Lettow's thousand men with four machine guns and no artillery. Not only were the casualties appalling but von Lettow was able to re-equip his forces with modern British rifles, the sixteen machine guns, half-a-million rounds of small-arms ammunition,

Telegraphic message of success by Governor Dr Schnee about the disastrous battle of Tanga, in which the British lost a large number of troops and material in an attempted invasion of the port.

Lieutenant-Colonel Paul von Lettow-Vorbeck (second from right) with officers of the German *Schutztruppe* (defence force) and friends in German East Africa before the First World War.

enough field telephones to supply the *Schutztruppe* and enough clothing to kit out the entire *Schutztruppe* for a year.

The German press was jubilant and published imaginative illustrations of the battle. Von Lettow said with admirable modesty that 'Tanga was the birthday of the soldierly spirit in our troops'.

Tanga was to affect the judgment of Smuts and his staff. Indian troops were worthless and naval landings were an invitation to disaster. If he had thought otherwise, the campaign might have been fought along other lines.

So the deadly encounter of the South African general and the German colonel came nearer. It was to be a strategy of 'your move' followed by 'checkmate' as the brilliant adversaries sharpened their wits to outdo each other's latest manoeuvre.

Why was Smuts there? What was German East Africa to a former Boer general? He was now righthand man to the Prime Minister, Louis Botha, and his Minister of Defence. Why had the colonies of Germany become the concern of a South Africa so recently at war with the British Empire? Partly, it was because of Smuts's belief in the real possibility of a German empire in *Mittel-Afrika*. No Boer wanted that.

Fear of German Rule

When Meinertzhagen asked a Boer officer why he had come to help the British – was it loyalty to the Empire or expediency or what? – the reply was: 'Although we respect the flag and the British race and would sooner be under British rule than German, we do not love the British. Our dream is eventual independence.' His hope was that having proved loyal in the British war 'we shall receive our complete independence'. It seemed a powerful enough motive to bring thousands flocking to answer Smuts's call.

What of Smuts himself? What was the South African position when this war was declared? In 1912 Smuts gave the House of Assembly a masterly review of the principles governing the defence of South Africa.

To staff officers in Bloemfontein he said:

> We want a force that will be able to defend South Africa against anyone who may come against us . . . things may happen that nobody foresaw . . . At present the nations all seem to be preparing as if doubtful of each other . . . We want an organisation that shall be not Boer or English, but a South African army . . . do your duty in a broad national spirit.

The Red Rebellion

Only a few months later the country was plunged into turmoil and rebellion. The mining trade unions represented a mostly immigrant British work force at skilled level. Their leaders declared a general strike and mass demonstrations by thousands of men who refused to disperse from Market Square, Johannesburg. Red flags were waved and Bolshevik slogans shouted. They demanded a Workers' Republic. The offices of *The Star* newspaper, supporting the 'Rand Lords' were sacked and burned down.

Smuts rushed Imperial troops to Johannesburg and dragoon sabres flashed as they charged the packed square. Next day the strikers marched to storm what they saw as the citadel of capitalism, the Rand Club. The troops fired. Twenty-one were shot dead and forty-seven wounded. Smuts and Botha parleyed with the leaders of the strike in the Carlton Hotel, two defiant figures symbolic of order in a maelstrom of hatred and anger.

Forced by armed strike leaders to agree to their terms, Smuts later explained:

> We made peace because the Imperial forces informed us that the mob was beyond their control . . . Anything could happen in Johannesburg that night; the town might have been sacked and the mines permanently ruined.

In the biography of his father, J C Smuts wrote: 'Botha and he drove away through the hostile mob. Botha replied to some of their jeers and threats; but my father sat white and mute with anger. Not a word passed his lips, but in his heart he had decided that such a state of affairs should never rise again.' His first action as Minister of Defence was to organise the Defence Force.

Don't Hesitate to Shoot

With the labour movement cock-a-hoop, the leaders of the strike tried again in January 1914. This time Smuts declared martial law and ordered the Rand Light Infantry to: 'exercise the greatest severity . . . don't hesitate to shoot.' Smuts seized the nine British ringleaders and summarily deported them. The Labour movement raged. Smuts replied: 'A smashing blow had to be struck at syndicalism in this country. I gave that blow.' In ten days he had smashed the general strike and the union leaders' attempts at revolution.

Politically the new Union was in a state of disunity. The Boers were divided in violently opposed factions in which the British took little part. Some were for Botha and a nation of British and Dutch equal and united, others were for separate races with the Dutch in control.

Suddenly, six thousand miles away in Europe, the nations were at war. 'In South Africa,' wrote H C Armstrong in his biography of Smuts, *Grey Steel*: ' . . . the Dutch were only vaguely interested. They sat in cinemas and watched the newsreels showing the German advances and the retreats of the English and French . . . this was no affair of theirs.'

However, Botha and Smuts saw it differently. As early as 1911 Botha had assured London that South Africa could defend itself without Imperial troops and would invade German territory if asked. Ten days after war was declared he had personally agreed to a British proposal 'to attack the Germans in South West Africa and destroy the big wireless station at Windhuk'.

Smuts Urges Parliament

Smuts urged Parliament to support Botha's decision.

England has treated us well, given us back our liberty, and now she needs our help. There are German battleships in South African waters and they threaten our trade. They are in communication with Germany through the wireless station in the southwest . . . The British Government has said, 'There is work for you to do,' and I ask Parliament to let us do it. It is a duty we owe to ourselves also. The Germans are bad neighbours.

Many of the Boers resented the idea of a call-up against the Germans, and their anger was whipped up by German agents at work all over the country. To many Boers this was the God-ordained time to strike and seize back their republics. The Germans were almost in Paris . . . the British were being whipped. Beyers, the Commandant-General of the Defence Force, had been appointed by Smuts. Now they disagreed. Beyers was convinced that the Germans would win. He had seen their army manoeuvres. He had followers ready to support him, including men with important commands in the Defence Force. The plan was to rise on 15 October, the very day on which the South African contingent would be leaving for German South West Africa.

Germans in South West were on the border ready to raid over the frontier into the Cape as the first South Africans disembarked at Lüderitz Bay, well out of the way at the southern port of the German colony. It was the great opportunity.

It is not the purpose of this book to chronicle the tragic events of the revolt or the campaign that so quickly defeated the German forces in South West Africa. But in an examination of Smuts's motives for sending South Africans to German East Africa it should be noted that Smuts wished to take command of the South West expedition.

But the Boer volunteers were Botha men and would not fight under Smuts, who remained in Pretoria as Acting Prime Minister. He was quickly critical of the progress of the campaign, especially the timidity of General MacKenzie.

Smuts's Northward Ambitions

An expansion northward of South Africa had been in Smuts's mind for years; since republican days in 1895. He was a man who needed to be at the heart of things, to drive the chariot of destiny, his own and that of others too.

'Fierce, sharp and resolute,' so British Intelligence had assessed him. The man who had spoken of 'those old-world monsters of Empire' was now confident that he could add first German South West and then German East Africa to the territories of the Union; yet within the free and fraternal bounds of the British empire.

Other Boers had the same dream of acquisition – but outside the British empire. As Smuts's biographer Hancock noted:

> In 1914, however, the government's case was grounded upon the argument of German aggression . . . it would have been too embarrassing for it to avow aggressive purposes of its own. Then, too, there was the clear evidence of Germany's 'eager eyes on the Union' to make attacks legitimate.

Strike first! There never would be a better time to establish a South African hegemony over an enormous area of Africa. Three precious months had been lost in getting control of the ferment in the Union, and some of the troops had to be recalled. By New Year 1915 the Germans still held the whole country except the two ports of Swakopmund and Lüderitz. There had been infuriating administrative bungling on a vast scale and much friction between Boer soldiers, all conscripts and British officers. And 'the old chap', General MacKenzie, was unwilling to take the offensive. Botha asked Smuts himself to come to the southern front: 'Stand fast and hurry through and come in yourself at one end – then we shall finish everything by May.'

By the second week of April 1915 Smuts was at the front. He chased the Germans north into Botha's net after heavily defeating them at Gibeon.

'I have finished my job,' he wrote, 'and have now returned to the Union after disbanding part of my force and handing the balance over to General Botha . . .'

On 12 July he issued a general order. It described the conquest of German South West Africa as 'the first achievement of a united South African nation, in which both races have combined all their best and most virile characteristics'.

Relentless Pursuit

It had been a hellish campaign. In typical style Smuts had driven his men and animals across the desert in a relentless, unremitting pursuit that took no account of hardship, lack of water and rations, foundering horses and transport oxen and the exhaustion of his men.

This was a prelude to what was to come. In both tactics and ruthless determination he had established his style of attack, a style that depended much on his own energy, his force of will to impose on the weak flesh of his men, his own determination not to weaken.

As he said to disbanded burghers at Potchefstroom: 'If you tell them of the march from Nonidas to Karibib they will not believe you; if you tell them how little water you drank and how few biscuits you ate, they will not believe you . . . There is always success on the road to duty!'

However, there was serious division at home; bitterness between the white races; glorification of the Boer martyrs of the rebellion; hatred of Smuts and Botha.

Smuts was warned: 'Do be careful about sending men out of the country. We shall want them all when the civil war comes, as come it will, if things go on as they are now.' So wrote the Parliamentarian John X Merriman.

In South West Africa Smuts had come across a copy of a book that caused him to muse on the wide gap between Kant and Goethe and the spirit of the *Junkers*. It was already being whispered in London that he might be going to London to the Imperial War Conference. But Smuts did not yet see his duty there; not yet outside Africa.

Invitation to Command

It was in November 1915 that he received an invitation to take over the command of British troops in German East Africa. He had watched the disastrous course of that war with interest, finding support from men like Merriman, who argued that it was a proper sphere of interest for the Union. 'If that country were conquered by us,' he said, 'we could probably effect an exchange with Moçambique and so consolidate our territories south of the Zambezi and the Kunene.'

Indeed, as Minister of Defence Smuts had already approved the sending north of two regiments to face the enemy on the north-eastern frontier of Rhodesia. A call had come from the Imperial Government for volunteers to push back the enemy between Lake Tanganyika and Lake Nyasa. Within two weeks two regiments, designated the 1st and 2nd South African Rifles, were mobilised and equipped with machine guns, signals, medical and wireless sections. With a battery of 75 mm mountain guns captured in German South West they sailed up the Zambezi and Shire rivers. From Limbe they marched over five hundred miles in fifty-four days to join the Rhodesians, most of whom had also returned from the campaign in South West.

Follow the Drum

Back in the Union, Smuts called a national conference in Pretoria on 13 November 1915. Delegates from all over approved the appeal of Sir Charles Crewe, director of recruiting, for ten thousand men. A wave of enthusiasm swept the country and in a fortnight Smuts had his recruits. Many had only recently been discharged after service in German South West.

In Johannesburg nurses and women of patriotic societies and Boy Scouts with Union Jacks paraded the streets to the cry of: 'Fall in and follow the drum!' Private motor cars led the way with posters exhorting: 'Recruits come with me to the Wanderers' (sportsground). Drums were thumped and every balcony was packed with flag-waving enthusiasts. Seven thousand men marched four abreast in their civilian attire to sign on. Hastily trained and scantily equipped, they were paraded before Smuts and the Governor General, Lord Buxton, both mounted, and were embarked with patriotic fervour from Durban in SS *Laconia*.

They were the first of twenty thousand men that Smuts had decided were necessary for East Africa and France. But this force was earmarked for East Africa.

The British Government had so far regarded this theatre as a sideshow. It had discouraged any military adventures by its generals there. What limited actions they had ventured upon had been without exception disasters. The Germans were masters of the frontiers and of the only rail connection between Mombasa and Nairobi.

It may be asked at this late point in the century, why a country of such limited resources in men and wealth should be eager to send volunteers to the ghastly impasse that had developed in Flanders. That would be to underestimate the potency of the rallying cry: 'King and Country!' Many volunteers were still committed in spirit to the Motherland. South Africa was a secondary loyalty.

The Call of the Blood

What was their motive? Part of the answer is to be found in a collection of personal experiences by a soldier who signed his name simply F C. When Private F C Cooper's book was published in Cape Town in 1917 the war in East Africa was still far from over. Ten thousand men of many races had died there for the British cause. Two thousand of them were South Africans. Why were they there?

Private Cooper opened his book with a chapter headed 'The Pathway to War'. He had just been demobbed after volunteering for the 1915 campaign in South West Africa and was wondering 'what next'?

'Our little party of six dined in immaculate evening dress a few weeks after the return. The dinner had been proposed one day over a lean meal of bully and biscuit and we had derived great comfort from the recitation of the dishes proposed for the menu of this great feed of the future.' The dinner turned out to be a farewell. The writer joined the ranks of the infantry brigade sailing for East Africa; two others were about to sail for England to receive commissions and to fight in France.

'Lying on my straw mattress in the training camp, or rolled in my blankets on the hard veld under the stars, I have listened to my comrades chatting away on a range of subjects varying from higher mathematics to the quality of the last bully-beef issue.'

Why they joined up was never discussed. Cooper put it down to duty, a greater or less proportion of patriotism, a love of adventure and a temporarily carefree life. 'Some in sorrow for what they must leave behind, and some who would sooner face a German bullet than the scorn in a girl's eyes.' But for the man who wanted to see the world 'everything was provided for him – free passage, free meals, free clothing; no worry about tickets, luggage or hotels, no need to wonder how much to tip the porters and stewards. Everything necessary was supplied by a generous government, which asked a man in return only a few simple services such as perfect discipline, reasonable care of his rifle or horse . . .' And a willingness to be killed.

Sons of their Time

Cooper was an intelligent, literate, educated man, and though he writes with conscious irony and underplays his emotions, he was a son of his time. On the trooptrain taking his brigade from its training ground at Potchefstroom to the troopship at Maydon Wharf in Durban he was 'profoundly moved' by a sight of the graves of his countrymen round Colenso, Spion Kop, Ladysmith, and the dozen other historic battlefields. 'I think even the gayest hearts among us felt that the presence of those great dead made the ground on which we stood holy.' Men who had fallen for Queen and Empire.

There stands the reason in the unabashed commitment of an English-born South African. He was carried away by the great tide of emotion of the hour and the frenzy that had gripped the peoples of Europe. He did not know that what was happening was a 'showdown' between rival empires. He was a willing pawn in the imperial game between the greatest colonial power on earth and a nation that aspired to be at least second.

Frederick Russell Barratt was typical. At twenty-three, this son of a Methodist minister landed in Cape Town in January 1901. At that time, he wrote in a memoir: 'Hundreds of young Britishers were flocking over the seas to take their chance in a country still in the making. Some of them had come over to South Africa to take part in the war.' Barratt thought he would 'do a little soldiering' before resuming his career as a schoolmaster. When the war ended he became a civil servant.

He was working in Pretoria when the war in Europe broke out. At the age of thirty-nine he volunteered to leave his wife and children.

> To us 'home-born' men the call was especially strong, partly of patriotism, partly a feeling that one ought not to be out of it when others went. Some would not wait for the formation of South African units but paid their passage to England to join British regiments.
>
> There was certainly no reason why the Afrikaner should feel impelled to fight for the British Empire but an astonishing number did volunteer. Some of them couldn't even speak English.

The mystery of why so many Afrikaners from all ranks of society volunteered was explained by Deneys Reitz:

I had no animus against the German people, but I thought then that a victorious Germany would be a disaster for human liberty. Also, my chief was going, and I could not hang back while so many of my countrymen were moving forward to an adventure in the wilds of Africa.*

Dudley Phipson, just discharged from the German West African campaign and still only twenty-three, went immediately to the Secretary for Agriculture in Pretoria and asked for permission to join up again. It was refused. The department was short-handed. A few days later: 'the telephone rang . . . I was to be released at once. I dropped my pen and within half an hour I was heading for Pretoria from Onderstepoort, the mules going at a hand-gallop. I intended to enlist in Pretoria and catch that evening's mail train to Cape Town to join the South African Field Artillery for service in France.'

Patriotic Frenzy

This sense of a need to serve extended to all the gold-mining towns of the Witwatersrand. Its large immigrant populations spread along the reef were in a frenzy of patriotic enthusiasm. In a memoir of those years, a Benoni woman, Winnie Simpson, recalled the scene as she saw it as a child of seven:

> Few families were not affected. All military service was voluntary, and the men signed on for a campaign at a time. Early in 1915 Daddy joined the local Citizens' Voluntary Training Corps. They drilled in the Market Square. Alongside of Daddy's love of his family and devotion to home life, he was very strongly a born soldier. A mounted regiment was raised and No 2 Troop, A Squadron of the 1st South African Horse was recruited from Roodepoort, with our school principal, Mr Carter, as the lieutenant in charge of it, and the major was a Mr Stewart ('Mudguts') from Krugersdorp.
> The training was at Roberts Heights, and there were few weekend passes. Mother went to Pretoria to meet him before the regiment left. Mother must have been very heavy-hearted as the time for departure drew near, but she was as brave as everyone had to be. When Daddy left by train for Roodepoort I earnestly begged him to stand behind a big tree while shooting Germans, and just put his rifle round.

---

* Later Colonel Deneys Reitz commanded the 7th Battalion, the King's Shropshire Light Infantry and the 1st Royal Scots Fusiliers.

In May 1915 the sinking of the *Lusitania* caused widespread indignation, and this was expressed by some citizens in the burning and looting of the German shops in Roodepoort.

Trooper Simpson went to war with a present of a green morocco leather cigarette-case, and he reached East Africa in time to qualify for the 1914-1915 Star.

Describing the thousands of men gathering at Potchefstroom and Roberts Heights training camps at the end of 1915, Frank Reid, a barrister with the rank of private in the 9th South African Infantry, wrote:

> They were on the whole of a most excellent stamp – the pick of the available manhood of the country. Among them were men of every profession, trade and calling – parsons, barristers, attorneys, architects, civil servants, schoolmasters, engineers and men prominent in every branch of sport.

Cape Coloured Enthusiasm

Equally enthusiastic about serving were the mixed-race people of the Cape. A large number of Cape Coloured men had already served in the German South West African campaign as artillery and transport drivers, motor drivers and mechanics, officers' servants and on other non-combatant duties. But it was not until September 1915 that there was official sanction for their enrolment into a separate infantry battalion to be known as the Cape Corps. 'Until then,' wrote John X Merriman, 'prejudice had stood in the way.'

What kind of men were they? A J Desmore, who served with their 2nd Battalion in the last and fiercest part of the entire campaign in East Africa, described them:

> The bulk form the labouring class of South Africa . . . mainly as farm labourers and, in lesser degree, in skilled trades in the towns. The labouring class have very robust physique. They have perseverance and a power of endurance . . . a marked cheerfulness under extreme circumstances makes them natural soldiers.

Most recruits came from the Cape, but 'almost every train from the north brought its batch of warriors to Cape Town and the City Hall was daily the scene of much excitement.'

Their forefathers had served for over a century in the various frontier wars of South Africa and had worn the red tunic of the British as well as the uniform of the Dutch in innumerable native campaigns as foot-soldiers and cavalry. As late as 1896 they were in Colonel

Baden-Powell's column raiding into what became Rhodesia. He wrote: 'There was some tough fighting and the newly arrived corps of Cape boys, much to everyone's surprise, showed themselves particularly plucky in storming the kopje.'

This was the last campaign when the Cape Corps served. Now it was eager to be reformed and to fight as a unit. As Desmore put it: 'They prayed to be allowed to share in the toils of the Great War.' And particularly in a fighting capacity.

The battalion was attested in December 1915 and in six days it was over a thousand strong, and hundreds were turned away. They were a special breed of men, as brave as they were unpredictable, as tough as terriers and with the special virtue of cheerfulness. General Sheppard later wrote of them: 'The only men in my column still singing at the end of the march were the men of the Cape Corps.'

Commanded by Lieutenant-Colonel G A Morris, they sailed north on 9 February 1916 to suffer every privation of Smuts's army and, unlike the bulk of the South Africans, to be in at the death in 1918.

THE CALL OF THE BLOOD

THE entire British Empire has given a ready assurance to the Mother Country of the desire to share and stand by her in the present struggle.
(The *Cape Times*, 7 August 1914)

3

Smuts Answers British Call to East Africa

At this time a curious paradox was evident in the thinking of Smuts. This man, so eager to face the hardships of war, had just returned from a victorious campaign in German South West Africa, where he had earned a reputation for hard driving, pushing his men with relentless energy. Privately he was questioning the spiritual dilemma that faced the soldier.

'Will mankind, sick of all this horror, turn inward and purify its spirit, or will it become debased and demoralised and brutalised by its horrible experience?'

At that moment there came a call from the War Office in London to take command of a new army in East Africa where Brigadier-General Edward Northey commanded a force of five thousand men. Difficulties abounded; the German guerrilla fighters were harrying his lines of communication. He was in no state to fight an attacking war.

Smuts seriously considered the call, which came to him in November 1915; but he turned it down, pleading the exigencies of the political climate. Many round him were arguing that German East Africa must be the next battleground if the Union were to secure its own safety and interests.

Smuts knew that, but he hesitated. He professed relief when the command was then offered to General Sir Horace Lockwood Smith-Dorrien. This officer was one of five who had survived the Zulu spears at the massacre of a British force at Isandhlwana. He had commanded a brigade in the Boer War. In France in 1914 he commanded the British 2nd Corps in those desperate first days of the German onslaught through Belgium. His turning at bay with his retreating army at Le Cateau had stopped the retreat from Mons from becoming a headlong rout of men overwhelmed by enormously superior numbers. In the shattered village the controlled fire of his men, armed with the .303 Lee Enfield rifle with its ten-round magazine, had cost the Germans such heavy losses in their tight formations that they could not pursue further.

Springboks for the East Coast Campaign. Two reviews of the 2nd SA Infantry Brigade were held at Potchefstroom, one by HE the Governor-General, and the other by General Smuts, Minister of Defence.

Smuts discussed the new appointment with his old comrade Jacob Louis van Deventer, just back from the campaign in German South West Africa. The Boer commander reminded Smuts: 'I captured one of his convoys. He was a young brigadier, in command of the 19th Brigade . . . some of the *kêrels* we gave a hard time at Modderfontein.'

Smith-Dorrien had emerged as an officer with real concern for his men, and he was dismayed by the reckless and futile tactics of his commander at Modderfontein. Kitchener had coldly ordered his regiments to charge the well-entrenched Boers. It was a day that cost 1 270 men, dead, wounded and missing.

In East Africa Smith-Dorrien was given command of two fresh divisions, among them the 1st South African Mounted Brigade under Van Deventer, whose opinion of British generalship in Africa was as low as that of Smuts. Critical of the appointment of Smith-Dorrien, Richard Meinertzhagen noted: 'If he thinks he is going to conquer German East and bring von Lettow to terms, he's mistaken. He'd do it less likely with ten divisions.'

Brigades Sail North

The end of December 1915 saw two brigades of South Africans embarked for Mombasa. These were 2nd South African Infantry Brigade under Brigadier-General P S Beves and 1st Mounted Brigade under Brigadier-General J L van Deventer. Both officers had commanded in South West Africa. Under Lieutenant-Colonel S A Taylor were five batteries of South African Field Artillery armed with thirteen-pounders. The necessary administrative units, supply columns, field ambulances and railway companies were shipped with them.

Meanwhile the 3rd South African Brigade under the command of Brigadier-General Berrange and a second mounted brigade under Brigadier-General Coenraad Brits were preparing to sail, while 2nd Mounted Brigade was in training to embark in April under the command of Brigadier-General B Enslin.

On New Year's Day, 1916 Van Deventer's mounted brigade trotted jingling through the streets of Nairobi with the 1st, 2nd and 3rd Regiments South African Horse. The Boer officer with the guttural croak, legacy of a throat wound by a British bullet, met the British generals under whom he would be fighting. Brigadier-General Michael Tighe, a florid-faced, heavy-drinking Irishman, had led a brigade that had been thrashed at Tanga and was now in command, awaiting Smith-Dorrien.

The hearty Boer may have confided in private to his officers his opinion of Tighe and his staff. Meinertzhagen was outspoken in his diary. Tighe commanded a 'rotting, undisciplined, weak, planless, gutless lot of buffoons in uniform'. No matter how the British staff bluffed it out, none had recovered from the three defeats that they had suffered already.

Tighe, according to Meinertzhagen, had been drinking 'much more than is good for him and is now fast in the clutches of gout and liver and, I fear, incipient delirium tremens'. However, he was, despite his intense irritability, 'a man of great charm, a good soldier and straight as a die'. It was just a pity that he was 'drinking himself to death in the middle of the greatest war in history. Sad'.

From Durban to Mombasa. The SS *Laconia* leaving Durban with a 'full cargo' of Union soldiers for German East. Note her two big guns on either side of the stern end of the middle deck. (The *Laconia* was sunk by a German submarine in the Atlantic during the closing days of February 1917.)

From the very beginning there was a clash of cultures. To the British officers Van Deventer and his staff were a rough lot 'hardly able to speak the King's English'. They were not impressed by the Boer generalship that had so swiftly cut down the German threat in South West Africa. The Boers were seen as specimens of a race defeated and conquered, and here they were wearing the uniforms of British officers. It was grotesque. 'Why, these fellows have no traditions whatever . . . uncouth is the word. Quite at sea in the mess!' was a typical comment.

Nairobi's Contempt for the Army

This hardly veiled contempt boded ill for the coming battle when Tighe would make his attempt to clear the Germans from British East African soil at Salaita Hill. Van Deventer found that the citizens of Nairobi despised the British army for its defeats and humiliations and for the imposition of martial law. They resented the puffed-up self-importance of pukka officers from India who looked down on all about them and bemoaned the sporting life that they had left. All were debilitated by long years of inactive service in a docile India of parades and polo; chota pegs and gymkhanas.

The intelligence officer particularly detested Brigadier-General Wilfred Malleson, a soldier who was as vain as he was vacuous in commanding troops. 'A bad man, clever as a monkey, unreliable and with a bad record behind him . . . he knows little about active operations and comes from a class that would wreck the empire to advance himself.' He went so far as to predict: 'within six months Malleson will not have achieved a single success and will have cost us many hundreds of valuable lives, and within a year he will be sent summarily home'.

This in fact, was the man whom Tighe chose to lead the attack on Salaita Hill. Van Deventer noted, in his bluff Boer style, that there was not an officer among the staff who had won a battle yet, and that included Brigadier-General J M Stewart, who had been senior staff officer at the Tanga fiasco and had tried his hand at command at Moshi only to be thrashed. He was 'a great gentleman of great charm,' noted Meinertzhagen, 'but a hopeless, rotten soldier'.

The injection of the South Africans should have come as a blast of vigour. They had tasted victory in a hard campaign, but the gentlemen of the staff at Nairobi considered them a pack of amateurs, not gentlemen enough for staff college officers and positively loutish in the vulgar confidence with which they assured everybody that they would soon teach the Germans and their blacks a Boer lesson with the sjambok.

The Governor, Sir Henry Belfield, had given the settlers a lead in coldness to the military. In a notorious speech, much welcomed by the settlers, he had declared: 'I wish to make it abundantly clear that this colony has no interest in the present war except in so far as its unfortunate geographical position places it in such close proximity to German East Africa.'

The South Africans received a chilly welcome from both settlers and soldiers. The only soldier who showed wholehearted approval of their arrival was von Lettow. He wanted them to arrive in ever-increasing strength 'and thus be diverted from other and more important theatres of war'. He noted, with some regret, that the Boers whom he had so much admired on their own ground were now about 'to take a decisive and in a sense tragic part in anglicising the German part of Africa'.

He welcomed every piece of intelligence about the forces being built. Mombasa had been transformed from a somnolent Arab port into a military depot and transit camp and was the busy terminus of the Uganda Railway line to Nairobi. Its docks were crammed with unloaded artillery, staff cars, lorries, ambulances and armoured cars. Thousands of horses and mules were emerging from the holds of transports.

A Private's First Impression

As a veteran of South West Africa Private F C Cooper noted the contrast from the landing on 'the inhospitable sands of Walvis Bay to the forests of coconut palms' as the infantry troopship nosed up the narrow channel to Kilindini harbour. They had been seven days at sea, crammed into the steamy messdecks.

He and his comrades, after unloading regimental kit and stores, explored the ancient Arab town with its British additions in the form of 'some good government buildings, private residences and shops, as well as a cathedral of oriental architecture'.

After one night under the tropical stars in base camp the reinforcements were packed into open trucks, and the Ladies' Comforts Committee which had welcomed them ashore with tea and cigarettes were supplanted by bawling sergeants and transport officers.

'The oven-like bogies were shared with thirty-nine others, fly-bitten horses, sparse battery mules, solid-tyred motor lorries and Swahili stretcher boys.' More than half the men had to make the journey up-country standing. A harassed transport officer to whom they complained snapped back: 'When you reach Flanders you'll find double this number in a truck!'

The train began its long climb through forests of coconuts and bananas, wrote Cooper. These gradually yielded to rubber plantations and fields of maize. 'We climbed steep gradients at a walking pace and rushed down inclines with a reckless speed that would have blanched the hair of a Cape branch-line passenger.' At the bottom of many a hill lay derailed trucks.

Then out into open country, teeming with game. Forests, thorn bush; then the emptiness of the great plain and their destination, Voi. This was the huge military camp and training base about two hundred miles from Kilimanjaro. In the clear air of the plateau it was not too far off to see the snow-capped summit of the immense mountain, rearing its bulk nineteen thousand feet into the equatorial sky.

Here the raw troops began 'the purgatory of training', the fighting of mock battles and the heat and dust of manoeuvres as they rehearsed attacks with machine guns firing, and at the bugle call, charging through the bush with fixed bayonets and yelling war cries. 'Wars are still won with the bayonet . . . the infantryman and cold steel.' Such was the received wisdom.

The newcomers found the men already there in low spirits. The Germans held every foot of their territory after more than a year of skirmishing, and they had two positions on British soil, at Taveta and with an advanced post at Salaita. Gruesome tales circulated of the German askaris' prowess with the bayonet. The troops were always on the defensive, always apprehensive of attack, never hitting back. They were weary of being rushed from place to place, always too late to oppose the aggressive attacks of von Lettow's men. Constantly ambushed, their supply trains derailed, their bush trails mined, weakened by tropical diseases, they were a sorry army.

Stand-to at Maktau Stockade

The worst place to be stationed, the South African newcomers were told, was the advanced post at Maktau. There the defenders had cleared the bush for half a mile round the camp. 'We stood-to every morning and evening in perimeter trenches, facing towards the boma of cut bush stacked all round as an impenetrable obstacle'. There was a sense of a beleaguered garrison waiting for the onslaught, which came in sudden attacks on patrols venturing beyond the stockade or on supply trains bringing up rations.

The railway line had been pushed on from Voi along the old caravan route along which slaves had marched in weary columns. The line was punctuated at intervals with the gaunt iron carcasses of trucks and locomotives derailed by mines. Here at Maktau supplies for a growing army were piling up.

There were pyramids, some thirty feet high, of hay and animal fodder. Just outside the perimeter was the cemetery, where rested those fallen in the encounters when the enemy attacked our advanced post.

So wrote Brigadier-General J H V Crowe, Smuts's Chief of Artillery. His batteries were learning to shoot in bush country. The thirteen-pounder guns of the South African battery, relics of the Boer War, were pulled into battle positions by teams of oxen goaded forward by yelling, cursing Cape 'boys', as they were called by all. Heavy four-inch naval guns sent from England arrived with wheels too thin to support their weight in the dust and mud of bush tracks and had to wait weeks for the arrival of steam traction engines to draw them.

Formidable Difficulties of Supply

Such preparations took months of the dry season. In the coming campaign men would have to march and hack their way through jungle and elephant grass, head-high, totally dependent on supplies getting through to them. Food, ammunition, medicines, fodder for cavalry horses, mules and oxen, fuel for motor cars, would all have to follow the army as closely as possible in a country totally unsuited for an army that could not support itself from the land. The enemy, however, would be falling back on his supply bases and could forage as he retired, leaving nothing for those who followed, the fertile fields stripped or burnt.

The askaris could live adequately on the land, but for the British forces the only food that they could rely on from East Africa was fresh meat from the slaughter-oxen driven with them, salt bacon, dry mealies, coffee and groundnuts. As Brigadier-General Collyer, Smuts's Chief of Staff, noted: 'South Africa could have supplied unlimited quantities of biscuits and preserved meat but for the

An ox-team hauling a field gun in German East Africa.

An askari soldier. Recruited from local East African tribes, askaris made up approximately ninety per cent of the *Schutztruppe*.

lack of any tinning plant in the Union.'

The Germans were already well-equipped with porters to carry guns, ammunition, food. Each askari company had an allotment of 250 men, and each one of those was a potential askari. Von Lettow boasted that he had 'hundreds of thousands of carriers working for the troops'. His troops were recruited from tribes that had for years been used by slave traders and were, in Collyer's words 'apt disciples of the cult of force'.

Weeks before Smuts arrived, staff officers were wrestling with logistic problems. Once the border railway lines were left behind, the attackers would have to depend for supplies on a force no larger than three mechanical transport companies, one bullock cart company and six ox-train companies. The bulk of stores would be carried on the heads and slung on the poles of nine carrier companies of thousands of chanting blacks, who also had to be fed.

Smuts was aware of the difficulties that he would have to master. The ravages of tsetse fly, horse sickness and other animal diseases guaranteed that the life of transport and cavalry would be short. In some areas there would be insufficient water for the men, let alone the mass of transport animals following them.

While the dry season lasted wheeled transport could use the few roads and tracks; but once the rains burst in this land of torrential rivers, bridges would disappear and the streams would become oceans, while the Germans would destroy railway lines, signal communications, bridges and culverts, rolling stock and locomotives.

In Brigadier-General Crowe's assessment:

The transport question was beset with every kind of difficulty. It demanded expert knowledge, forethought and imagination. We knew conditions would be unlike any previous campaign in which forces of this size had been engaged.

51

And so it turned out. For in truth, no one had any idea how bad it would be once the juggernaut was on the move. Perhaps only von Lettow knew what was in store. He had been busy raising and training his forces. During 1915 the number of his field companies rose to thirty and rifle companies to ten. He had shrewdly mixed Europeans with askaris so that there were no separate black and white companies but a unified company with a common *esprit de corps*. The greater number of recruits came from the populous districts of Tabora, Muansha and the district round the Northern Railway.

By the end of 1915 he had raised a force of three thousand Europeans and over eleven thousand askaris. They were not all fighting men: they included administrative staff, hospitals and field postal services. He was well aware of what was coming. As early as June 1915 he had intelligence that General Louis Botha was coming from South Africa with fifteen thousand Boers. It was only a rumour, so far, for with little wireless communication from outside he had to depend on limited sources.

On the frontier, his fighting patrols told him that the enemy's railway system was pushing nearer to German territory. Attacks were constantly being made on working parties 'but the line continued to make progress to the west'. Once it became obvious that the enemy would attack from the north it would be time to remove all military stores to the south.

At that point von Lettow was uncertain whether the attack would come from the enemy preparing to advance in the Kilimanjaro country. 'I still thought it possible that the main force would operate in the Bagamoyo-Dar es Salaam area'. But by New Year the army under Brigadier-General Tighe was within three miles of the great mountain 'where he established strongly fortified camps'. These were supplied by pipelines from the springs in the Bura Mountains and pumped into reservoirs for the supply of thousands of men and animals on the dry plains.

Only a few miles away the Germans had discovered excellent wells on the old caravan route through Taveta. From there the men defending Salaita Hill had to carry their entire supply of water by donkey cart, for the hill was waterless. An attempt was made to find water with the help of a water diviner in the force. The men at Salaita dug a pit more than a hundred feet deep, but none was found; so every day the donkey cart safari had to trek the eight miles to Taveta, running the risk of ambush.

But it never came. Von Lettow was amazed that the precarious link was never seen as vital. If it had been cut, the crucial hill would have been abandoned without a shot being fired. But as long as they had water the Germans could turn the slopes of the barren hill into a fortress defended by three companies and two light guns.

Major Kraut was Waiting

Major Kraut's men looked out over the flat thorn country from a feature that rose like an easily assailable hill out of the surrounding sea of bush and flat-topped acacias, typical game country of the plains. It was, in von Lettow's assessment 'an almost impregnable fort'.

On New Year's Day, 1916, Meinertzhagen noted in his diary the arrival of the first South African mounted men. General van Deventer, he wrote, was a fine figure of a man, not unlike Botha.

> I spoke to many officers and men. They all seem confident that they will finish the campaign in a few months. I tried to explain to them that they had not the slightest idea of climatic and health difficulties, neither had any of them any experience of fighting in thick bush. I told them I thought perhaps two years might finish the campaign. They smiled and told me I did not understand the Boer. This Dutch brigade should do us well, for the men's physique is splendid and their morale high . . . at the back of their heads they have the idea that if they get the country they will be allowed to keep it.

Meinertzhagen's assessment of a two-year struggle was in fact an underestimate, though close. But, as he often complained, he was an intelligence officer that nobody listened to.

Von Lettow was now aware of 'considerable bodies of troops, amounting to a thousand or more men, who deployed in the direction of the mountain [at Salaita] but did not approach it closely. These were

German askaris in military training in 1915.

exercises by which the young European troops from South Africa were to be trained to move and fight in the bush'.

Smith-Dorrien to Command Imperial Army

The news that General Smith-Dorrien had been given command in East Africa caused a flutter of apprehension among the generals and British staff officers under the discredited General Tighe. Smith-Dorrien was not a man to be deceived by poseurs, bluffers and rank incompetents. Tighe, drinking heavily, saw the writing on the wall and hoped to restore his position by retaking Taveta and thrusting over the border, to throw the Germans off Salaita Hill and defeat von Lettow's main force on the spot.

From London, Smith-Dorrien approved the plan and took ship for Cape Town. The plan was nothing if not ambitious. It was to smash a quick breach between the Pare Hills and the immense sprawl of Kilimanjaro, a gap only a few miles wide. It was known as the Taveta Gap. Once through it, Tighe intended to destroy von Lettow's army.

The strongest force in the resurrected army so far were the South Africans with fresh mounted riflemen, full-strength battalions of infantry and five field batteries.

The remainder of two divisions were a thoroughly imperial mixture of British, Rhodesians, Kenyans and Indians, including the 130th Baluchis, grim fighting men from the Afghan border. They had been blooded in Flanders, had no fear of heavy gunfire, bore their casualties stoically and were fearless in assault with the bayonet.

There were no askaris of the King's African Rifles, for no serious attempt had been made to raise further battalions of these formidable bush fighters. In short, there was not an officer or man in Tighe's force who had the smallest experience in the bush except for the 2nd Rhodesians.

On the staff of East Africa Force was Brigadier-General C P Fendall, who wrote that Smith-Dorrien had been confident that when all the reinforcements had arrived, he would not have 'great difficulty in defeating the enemy'. However, he had reservations about the quality of some of the troops. The newly raised South Africans were untested material. Some had fought in German South West, but the rest were likely to be raw.

Commander Struck Down by Flu

On 24 December 1915 the staff contingent of East Africa Force of forty-three officers and nearly two hundred men with motor cars, batmen, baggage and drivers, left Paddington Station at midnight.

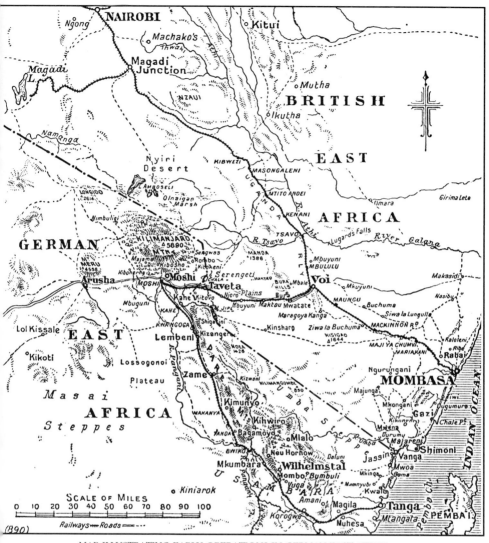

MAP ILLUSTRATING EARLY OPERATIONS IN GERMAN EAST AFRICA.

We arrived at Plymouth in the early morning to find a high cold wind blowing. The Commander-in-Chief had had a bad influenza cold for several days . . . he came off to the ship in the afternoon in a piercing wind. A day or two later he was desperately ill with pneumonia.

Smith-Dorrien barely managed to stagger off the ship in Cape Town and went to Muizenberg to recover in Sir Abe Bailey's house, a fine Cape Dutch mansion overlooking the warm blue-green waters of False Bay. A young captain and Member of Parliament, Piet van der Bijl had been one of the South Africans appointed to his staff.

55

I reported to him at Rust en Vrede to be told he was seriously ill. I never saw him. I was handed a huge trunk filled with documents, codes and ciphers, so secret that, not daring to leave my compartment on the train to Pretoria, I had all my meals there.

When he arrived at Pretoria Van der Bijl heard that Smuts had been offered the command. General Collyer, just back from South West on Botha's staff, told him: 'I am going as Smuts's Chief of Staff, and you will be Staff Captain. Mrs Smuts's brother, Tottie Krige will also be attached to the personal staff.'

When the British officers, newly arrived on the way to East Africa, stopped at Cape Town, they took train to Pretoria to meet Smuts, Union officials and the Defence Force chiefs. They noted that the Smuts command structure looked like developing into an all-Boer staff. They had been appointed by Smith-Dorrien, and they would never see that gallant soldier again.

'Many decisions were made in Pretoria. South Africa was to be the main source of supply for the force. On paper these looked excellent,' wrote Fendall, 'but we did not get the whole-hearted co-operation they required. Obstacles were put in the way of East Africa Force by people over whom we had no control.'

From Pretoria Smith-Dorrien's chosen officers took train to (Maputo) Lourenço Marques on 27 January 1916. This was only two weeks before the new offensive and three weeks before the arrival of Smuts as the new Commander-in-Chief.

Nairobi – an Administrative Mess

What the staff found in Nairobi was an administrative mess by generals and staff of the Indian Army temporarily commanded by Tighe, described as 'an impetuous Irishman who was never so happy, never so cool as when under fire'. He was a disgruntled man, having had to make plans and preparations for a campaign to be carried out by a commander who came victorious from another theatre. Brigadier Simpson Baikie's staff were angry, too, at being downgraded by the arrival of staff officers of higher rank from England. And they showed it aggressively. Fendall described Tighe's staff as dithering, still thinking in terms of peacetime Indian Army economies, with no imagination or forethought for what was coming.

According to Major Piet van der Bijl on Smuts's staff, 'several had been sent there by the War Office in London or Headquarters in Simla, to get them out of the way. Living very comfortably, they dressed for dinner every night, not in mess-kit but in posh tusser silk khaki uniform'. Dismayingly inefficient, and now bitterly resentful at being

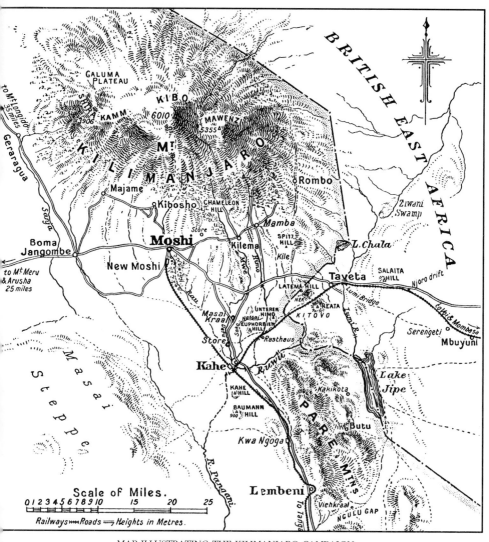

MAP ILLUSTRATING THE KILIMANJARO CAMPAIGN

shoved aside, they were a recipe for disaster if the new C-in-C turned out to be weak.

At Salaita Hill, the Germans were still in possession. Tighe, drowning himself in whisky, was about to be downgraded from Acting Commander-in-Chief to a Divisional Commander. Since he preferred action, he showed no resentment towards Smuts. The new staff, however, soon showed little confidence in the South Africans, the mess they had inherited and the news that Smith-Dorrien would not be coming after all. Smuts's appointment was a shock to most. Heads were going to roll.

'Some thought he would get rid of all the staff and put in his own men from South Africa. He was used to their ways of running a campaign and not that of regular British Army staff.'

Van Deventer's mounted brigade with many loyal Boers were openly delighted to be commanded by one of their own. Fendall observed: 'The infantry, largely composed of Englishmen*, were not so enthusiastic about it. They did not relish having to serve under a man of another race.' What would Smuts do? Memories of the Anglo-Boer War were still too close for some.

His biographer Hancock quotes him as only accepting at the urging of the Cabinet 'with many a pang and misgiving'. But Armstrong, the author of the Smuts biography, *Grey Steel*, says that with seventeen thousand South Africans already in German East Africa Smuts believed that 'a South African general ought to be there to lead them and look after them'.

When he accepted the command it was in the face of his enemies' sneers. *Die Burger* wrote that 'he was escaping his difficulties . . . had to go because of Cabinet disagreements . . . was after an English general's pay in addition to his salary as a South African Cabinet Minister'. Smuts told Botha that he could finish the campaign in a few quick strokes. Armstrong describes his last hours in South Africa in moving terms:

> He wasted no time, went to his house in Irene to pack up, and down to the little local wayside station to catch the night train to Durban. Two staff officers from Pretoria and a few local friends saw him off. He came hurrying along at the last moment with his family . . . his children barefooted and lusty urchins of the farm. He said goodbye briefly under the station lamp, picked up his eldest son, carried him to his carriage, and then, with a sigh, as if he could not bear to leave him, put him down, climbed up into the coach, and steamed away into the darkness.

On that hot February night Smuts travelled with soaring spirits. He was sick of the bickerings of the political scene and weary of desk work and being the villain of the piece on all occasions. He was eager to prove his generalship.

Of the night of 11 February 1916 his son wrote: 'I had grown weary of the protracted proceedings of the evening, so my father carried me to the platform in his arms and took me into the train with him. At Durban he paused for only twenty minutes before boarding a steamer for Kilindini.'

---

* Worked on a basis of names only, a breakdown of men killed or who died of disease shows 82% of the infantry were English and 56% of the mounted men were Afrikaners. These figures cannot be taken as accurate as many names were interchangeable but they indicate, surprisingly, the large number of English mounted men.

He went, not without military criticism of the appointment. Brigadier-General Crowe noted with professional doubt that 'he was a man who was not a soldier, who had practically no experience in handling any considerable force'. But he granted that Smuts's operations in South West were characterised by 'peculiarly daring and successful strategy'.

In short, being a professional soldier trained in the hidebound traditions of the military college and a part of the petrified military structure of command was quite likely (as it had proved) to be more of a hindrance than a help. It was a bold stroke, Crowe conceded, this choice of Smuts.

What did Smuts know of the command that he was sailing to take up? There were two divisions, the 1st and 2nd East African. The 1st, under Major-General J M Stewart, had the 1st South African Mounted Brigade with divisional troops. The 2nd, under Major-General Tighe, had the 2nd and 3rd South African Infantry Brigades and divisional troops under command.

Concern Felt in England

He knew that both generals had a sorry record and that throughout England there had been intense dissatisfaction about the failures in East Africa. Questions had been asked in Parliament, and the newspapers had urged the Government to bestir itself. He knew all too well that at home in South Africa the British failures had been a matter of contempt. Now he felt secure. His recruiting campaigns had raised some 35 000 men, of whom the spearhead were now to be tested.

He came with his own ideas of tactics that owed nothing to British generalship. His own tactics had worked well in German South West. Why not here? Above all, he saw his adversary von Lettow as a formidable opponent. A man as skilled, wily and inflexible as himself. If he could beat the German on the great plateau of semi-desert and thornbush it would be over quickly. After all, Botha's victory in South West had been a model desert campaign. Water and transport difficulties, considered insuperable by the enemy, had been overcome and a brilliant and daring strategy resulted in the rapid collapse of the enemy. He had to admit that 'during the nineteen months before his arrival in East Africa the enemy had been superior to us both in strategy and effective striking force'. He realised, too, that the Germans had not attempted to invade in force.

Von Lettow had known that the real struggle was to come, and he devoted his attention mainly to the recruitment and training of a large native army under German officers. Smuts was all too well aware that he was coming to command an army demoralised and humiliated,

German East African native troops in the early days of the war.

with no confidence in itself. Doubtless, he hoped that by the time he arrived, the large army now assembled would have shown its teeth; particularly the enthusiastic new blood brought by his South Africans. They were to be given their chance at Salaita Hill.

ARE YOU THE ONE ?

SIGNALLER: "Hold on ! 10,000 South Africans coming." [A Contingent of 10,000 South Africans were being recruited for British East Africa.]
(The *Cape Times*, 25 November 1915)

4

Salaita Hill – A Shock Defeat

Early in February 1916 the South African force in East Africa consisted of two brigades. Van Deventer was there with his 1st Mounted Brigade, all experienced riders and good shots, men after his own heart and mostly of his own people. There were four battalions of infantry under the command of Brigadier-General P S Beves in his 2nd Infantry Brigade. The 1st Infantry Brigade was already in France. Five field batteries of artillery were ready on the scene of operations. All were now at Mbuyani where, on 13 July the year before, the British had been repulsed. Now the Germans had drawn back from there.

In the first week of February the railway from Voi had been extended up to the Njoro Nullah, a dry watercourse three miles from Salaita.

General Tighe's plan of attack was ready. The senior South African officer was to be General Beves, commanding 2nd Infantry Brigade. He had been an infantry captain in the Boer War, and recently he had commanded a brigade in German South West.

Smuts sailed north in the knowledge that the day of the attack would coincide with his embarkation. If he had little confidence in British generalship, he was certain that his men would give a good account of themselves. He had entire faith in Van Deventer and the loyal Boers who made up much of his mounted force. The old veld warrior was as tough as old boots, a tried and tested comrade from the Boer War onwards. He did not know Malleson, the officer to whom Tighe had entrusted the South African Brigade and the conduct of the operation . . . only that both he and Tighe had been in the fiasco at Tanga. But this would be different. This was not a coastal landing with Indian troops, seasick and demoralised before they set foot on the beach, poorly trained for service in Indian conditions. 'Wretched, chattering, hysterical gunfodder'* who had thrown away their arms before a handful of askaris.

---

* Meinertzhagen's comment.

Brigadier-General Beves, Commander of the column which pushed south over the Rufiji as part of Smuts's renewed offensive early in 1917.

He had no doubt of the outcome with his men led by his own Brigadier-General Beves and Lieutenant-Colonels Byron and Freeth. He had once called the Boers 'the best soldiers in the world', and he had no need now to think otherwise. So he sailed north on the sparkling bosom of the Indian Ocean.

It was in the week before the coming battle that von Lettow noted the first appearance of hostile aeroplanes. 'They bombed our positions at Oldorobo Mountain [Salaita] and Taveta. On 27 January one of these airmen, while on his way back from Oldorobo, was fired on and brought down by our advanced infantry. The English had told the natives that this aeroplane was the new *munga* (God), but now that this new *munga* had been brought down it rather increased our prestige than otherwise.' His askaris were also greatly impressed that German arms had defeated the flying god.

Things had not gone easily for the 26th (South African) Squadron of the Royal Flying Corps. At that altitude the rudimentary BE2C biplanes had the greatest difficulty in gaining height and were thrown about by the violently rising thermal currents. Private E S Thompson noted in his diary how he 'saw an aeroplane start off for the German lines south of Kilimanjaro. Another aeroplane rose about ten minutes later and after flying in a large circle suddenly swooped down. The propellers hit the ground and broke and the plane swerved round and turned completely over. This is the second plane we have lost this week.'

Urgent Need for Air Reconnaissance

Captain Leo Walmsley's account of the campaign tells how the squadron of eight machines camped with its canvas hangars on the flat grassy plain at Mbuyani. It had taken several days to bring up the aeroplanes from Mombasa, unpack them from their wooden crates and assemble them for flight.

The need for aerial reconnaissance behind the enemy lines was hourly becoming more urgent, and as soon as the first machine was ready we were ordered out. Captain Creed cleared the trees at the end of the aerodrome by inches only, and it was nearly half an hour before we reached six hundred feet.

Some of the open spaces were literally brown with game. At the western extremity of the plain rose the mighty slopes of Kilimanjaro, its highest peaks floating on a great bank of cloud, its snow fields and glaciers aglow in the evening sunshine.

Farther south the ragged cliffs and ridges of the Pare Mountains leapt from the plain, dark and portentous, for they formed the natural barrier between the British and German armies and behind them lay the vital Tanga-Moshi Railway, which later became the main objective in General Smuts's offensive.

The airmen were touchy about their relations with the general staff. 'From the beginning,' wrote Walmsley, 'the aeroplane was regarded with disfavour by the Dutch General Staff . . . they looked on it as an expensive toy, useless either as a substitute for or as an auxiliary to cavalry, particularly Dutch cavalry.' Their claims were 'frankly discredited', their observations regarded as inaccurate.

This was the squadron that would be giving vital reports on the defences at Salaita Hill. Its members were British pilots of the Royal Flying and South Africans who had volunteered for training as 'officer-aviators' in 1913 and learned to fly in Kimberley. They had flown on reconnaissance patrols for Botha and Smuts in German South West and had had a taste of frontline battle against the Germans in France. It was from there that they were called back to Britain to regroup and form the nucleus of No 26 Squadron RFC, known as the South African Squadron.

It was snowing at Southampton on Christmas Day, 1915 as the greatcoated pilots and observers embarked under the command of Major G P Wallace. Now at Mbuyani, they had among their ranks East African settlers and former civil servants and officers transferred from RFC squadrons.

Staff did Not Like Initiative

Walmsley, himself British, noted that the British pilots were regarded as 'outsiders', and this led to an extraordinary amount of jealousy, favouritism and ill-feeling. Some of the best pilots were 'manoeuvred out' for showing an initiative that the staff did not approve of in this upstart arm of the services. Indeed, that had been the attitude of the South African staff even in South West Africa, where aircraft were regarded as expensive toys apt to crash and a poor substitute for horsemen.

Neither did these airmen take kindly to discipline of the military sort. Walmsley admitted that 'compared with the infantry, ours was a soft enough job. There were no enemy aircraft to worry us and few anti-aircraft guns. While the poor tommies were floundering in the swamps or staggering across the scorching, waterless veld, we were flying in clear air above – well fed, clean, healthy and safe. While they were rationed we were feeding on Fortnum and Mason hampers, grumbling when we had to take water with our whisky instead of Schweppes.'

Obviously, then, there was a gulf between the sweaty horsemen, the footslogging infantry and the airmen from the very beginning. There is no doubt that this ill-feeling, suspicion and distrust contributed to the disaster at Salaita Hill. A pinch of prejudice led to an avalanche of mishaps, and the military put the blame for what happened on the airmen as much as on their own mishandling.

From Mbuyani observers in their eight obsolete biplanes began to fly over the German posts to assess their strength. The elongated fusilage of the fragile BE2C biplanes gave them the appearance of dragonflies as they drifted over the treetops at speeds little more than 60 mph, or 100 in a dive. They were rejects from the Western Front, already much repaired and subject to hair-raising engine failures. The observer was the senior airman, rather like the captain of a ship, and the pilot only the operator, the helmsman as it were.

Observers flying over Taveta from their aerodrome only seven miles away had been unable to see any sign of German movement there. But even when movement was seen it was practically impossible to tell the difference between German and British khaki.

On 3 February the South Africans were sent out on a reconnaissance patrol in strength to test the defences on Salaita Hill. The infantry skirmished forward and artillery bombarded the hill. Smoke drifted away, and the infantry opened fire; but there was no response. The question now arose: Was this post on the flanks of the big movement through the gap into German territory a position to be taken seriously?

Beves was an officer who cared for his men, although he knew how to drive them hard, and he was soon to earn a reputation with the Germans for making frontal assaults with no regard for casualties. From the beginning of the planning he was uneasy about his three battalions to be committed under General Malleson.

Malleson's reputation as a *flâneur*, his fondness for women and champagne, his deafness to good advice and his theatrical style all combined to trouble the careful Beves. Tighe, usually genially tipsy and eager for combat in his belligerent Irish way, had given the 2nd Division to his old Indian associate for the operation.

Malleson saw it as a walkover. He brushed aside an assessment from Meinertzhagen that there might well be something like fifteen hundred men with artillery up there. His booted legs astride, cigarette-holder at rakish angle, Malleson drawled that he reckoned on no more than three hundred riflemen, the blacks notoriously poor shots, a few machine guns and no artillery.

Kraut's Hill was a Lethal Trap

The German commander was Major Kraut. He knew the border territory round Kilimanjaro well. He had been waging guerrilla war there for months, and he had beaten off a British attack at Longido, an extinct volcano near Mount Kilimanjaro. By a swift manoeuvre he had put to flight a force of a thousand. Major Kraut was fully prepared. He had months in which to work out his strategy of defence and counter-attack. His rifle pits and trenches were dug and wired, his guns ranged, his machine guns sited to fire over open ground, their ranges carefully marked by poles stuck up in the lethal stretch of ground cleared of bush. His reserves were in position to counter-attack.

In short, he welcomed the test of strength against the low, sprawling hill that he had turned into a fortress. He had not shown his presence to the force that had come probing on 3 February. On 9 February he got his second chance to deceive the South Africans as they made another cautious reconnaissance.

Private Thompson of the 7th was in it. He describes with touching *naïveté* the training of the green troops, so recently in civilian life. Between filling machine-gun belts, doing gun drill and learning how to apply field dressings, he went with his mates to the YMCA canteen to buy things for a friend's birthday. 'Bibby and I bought some Eno's Fruit Salts, potted meat, preserved pineapple, chocolates and soda water'. A regular schoolboy feast. Next day the youngsters moved out. The night before their officers had told them to be ready to march at five a.m. 'Great bustle getting ready. Told we were to attack a bridge and hold it. Great excitement!'

Here is his account of the advance march on 9 February.

9 February (Wednesday)
Reveille 0330 Saddled the mules. Breakfast. On the road 0530. Fine morning for marching. The 5th, 6th and 7th Regiments were accompanied by a Baluchi Regiment and Field Telegraph Corps. Firing was heard on the left flank (5th Regiment) and we heard that they had met an askari patrol. We could now see that there was a German fort on a hill about three miles away flying two flags. We all thought we were to attack this and so loaded our

rifle magazines. We advanced for another hour through the bush and then came into a clearing and as they could see us quite well we expected every minute they would open fire, but they never did. Suddenly word was passed along that enemy were sighted at 400 yards ahead, so we doubled into cover and unpacked the guns. The range was now given as 800 yards.

Ordered to Retire

The askaris could be seen running down the hill from the fort to man the trenches. The fort was right on the top of a small hill and had three lines of trenches. It ought to be a tough place to take as the ground is so exposed. After about 15 minutes we were told to pack up and retire and then began to feel tired and disgusted . . . it is reckoned we went about twenty-four miles altogether. The mules were pretty tired as they had the heavy guns and saddles on for nearly twelve hours. We never took our packs off once.

Later we heard that General Beves was very pleased with us. He wanted to attack but it would have been no good as the railway was not near enough . . .

Had Kraut's men deliberately exposed themselves as they rushed to occupy the trenches plainly visible at the top of the hill? Did no one ask this question or suspect the obvious? Observer Leo Walmsley flew over and reported: 'We had no difficulty in identifying Salaita Hill with its elaborate system of trenches and entanglements. Machine guns flashed as we passed over at a thousand feet . . . it was very annoying having no means of retaliation. I pulled out my Colt automatic and emptied the magazine at the hill.'

South African artillery at Salaita, part of Tighe's 2nd Division which moved east along-side Van Deventer.

Major-General J J Collyer CB, CMG, DSO.

Aerial reconnaissance had not revealed the presence of six more field companies between Salaita and Taveta, all of them battle-tested Germans and askaris seasoned in frontier skirmishes and daring raids. All that was known, as Collyer wrote, was that 'the hill was well entrenched, with some clearance of bush on the east and south-east approaches.'

Malleson's plan was delivered to Serengeti camp. From it Beves learned that his infantry were to attack from the north to deal with any possible counter-attack. Beves did not like what he read; neither did the major of his brigade. It had all the earmarks of a foolhardy, illconsidered frontal attack; and even though it would be made in two-brigade strength, numerically far superior to the enemy, Beves wanted some assurances for his battalion commanders who were questioning the wisdom of the movement.

The Over-confident Malleson

They drove to Malleson's headquarters, where they were met with a supercilious response when Beves put his point of view.

'My brigade will be seen from miles away. There will be no element of surprise. When I've committed my three battalions frontally, according to your orders, what is to deal with a counter-attack from Taveta?'

'My dear general,' drawled Malleson, 'you'll have adequate artillery support. In any event, the assault will be over before they can reach Salaita.'

'It's only seven miles, Sir.'

'Two hours' march!'

'I'm asking for another battalion to take care of my exposed flank.'

'You'll have Belfield's Scouts thrown out towards Taveta in plenty of time to warn on any more from that direction.'

'I would point out, Sir, that artillery co-operation in that kind of bush on the north side will be unable to break up a counter-attack. I am asking you to reconsider.'

Malleson replied that the Commander-in-Chief's order stood. There would be no discussion. 'In any case you'll be attacking in strength against about three hundred askaris. Your brigade's admittedly green, it'll be stiffened by the Loyal North Lancs, the 130th Baluchis and the 2nd Rhodesian Regiment; not to mention two armoured cars and a machine-gun unit.'

Seething with controlled anger Beves told his infantry commanders: 'The attack is on as scheduled. Your battalions will move out independently from Serengeti at 0500 tomorrow.'

'What about further orders when we've taken the hill?'

The question came from Lieutenant-Colonel Byron, commanding the 5th, while the commanders of the 6th and 7th stood by.

'My orders are to eject the enemy. No doubt further orders will be given. That's it, gentlemen. Good luck!'

This was the evening of 11 February.

The regiments had marched from Mbuyani to Serengeti, leaving their kit at base there and taking only what they considered necessary for their first battle.

Private Thompson took one blanket, slacks, socks and his cholera belt. It began to rain at Serengeti, and 'a good many of the chaps took off their clothes and tried to get a bath in the rain, but they were worse off than before.' Later that night he wrote: 'Got marching orders and were told that we were to attack Sileta [sic] Fort. Great excitement!'

His regiment, the 7th, was to lead the attack. Only a few days earlier Thompson had noted in his diary: 'Heard that a Rhodesian got lost on patrol and had been found with his arms hacked off and his eyes taken out.' This grisly intelligence, whether true or not, may have been the origin of the word that passed among the young soldiers: 'We are to take no prisoners.'

Such was the fearsome reputation of the askaris, all recruited from warlike tribes, among them cannibals* who not many years back had disembowelled and beheaded their prisoners. Von Lettow wrote of recruits who brought in ninety heads of their enemies to prove their fighting worth to him.

Day of the Fatal Attack

Morning of 12 February.

At headquarters of 2nd East African Division, Major-General Michael Tighe was hopeful that all would go well before the arrival of the new

---

* Meinertzhagen wrote of his cannibal Corporal, Simba Manyema. When he found him after a skirmish with the Nandi with five hands in his belt, the corporal said they were regarded by his people as the tastiest part of a man. 'But the best of all is the buttocks of a young girl.' Kenya, 1904 as recorded in *Duty, Honour, Empire* by John Lord.

General M J Tighe.

Commander-in-Chief. Until then he was in charge of an operation that he had devised and that had been passed by Smith-Dorrien and the War Office. Malleson could hardly fail with two brigades. By the time Smuts arrived on 19 February they'd be through the gap in hot pursuit, with the Germans falling back on their railway terminus at New Moshi.

He motored to Malleson's headquarters at Mbuyani and breakfasted on champagne with a confident Malleson. Meanwhile at 2.30 a.m. Beves's force marched out on to the road and waited for daybreak. At 5 a.m. the long column marched off in fours in column of route. It was a fine cool morning. The night had been chilly and the dew was heavy. The tramp of four thousand men and the wheels of gun limbers and mule-drawn ambulances soon raised the dust.

Three thousand yards north of Salaita the regiments formed up in mass and advanced a further thousand yards. Then they adopted a more open formation and waited, a thousand yards short of the hill. The artillery mules were unloaded and led away. There was no field ambulance forward and the nearest dressing station had been set up two miles back. Regimental stretcher-bearers, with their scanty knowledge of wounds, did not expect many casualties. Machine guns were

Photo (a)

Photo (b)

Photo (c)

Battle of Salaita Hill – from the enemy's side. These striking photographs of actual operations in the German East campaign were taken by a German photographer. In the first
photograph (a) a thorn-scrub zariba can be seen in the foreground, while halfway up
the hill is a solid stone rampart. The second photograph (b) shows the enemy shelling
the advancing British forces as they advance through the neck, seen on the right-hand
side of the picture. The third photograph (c) shows the enemy's field guns in action.

still loaded on the mules in the rear and they would not go forward until firing began.

Bright sunlight gilded the bush, striking on tall acacia trees and the thick trunks of the bulbous baobabs characteristic of the plains.

The young soldiers waited, sweating in full marching order, joking and eager as hounds to be let loose. The bush ahead was thick. Regimental commanders and their staff stood with their runners ready to keep contact with each other and General Beves when the order to advance came.

There was no signal or field telegraph section with them and no communication with Malleson's headquarters. Unless things went with absolute precision it was a first-rate formula for disaster. But who thought of that! Back at his headquarters, Malleson waited. If things got rougher than he expected he had the East African Brigade in reserve at Njoro with additional artillery. The Baluchis and the North Lancs were of proved steadiness.

While they were waiting, kneeling and crouching, Thompson looked up to see an aeroplane fly over and circle the summit of the hill. He could not know it, but the observer dropped a note on Malleson's headquarters. It reported that Salaita appeared to be too strongly fortified to attack: 'Request permission to drop bombs on trains bringing up German reinforcements from New Moshi.'

The information and the request were ignored.

Ready to Make Counter-Attack

On Salaita Hill Major Kraut was ready. He was in constant communication by telephone with von Lettow at New Moshi on the railway line. The plan was to engage the attackers and pin them down while Captain Schulz's detachment at Taveta counter-attacked on their right flank. Other German detachments of several companies were ready west of Taveta on the road to New Moshi.

Where Beves made his headquarters the hill ahead dominated all thoughts. It was surprising, now that they were so near to its gently rising slopes, how bland and peaceful it seemed. No flags flew at its crest that morning as the battalion commanders scanned the hillside for movement.

Suddenly a few ranging shells whizzed over and crashed farther back among the trees, sending up pillars of red earth and sooty smoke. Light stuff; but it sent the young soldiers of the 7th ducking and diving for cover.

At 8 a.m. Beves ordered the advance. The 7th in the centre, with the 5th on its left, moved forward through thick bush sloping gently southwards. The 6th battalion took the right of the 7th. With the exception of two companies in reserve the whole brigade was in the attacking line with the mountain battery in the rear of the extreme right of the advance.

'Our howitzers now began firing,' wrote Thompson. 'And it was a fine sight to see the shells bursting round the trenches. When we got closer the enemy began firing at us with rifles, so we got into cover and began to unpack the machine guns, get them into position to fire into the trenches we could see.'

This was the moment when Kraut decided to open fire with his machine guns and two light guns. It was 9 a.m. The advance of the 7th had stopped three hundred yards short of the slope. Enemy fire was sweeping through the mostly open bush from trenches at the foot of the hill.

Line of Dummy Trenches

Nobody had expected that. The 6th had already crossed a line of dummy trenches, and Beves now saw that it seemed likely that the trenches reported on the crest of the hill were also dummies, unoccupied. The trap had been well set. German machine guns were scything through the bush and stripping the bark from trees far behind. The attackers were dropping in bunches, crying out, attempting to crawl away. From the hidden gunpits white puffs of smoke marked the positions of the askaris firing their old rifles with heavy lead bullets.

Cries of 'Stretcher-bearers!' were going up on all sides.

Thompson was right up in front. 'The wounded started coming back past our gun position. The 5th Regiment began to retire and acted disgracefully, refusing to halt and take up firing positions when ordered.' Regimental Sergeant-Major Molloy* of the 5th saw it differently:

> The 7th opened the attack and we supported their left and immediate rear. The 6th passed Salaita on the north side about 1 500 yards off and inclined westwards to a thick forest to intercept reinforcements from Taveta. The enemy allowed us to start the attack and opened up on us at about 400 yards range. Their artillery fire was nothing to write home to mother about.
>
> Shortly after the action began our regiment was ordered to move to the right flank of the 7th and fill the gap between them and the 6th as the enemy had by this time come up from Taveta.

---

* Molloy served as a Major in the Second World War and earned the MC, 3 MIDs; appointed an Officer of the Order of Aviz (Portugal) and the Silver Medal for Valour (Italy). Other soldiers in his family were Lt J Molloy, who fought at Waterloo, and later became an artist, and Surgeon Colonel O F Molloy, who served in Egypt and India, and also became an artist.

This was the advance of Schulz's detachment along the rear of Kraut's detachment. Von Lettow had given the order when the moment was ripe, and he had news that the 'effect of our machine guns and artillery was good'. Now Schulz with his eager askaris was moving towards the South Africans under cover of the hill and protected from artillery fire.

Von Lettow Sees for Himself

Von Lettow himself went by car to Salaita Hill, and Kraut told him that the enemy had attacked 'our strongly entrenched front and been repulsed with heavy losses'. From the hill they could see Schulz's detachment deploying for the charge against the South Africans' right flank.

It was exactly as Beves and his commanders had envisaged. He gave the order for the 5th to fill the gap between the 6th and the 7th. When he received the order Colonel Byron of the 5th shouted to Molloy: 'Take my horse and report to General Beves. Tell him we are moving in accordance with his order.'

It was that order that had created the confusion. Molloy galloped past scenes of disarray to Beves, who told him: 'Go back to your CO and cancel that last order. Have him retire the 5th some 1 200 yards to its rear to protect the 10th Mountain Battery.'

This battery was now exposed to the coming attack of Schulz's detachment and had already pulled back some eight hundred yards on its own initiative. Confusion was now worse confounded. The 7th were in a bad way. As Molloy recorded it:

> Meanwhile Colonel Freeth of the 7th had made an urgent appeal to Colonel Byron to protect his left flank while he retired his regiment after ours. I found our gallant old CO in the firing line in the open and about two hundred yards from the enemy. Very properly, and without a moment's hesitation, he took the responsibility, disobeyed the general's orders and sent D Company to the help of the 7th. Our company remained on the scene half an hour after the retirement of the 7th. At this time the 6th were being pressed back by the enemy from Taveta. We sent another company to their help and shortly after they retired through our lines. We were then ordered to form a rearguard for the general retirement of the whole force.

RSM Molloy describes the confusion: 'The bush was dense, and men of every regiment were very much scattered and wandering about. We could do very little against the enemy owing to the stragglers, lost and

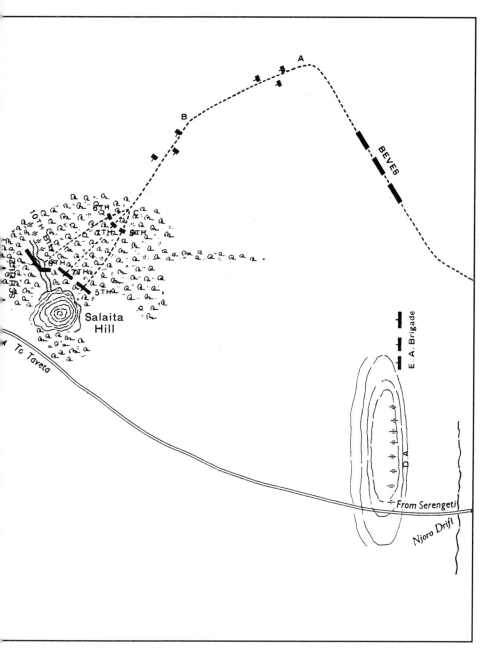

SALAITA HILL ACTION
12 FEBRUARY, 1916

(*The South Africans with General Smuts in German East Africa 1916,*
Brig-Gen Collyer, 1939)

wounded between us and the enemy. The wounded, poor chaps, had to be carried away on groundsheets.'

So far the casualties were from the enemy in front. Now like a black avalanche came Schulz's detachment of six hundred askari riflemen with fixed bayonets, loping forward yelling *'Piga! Piga!* Shoot! Shoot!'

Panic and Confusion

There is no panic like that of a lost engagement. Beves's scattered formations fell back in confusion, leaving its dead and wounded behind.

'Considerable confusion,' was how Collyer later described it. Von Lettow, observing from Kraut's camouflaged bunker on the hill, described it as 'disorder'. Indeed, the 6th Regiment fell back so far in the face of the charge that it was only stopped when it reached its starting point of that morning. Meanwhile, several platoons of the 7th lost touch and retired in disorder on the East African Brigade, itself held up by heavy fire from trenches in thick bush on the eastern face of the hill.

Young Thompson's diary, written that night, records how he and his comrades fell back among the Indian Mountain Battery, also in retreat. 'We lay down for about half an hour with bullets zipping past all the time. My mule bolted for the German lines, so I let him go, and I loaded my rifle and got behind an anthill . . . snipers were getting all round us. We were being shelled all the time . . . and then the Baluchis guarding our rear got behind us, so we retired further.'

In fact, it was the Baluchis who saved the retirement from total disaster. They met the askaris' charge with steady fire and fixed bayonets, and Schulz's counter-attack withered.

Thompson tells how several men of D Company of the 7th had got into the first line of trenches, but as the 5th would not support them, they had to abandon the place.

Hans Gosch was killed during the retreat. He was bending over when he was shot through the back, the bullet coming through his jaw and smashing it. The poor fellow said 'Take me out of this. I guessed this would happen, as it's my birthday.'

Towards the end of the day I was so tired I didn't care what happened. We had nothing to eat all day except three biscuits and a cup of coffee at about three in the morning before we left camp. When we got back to camp we had to entrench ourselves and bury the poor chaps who had been killed.

Some of Schulz's men had pursued them all the way.

Germans Bury the Dead

The slopes of Salaita Hill and the bush all round its foot were dotted with the fallen. 'We buried more than sixty Europeans,' wrote von Lettow. Dejected prisoners and wounded were brought in and questioned. They readily gave information about the identity of their regiments. The Germans were amused at their belief that they would be shot and at their hope of getting farms and plantations, which was why they had joined up.

Diaries found on the dead gave evidence 'that strict orders had been given to take no prisoners'.* The German commander commented dryly: 'As a matter of fact they had taken none.' But his senior officers were indignant. If that were the attitude of General Malleson 'we might have to regulate our conduct to prisoners accordingly'.

Von Lettow himself did not set much store by 'the nonsense that men wrote in personal diaries' then or later; but he demanded an answer from Malleson. Had he, in fact, given such an order? Von Lettow accepted Malleson's repudiation 'as the word of an officer and a gentleman'.

After the defeat Private Thompson recorded the feelings of the lower ranks.

13 February 1916
Heard that Hans Gosch died early this morning and went to his funeral which was very sad. Jock Young and Ben Thompson never turned up so we feared the worst. A long hospital train came to take away the wounded. Early in the morning the Baluchis, Rhodesians and Loyal North Lancashires went out to see what could be found. They brought in three men who had their throats cut. The colonel addressed us and told us he was proud to command us. In the afternoon we marched back to Mbuyani owing to lack of water at Serengeti. The band played the 5th in as though they were conquerors of the world. We had no band to play us in . . .

As a colonel†, he wrote years later: 'The South African losses at Salaita Hill are given as 138, of which eighty-three were from the 7th SAI. Six killed, forty-seven wounded and thirty missing. Only three of the missing were ever heard of again. Jock Young [with whom he enlisted] was one of them and I feel sure that his lack of sense of direction caused him to wander into thick bush, where he probably got lost.'‡

---

* In fact, such exhortations may well have been given at NCO level to get the men's blood up.
† Colonel E S Thompson later commanded the 2nd Transvaal Scottish Battalion.
‡ In South West Africa there were 113 killed and 311 wounded; at Salaita Hill total casualties were 172, of whom 133 were South African. Footnote by Hancock.

Graves of British officers and men in a 'war cemetery' (at the foot of a Baobab tree), who fell in the botched action of Mbuyani Hill in July 1915. Salaita Hill dead were similarly buried.

No News of Missing Men

No news was ever received of the missing, in spite of enquiries to the Germans through the Red Cross. 'It remains a mystery,' wrote Thompson even though he eventually found his friend's grave in the Taveta cemetery. He was one of the last two buried there.

But at the time, in the shock of defeat, the young soldiers were full of rumours that the missing had deserted and made for Nairobi through lion-infested country. Gunner G E Lewis of the 4th Battery SAA noted on the evening of the battle that his horse, though exhausted, suddenly broke into a gallop. 'Next day a party of our men came across two lions about that same place.'

'The moral effect was considerable,' wrote Collyer.*

---

* In his 1939 history of the campaign General Collyer wrote that want of steadiness at Salaita could be attributed to lack of experience rather than to lack of training. 'A high proportion of men had had Active Citizen Force training and even previous war experience.'

Van Deventer was appalled. 'Man,' he declared to his staff, 'they lost more in a morning than I lost in the whole South West campaign.'

Malleson was complacent. The losses to the East African Brigade had been slight. He could praise the Baluchis and lay the blame squarely on the ineptitude of Beves, who indignantly demanded to know why the East African Brigade had not advanced with his own. 'They moved only at 10.45. By that time I had to order a general withdrawal.' The South Africans blamed Malleson's dilatory and remote style of command as totally ineffectual against a soldier of von Lettow's ability.

To the British officers, however, there was a certain satisfaction in having had to rescue those South Africans who had come there despising the Indians as coolies and the askaris as kaffirs. The final humiliation was the returning by the Baluchis of abandoned machine guns with a note to remind the owners that they were 'sepoys, not coolies'. Further evidence of a panicky flight were about a hundred rifles retrieved from the bush.

Dismay at Latest Failure

However, at staff officer level and in official circles in Nairobi there was dismay at another 'British failure'. Everyone waited with some apprehension for the coming of the new Commander-in-Chief. General Tighe would have to face the cold eyes of the abstemious Smuts in a week and explain why he had given command to an officer who had been only a communications officer in India.

Malleson, Tighe and Charlton at Salaita Hill, scene of the shattering British defeat at the beginning of the offensive against the German stronghold of Kilimanjaro. Tighe's defeat at Salaita made a lasting impression on Smuts; henceforward he determined to out-manoeuvre von Lettow-Vorbeck rather than engage him in a stand-up fight.

At the War Office, Lord Kitchener received the news as another disgrace to the officer corps of the Indian Army. The South Africans, after all, had soundly defeated the Germans on their own ground and under their own officers. He also waited for the arrival of Smuts, the man who should put things in order.

Those who were not committed to the battle that day went on with routine camp life. Gunner Lewis wrote in his diary that he 'bought some tinned apricots and golden syrup at the YMCA canteen and after having some coffee and cake returned to camp.' Two days passed before he mentioned the battle, giving rather more importance to his entry: 'Welcome arrival from South Africa of cakes, almonds, raisins and smokes.' And almost as an afterthought: 'General Smuts will be here in a day or two.'

Smuts was still at sea. In Cape Town, Louis Botha had received a cable of the disconcerting news. The public was not informed. Philip J Sampson, editor of the military magazine *Nongquai*, wrote in his 'Conquest of German East', March 1917: 'To say that Salaita Hill fight created a painful impression in South Africa is but mildly to express it, especially as it was many weeks before details were allowed to come through.'

Smuts arrived at Mombasa on 19 February. Although he was expected at Nairobi, he chose to go straight to the scene of the battle. Next morning he was scanning the fatal slopes, noting the bare lump of hill plainly showing the line of false trenches near the summit. He turned to Collyer. 'This is how De la Rey caught Methuen at Modder River . . . at the foot of the hill instead of the kopjes.' No Boer officer would have been deceived by the trap. They had learned the mistake of holding the hilltops at both Belmont and Graspan, at Talana and Elandslaagte. Hilltops became deathtraps with field guns firing shrapnel that burst in lethal showers overhead.

King George's Good Wishes

From there he rode off on a personal reconnaissance of the enemy lines in the Longido area and scanned the German camps with his well-used field-glasses. That afternoon he left the South African base at 2.30 and set out by car for Nairobi with Collyer.

He arrived on 22 February to find a message from King George V: 'Hearty good wishes to you and your troops for every success in the forthcoming campaign.' Botha, all too keenly aware of Smuts's anger and humiliation, wrote: 'My heart and soul are with you and I shall do everything to help you, be assured of that. Just tell me what can be done. Your going has everyone's blessing. Be careful and let Van Deventer always keep a captaincy with you. God bring you back safely to us will always remain my prayer. May your work be blessed.'

No one in that sanguine age ever saw warfare as other than 'work'; and the blessing of the Almighty was taken as a matter of course.

Private Thompson, noting the time of Smuts's hurried departure in his diary, observed: 'Looks like rain.' The big rains were due in March. Smuts knew very well that if he did not break through the Taveta gap within the next three weeks his army would be immobilised, with all the effects of tropical sickness on man and beast. Smuts was a commander in a hurry. He knew very well that there was no time to work out an elaborate strategy of his own.

At Nairobi he shunned the social round arranged by the Governor and the Poona crowd. The ubiquitous Meinertzhagen, as Chief Intelligence Officer, 'found it a pleasure to run over the situation with him on a map, after the laborious processes and artifices one had to resort to with Tighe. Smuts grasps points at once and never wants telling a second time.'

Meinertzhagen warned him that he would find the German native soldier as good as his South Africans:

I told him bluntly that he would have great respect for what he now terms 'damned kaffirs' who could be driven with a whip.
'Sir,' I told him, 'before this campaign ceases there will be more than one instance of them giving you a licking. Dense bush is just what von Lettow wants for his manoeuvres.'

Smuts replied that he intended to manoeuvre von Lettow out of his positions. He was not going to go in for any British head-on tactics. As he observed to his staff later, when he examined the Salaita fortress on the spot: 'British generals seem to take fortified positions as a personal affront and attack it head-on. We believe in going round it.'

Meinertzhagen argued that manoeuvre in this territory would only succeed at 'great expense in men and money. Every man killed in action means ten invalided with disease.' He urged a decisive action that would bring the campaign to an end as soon as possible, right there at Kilimanjaro. 'Von Lettow is concentrated here and ready for a fight. You should bring him to battle . . . surround and annihilate him, no matter what our casualties may be. Our troops are fresh and eager. We know the ground, so why manoeuvre?'

Smuts replied, 'I do not intend to go home with the nickname of "Butcher Smuts". I can't risk another heavy casualty list'.

In fact there was a plan ready. Would Smuts and his staff accept it? It had been drafted by Tighe and accepted by Smith-Dorrien and the War Office. He discussed the Tighe plan with his staff. What was eventually decided was not unlike the Meinertzhagen strategy: bottle the enemy in by an encircling movement and strike hard from the front.

If it worked von Lettow's main force could be destroyed. Taveta would be the trap. A shrewd blow from the front would send him back into the path of the encirclement of Jaap van Deventer's mounted brigade. If it did not mean destruction it would at least clear the Germans from British East Africa at a stroke.

It was better, he and Collyer agreed, to change the British plan as little as possible. There was no time otherwise. 'He knew little or nothing of the officers of the British and Indian armies who held command under General Tighe.' After the battle he would make his own decisions about their worth.

Von Lettow was well aware of what was going on. He knew that Smuts had taken command. He had his dispositions ready. He had over five thousand rifles supported by forty-nine machine guns and eighteen field guns spread through the area under five able commanders, all under his personal command with Major Kraut as second in command. Smuts had been only two weeks in the area; the Germans had been preparing for over a year. Von Lettow's troops were well concealed in thick bush, well entrenched, and his companies had cut down bush to prepare deadly lanes of machine-gun fire from hidden positions.

The daily flight of aeroplanes along the railway line to Moshi, bombs dropped on Salaita Hill and the increase in patrolling by the British, who had brushes in bush with his own, all pointed to the conflict that von Lettow expected. The thing was to keep on harrying the newcomers in every way.

'During the night,' wrote Private Thompson, on 21 February, 'some Germans blew up our boreholes at Vuria, so we marched out twelve miles north of the camp, leaving two lines of men all the way, hoping to intercept any Germans who passed that way.' Next day 'a white German and askari were captured during breakfast. The German looked very dirty, and we took his revolver, water-bottle and a good many papers off him . . . rum dished out. Heard that a German had been caught in the camp in one of our uniforms. He is liable to be shot.'

General Advance Begins

On 7 March the general advance began. Gunner Phipson's 4th battery moved out of Mbuyani camp after dark and:

> . . . trekked all night through the bush, having muffled as far as possible all parts of the guns, limbers and harness that were likely

to make any noise. The order was 'no smoking or talking'. At dawn of the 8th we found ourselves near the Lumi River and halted to await orders. Several severe actions had been fought during the night by the infantry at Taveta and other places.

Soon after dawn we were ordered to cross the river, which we did by digging a drift and helping the mule teams to pull the guns and ammunition wagons through. General Smuts suddenly appeared on the bank and sat on his horse watching us go through and making remarks of encouragement. Almost immediately the order came to move forward into action.

Later in the morning there was a sound of heavy rifle fire moving back down the river towards us. The enemy was pressing back the South African Horse and the situation looked quite serious.

'We were ordered to get our guns ready for action in a rough square with a gun at each corner. We loaded with Fuse 0, which means that the shell would burst almost immediately it left the muzzle and spray shrapnel bullets out in front. The fight, however, gradually drew away . . . though snipers were busy at us all night.

On that day von Lettow's detachment on Salaita Hill noticed 'huge clouds of dust moving from the enemy's camp' and 'numerous motors were also seen.'

General Smuts, Brigadier-General Beves, Brigadier-General Sir Charles Crewe and Colonel Grant (Camp Commandant).

SOUTH AFRICAN OFFICER (addressing as he thinks, a Private of the Cape Corps): "Hi booi, waar is de General Headquarters?"

PRIVATE JONES (of the West Indian Regiment): "I am not a boy, sah, but a Briteesh Sojah. An' I do not spik dat language; I only spik Ingleesh, sah !"

(*'Jambo' or with Jannie in the Jungle*, AW Lloyd, undated)

5

'The Most Extraordinary War'

The tower of dust was being raised by thousands of marching men, the trampling of mules and spans of oxen drawing supplies after the 2nd Division, with General Tighe somewhere in the column. He was eager to see his plan in operation, and with fresh men and cavalry he meant to breach the gap between Kilimanjaro and the Pare Mountains in short order.

Meanwhile Jaap van Deventer was leading his four thousand horsemen round north of Salaita. Von Lettow saw the ominous dust cloud and knew that 'the enemy does not intend to get his head broken a second time on that mountain.' He also knew that it was time to abandon the hill and fall back on the carefully prepared deathtrap contrived on each of two hills that reared above the pass that Smuts's army would have to take.

Latema and Reata. 'They sounded like girls' names' wrote a signaller; 'and they were right bitches!'

Smuts had no option but to attack von Lettow on his own chosen ground. It was a situation that he seized with characteristic alacrity. He wanted the initiative, and he meant to keep it. In the past three days of skirmishing and manoeuvring he had seen the German withdrawing from his long-held positions. Smuts's men held the initiative, however awkward their manoeuvrings appeared to the critical eye of von Lettow.

It was a formidable army that Smuts had at his command. Tighe's 2nd Division had nearly five thousand rifles with thirty-four machine guns and nineteen guns. Van Deventer was jingling along with three regiments of horse, four battalions of infantry amounting to nearly six thousand rifles, twenty-eight machine guns and fourteen artillery guns.

In reserve Smuts had General Beves's 2nd South African Infantry Brigade of five battalions numbering nearly four thousand men, sixteen machine guns and six guns. At the same time his 1st Division under Major-General J M Stewart was marching to encircle Kilimanjaro from the west with four thousand riflemen, on foot and mounted, twenty-two machine guns and eighteen guns.

Altogether about eighteen thousand men. Against Smuts in the Kilimanjaro area at this date were over five thousand German rifles; of these seven hundred were European with forty-nine machine guns and twenty-five guns divided among five detachments led by officers of much skill and daring, resolution and great personal bravery.

Forward into Battle

Indeed, never before in the history of that vast territory had such armies been ranged against one another. Tribal warriors of East Africa, now fully trained and masters of the bush, German machine-gunners and artillerymen and the most polyglot mixture of British imperial troops ever assembled on one battlefield. Stocky Lancashiremen of speech all but unintelligible to the settler soldiers of the 2nd Rhodesians; Baluchis from the North-West Frontier, long enemies of the British; King's African Riflemen from subjugated Kenyan tribes; fighters from the mystic hills of Kashmir. Punjabis who had fought with fanatical courage in the Indian Mutiny; Royal Fusiliers with their mixed bag of scoundrels, remittance men, alcoholics and heroes and adventurers.

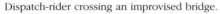

Dispatch-rider crossing an improvised bridge.

There they came, marching in the red dust of the Kilimanjaro plains alive with great herds of wild animals, unspoiled as on the day of creation. Fording great rivers they marched and sang, while behind them clattered and creaked the paraphernalia of a mighty force, driven forward by the jesting, irreverent masters of horse and mule and oxen, the men of the Cape Corps Battalion.

With them marched their black porters, chanting under their loads, soon to be dressed in nothing but their cotton rags, but now in khaki, advancing with their masters into a campaign in which they had not the slightest interest, except the few rupees a month that they earned. They marched against an enemy who was already master of the bush, had cleared his deadly, ambushed open ground, dug in his riflemen, sited his machine guns across the clearings and laid his telephone communications across miles of hills. And what was more in his favour, he was lying ready in wait, his exact positions unknown until the first ranks of advancing men fell before his machine guns.

Depended on Stewart's March

Already Smuts and his staff knew that if he failed to cut off the enemy retreat they were in for a struggle that Collyer described as 'the most extraordinary war'. Smuts knew that if General Stewart's division did not get a move on in his approach round Kilimanjaro with a waterless march of thirty-five miles, the whole thing would fail. He had urged on Stewart the need to move fast. But already Stewart, having loitered, wasting two days on the way, wires Smuts to say that he can't reach his objective till four days later than expected.

'The whole of these operations depends on Stewart,' writes the incensed Meinertzhagen, 'and here he is, dawdling along. Tighe, now completely under the thumb of that snake Malleson and soaked with drink, likewise is quite inactive. We are all furious. Smuts, poor little man, is livid with rage, but scarcely dares to move against these dilatory officers so early in the day.'

Meanwhile the advancing attackers bivouacked for the night in territory swarming with lions and loud with their throaty roars, terrifying to townbred soldiers and so dangerous to horses and oxen that no bivouac could be made without fires and thornbush bomas. It was indeed a most extraordinary war, beginning as it was with incompetent or drunken or dilatory leaders more used to the comforts of military clubs and parade-ground ceremonial.

As a background to all this reared the huge snow-clad crater of the highest mountain in Africa, aloof and majestic above the searing plains and the foothills with their thick forests and streams and lakes teeming with crocodile.

Where Eden turned to Hell

Here was the strangest, most romantic battlefield of the war, where two colonial powers would fight for possession of a vast territory where neither could have any right of dominion except by defeating the other. The pawns in the game were the half-trained South Africans with their inexperienced officers. Amateurs for the most part, and those who had fought before with not an iota of experience in this country that some called Hell and some called Eden. Smuts spoke of his men as 'my young burghers', for indeed many of his force were Afrikaners; and now he was their commander, confident that their offensive spirit was high once more.

Major-General Sir Michael Joseph Tighe, KCMG, CB, CIE, DSO who commanded in the earlier East African campaign prior to General Smuts.

The conduct of the battle was in the hands of Tighe, and the plan had been passed by the War Office with small alteration; but as Commander-in-Chief it was now Smuts's own plan, for good or ill. Salaita Hill was Tighe's first objective. He approached with two infantry brigades, and according to Meinertzhagen no attempt was made to see whether it was occupied. The intelligence officer found Tighe 'sleeping most of the day under a tree, taking no interest in the proceedings. With him was the entire strength of the army artillery.'

Next day he sent in a brigade in a frontal attack in the old costly manner. The hill was empty. The Germans had left their masterpiece of defensive digging in the darkness.* With Smuts on the move with the mounted brigade and a brigade of infantry, the Germans now awaited the outcome at the twin hills astride the road that ran through the *nek* to Moshi.

So far the operation had resulted in the taking of Taveta, which had been in enemy hands for a year and a half. So far so good.

---

* At the foot of a giant baobab tree the graves of those who had fallen on the slopes on 12 February were found where the Germans had buried them. The trees were so often used to shade soldiers' graves and those of settlers that tribesmen called them 'white men's graves'.

'I am convinced,' Smuts told his intelligence chief, 'von Lettow will retire through Arusha to the Central Railway.' Meinertzhagen argued that he would retreat down the Usambara Railway, and he was right. Now, as the huge force advanced, it had to keep contact. It was dangerous work.

'Today,' wrote Meinertzhagen, 'an enemy long-distance patrol killed a wounded man in an ambulance and shot the driver of a car. They also mutilated two dispatch riders carrying information to Smuts at Chala.'

Talking to an old Boer settler before the battle, von Lettow observed that Smuts seemed to be reckless 'in exposing so many youngsters to this kind of warfare in tropic bush'. Indeed, as Collyer noted, his chief's knowledge of the ground was as defective as von Lettow's was complete. Every foot of the advance against the twin hills was under observation, and information on every movement passed rapidly.

Smuts saw the movement forward as a kind of probe to feel whether the enemy were strong enough to threaten his advance by counter-attack. Malleson, who had by now failed thrice, was given the job of clearing the pass. Why Smuts did not overrule this decision it is hard to say. Somebody had to command the brigade; and time was limited.

Too Late to Change Generals

It is not known whether Collyer argued the case. In his account of the action he wrote, with icy sarcasm: 'The scheme adopted by General Malleson was simplicity itself . . . a frontal attack' without any attempt to cover his flanks. Smuts did not intervene. It might turn out to be another Salaita Hill, but it was too late to change generals. If it came off, well and good. If it failed, Smuts had his scapegoat: the man whom he had been obliged to accept and the plan he had not devised, only making small changes to suit the movement of his mounted force.

Collyer did not expect it to succeed. It was a month since Malleson had attacked Salaita Hill, and once again he was ordering a frontal attack. The men would have to charge uphill through thick, head-high bush in which they quickly lost touch with each other or had to bunch together to force a passage through thorn scrub.

However, Malleson did not intend to send the South Africans into the first attack. He had the well-proved 130th Baluchis and the 3rd KAR, with the 2nd Rhodesians in support, altogether about fifteen hundred rifles. As they approached, just after noon on 11 March, they were plainly visible to the watchers on the hills coming forward in extended order across the wide and empty plain, dotted with parklike trees. It

General Wilfred Malleson – denounced to War Office by Smuts after battle of Latema-Reata.

was a scene of pastoral tranquillity. Bayonets glistened as the khaki lines approached the slope, where the gunners on the hillcrest waited behind their skilfully prepared emplacements, well-hidden in bush and with the muzzles of the machine guns just clearing the embrasures. The advancing men were walking right into machine guns and rifles dug in on the slopes of Latema. At once men began to fall, and the advance faltered. The British guns, firing from 3 500 yards in the rear, dropped their shells short, which added to the confusion among the men pinned down. Wounded began to stream back. Not a German was seen, but the bush below the hill spat flame at every movement. Thompson counted wounded men going by on stretchers. 'The casualties seemed to be heavy.'

Above the attackers Latema hill reared seven hundred feet high. Major Kraut had three companies to face the advance of what he reckoned to be 'several thousand with heavy artillery'. He reported this to von Lettow, who replied: 'The attack has little chance of success; but I am sending you two companies in support. I believe that Smuts is only using this to keep us occupied while he makes his decisive move round our left. I have reports of large bodies of horsemen.'

These were part of Van Deventer's brigade, exhausted by their hard ride since 9 March without water, rest or rations. The Germans observed them dismounting and stripping a banana plantation of unripe fruit. 'It was a moment of great tension,' von Lettow admitted, 'but I believe we can give at least one of Smuts's detachments a thorough beating.'

As the afternoon wore on the attackers set up their maxims; whereupon the gunners were at once cut down by the hidden enemy. The Baluchis dug in where they were, firing from shallow rifle pits dug with their bayonets. The KAR, toiling upwards toward the crest of Reata with bayonets fixed, were losing men at every yard.

Von Lettow was receiving good reports. 'The enemy was obviously suffering severe casualties. Hundreds of stretchers were being used to get the wounded away'. It was going in his favour even better than he knew.

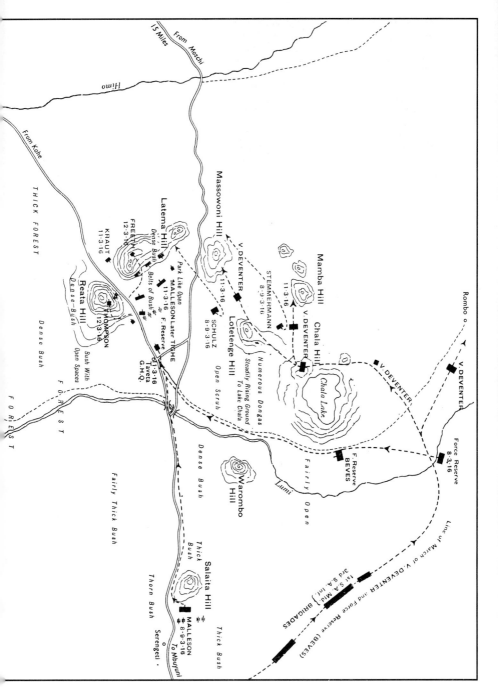

OPERATIONS EAST of TAVETA
From 7 MARCH to 11 MARCH CULMINATING IN ACTION AT LATEMA and REATA
11-12 MARCH 1916.

(*The South Africans with General Smuts in German East Africa 1916,*
Brig-Gen Collyer, 1939)

One of the well-emplaced German maxims on the crest of the Latema-Reata hills. It commanded the open plain over which the South Africans advanced. The defences were stormed when Smuts rushed reserves to take and hold the crests.

Malleson Abandons his Command

Back at Taveta Malleson had been receiving evil reports for two hours. Now he asked Smuts to relieve him of his command. He had been ill all day, he confessed, and was now too sick to continue. 'Malleson's condition has become worse,' Collyer told Smuts. 'He appears to be incapable of further effort.'

The time was 4 p.m., five hours after the advance had begun.

Meinertzhagen recorded that moment with trenchant pen and infinite contempt.

> I could scarcely believe my eyes when I met Malleson in a car, reclining on a soft cushion and smoking a cigarette and making good headway from the battlefield towards Voi. I stopped his car and spoke to him, asking him what was the matter. He said he was feeling very ill, had handed over his brigade and was off to Voi.
>
> I said nothing, I felt like shooting the cur. Just imagine any general leaving his brigade in the middle of a fight and taking a car as fast as it could carry him back to the rear. He did not look in the least ill! Apparently he got hold of a doctor during the action, a man named Halloran, and told him he had acute abdominal pain. Halloran winked at me and inferred that the pain was not very serious.

For the moment Smuts contained his cold anger and contempt and gave direct command to Tighe. The Irishman at once gave the order for the Rhodesians to attack, carrying the King's African Rifles forward with them, with the Baluchis in support on the right.

The Rhodesians went into the attack with magnificent dash, and in the densely wooded slopes the fight developed into a number of small engagements with fierce hand-to-hand fighting. Positions were taken, lost and retaken, bayonets and clubbed rifles were used, men were falling fast on both sides. When the Germans counter-attacked from Reata the Rhodesians had to fall back. Somewhere on the way down Colonel Graham stood forward when a voice called to him in English. At once he was cut down by a burst of fire.

A small group of Rhodesians had stormed the top of the ridge with the bayonet. Their fierce rush was helped by a single man of the Loyal North Lancs and a KAR askari with a machine gun. While all others fell back they scraped positions in the rocky surface. There they waited with their askari prisoners. Suddenly the figure of a European appeared silhouetted on the skyline with an askari carrying a box of ammunition. When the prisoners started to murmur a Rhodesian shot down the German. 'At once there was a tornado of fire from a body of Germans close behind him. As the two groups clashed in the darkness there were screams and yells of "Rhodesia!" "KAR" and "Washikauser" as the men tried to identify themselves. If the wrong answer came it was either a quick shot or a lunge with the bayonet.'

Midnight Struggle for the Crest

In his vivid account of the struggle told by survivors, Philip Sampson describes the midnight hours on the hill.

> The little garrison of thirteen men took refuge in half-formed trenches. Up the slope behind them askaris began to crawl and shoot, their fire being promptly answered. Some of the askaris got to within two or three feet of the defenders before they were laid out. By the time the attack ceased only four Rhodesians were unwounded. The groans of their comrades could be heard, but nothing could be done to help.
>
> When the firing ceased the four began to improve their defences; and then the wounded men, who thought they had been abandoned, begged to be brought into the trench. This was hardly done when in the darkness a German askari came quietly on the scene and was seen standing over the wounded. 'Get down!' he was ordered, being mistaken for one of their own.

The askari disappeared, reported that the ridge was strongly held and within a few minutes there was a demand for surrender. 'No surrender!' they shouted and another fierce attack followed, to be stoutly repelled by the gallant four who, owing to the darkness, were compelled to hold their fire until their foes were only a few feet away.

Once more the attack died away. The four crouched, waiting, eyes on the wall of darkness before them. 'Water . . . for God's sake a drop of water!' cried one of the wounded.

So they held on through the night, waiting for dawn and the inevitable attack, with the dead sprawled about them.

With the apparent failure of the Rhodesians, the KAR and the Baluchis to take the hill, Tighe decided to put in the 5th and 7th SAI. At midday these regiments had been detailed as Force Reserve. From their bivouac at Taveta they could hear the naval guns and howitzers bombarding the hills. 'No sooner had tea been eaten,' wrote Private Thompson, 'than we were ordered to saddle-up. We knew we were off for a scrap, and a night one at that, so we knew it was going to be heavy.'

So they set out with their mules bearing the machine guns, and the news came that the assault on Latema had been beaten back. 'The men up there had been ordered to dig in and hold.'

Colonel Byron of the 5th was given command by Tighe. He ordered Lieutenant-Colonel Freeth with the 7th to form the first line and Major Thompson of the 5th to command the 7th second line. Freeth was to storm the crest of Latema; Thompson to take and hold Reata. Colonel Byron himself led the attack to secure the nek between the two hills. The enemy was waiting on both sides of the nek, with numerous machine guns and quick-firing field guns in support.

It's Hell up There!

Colonel Freeth gathered his battalion round him in the dark. 'When a shot is fired, that will be the signal to advance. Each man is to fire ten rounds rapid into the bush at his front and immediately charge, cheering. After a hundred yards you are to load, fire and charge again!'

It was 8 p.m. when the advance began. Numerous stretcher-bearers passed them on their way downhill carrying dead and wounded. 'How's it up there?' they were asked; and the reply was: 'It's hell!'

They had not climbed far when the Germans began a fierce counter-attack. As they rushed downhill on the 5th and 7th Colonel Byron was heard to shout: 'General advance! South Africans!' and the

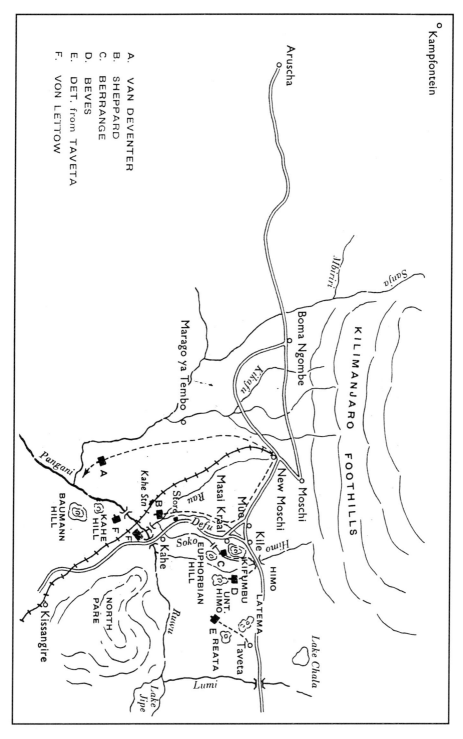

OPERATIONS for the OCCUPATION of the
RUWU RIVER LINE after the ACTION of LATEMA-REATA 11 MARCH 1916.

(*The South Africans with General Smuts in German East Africa 1916*,
Brig-Gen Collyer, 1939)

sections of men moved rapidly forward through the ranks of the Baluchis and the KAR and took up positions for the charge.

Then came Byron's order to fire. Officers' whistles shrilled. A fusillade burst from a thousand rifles. There was a pandemonium of cries and confusion. The 5th and 7th advanced, knelt to fire again, and then on and upward.

> For a solid hour this weird fighting in the darkness went on, the night stabbed with flashes from rifles. Moonlight filtering through trees glinted on bayonets as they pressed higher, pausing to fire and then press on. In front of them could be heard hoarse yells from German officers and the askaris, who fought stubbornly and valiantly.
>
> Advancing with controlled fire, responding to their officers' whistles, they pressed up the slopes towards the nek. At nine p.m. Colonel Byron ordered the storming parties to make for Latema and Reata's crests while he attacked the nek. At 150 yards from a thick belt of scrub the order was heard: 'Five rounds rapid!' A burst of fire from hundreds of rifles. Then the order: 'Into the bush in front . . . charge!'

The men cheered and charged into the bush, to be met with howls of defiance and volleys of bullets. The sound of the night battle, the curving tracks of tracer bullets and the stabbing muzzle flash of rifles and machine guns, the soaring signal flares and the sudden flash of shells bursting, were turning the twin hills into a lethal fireworks display. Men charged across the moonlit spaces in groups – the night was somewhat cloudy – and aimed at muzzle flashes. Where they made contact they fought with bayonet and clubbed rifle in the dark tangle of bush.

A cry of 'Are we downhearted?' was answered by a yell of 'No!' 'Shall we win?' was followed by cries of 'Yes!' and 'Tipperary'* was taken up all along the line.

The enemy yelled derisively: 'Come on, we'll give you Tipperary!' Again the South Africans met them with the bayonet, and the slopes were strewn with their fallen.

Tighe Calls for Reserves

At 9.15 p.m. Tighe's message reached Smuts: 'The two battalions of South African infantry with me are just going in with the bayonet. I must have another battalion in reserve.'

---

* A song popular among the troops in France expressing the longing for home.

Smuts and his staff were taken aback. Was Tighe already hinting at another failure in the making? 'But it was too late to stop the two-battalion assault going in. They were already well committed when Tighe told GHQ of his intention,' says Collyer. They could only hope for the best.

By midnight Colonel Byron's attack in the centre was only thirty yards from the enemy's main position in the col. They were resisting stubbornly with three machine guns posted to catch the attackers. In one concentrated burst of fire as the South Africans made a rush, the maxims cut down twenty-two men, killed outright. Colonel Byron was slightly wounded and Major Mainrose, RE Brigade Major, was killed. Byron rallied the last twenty men and reached the top of the col, only to fall back.

In the darkness after the moon went down Captain Koehl's two companies pursued the retreat with deadly energy all down the slopes to the plain. Wherever the retreating men tried to rally, his machine guns drove them back. A young machine-gunner, Thompson, wrote:

'After the moon went down the fire slackened so I slid back on my tummy for about fifty yards and found a little trench, so I got into it and began digging deeper with a bayonet.' He had hardly dug in amid cracking bullets when he heard an officer shout: 'The 5th and 7th have retired.' So Thompson hastily followed and rejoined the other gun-teams.

'One of our young muleteers, Mennie, had been shot through the head and was carried away unconscious . . . We entrenched ourselves and slept for about half an hour.' Thompson had no stomach for glory; and in that he was certainly not alone that night. The heroes who reached the crests held on through dark hours of 'heavy and continuous firing' with Smuts's staff desperately trying to obtain a coherent account of the situation.

Appeals to Tighe for information brought no reports to Smuts. Wounded and lost men kept coming back with garbled accounts. Collyer described a young officer of the KAR stumbling in. He was badly shocked, and reported that the enemy seemed to be making an attempt to get round Tighe's left flank.

'Owing to his unpleasant experience,' wrote Collyer, 'one had to make allowances that his report was not in the least improbable. If a way round existed the enemy could presently be attacking the reserve at Taveta, where there were now only two battalions, the 6th and 8th.'

Smuts Makes his Decision

At 3.30 came news that all Tighe's attacks had failed. Tighe's staff officer reported to Smuts: 'The general is trying to collect the troops and restore order in a situation which seems very confused . . . He is also asking for reinforcements.'

Smuts made a cold calculation. It would be reckless to risk any more lives in frontal attacks. Lesser men might have attempted it to save face. It was, after all, his first offensive action in the new campaign.

Without hesitation he said: 'Tell General Tighe: no further reinforcements. He must withdraw to more open ground, dig in and await daylight.' The time was 4.30, and his hope was that Van Deventer's turning movement would force the German to leave the hills.

'What of Major Thompson and the two hundred men of the 7th, Sir? What am I to tell General Tighe?'

'Regard Major Thompson's detachment as a casualty,' said Smuts with icy logic.

Hardly was the order given when patrols sent out to get in touch with Colonel Freeth and Major Thompson returned with the news that the enemy was in full retreat. Thompson and Freeth were holding the crests.

Captain van der Bijl, as Smuts's ADC, gave a vivid account of that moment as Smuts's staff experienced it.

Towards dawn the firing in front of us died down, but no one knew exactly what was happening. Had we held the two ridges, or were the enemy in possession? Was it victory or defeat? As the top of the ridges became faintly visible, we all studied them through our glasses with anxiety. On our side of Latema we could see a few men building schantzes – obviously our own men, for the enemy had long ago prepared all he required.

The light strengthened until we could read a hand-signaller telling us that Lt-Col Freeth's 7th SAI with a couple of dozen men was holding on. However, he could keep no more men with him, as the rest of his force had run out of ammunition and after fighting half a day and all the night had neither food nor water. Some odd men from the Rhodesian Regiment and the KAR, detached from units in the dark had gallantly climbed to the sound of firing and found their way to him.

Collyer told me to empty all our staff vehicles, including the general's personal car, and rush reinforcements, saying: 'If the Germans find the positions so lightly held they will attempt to re-occupy it'.

Rushed Forward on Tin Lizzies

Men of the 8th were ordered forward on foot while Van der Bijl, 'loading any armed men I could find into the cars and vans sat astride the bonnet of the leading Tin Lizzie Ford'. When Van der Bijl climbed Latema he saw the evidence of the deadly night.

'Winding footpaths and game tracks passed through the thick bush with visibility only a few yards. At every bend I saw dead men, caught by waiting machine guns. On the summit, in an open area of about twenty by forty yards lay a number of Germans, all shot through the head.'

It was there that the brave Rhodesians had held the crest.* As the remnant waited in the grey light, in the dawn hour of crisis and counter-attack they heard the sound of boots on rocks.

'Halt! Who goes there?'

'South Africans – 7th Infantry!'

Freeth's men found only four unwounded. These ran forward to grasp the hands of their rescuers. Four others lay dead and five more were badly wounded.

With those of Colonel Freeth's men who reached the top they turned the three abandoned German machine guns on their former owners, and when the belts were expended they counted over a hundred dead on the hilltops with the sprawling crew of a three-pounder gun. On Reata, Major Thompson's 170 men were waving and cheering wildly. Both Freeth and Thompson were awarded the DSO for their gallantry that night and Captain Fulton the Military Cross. RSM Molloy of the 5th noted that Latema Nek 'has been renamed Byron's Nek after our gallant old CO. This morning he was promoted Brigadier-General of the 1st Brigade.'

In the critical hours of that night von Lettow had been telephoned before midnight by Lt Sternheim, commanding the guns of Major Kraut's detachment: 'The enemy have attacked and penetrated the Reata position in great force.'

Von Lettow had seen the danger. If the enemy pressed forward, his communications would be cut. 'I therefore ordered the troops at Kitovo and Himo to fall back to the Reata-Kahe road. That was done with difficulty, and men were lost. A few stragglers came towards us; when we said that we were Germans, they did not believe us and disappeared again. On the new road we found the dressing station. There, also, the reports of the numerous wounded were so contradictory that one could only gather the impression of very heavy fighting in the bush at close quarters . . . ' But of the result von Lettow was as much in the dark as Smuts.

By morning it seemed to von Lettow that the enemy had cleared out of the Reata mountain as far back as Taveta, leaving a great quantity of booty which was being collected by his men.

---

* Colour-Sgt G Green and Corporal W H Ballinger were both awarded the Distinguished Conduct Medal for conspicuous gallantry that night.

Von Lettow saw his Error

Von Lettow observed for himself the grim scene. 'The close-quarter fighting in the dark had left English [sic] dead lying in the bush far in the rear of Kraut's detachments, proving that some units had got behind Kraut's line. It was clear, however, that the enemy had been repulsed with heavy casualties.'

It was then that the German officer realised he had been over-hasty in ordering a withdrawal of his left wing as by doing so, he had actually made the Reata position untenable. 'The more so as it had no supply of water.' It was too late to bring back the units that he had ordered to retire. And in any case, he was completely out of touch with them. 'I decided to withdraw from the Reata position.'

That decision enabled Tighe's force to disengage with no interference by the enemy. 'This was just as well,' noted Collyer in his matter-of-fact style. For if he had not retired, Tighe might well have expected a sharp counter-attack on his disorganised forces. That would have been a disaster not without precedent.

'With this action,' Smuts wrote in his report, 'the first phase of the battle for Kilimanjaro came to a conclusion. Our casualties in the engagement were about 270, which cannot be considered excessive in view of the important results gained.' The Germans, he pointed out, usually so careful about removing their fallen, had left some fifty to seventy dead and wounded, a sure indication that confusion had overtaken both sides in the bloody fight for the summits of Latema and Reata and the securing of the road through the nek.

Smuts found time, as always, to write to his wife.

Himo (East Africa)
14 March 1916

Dearest Mama,

It is a little quieter today and so I want to send you a line. We have a memorable week behind us. On Tuesday night a week ago we left to encircle the enemy from the right, and we worked so fast that by Sunday morning the enemy were in full flight southwards and the whole of the Kilimanjaro and Meru country was in our possession. The spirit among our young burghers was excellent. The battle of Kitovo* was a repetition of Spioen Kop. We charged continually and were always beaten back, but about eight o'clock on Saturday evening I sent 2 000 Afrikaners for the final charge, and the high bushy ridges of Reata and Latema were taken by two parties of Transvaalers while the rest were again repulsed . . . it was a joyful victory.

* The area of the battle.

It is interesting to note how, writing in Afrikaans, he equates his mainly English-speaking infantry with his own language group in this simplification of the events.

However joyful the victory, he had been robbed of total success. Stewart's 1st Division had failed him. Although expressly ordered to make a wide flanking movement and cut off all retreat, his horsemen and infantry had reached the crucial point four days late. Von Lettow's main body had passed through unhurried, and the six companies sent to oppose Stewart's division had withdrawn unscathed.

It was left to Meinertzhagen to fill in the details of that failure, which Smuts was too noble to mention in his report.

13.3.1916. Stewart has at last reached the crossroads at Boma Ngombe, having averaged four miles a day on a good road . . . and no more opposition than scouts. Colonel Jollie[*], commanding Stewart's mounted troops, retired on the first occasion the enemy was met with and absented himself for four whole days. Marvellous! But it is all our own fault for not having Stewart, Drew and Jollie removed when we could have done so. They are all dangerous, inefficient soldiers and quite unfitted for command. Drew is downright stupid, conceited and unable to give a decision on any point. Jollie is a decrepit old woman without the courage or energy of a hedgehog . . .

Smuts Determined to Weed Out Failures

Smuts was now determined to clean up. 'I am not going to have my strategy ruined by ignorance and slackness in subordinates. I am not going to allow Stewart to return to India without making it quite clear to the War Office that the man in unreliable. I am now beginning to understand,' he fumed to his Chief of Intelligence, 'how it was that we always outwitted your leaders in South Africa. Are they all like this?'

Despite the swollen streams and broken bridges Smuts determined to give the enemy no rest, but to drive him south to the Ruwu River before the rains set in. On 13 March, memorable because on that day most of his forces crossed the frontier, where some cheered and some jeered at the black, white and red boundary post, the 2nd South African Brigade left Taveta, having buried their dead there, and moved westwards along the Moshi road. The 3rd Brigade on their right pushed on through much higher ground along the slopes of Mount Kilimanjaro, and they met at the river Himo, a beautiful place with plenty

---

* 28th Cavalry, Indian Army.

In the forests of Kilimanjaro troops of General Smuts's command cross a river in his February 1916 offensive.

of water, farmhouses and plantations of rubber and banana trees. There Smuts pitched the tents of his HQ.

'At 11.10 we crossed the border, which was marked by a pile of stones,' wrote Private Thompson. 'We were very happy. Orders were to wash ourselves and our clothes in the river [Himo] as we could not move till the bridge over the river was repaired. The water was fine but chilly, as it comes from the snow of Kilimanjaro. A lovely river with ferns all round. While having lunch General Smuts came near our position with his field glasses . . . and climbed up a tree to see more clearly the surrounding country.'

Advance on Empty Bellies

General van Deventer's 1st Mounted Brigade, which had pushed on up to the Mambo Mission and over Himo bridge, now reached Moshi, the terminus of the enemy's Northern Railway, with the retreating Germans only a few hours ahead of them. There he was to be stuck for several days without rations till the road from Taveta was repaired and crossings were made.

At HQ staff officers were taking a cold hard look at the way in which things had gone. Men had fought with empty bellies after long marches. Gunner G Lewis of the 4th Battery SA Artillery recorded a typical grouse:

'Last night we no sooner got the fires going than "Saddle up!" and off we go minus food. Later we got half a plate of mealie meal, our first mouthful since noon the day before. Then we were off again at 4.30, with empty bellies and digging in the fields for sweet potatoes.'

Although they were near to the railhead there had been a total failure to get supplies forward. If that were to continue, the staff saw perfectly clearly, and men were so badly supplied in a battle that had lasted only three days, how were they to accomplish the hard marches ahead in country full of fever and burnt and stripped by the retiring enemy?

What they had gone through was nothing compared with what was coming, Collyer noted. 'It gave ample food for thought,' he wrote with dry humour. Food, or rather the lack of it, was soon to be an obsession with all.

The battle of the Ruwu River lay ahead. Smuts, denied his enveloping movement that would have brought von Lettow to climacteric battle, was determined not to miss the next chance. He believed himself to be in a good position to trap von Lettow at the Ruwu River, where it became the Pangani and the massif of the Pare Mountains began. 'I believe I can finish the campaign at a stroke . . . If we fail here, von Lettow will fight a rearguard action down the length of mountains into the river valley of the Usambara.'

Smuts Scouts Ahead of Troops

With Meinertzhagen at his side he rode far in advance of his outpost lines. When the Chief of Intelligence remonstrated he retorted: 'I can't attack Kahe without having a look. If Stewart won't look, I must.' He took no heed of the danger of enemy patrols, and confided that he had no faith in General Stewart as the man to carry out the encircling movement.

'Van Deventer will do it . . . We have to cut von Lettow off.'

He was eager to move his men at once, but Meinertzhagen told him that the country was so difficult that he had not been able to get a clear picture from his agents. 'I only knew that von Lettow was somewhere there and presumed he had his main force with him.'

The question was: would the German be preparing for

Brigadier-General J M Stewart, CB incurred the wrath of Smuts for his tardiness.

defence or for attack? Someone had to answer that question. 'Personally I think he's up to some devilment, and I mean to try to find out.' He urged Smuts to contain his impatience for another twenty-four hours till he returned with better information.

So far Smuts only knew what formidable natural obstacles faced him. His patrols had been reconnoitring very dense country where there were only game tracks to be followed. Rivers, dense tropical forest and mountain were obstacles all of which would be used with skill by his enemy. To advance there was to court the unknown. All he could do was to prepare and dare.

On the night of 17 March Meinertzhagen set out alone to reconnoitre the enemy positions at Kahe. Carrying a rifle, bayonet and thirty rounds of ammunition, he followed the railway line. At Kahe station he ran into force of about four hundred men with sentries posted. The railway bridge was still intact and well guarded.

'Stark, Staring Mad'

'Snoring, talking, changing sentries, patrols coming and going all kept me fully informed of the main camp, which was near the Pangani Road bridge. I estimated the enemy force at the bridge as 1 400 men.'

To get back he had to swim the river, and he ran into a sentry. 'The man could not possibly see my uniform, so I spoke to him; and before he could give an alarm I had my bayonet right through him, a beastly job but vital. I was back at New Moshi by 10 a.m. and at once telephoned to Smuts, giving him full details of my reconnaissance.'

Smuts accepted the intelligence, but rebuked him: 'Meinertzhagen, you are stark, staring mad. It is not your business to do this sort of work, so please do not do so again.'

Meinertzhagen replied: 'I enjoy it!'

Next day Smuts ordered an advance towards Kahe. This time there would be no British brass-hats to foul up. The plan would be his. Stewart resigned after a stormy interview. Malleson was sacked. Smuts refused to see him and hear his excuses. 'Tighe has received his orders for India,' noted Meinertzhagen. 'It has not taken long for Smuts to smell out the rotters.'

Van Deventer's 1st SA Mounted Brigade left Moshi on the afternoon of 20 March with the 4th SA Horse and two field batteries. They rode hard all night, and at first light, as he prepared to attack, the enemy retired over the railway bridge and blew it up. Not to be denied, some of his force swam their horses across and seized Kahe Hill on the Pangani River, a mile south-west of the bridge, and went on to seize Baumann Kop, farther to the south-west. It looked good. Van Deventer told Meinertzhagen, who rode with him, that 'he did not wish to have a lot of casualties, and if he could manoeuvre the enemy from their position he would be satisfied.'

Van Deventer's Costly Delay

From his position of vantage he sent out a mounted party to intercept the enemy, seen moving along the waggon road that ran parallel to the railway line. The attempt failed; his men were repulsed and fell back while the Germans, now alert to the value of Kahe Hill as the key to the Ruwu position, made repeated attempts to capture it. Two 4.1 inch naval guns, one on a railway truck continually in motion, fired from eight miles away. Van Deventer's move to cut off the main body was stopped. 'I plan,' Van Deventer said, 'to get all my force, including the guns, over the river during the night and seize the waggon drift in the morning.' It would prove to be a belated attempt and a costly one.

When he received this news Smuts knew that it was time to send in Sheppard's 1st Division. No doubt he expected Van Deventer to continue his outflanking move to cut the railway line and the route of von Lettow's retreat. Amazingly, Van Deventer chose not to move. His men had looted houses, stores and shops and the Kilimanjaro Hotel in Kahe. Goods were scattered in the road and smashed in pointless destruction from one end of the village to the other.

Smuts's 1st Division under General Sheppard were ordered to march to Store, cross the River Soko and attack the enemy in his well-prepared positions. The 5th, 6th and 8th SAI under General Beves's 2nd SA Brigade were ordered to join him at Store. The guns went forward to bombard the enemy in their almost impenetrable fortifications.

Gunner Phipson of the 4th Battery recorded the order to hook-up and saddle-up. The Cape drivers who rode the mules pulling the guns and ammunition waggons had 'got into some potent native liquor and were all too drunk to sit in the saddles. We eventually managed to get the teams harnessed and heaved the drunken drivers into their saddles, only to see half of them fall

Major-General J L van Deventer, whose march to Kondoa-Irangi was an epic of a campaign noted for its hard marching and heavy loss of men and animals *en route*.

105

off their mules again. After a few miles of this we came into action, and after letting off a few rounds a frantic order came to cease fire.' They had been firing on their own Indian troops; fortunately 'the shooting had not been good'.

The German headquarters, in a plantation building about a mile from Kahe, was brought under fire, but to little effect; but by late afternoon von Lettow knew that Sheppard's force was at Store. He took it as no more than a screening column, easy to dispose of. It turned out to be a fatal miscalculation.

Sheppard's advancing 130th Baluchis came on the Soko, a considerable rain-swollen river flowing into the great Pangani, and began to ford it. Twice they attempted to advance across open ground, but by sunset they had to give up and dig in opposite the thoroughly alerted enemy. Sheppard prepared to attack in the morning, when he would be joined by Beves's South African Infantry. He was confident that Van Deventer's march was going well, but the dense bush and lack of communications kept him ignorant of the fact that Van Deventer was only five miles away.

It was 8 p.m., and already dusk, when Sheppard's encamped troops were aroused by a tremendous outburst of fire. 'It came at a suddenly given signal,' recorded Captain A Buchanan of the Fusiliers. It was the beginning of a 'deafening, close-grappling, vicious battle'.

Terrifying Din of Battle

Firing massed volleys and then charging, groups of about six hundred *Schutztruppe* flung themselves furiously against the 1st Division, bivouacked and preparing food in leisurely fashion. The din of battle in the thick bush, the choking fumes of gunfire and the terrifying howls of the askaris was unforgettable. They made charge after charge, piling their dead and wounded before the shallow hastily-dug trenches of the defenders who were tearing at the soil with their bayonets and fingers.

RSM Molloy arrived with the 5th 'at dusk, in the nick of time. I passed the order to dig in. The men grumbled, but a swish of rifle-fire into them set them digging like navvies with their bayonets.'

The moon was now up. Major W F Barr's men of the 6th dug in 'with our bayonets, the only implements we had to burrow a few inches below ground-surface, and strewed thornbushes in front of us to check the enemy attempts at close quarters. They came off second-best, leaving a number of dead in front of our boma.'

The main attack seemed to be directed at the 29th Punjabis. Molloy described the fury of the attacks: 'The askaris had been primed with liquor. They charged the trenches at least a dozen times, but were repulsed heartily by the gallant Punjabis, who certainly bore the brunt of this attack. The tear and crash of maxims and rifles was incessant from 7 p.m. to about 2.30 a.m. Just before dawn they retired to splendidly prepared positions. We followed them and immediately attacked.'

The South Africans' orders were to charge across a clearing varying in width from six hundred to twelve hundred yards. The men went in in broad daylight against hidden machine guns, while heavy shells from the naval gun from the *Königsberg* pounded away at their transport concentrations from miles behind.

'The South African infantry were beaten off with heavy loss,' wrote von Lettow. 'The enemy realised that he could not advance over the field of fire in front of our trenches with any hope of success and endeavoured to envelop our right flank.'

'Damn the Consequences'

Colonel Molyneux, commanding the 6th SAI told his men: 'We will fight the enemy from our side of prepared enemy positions.' The fight went on all day, with varying fortunes. The attempt to outflank the German position was met by a furious charge of askaris who worked forward so near to the South African machine guns that they were on top of them before they were seen. Deadly close fighting was terminated with the bayonet, and the wounded and dead lay concealed by the thick vegetation where they fell.

When he came forward to see for himself, General Beves found the 6th well dug in. He told Major Barr's men: 'Stick it out and damn the consequences. But when the moon rises about 9 p.m. be ready for another attack like last night!'

Towards dawn they heard the bugles blaring. All along Sheppard's embattled line men braced for the fusillades of rifles and machine-gun fire that would announce the charge. But none came. Late in the afternoon von Lettow had received an ominous report: 'Strong enemy forces advancing in our rear towards the railway at Kissangire.'

'I was therefore compelled to issue an order for immediate withdrawal,' he wrote. While Sheppard's men waited for the night attack, von Lettow withdrew his forces across the Pangani, leaving behind the *Königsberg's* gun in its emplacement, blown up.

Down to Last Reserve

But it had been a close-run thing. Molloy wrote to his friend Middleton, promising him a piece of the gun that he had salvaged:

It was a pretty fight, well handled by the general in command, who had the confidence of all. To show how close it was, our last reserve, amounting to about a hundred out of a force of five thousand, was held in readiness only some hundred yards in the rear of our firing line – and had not a few casualties. From the 7th to the 21st March we had marched and fought day and night, and the 5th took part in every action.

When it was certain that the bugles of the night had sounded retreat, men swarmed forward to look at the enemy defences, and soon saw how skilfully they managed to cover their withdrawal under pressure after an attack. The volume of machine-gun fire they used to delay pursuit was like a tornado, making pursuit a deathtrap.

Major Barr of the 6th SAI wrote: 'I found cartridges piled at the foot of a tall tree, enough to fill a mealie sack. The trunk of the tree was dyed red with the blood of brave men who had died so that their fellows could move back.' Thirty feet up in the tree there was a machine-gun platform. At its foot there was a breastwork for another, and a few yards to the side was a third. 'And could those three machine guns spit out bullets!'

No wonder the brave Baluchis lost almost an entire company attacking, and Selous* wrote that his company of Fusiliers had been hopelessly pinned down with 'the sweeping fire of three or four machine guns pressing them flat to the ground'. He described the German dead that he saw that morning 'laid out in rows like pheasants or hares after a drive'. Nearly two hundred of the six hundred attackers had been cut down through erroneously taking Smuts's main body for a mere screening force. It was a loss von Lettow could not afford to repeat.

Von Lettow had hastened back to Kissangire, abandoning his good position after first blowing up the railway bridge and withdrawing fifteen mules down the line. At Kissangire station, which he reached in the early hours of the morning on 22 March, he found that 'our withdrawal had been unnecessary'.

Von Lettow Loses Battle of Kahe

Whether it was his casualties or the threat offered by Van Deventer's immobile mounted men, it made no difference. The battle of Kahe had been lost. It was striking proof, von Lettow noted, of the difficulties encountered by a commander in the African bush, where he had to

---

* Captain F C Selous is better known as Selous the Scout. He was in the column Cecil Rhodes sent in 1890 to found Fort Salisbury in what became Rhodesia. He was already a famous name as a hunter.

5th Battery of the SA Field Artillery on trek.

assess the accuracy of reports delivered by men confused by the ebb and flow of battle.

'Personal observation' was the only means by which a commander could know for certain; a judgment that would have been confirmed by his opponent, who climbed trees and mountains and rode ahead of his advanced posts to see for himself.

However, for the German commander the Kilimanjaro battleground was lost, and it was time to redeploy his troops. His plan now was to close the passes through the Pare Mountains. His men were in good heart and believed they had dealt a heavy blow to a far superior enemy. And indeed they had.

In Smuts's camp it was time for congratulations.

Only Meinertzhagen struck a sour note but a true one. Kahe station was only five miles from the scene of the battle, but 'Van Deventer had made not the slightest gesture to support Sheppard's right flank. It was a great opportunity lost. A great chance which may never recur, for with a little push we might have rounded up his main body and finished the campaign. Smith-Dorrien would have done it'. The South Africans, he wrote, 'are not trained troops, and their officers are the least efficient part of them . . . Sheppard fought like a hero . . .

but he lacked support [from Van Deventer] at the critical moment to gain a crushing and decisive victory.'

However, he conceded: 'We are now secure in the Kilimanjaro area and can rest until after the rains. These may commence any day now.'

From South Africa, the Prime Minister, Louis Botha, wrote to Smuts: 'What you wrote in your letter from Nairobi before the attack you have carried out beautifully . . . in so short a time you have made yourself master of the situation. The despondency among our friends has been relieved, and there is now only a feeling of gratitude that you have advanced so amazingly and have driven the enemy out of English territory . . . we are all astonished that your losses are so slight.'

Smuts moved his headquarters to Moshi. In his report to their Lordships at the War Office he dealt mildly with his old comrade's failure. Van Deventer, he wrote, had had to retire after a brush with the enemy. 'He waited for the following day to develop the turning movements after his whole brigade should have been brought across the Pangani.'

Von Lettow admitted his error of judgment. 'Our casualties unfortunately included three company commanders. Lt von Stosch and Freiherr Grothe died of their wounds. Captain Augar only became fit for duty again after a long time and with an artificial foot.'

Into Deadly Pangani Valley

So ended the first of the bloody encounters in the valley of the Pangani River. It was to be a Vale of Tears in weeks to come, and a slaughter-house for the wretched animals on whom the army depended. In truth, no one but von Lettow had the faintest idea what lay in store for them.

Twice now Smuts's enveloping strategies had failed. He had depended on swift movements by trusted commanders. First Stewart and then Van Deventer had let him down. At least he could console himself that von Lettow had made a costly error.

'Hundreds of dead bodies were subsequently found buried in the enemy trenches and lying in the thick bush, while a big pile of field dressings on the banks of the Ruwu River told its significant tale,' wrote Philip Sampson in his chronicle of what he called 'the Soko Nassai action'.

Smuts saw for himself: 'Heaps of bloody field dressings told something of the German casualties. Ours,' he admitted, 'were 288. Our men fought like heroes.'

Lord Kitchener telegraphed Smuts congratulating him and all ranks of the army 'on the dash and energy of the operations in a region whose difficulties are not unknown to me'. In Britain there were rejoicings. The General from Africa was giving them what they needed. At home there were bitter attacks on Louis Botha for the rising cost of the war 'that no one wanted here in the Union'.

Thus ended the third and last stage of the great battle for Kilimanjaro with Smuts's forces in possession of the mountain and its slopes on all sides, the terminus of the Northern Railway and the richest part of the German colony as far as the Pangani River. In his dispatch Smuts praised General Tighe for his preparations for the offensive, his command in the actions at Latema and Reata and his loyal co-operation. He also praised Van Deventer for his 'swift execution of the turning movement for which the rapid success of his force was largely due'.

Nor did he omit to praise the Royal Engineers and the Railway Regiment for building bridges and surveying and laying the railway at the rate of a mile a day.

'It must be remembered,' wrote an engineer, 'that from Mbuyani there were seventeen rivers and streams within a distance of twenty miles, and in nearly every instance the bridges had been destroyed by the enemy.'

Small wonder, then, that the transport of supplies was days behind the needs of the fighting men.

Dastardly conduct of Colonel von Biergarten at the Battle of Bado-kidogo in taking cover behind one of the Civilian Population who was peacefully taking home the Sunday joint.

(*'Jambo' or with Jannie in the Jungle*, AW Lloyd, undated)

6

Poor Equipment, Low Rations Hard Marching

Having transferred his headquarters to Moshi in the cool and pleasant highlands and placed a chain of outposts along the Ruwu River, Smuts set to work to reorganise his forces for the next move, concentrating them as far as possible in the healthy regions to rest them after their trials. The rains were near. Equipment for the men was rudimentary and inadequate.

'Our clothing consisted of a mosquito shirt, a spine protector, a pair of shorts, puttees, boots, helmet and groundsheet. One dug one's trench with one's bayonet, cut grass and branches to lie on, secured the groundsheet at the corners, sloping slightly towards the feet, and so shed the rain into an empty biscuit tin.' So wrote Major W F Barr of the 6th SAI.

Resting, the rank and file had time to indulge in army-style grousing and moaning. There was dismay at the number of graves in the cemeteries, the sound of the Last Post and the volleys of firing parties. Letters home even under censorship began to reveal that there were grave deficiencies. True, the men still had plenty of enthusiasm and their admiration for Smuts was still great. What the letters made clear – and the staff were well aware of it – was the inability of the service corps to cope with its task.

The short period of action produced pen pictures of hungry men scavenging in fields for sweet potatoes, stealing crops and stock from peasants' fields, shooting game for fresh meat, stripping plantations for unripe fruit; even chewing coffee berries on the march.

Rations did not come up in time, and men set out on life-or-death operations with nothing but a cup of coffee and a few hard-tack biscuits in their stomachs to sustain them for hours of marching and digging and fighting under the equatorial sun. Diaries tell of getting a fire going to cook a hasty meal, only to be ordered to *opsaal*, carrying their half-cooked or raw meat dangling from their rifles, covered with flies. Every man carried a fire-blackened jam-tin at his belt.

The main rations were salt bully-beef, biscuits that had to be crushed to be edible, sugar, flour, oatmeal, tea and the eternal plum-and-apple jam. That was the ration in theory. What was issued was often far short of that. So were fresh vegetables and fruit that in a land of plenty were never seen.

Men wrote of going for eighteen hours with nothing to sustain them, while 'some officers are only concerned for their whisky supplies and their dainties'.* The journals of soldiers are full of details of food, or the lack of it. Thompson never makes an entry without describing what he ate.

'Had a lovely tea of bully-beef on toast with onion sauce. It was most enjoyable . . . managed to buy a few bananas from a native for a cent each . . . flour issued instead of bread, so made a few dumplings.' Already they lived and looked like gypsies, each man cooking for himself over his own fire, or in pairs. The crudity of the food and the manner of its cooking in hot embers brought on diarrhoea.

Nothing is mentioned more frequently: 'Had nothing to eat all day and vomited twice . . . Bibby is very bad with dysentery and sent to Nairobi . . . feeling a bit better from the fever, but still bad with diarrhoea . . .'

Wretched Medical Services

Such writings were made at the time of the breakthrough into German East Africa when supplies and medical help were within a score of miles from the front. Diarists recorded the inadequacy of the medical services, and the men sent back in lumbering waggons over roadless country and boulder-strewn river drifts suffered agonies. The best ambulances were those drawn by eight mules on bush tracks where motor vehicles could not move. Makeshift hospitals behind the lines were native huts where men were laid on the ground among filth and vermin, without even cut grass to lie on; if they were lucky they might have a stretcher.

Private Thompson's diary for 4 April: 'Taken to the Indian hospital on a stretcher. Put in a tent on the ground. Given no food. 5 April: No food for 18 hours. Hospital cook then brought half a loaf of bread and some jam.'

Another diarist wrote of being refused water by an Indian orderly who demanded a rupee for a quart. A gunner of the 4th Battery SAFA,

---

* Gunner Phipson was struggling to extricate an officers' mess-cart when some commando-type Afrikaners of the South African Horse dismounted to help. 'What are we pulling here?' one asked. When told that it was an officers' mess-cart, they dropped the tackle and rode off.

A supply train on the Uganda Railway, the British lifeline between Nairobi and Mombasa.

G E Lewis, wrote of the horrors of neglect in an improvised hospital:

> While off-saddling I suddenly came over sick and cold and was told to report to the doctor without delay. A few moments later I was vomiting violently. There was no place for the sick, and there were four of us lying on soaking wet ground for well over an hour and no covering – all the while vomiting. After a while we were taken to an empty house and laid on blankets on the cement floor.
>
> All night we were left in agony, without medicine, the medical corporal being unable to do anything for us . . . our water bottles empty. Towards evening two other fellows were brought in, both corporals. Oswald van der Hoven had eaten a root that they took for sweet potato. Van's face looked purple, he said he was feeling awfully ill. Corporal Farrar raised his head and tried to administer a little stimulant but failed. I could not watch him any longer, so I put on my boots and went to look for a doctor.

Fifteen minutes later he stumbled on a Hospital Kitchen notice and found a temporary hospital manned by East Africans in what had been the Kilimanjaro Hotel. 'They sent a stretcher and a medical man, but poor old Van was gone.'

115

At 8.30 next day an ambulance came for 'us artillery fellows'. It took three hours to do a four-mile journey to their camp on the slopes of Kilimanjaro. 'We were put into a coffee mill and placed on the earth to sleep. Next morning our Colonel visited us and got into a towering rage when we reported our treatment. He sent for the doctor, and we got food and beds within an hour. The Colonel even sent his own stretcher up.'

From the hospital train to Voi 'we were taken into the Imperial wards – we were glad, as the South African wards are inferior in every way. An orderly allotted us each a bed – fancy, clean sheets – new pyjamas and a glorious hot bath. Nurse Alice Middleton of Bulawayo, a charming lady, was indefatigable in her efforts to assist us.'

Forty Sick to a Cattle Truck

Two days later Lewis described the journey to Nairobi by 'Cattle Truck Express. What a fearful journey – an iron truck – a little straw strewn on the floor and forty-odd sick men huddled up in every conceivable shape and form – some with fever – some with dysentery and other diseases, groaning in their pain in pitch darkness . . . '

Gunner J K Jackson of the 2nd South African Artillery recorded that the menu at Kilossa Hospital for convalescent fever patients was 'breakfast – mealie-meal porridge, no milk or sugar, coffee and a slice of dry bread. Lunch – stew and dry bread. Tea – dry bread and a pint of tea.' When he left hospital for a three-day train journey to base hospital he was issued with one loaf of bread, three pounds of flour, bacon, raisins, tea and sugar, but no means of cooking the flour in the cattle-truck packed with twenty-seven men.

Smuts's campaign was hardly a month old, and for his men this was only the beginning of a medical disaster that was to affect thousands of men in the next months. It is likely that not since the Crimean War in the 1850s had an army so suffered from disease. Far worse was to come as the lines of communication lengthened, the rains set in, the tracks dissolved, and the transport horses, mules and oxen began to die in thousands, their inflated skeletal carcases marking the long, long treks and forced marches that were so characteristic of the campaign.

While Smuts was still formulating his plan for the pursuit, Gunner Lewis noted that he was sent to guard a quarantine camp where six hundred Transvaal African volunteers were down with smallpox. 'There are five of us left now guarding them – eight have been taken to hospital with fever and dysentery . . . trains from the front with wounded and sick arrive every day.'

A wartime sketch of Jan Christiaan Smuts, PC, KC in the uniform of a Lieutenant-General of the British Army.

In his report to the War Office, Smuts admitted that the number of sick who passed daily through the hands of the medical authorities, 'more especially since the cessation of active operations, has been very great . . . Exceptionally heavy work has been thrown on medical officers and personnel . . . Great credit is due to the Surgeon-General, G D Hunter, and his assistants.'

Smuts, of course, was not immune to the pain of sickness and the hardships and poor rations of his men. He chose to share them. Nothing, he determined, would deflect him from his purpose.

Comparison with War in France

In Britain and in South Africa, his advance into German territory was received as the work of a military genius. Only a man of Africa could have done it. Indeed, next to the horrifying casualties on the Western Front in the same period, any victory, even such a small one, gave the unaccustomed taste of ultimate success.

In Europe, the Germans had failed in the battle of the Marne to win the war with one sledge-hammer blow against their numerically superior enemies and suffered three-quarters of a million casualties. France had lost three hundred thousand killed and six hundred thousand wounded, captured and missing.

For 1916, the plans for the bloody battles of hopeless attrition on the Somme lay on the tables of the general staffs of France and Britain. Forty-five French and twenty-five British divisions were to go over the top arm in arm, or as Joffre put it: *bras-dessus, bras-dessous.*

The wars in Europe and in Africa were not to be compared. While Smuts and von Lettow had been fighting with at most ten thousand men in action, the Germans in Europe were placing more than twelve hundred heavy guns to destroy the French fortress of Verdun. Small wonder that the British and South African public displayed almost hysterical delight at 'our great African victory'. Where Smuts was counting his casualties so far in hundreds, the French and Germans were counting theirs in hundreds of thousands, with much worse to come.

In the remoteness of Africa that unimaginable devastation was inconceivable. Here the war was as much against the nature of Africa as against the enemy. Indeed, it was the worst enemy.

Not that it was all suffering and misery. Back in the tranquillity of pretty little Nairobi, where brass hats flourished and little had changed except the arrival of convalescents, Private Thompson was rejoicing.

'Went into town for the first time, ordered a table for dinner at the Hotel Stanley, booked seats for Theatre Royal, where during a Charlie Chaplin film we nearly collapsed from over-eating and laughter.'

Next day they dined sumptuously again, and this time they went to the Palace Theatre after a 'glorious repast finishing with cheese, black coffee and cigars. All for the most moderate figure of 1 rupee 50 cents – or two shillings in English money.'

Meanwhile the African battlefields awaited the next wave.

The Germans were ready for the next round, having given ground only to establish themselves in even more favourable positions, barring Smuts's southward advance by occupying the mountain passes through which the railway ran south and by which his supplies came up. The passes were closed. The spirit of the troops was good, and 'the askaris were imbued with a justifiable pride in their achievements against an enemy so greatly superior,' wrote von Lettow.

Settlers Forced to Trek

What of the German, Greek and Boer settlers of the Kilimanjaro country who had raised beef, coffee, cotton and bananas? The Germans left their homesteads and fields with bitter hearts, trekking south down the railway through the Usambara Mountains. Those in the north-west loaded their goods on to ox-waggons and made the desert trek to the far south. Many Greeks stayed on their coffee plantations in Kilimanjaro and the Boers of British nationality stayed on their cattle farms round the Meru Mountains.

Military supply trains rolled north regularly into the new terminus at Lambeni, and 'the companies not in mountain front line worked diligently at their training.' The country was carefully prepared to meet possible battle conditions, passages were cut through the dense rhinoceros bush, and a field of fire was cleared where necessary. 'Personal reconnaissance took up much of my time,' wrote von Lettow, 'and led me to companies encamped in thick bush and on the dominating heights.'

From his reminiscences we get the impression of a commander who was relaxed and confident, knowing his own worth and the

Ruwu bridge, a suspension bridge repaired by Indian Sappers after the Germans had destroyed it.

tenacity of his men; a man keen to pit his skill against a worthy adversary. He was not so harassed by events that he could not relax with his men, enjoying the pleasure of locally-grown coffee with 'beautiful rich milk, prepared from the ground-down kernel of a ripe coconut' while he enjoyed the rustic charm of a grass hut, 'comfortably furnished'.

However, an unexpected blow was on its way.

Where was Smuts, the agile adversary, the man who had achieved so much since his arrival on 19 February? And yet his achievement was so frustratingly small. Ahead of him stretched an interminable campaign, forever just beyond his power to bring to a victory. It was an intolerable situation for a man of his temperament, but at that moment he was confident as he outlined his strategy to his staff. There was not a moment to lose if he were to dispose his men in the best manner to get through the rainy season, which threatened to lay low man and beast in unprecedented numbers.

But first he needed to feel comfortable with men whom he could trust: men of his own people to command in his own imperious style. Reorganisation was needed to get rid of the Indian Army element. On his personal staff he retained an officer of the 7th Hussars and as ADCs one of the 124th Baluchis and his wife's brother, Captain P S Krige. His old associate, Brigadier-General J J Collyer, was head of his general staff. Captain Piet van der Bijl was his GSO3, and Deneys Reitz was loosely attached. Reitz had ridden with him on his famous raid into the Cape and later commanded a British line regiment in Flanders.

Sound men; men of his own blood. Impetuous, daring, and not bound by the rules of conventional warfare.

He had angrily refused to hear the excuses of General Stewart and he had denounced Malleson to the War Office for his poltroonery at the battle of Latema-Reata. 'I want only good commanders that I can trust,' he told Meinertzhagen.

Tighe also had to go; but Smuts did not despise this choleric, impetuous man, whose health was at last broken by alcoholism. In typical face-saving manner Stewart became Governor of Aden and Malleson got an 'important' command in India, to control the new menace of Bolshevism there.

War Office approves Changes

The War Office accepted Smuts's new arrangements: three divisions instead of two; the 1st to comprise two East African brigades of Indian and British troops; the 2nd and 3rd to be South African, with Boer commanders. Old comrades-in-arms, trusted friends. Jaap van Deventer to command the 2nd; Coen Brits to command the 3rd.

Richard Meinertzhagen as Chief of Intelligence was a man of independent mind who had a habit of breaking the British moulds: outspoken, impatient of fools, brave to the point of recklessness; yet a man of remarkable foresight. Sometimes it seemed that he knew the right answer before the question was asked.

With his new organisation in force, his own commanders at his hand, Smuts was ready to try conclusions without delay. Until now the British and Indian Army officers had thought that the South Africans had not embarked on the campaign with serious intent.

'Neither the people as a whole nor the men who came up to take part in it expected a long campaign as far as fighting was concerned. A few weeks, at worst a few months. There was the general idea that the object for which they were fighting was not worth the loss of South African lives. Their commanders feared social and political ostracism.'

Such was the opinion of Brigadier-General C P Fendall as he watched this amateur army with its amateur commander-in-chief prepare for the next advance. He respected Smuts as a great man; but a great general was another thing.

'His idea was to use his superior strength to make the enemy leave his chosen position and then to use his mounted troops to intercept and force him to fight on his chosen ground.'

So far he had been let down. What now? The enemy had been forced to retire, but it was by no means demoralised.

Smuts had a long discussion with his Chief of Intelligence. Meinertzhagen told him that his extensive network of spies reported that it looked as though von Lettow was going to fight stubbornly for the rich cultivated settlements of the Usambara Highlands and do everything he could to defend Tanga and the main port of Dar es Salaam. Here was the hub of German colonial government. Once that fell it would be all over. So ran the conventional wisdom of the time.

A Calculated Risk

Smuts told Meinertzhagen that he was against chasing von Lettow down the Usambara Railway with the rains so near. He intended to push a force south towards Arusha and Ufiome in the west. The idea was to occupy Kondoa-Irangi before the Germans could gather strength there. His intention was to cut the Central Railway running from east to west across the territory.

Meinertzhagen agreed that that was a sound policy. But it had to be done quickly. 'At this moment,' he told Smuts, 'our supply and transport can cope with this move, and they are anxious for us to do so at once. But the rains should be on us in three weeks' time, and we shall have to stop wherever we happen to be. The whole country becomes impassable.'

Could it be done in time? Was it worth the risk? Could Van Deventer's mounted men and infantry ride and march fast enough to keep ahead of the rains?

Smuts and Van Deventer had spoken to Boer cattlemen settled in the Arusha area. They were told that the farther they rode south the less chance of rain there would be. It was high ground all the way. The rains would have no effect on his march or bog down his transport; and there would be little risk of malaria and animal diseases.

With that assurance Smuts and Van Deventer agreed. The march south to cut the railway line was the soundest strategy. Unfortunately it was more sanguine than accurate. The Boer farmers had never in fact ridden so far south. Their opinion was founded on hearsay. Smuts was about to order his 2nd Division to a march that had all the marks of a hastily prepared disaster.

It was to take place in the blazing heat of tropical Africa, with torrential rain bogging it down as effectively as Napoleon's Grand Army in the Russian snow. It would be an endeavour of human and animal endurance that no one foresaw.

'Opposition will be slight,' Smuts believed. 'There is practically no enemy in this huge area. I have decided to push the whole of the 2nd Division into the interior under Van Deventer and to keep the other two divisions with me in rain quarters facing the enemy concentrations south of the Ruwu [Pangani] River.'

121

Indian troops crossing the blown German railway bridge at Kahe.

He hoped to occupy an immense tract of country within two months. At the same time the move would draw off large forces from the Pare and Usambara Mountains 'to stem the tide of invasion'. If necessary, he could even send Van Deventer more troops and still have 'an easy conquest against the enemy's weakened defences in the coastal mountains'.

Collyer has his Doubts

It looked like a typical Boer raid on a large scale. A dashing two months on commando for the energetic Van Deventer. Boer daring and initiative would be enough. Collyer had his doubts. 'Like most Boer generals,' he wrote in his dry, precise manner, 'Van Deventer had led only small bodies of men, never stronger than a small regiment. He had no experience whatever of the innumerable details of staff work. He was a typical Boer in outlook, insistent on his men obeying him; not so eager to take orders or carry out the plans of staff officers.'

Nor had he any idea of what the movement of a large body meant in the supply of a division with food, water and munitions, or of keeping on the march miles of loaded porters, ox-waggons, mule-drawn ambulances, watercarts – the whole cumbersome baggage-train needed to keep a division on the move.

'Van Deventer,' says Collyer, 'was a splendid physical specimen of his race. He spoke with a husky voice, the consequence of a severe throat wound received in the Boer War . . . he was righthand man to Smuts in his Cape raid and responsible for several tactical successes, of which the capture of a squadron of the 17th Lancers at Modderfontein

122

was a notable instance . . . He was energetic, courageous and competent, and a loyal adherent to General Smuts.'

As a regular British staff officer, and Smuts's Assistant Adjutant-General, Colonel C P Fendall also admired Van Deventer as 'a big man morally as well as physically. Clear-headed, he always saw the point of an argument at once, and could and did look at all sides of every question. He had a very high standard by which he judged the conduct of all men. His plans were always logical, always based on the idea of what he would do in the position of the enemy commander.'

So, with false information and a great deal of reckless optimism, Van Deventer prepared his brigades to march. First to Arusha, then on to occupy Kondoa-Irangi and to cut the vital railway line at Dodoma. It was to be a lightning strike that would catch the Germans off their guard. On 3 April he sent forward scouts who came riding back to Arusha, hell-for-leather. They had been fired on from an isolated hill at Lol Kissale, forty miles to the south across the Masai desert. Their horses had smelt water at the springs there, but they were unable to drink. The Germans had opened fire.

In his mountain camp on the distant east coast von Lettow was suddenly made aware of what was happening by a fragmentary report from Captain Paul Rothert, camped with his 28th Company at Lol Kissale. 'Have been attacked by superior forces . . . ' With that the heliograph message broke off. The message was dated 4 April.

Van Deventer's Night Ride with 1 500

Van Deventer had wasted no time. The order to *opsaal* and ride went out at once. Rations were already short at Arusha (so wrote Gunner

Phipson) 'but it was decided not to wait for rations to come up before we set out with two batteries, the 2nd and 4th.' With all possible haste Van Deventer's fifteen hundred horsemen set out, riding hard all night. They reached the springs at dawn. It was the only watering-place for a hundred square miles.

General J L van Deventer, Commander of the 3rd South African Infantry and SA Mounted Brigade. Smuts planned to approach Kilimanjaro from the east and north; Van Deventer's task was to seize the Chala Heights and take Taveta from the east.

123

From the rocky knoll Captain Paul Rothert's 28th Company saw the hard-riding Boers encircle the hill. Their horses were half-crazy at the smell of water, the riders' bottles were empty, with no prospect of any until they had beaten the Germans. The askaris were dug in on the crest of the steep and rocky hill. In the typical style of a Boer attack the riders dismounted and skirmished forward from rock to rock, climbing towards the white puffs of smoke that marked the fire of the old Model 71 rifles. Van Deventer was investing the hill with three regiments.

The 2nd SA Horse had already made a night march of fifty miles when the attack began at 9.30. The rest had been going hard since noon the day before. It took all day to encircle the hill, and by night-fall horses were falling dead. Next morning the battle continued, but by 4 p.m. the attackers had made little progress. Rain was setting in, and it was still impossible to water the horses. Darkness fell. The shivering dismounted troopers were still held up thirty yards from the Germans' main trenches, where five hundred men were waiting for them, their machine guns firing warning bursts at every movement.

The attackers were without food; they had ridden out in haste with only twenty-four hours' rations and fodder; and they lay soaked to the skin, half-frozen, with no prospect of rations getting through. No one had expected rain so far south so soon. All round them horses were lying bloated and staggering; for many had set out already suffering from horse-sickness.

Still the hill held out, its machine guns keeping the attackers at bay and inflicting casualties who could not be got out.

Van Deventer did not know that the German commander had been severely wounded on the second day and was no longer capable of command or aware of the besiegers' desperate lack of supplies. Van Deventer called his officers: 'Kêrels, we have to take that damned hill tomorrow or go back to Arusha with our tails between our legs. What's it to be?'

There was no choice. During the night the Boers tightened the circle round the perimeter of the hill, and at daybreak they opened fire with two field batteries.* The smoke drifted from shattered rock and torn bush as the men of the 2nd Brigade fixed bayonets and advanced. Almost at once they saw a white flag raised as the 28th surrendered. Some stubborn askaris refused to accept defeat and broke out with their wounded during the hours of darkness. The rest remained with their gravely wounded commander.

---

* Gunner Phipson wrote: '5th April. We continued in action the whole day. Continuous firing in the heat was a strain on the gun-teams. Our gun (B Sub-Section) fired 95 rounds – a heavy two days' work for a gun team in action under the African sun near the equator.'

Boer Families Released

The attacking Boers were astonished to find many Boer families, altogether ninety-two persons, who were delighted to shake hands with their brethren from the south. 'We were compelled to get out of the Kilimanjaro area when the Germans saw how it was going for them and forced to retreat with them.' For what reason? 'They wanted us to leave our farms in case we gave information about their strength. We were always under suspicion because we were too independent to fit into their colonial system.' That was confirmed by official documents found at Moshi.

These Boers told their rescuers that only about two or three hundred of the enemy had got away to the south in the direction of Ufiome, a mission station fifty miles farther on.

Among the captured were several hundred porters, who were glad to be out of it; but they were immediately impressed by Van Deventer to carry away the spoils of machine guns, ammunition and ample stores. Van Deventer marched them back to Arusha along with four hundred askaris and a few white officers. These were left under guard halfway between Arusha and Moshi, and Shackleton later noted in his diary how he 'tramped along through the rain and thick mud beside the prisoners, the guards' wet clothing clinging to bodies which told of fever and insufficient food.'

It was the first capture of a substantial German force, but Van Deventer had taken the springs and the hill only just in time. He left 250 horses dead, and the exhausted remainder staggered back to

In front of the German boma (fort) of Moshi, later occupied as Smuts's headquarters.

Arusha just in time to die. The loss of horses was soon to affect the fighting power of the division. Colonel Fendall commented gravely on the Boers' 'apparent indifference to the suffering of their horses'.

At Smuts's headquarters in Moshi rain fell in torrents but (as Smuts noted in a letter home) 'there is proper accommodation for my staff during the rainy season.' Prisoners and documents from Lol Kissale were examined. 'Hold out as long as possible,' von Lettow had ordered, 'to give me time to send substantial forces to Kondoa-Irangi.'

He had immediately divined Smuts's intention and was aware of its danger. It was a stroke he might have conceived himself. At once it changed the whole thrust of the enemy's attack.

On assessing the intelligence, Meinertzhagen urged that a full division should be sent. 'Kondoa is the decisive point . . . He will concentrate and try to annihilate Van Deventer's detachment. Attack it he must, and before the rains finish . . . It is his only chance, and he knows it.'

From the beginning of the campaign the percipient Chief of Intelligence had argued for a decisive battle. He had to be satisfied with Collyer, as Chief of Staff, ordering two regiments of the 3rd Infantry Brigade to follow Van Deventer's trail south with a howitzer battery and a machine-gun company.

It was a forced march south across the Masai plateau for 250 miles. The mounted brigade had already expended a complete remount of fresh horses even before the march on Lol Kissale, but it could not wait if the plan to take Kondoa-Irangi were to succeed. Two thousand fresh horses were needed.

'They will be sent after you,' Smuts assured Van Deventer.

'The 3rd Infantry Brigade will drive them,' said Collyer.

'Stop for Nothing!'

Stop for nothing was the order. Kondoa-Irangi had to be secured before von Lettow could switch men from the east.

'He'll do that as soon as he sees we are on our way from Lol Kissale.'

Van Deventer told his officers that it was *opsaal* with the prospect of fighting on the way at Ufiome and Umbula. The march was on. He took the head of his 1st Mounted Brigade and splashed south through rising streams. Behind his horsemen, trudged seven thousand porters whom he had commandeered and scores of supply waggons creaking along to the crack of the twenty-foot *voorslag*. In front of the riding column rain was falling in torrents.

The hope was to outmarch the rain and reach an area which, they had been told, was never subjected to tropical torrents that lashed

126

Kilimanjaro and as far as the coastal mountains. The fear was: how are the supplies to get through this to reach the brigade? With fighting ahead, and cut off from the rear, what were their chances? The answer was to press on regardless. Fifteen days to Kondoa! was the reckless expectation. If the horses held out, and they could capture fresh horses in encounters with the enemy on the way.

It was country teeming with giraffe, zebra, eland, wildebeest and lion. The Masai villagers herding their cattle stood impassively beside their flat-roofed huts as the white horsemen jingled by. Soon the lions would be devouring the carcases of the fallen horses that marked the passing of the brigade from the first day.

Ufiome lay ahead, a village on the border of the Masai country, where the Germans had a fort and administrative buildings and houses.

Digging trenches while in the throes of Fever and Dysentery.

(*East African Experiences 1916*, C W Shackleton, 1940)

7

An Epic of Marching in Tropical Rain

Van Deventer's infantry brigade, the 3rd, under Brigadier-General Berrange was ordered to set out on a march that was to be an epic of infantry endurance. The 3rd had already been in the action that had cleared the Germans from the Pangani River at Kahe. It had already endured hunger and thirst and the confusion of night fighting. Its men referred to one such time of privation as 'Starvation Kopje'. They had fought an enemy that they could not see, and they had hardly been withdrawn to rest in their tents at Himo when the order came.

'Fall in, prepare to march!' The howitzer battery and a machine gun company formed up with the 3rd and they marched off in torrents of rain towards Moshi. Private C W Shackleton recorded the scene:

At 2 p.m. on 1 April four companies of infantrymen, complete with well-laden ammunition mules, ox-drawn supply waggons and a few native carriers, moved off for Moshi. The rain had stopped and the ground had quickly dried under the hot early afternoon sun. Clouds of dust, kicked up by the heavily shod feet blanketed the sweating men, giving each individual a dull grey appearance – in keeping with his thoughts.

Two hours' walking brought us to a welcome stream. A halt was called while thirsty men, animal-fashion, put their mouths to the water and drank. One of them shouted in disgust. Almost hidden by overhanging weeds and grass, a dead mule lay in the water, its partly decomposed body a swarming mass of maggots . . .

[Next day]: The first streaks of dawn showed in the cloudless sky as the regiment continued its advance, following the trail of the mounted brigade through undulating forest-clad country, crossed two rivers and halted for the night before a third. We threw off our packs and went foraging.

Always it was thus. Food was the main thing in our lives, at least the lack of it. Hunger was the enemy. And thirst and exhaustion and the eternal fever. In a large clearing we found guavas, bananas, lemons and sweet potatoes.

That night it rained heavily. We had no tents, no shelter. We got no sleep, and it was a tired regiment that continued its march in the early hours of the morning. By dusk that day the regiment had marched in full kit without rations, getting some relief from chewing grass and sucking stones.

Shackleton and his half-section Somers came on the lungs and guts of a buck that someone had shot. They roasted the offal on the glowing embers. 'A man must eat,' observed Somers, chewing with his eyes shut.

At nine o'clock the food-waggon turned up and issued rations, the first since the march began. Each group of a dozen men or so gathered round a groundsheet with sugar, salt, tea, coffee and flour in little heaps, together with a few strips of bacon to be divided up among them. 'It was raining, and as each man feverishly pushed his supplies into dirty tobacco bags, or pieces of shirt sleeve, he cursed the thought of losing some of his precious food.'

After another sleepless night in the lashing rain, during which most men stood dozing against a tree, the march was resumed. The next night was the same . . . everything was soaked through.

Two Hundred and Fifty Miles

By the afternoon of the next day they had been seven days on the march from Himo. Two hundred and fifty miles lay ahead. The men were in such bad shape that 'walking with boots on was too painful . . . we stopped, removed boots and puttees and wound them round our feet as a protection against the hot sun, the torture of the earth.' By the time they had marched a further eighteen miles 'the grilling sand crept in between the protective puttees and the soles of our feet, badly burning and blistering them. Many times we fell and had to crawl to the shelter of the nearest shrub.

Ox transport: Indian supply waggons drawn by hump-backed Madagascar oxen.

'At sundown the following day, utterly exhausted and deeply burnt, we reached Arusha and staggered into the fort.' Shackleton's description of a medical orderly's attention to his feet is horrifying. 'Next morning the company left Arusha and pushed on southwards, following the trail of the mounted brigade.'

Somers and Shackleton were allowed to ride on one of the two-wheeled ox-drawn waggons for a few miles. The muddy trail took them through banana plantations, but eventually the four platoons, accompanied by kit waggons and mules carrying ammunition and machine guns, arrived at Lol Kissale. Shackleton describes the pleasure of discarding his worn-out boots and finding an odd pair. 'One pinched, the other slid up and down; and so, marching and resting, I managed to keep up.'

There, at the site of Van Deventer's success, a medical officer looking after the wounded found the men of the 3rd in such pitiful condition that he ordered the column two days' rest. Amazingly, morale never declined. Shackleton described their march as a grim fight; 'the dynamic which lay behind it was the strong instinct to live.'

Private Frank Reid (formerly a barrister) of the 9th described the struggle of his unit to reach Lol Kissale.

Sometimes it was through quagmire . . . Sometimes the road would be impassable. It meant getting out pangas, cutting down small trees, branches and long grass to lay across the track and so provide something of a foothold for the animals and prevent the AT carts sinking into the mud axle-deep.
In spite of all the shrieking of the miserable little Indian drivers – they could be heard all along the line – and unlimited twisting of the oxen's tails, one or two of the poor beasts could go no further and sank down exhausted in the mud. One memorable day we spent sixteen hours of foot-slogging and hard labour on the road to make less than ten miles.

Ordered to Press On

At length Lol Kissale was reached. There we had been promised a couple of days' rest. But it was not to be. Van Deventer at Kondoa was threatened by counter-attack, and infantry were badly needed to hold the place. Every man who was able had to press on.
By now the rain, mud and heavy marching had told their tale on the general health of the men, and especially upon their feet. Toes and heels were protruding from boots, which in some cases had given away altogether. That meant blisters and blood-poisoning and many men could go no further without rest.

So when we marched on the same afternoon, we had to leave behind no less than a hundred and fifty men of our regiment alone, nearly all of them foot cases. Ahead, the route to Ufiome stretched seventy-five miles without water fit to drink. Muddy pools and rain that fell in torrents.

While the infantry plodded on far behind Van Deventer's mounted men, the cavalry pressed on hard for Ufiome with its small garrison of about twenty whites and two hundred askaris. These looked out from their stronghold on the kopje above the mission station of Gwansawe to see the several hundred horsemen appearing in the fields. They were ready, but they were quickly overwhelmed, and they fell back into the mountains, leaving thirty prisoners, some wounded and a large quantity of supplies. Van Deventer sent his troopers on their exhausted mounts in pursuit to Salaga, twenty miles to the south.

'Here we were too spent to go farther,' wrote a trooper on 13 April. 'My company had lost half its strength through fever, and so many horses that we could not go farther without remounts. Luckily we took some supplies from the Germans, for nothing was getting through to us, our wireless had broken down because of the weather, and the orders were to press on regardless, hungry, soaked but cheerful.

'I was sent back to make contact with the infantry, and I found them battling forward through a sea of mud, all mechanical transport immobile and dead horses and mules stinking to high heaven all the way. Leading supplies and rations, I got back to find my unit at Salaga.

With their horses dead South Africans turned to Abyssinian mules. Very hardy and wiry, and practically immune from all disease, they easily carried the heaviest man.

Major Kraut leading one of his columns of mounted askaris. Kraut proved an agile adversary, thwarting every attempt to outflank him.

There were only some 650 men fit to answer roll-call – and in poor shape at that. The horses were all but finished, poor, lean staggering creatures. Many a shot was heard as men put a beast out of its misery.'

From fetid pools of water myriads of mosquitoes rose in maddening clouds to persecute the men, and tsetse fly was killing off even the fresh mounts. Richard Meinertzhagen was also coming forward with some of headquarters staff. 'We travelled laboriously amid torrential rain, deep mud, voracious mosquitoes, the roar of lions, clouds of tsetse fly and the loss of all our mules.'

The unnerving presence of prides of lion* instilled a fear of being left wounded in the bush and carried away by predators – a fear peculiar to this theatre of war. Although so many were ill, most men felt that it was better to be down with fever and to carry on than to struggle back to the rear, where conditions were no better and the makeshift hospitals were overflowing.

Quarter Rations and Dysentery

By this time Van Deventer's men were on quarter rations, dropping with the bloody discharges of dysentery and a diarrhoea, vomiting from eating nuts, berries and the unripe ears of maize. They had marched in tropical rain for nearly two hundred miles in less than three weeks.

'Van Deventer was always able to rouse us to further efforts,' wrote a trooper. 'When he was around he gave us the feeling that we could do anything he asked.' Van Deventer had been able to get so far only by using methods totally unorthodox to the professional military mind.

---

* 'The place stank of lions' wrote Lt J H Lowden, 7th SAI.

Collyer called it 'the commando mentality'. Seize what you need, where you find it and from whomever, regardless. The old commando leader did that with a vengeance. As far back as Moshi he was being cursed and reviled by staff officers, regimental officers and men. His freebooting troopers had helped themselves.

An artillery staff officer noted in his diary: 'Suspect Van Deventer has collared everything he can lay his hands on for supply purposes.'

He did not scruple, in time-honoured Boer fashion, to take what he needed where he found it. That included anything on wheels and columns of black porters impressed to struggle forward through viscous black cotton-soil mud over tracks that had been almost obliterated by streams that turned desert into lakes overnight.

Smuts himself wrote: 'Rivers swept away almost all our laboriously built bridges, the roads became impassable mud tracks, and all transport became a physical impossibility. The rains fell steadily, day after day, sometimes as much as four inches in one day.'

Even the tracks of the railway being pushed forward to meet the German lines were 'for long distances practically under water, and the attention of thousands of labourers was constantly required to prevent its disappearance in the mud.'

On 17 April Van Deventer's scouts made contact with the enemy four miles north of Kondoa-Irangi. They could see across the Bubu River bridge to the whitewashed walls of the fort and the wireless station and the pleasant bungalows by the river banks. It was hoped to seize the wireless station and the bridge intact, but it took two days to clear the village. The enemy left twenty dead and four whites and thirty askaris as prisoners. The wireless station, the bridge and supplies had been blown up. But this was rich cattle country, and they had not been able to drive away about eight hundred head.

There Van Deventer found a few more Boer families who had trekked south to avoid the war and were none too pleased to be liberated. Most of them saw it as more British empire-grabbing. Van Deventer sent riders back to report his epic twelve days from Lol Kissale.

A Trail of Carcases

'My horses are exhausted. Will be unable to move until receive remounts. Have lost hundreds of animals since leaving Moshi a month ago. Troops worn out by ceaseless marching and fighting.'

Smuts decided to send the whole 2nd Division forward to concentrate at Kondoa-Irangi and push out patrols towards the Central Railway. It would take time. In the meantime, Van Deventer's men must live off the land and what supplies could get through, carried on the heads of porters for a hundred and twenty miles from Lol Kissale.

Private Shackleton recorded the last stages of the march to Kondoa-Irangi in the kind of vivid prose possible only to one who was there.

As we moved out the waggons began to sink into the swampy ground. The oxen had to be outspanned and the waggons had to be unloaded and man-hauled on to higher ground. There was no rest for the men pushing the vehicles from behind.

Everywhere along the trail, stretching as far back as Lol Kissale, lay the carcases of horses, mules and oxen. Attacked by sickness and tsetse flies, the unfortunate animals had been discarded by the mounted troops. The stench of rotting bodies was sickening. Hordes of bush flies rose in clouds from the carcases as men circled past.

At night we set guards against lions, leopards, hyenas and jackals and built thorn bomas and burned big fires to protect the frightened oxen. It rained continuously!

We marched through another long day, from sunrise to sunset through the dank jungle. At the end of it they served us our rations – half a cup of flour per man. Nothing else. It was too wet to make a fire. I put my flour ration into my tin mug and held it out in the rain, then drank the thin paste.

That night his comrades had their first encounter with a lion. The huge beast sprang among the sleeping men and 'with a great leap disappeared over the boma with a blanket roll in its jaws.'

On 8 May, what Shackleton described as a 'decrepit band of haggard-faced men, their tattered clothing hanging on skinny frames', reached the small town of Kondoa-Irangi and looked across the river to the cheering sight. 'Of the 240 men of the regiment who left Himo on 1 April there were less than a hundred.'

Handful of Rice a Day

The remnant of Van Deventer's force was there to greet them, six hundred mounted men out of twelve hundred who had left Moshi along with the thinned-out ranks of the 11th and 12th South African Infantry. The retreating enemy had taken most of the food supplies in the town. Van Deventer's division was issued with a ration of a handful of rice and a piece of sugar-cane per man per day.*

_____

* Private Aubrey A Menkin of the 9th SAI related being picked up by an ambulance convoy during a forced march on flour and water rations. He overheard the medical officer order his batman to prepare breakfast of porridge, bacon and eggs, toast and marmalade and coffee. Menkin was not asked to share. He reflected: 'The Medical Section had to have comforts – if only for the sick!'

These were the men who would have to fight the battle of Kondoa-Irangi as von Lettow moved to concentrate four thousand rifles against Van Deventer's half-starved and exhausted division.

At Moshi Smuts found time to write to his old friend M C Gillett in England, describing the torrential rains.

'My advance troops are 220 miles from here and have to be fed and provided somehow.' From this he digressed in philosophical speculations about the soul of man. 'Mankind must feel the pulsations of a new spiritual life before the wounds will heal and the new order will arise . . . When this war is over and we have counted our dead and our losses . . . '

He concluded: 'No time will be lost in pressing this campaign to a conclusion. But it bristles with extraordinary difficulties and the hospitals are full of men suffering from all sorts of tropical complaints – sunstroke, malaria, dysentery, etc., etc.'

The Gamble Pays Off

When Smuts heard that von Lettow was reacting to his advance on Kondoa-Irangi he was quietly elated. 'The enemy had realised the tremendous threat which this expedition constituted against his whole system of defence.' Von Lettow, Smuts reasoned, had seen the movement as an encircling drive to cut him off in the coastal area and prevent his escape farther south.

A situation had arisen in which each commander was trying to outguess the other. Smuts had been advised by Meinertzhagen to believe that the Germans would place all their efforts on holding the fertile, highly-developed coastal districts, the railway line through the Usambara Mountains and the port of Dar es Salaam.

They would fight there, Smuts reasoned. And there the campaign would be settled in a few weeks. If that were not so, the urgency to send Van Deventer south to cut the Central Railway and round the rear of von Lettow's army would have been pointless . . . a mere grabbing of undefended territory while the main battle remained to be fought where most of German settlers, the governor and the administrative machinery were established.

But now, seeing the threat to his rear, von Lettow elected to weaken his force in the coastal provinces and move them hastily to the west to meet Van Deventer. The entire thrust of strategy for both generals was abruptly altered.

Time was of the Essence

By rushing his fresh men to Kondoa-Irangi the German hoped to knock out Van Deventer's division and still have time to turn back and deal with Smuts when he moved in the east. Smuts had already had word that the defences in the Pare Mountains were being drastically weakened. He saw well enough that von Lettow could move to fight Van Deventer and by cutting across country on the old caravan trails be back in time to face him at Handeni. And do it in twelve days!

'My advance had to be rapidly executed. I had to reach the Western Usambara in a fortnight. If I could achieve that and reach Handeni before the Germans I would have two forces almost the same distance from the Central Railway as the one at Kondoa.'

Von Lettow, he argued, could not be expected to make a stiff resistance to two columns only 170 miles apart. It looked like sound reasoning – if only the men and the supplies could hold up to carry it through. Human endurance was the unknown side of the equation. This was tropical Africa!

Meinertzhagen continued to urge his commander to get enough men to Kondoa-Irangi to defeat the German decisively there. 'We have to get at the enemy's main force . . . strategic points are useless except with that object in view.' He pointed out that Smuts's strategy 'again places von Lettow on interior lines, and he will only be too ready to profit from any mistakes that Smuts may have made.'

Time was vital to both commanders; but the advantage lay with the German's fast-marching askaris, his thousands of porters inured to

German askaris camouflaged for patrol operations.

the difficulties of the country, his intact lines of communication, his support from the white population, his efficient railway service with its extensive network – and still undamaged where he needed it most.

When von Lettow saw no immediate move by Smuts in the northeast he decided 'to direct my main thrust against the hostile group that had pushed forward to near Kondoa-Irangi.' To achieve that he had to transport his troops south on the Northern Railway and destroy it behind him, then march the men 125 miles to the Central Railway.

An Army in Single File

Fifteen field companies on the march in single file on one jungle track! They moved three or four companies at a time with a day's interval between. It was not easy, even for German planners. Even the tireless askaris struggled in the sticky cotton soil. Those following behind piled up. 'The troops could hardly move . . . the supplies, the baggage, could not come forward and the companies fast stuck seized the porters coming behind and used them to extricate themselves.'

It was devil take the hindmost, for, as von Lettow dryly noted, 'according to ancient African custom' his officers, desperate to move forward, wrecked the whole system of relay carriers. To appreciate the German supply problem it is necessary to visualise a line of six hundred porters carrying the load of a single lorry. Each porter carried only fifty pounds and he needed two pounds of food daily.

Before the campaign a single white official or soldier seldom travelled with fewer than eleven bearers to carry his tent, equipment and food. Now von Lettow had cut the porters to three to a man! However, the long marches in tropical heat and humidity were exhausting the Germans also; they succumbed to the same disabilities as Van Deventer's men. His animals died from tsetse. It was no picnic, von Lettow's march towards Kondoa-Irangi – even though he had the ample resources of a rich colony at his disposal.

Other problems were the failure of telephonic communications because the system earthed in the soaking ground, the breakages in supplies caused by collapsing porters and waggons that overturned with all their contents. Giraffes broke telegraph lines and cut him off from news about his men marching in front, and as 'the rain came down harder and harder, the roads became deeper and deeper.'

Water up to the Saddle

Swollen torrents were almost uncrossable. Von Lettow, his staff and his men had to 'ride for hours with water up to our saddles, or wade with it up to our necks'. Bridges were swept away by the swollen torrents.

Yet there is no hint in von Lettow's narrative of men falling out on the march by scores and hundreds. Most were Africans, barefoot and tough, on their own ground and led by acclimatised Germans. Pressing forward, he reached the Burungi Mountains where he had placed a detachment under Captain Klinghardt. There he made a valuable find. 'A new and excellent map of the district of Kondoa-Irangi had been left with a native chief when the District Commissioner abandoned the town.'

Food would be no problem. There was plenty of native food from well-stocked farms with grain, poultry, vegetables and cattle. As soon as the rear detachment caught up with him von Lettow was ready to march to Kondoa-Irangi with two naval guns, one a 3.5-inch and one a 4-inch, both moving on travelling carriages, with their well-trained naval gunners from the cruiser *Königsberg*.

By the end of April he was in the hills only twenty miles from Van Deventer and in a very good position to swoop down on the South Africans' straggling encampments strung round the town.

Van Deventer was soon informed that the enemy, according to captured porters, intended to make a 'big stand' here. That was all he knew. He was in the German town with its burnt-out fort, its church and European quarters along the river. Ahead lay mountains and jungle, where it would be impossible to locate his enemy. Behind him on the waterlogged road his reinforcements and supplies were bogged in. His hospitals were crammed with patients who could not be taken out to the rear. His men at Kondoa-Irangi were foraging in the fields for groundnuts, maize, pawpaws and bananas that might have been left unharvested.

Von Lettow had accomplished his move so adroitly that even as late as mid-April there was nothing to support 'a view that any actual transfer of men to the west had taken place.'

Van Deventer in Dire Straits

Despite his network of thousands of informers and spies Meinertzhagen knew no more about the situation than Van Deventer. 'I am fifty per cent below strength in infantry,' Van Deventer signalled. 'My mounted men are waiting along the road for remounts that do not arrive. Three fresh infantry regiments have never reached me, neither have my howitzers.'

How could they? In Collyer's unexaggerated prose the troops struggling to reach Kondoa-Irangi were 'in bad case, sickness becoming rife, clothes and boots wearing out . . . generally in circumstances which demanded from them fortitude and endurance to an unusual degree . . . their response was as always in this abnormal campaign to their eternal credit.'

The East African Carrier Corps was vital in a theatre where the total absence of communications away from the railway required all supplies to be manhandled.

Van Deventer sent out his mounted patrols to scout ahead. On 2 May he reported: 'Patrol on Saranda road waylaid. One man wounded, two missing.'

Von Lettow described the same encounter. He was sending out patrols regularly, and this case six white soldiers were seen at a waterhole. A native officer, Yuman Effendi, stalked them and, in his report of the action, killed all six.

On 6 May Van Deventer began to withdraw his patrols. He signalled headquarters at Moshi to urge the staff to make a counter-move down the coastal railway to take Tanga. According to Collyer, the staff laughed heartily at this suggestion. 'Tanga is completely protected by large swamps,' they replied. Van Deventer retorted that his men's boots were wearing out and 'my horse's shoes are going the same way.'

The staff were right about the swamps but these were an obstacle still to be faced on the advance down the eastern mountains. In the meantime Smuts's chief scout, the redoubtable Major Pretorius, came in from behind the enemy lines to report that the Germans appeared to be thinning out. Smuts and Collyer decided it was only a stratagem at this stage.

'He is likely trying to encourage us to draw off men to assist Van Deventer, weakening our force here in the east and prolonging our attack through the mountains in a climate they know to be deadly to man and beast with fever, dysentery and sleeping sickness.'

This reasoning decided Smuts not to send more men to the mounted brigade. 'Hold on with what you have,' he ordered.

He knew very well that the initiative that he had wrested from von Lettow at Taveta was once more with the enemy, and that the next move would be made by him.

On 5 May Meinertzhagen rode into Kondoa-Irangi to see for himself. He saw the funeral pyres of dead horses fouling the air with the stink of burnt carrion, hide and hoof. In the graveyard beside the church, now a hospital, fresh graves were dug daily.

Credit for Bold Move

'The situation is interesting,' he noted that day. 'Our capture of Kondoa took the Germans by surprise. They never suspected that we could move so quickly over bad roads in the rain. Neither did they credit Smuts with so bold a move. I doubt whether any British general with British troops could have planned and carried out the move in tropical Africa during the rains. Only South Africans born and bred to long distances and living on the country could have accomplished it.'

This was the typical British view of the South African. It took no account of the fact that most of the infantrymen and gunners who crawled into Kondoa-Irangi were townsmen with no more veld sense than the British themselves. Many were in fact British immigrants, only recently settled.

The diary of Gunner Lewis names some of his comrades.

'I met Fred Young-Freemantle from Stuttafords [a well known

emporium] in Jo'burg and Malcolm Teare from Leonard Rayne's theatrical company; also Little Jeffreys, a solicitor from Bloemfontein.' Lewis, a thirty-three-year-old solicitor had been only eleven years in South Africa when the war began.

So much for generalisations and preconceptions.

The hard facts were that on 4 May, a German force estimated at six to eight companies had been encountered by patrols and three days later elements were seen six miles from Kondoa-Irangi. Meinertzhagen was there to interrogate native fugitives flocking in on the promise of protection. He reckoned a force of about twenty companies.

'The immediate situation,' he told Van Deventer, 'is that von Lettow has about three thousand rifles and eight guns, not thirty miles from here. But he has little ammunition and many sick, so his position is by no means secure. His horses are dying fast, and few of his squadrons can muster more than half-strength.'

'The Taciturn Dutchman'

'Van Deventer,' Meinertzhagen wrote, 'was not very talkative, but he had implicit faith in his men. "Let them attack," said the taciturn Dutchman. "Are you well dug in?" I asked. No reply. "For God's sake do not despise the enemy," I said. "Damned kaffirs," says he, and then adds to Nussey, "Are we dug in?" Nussey smiles at me, and Van Deventer comes near a smile.'

By the time Meinertzhagen appeared on the scene Van Deventer was well aware that he was on his own and that Smuts had complete confidence in his old comrade's ability to hold out against von Lettow's best. Meinertzhagen assessed him as 'calm and collected, divulging his plans to none, not even his staff.' He was critical of the fact that the Boer general appeared to be content to wait. He had stopped sending out patrols, saying that he had no lives to waste on getting further information.

But what discomposed the impetuous Meinertzhagen most was the fact that he saw no signs of energetic preparations for defence. 'On the so-called defence line, except for a few yards of good trench, not a sod had been turned by the South Africans, nor had a yard of wire been put up.' He saw men lounging about stone sangars that 'would not give protection from brickbats.'

When on 8 May the enemy patrols pushed nearer, Van Deventer refused to send out fighting patrols. 'He is content to see what is in store for him. I do not think he appreciates what he is up against . . . but we shall know in a day or two. Von Lettow is rarely late for an appointment.'

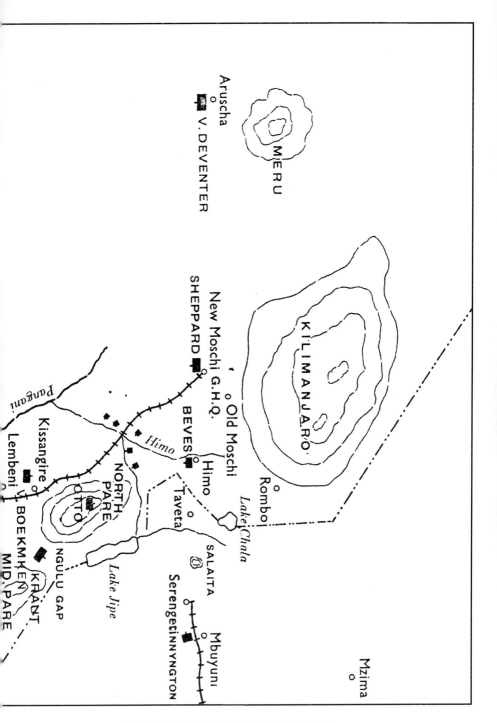

QUARTERS TAKEN UP FOR RAINY SEASON
1916

(*The South Africans with General Smuts in German East Africa 1916,*
Brig-Gen Collyer, 1939)

In fact, by 9 May von Lettow had completed his transference of troops and was ready to face Van Deventer's mounted men and the remains of his 11th and 12th Battalions. About a thousand rifles, or a third of his total strength, much of it dispersed round a five-mile perimeter. Small wonder that Meinertzhagen disapproved of this apparent Boer indifference to elementary precautions.

Boer Confidence?

Why were Van Deventer and his staff so casual? Was it the old Boer confidence resulting from battles won in Africa? Legend and history told how a handful of pioneers had destroyed the impi of Dingaan in a single bloody day of battle against a waggon train. Was it the phlegmatic temperament of men who did not believe that they could be beaten by kaffirs? So far the enemy's probing had been without much conviction. No mounted scouts had ventured as far as the perimeter.

There were four thousand rifles and twenty machine guns in the force mustering against Van Deventer and machine-gunners of high quality, as already demonstrated at Salaita and Latema-Reata. The deadly power of the machine gun was soon to be demonstrated in terrible fashion against the British within six weeks of that day. On the morning of 1 July the new British army was to go over the top at the Somme and lose twenty thousand dead and sixty thousand wounded to fewer than a hundred machine guns. That is six hundred casualties to one gun!

Not that the conditions were even remotely similar. The Boer had strong faith in the marksmanship of his riflemen and he had his own machine-gunners. He waited with what appeared unnatural calm for what looked like being a very serious attack. His men's fighting spirit was good, and he had eighteen machine guns and twelve artillery guns. The enemy was the attacker and could therefore expect to lose three times more men than the defenders.

An Unintended Battle?

The battle that was about to develop had created its own impetus. On the afternoon of 9 May a German naval gun fired a single shell from South Hill that went five hundred feet beyond the ridges held by the South Africans. The crash and the whitish-grey smoke from the naval gun, which was firing home-made shells with black powder, sent the outposts into retreat from their hold on Rock Rabbit Ridge. The approach to the main defences seemed to be undefended.

From the German perspective it was worth a probe in strength. Two companies were deployed in the valley between South Hill and

Range Rock Hill, commanded by Lt-Col von Bock and Captain von Kornatsky.

Inside Van Deventer's perimeter the effect was electrifying in the soporific quiet of mid-afternoon. Patrols were sent out by all units, fresh trenches were dug and barbed wire was hastily put up.

Von Lettow's assessment was that the South Africans were drawing back from their advanced positions, and that decided him to take possession of 'the low hills now held by the enemy'. He did not believe that his men could carry a charge across open ground to the main defences on the hills south of the river.

Surprise was impossible. He sent von Bock to examine the ridge that he believed he could occupy. The report came back to his headquarters: 'Hill unoccupied'.

Encouraged by that, von Bock advanced further and made for the next ridge. Night fell as they entered the valley and began the ascent in darkness, except for a sliver of moon. Von Lettow ordered up his baggage to settle in for the night.

'I myself went to headquarters camp a little farther back. I tried to relieve my great exhaustion with a cup of coffee and a little rum; but knowing that I had no more orders to issue, I soon fell fast asleep. About 11 p.m. I was wakened by remarks made by Lt Wunderlich in command of the 3.5-in naval gun.' The officer drew von Lettow's attention to flashes that he saw from the direction of the enemy in the hills that had been reported unoccupied.

'Soon there could be no doubt that the flashes were caused by rifles and machine guns, and when the wind shifted the sound of fighting became clearly audible. Contrary to all our expectations, a stiff fight was taking place on our front.' It was far off in bushy and rocky country. The moon was already waning. It was too late to send reserves.

'I had to leave the fight to take its course.'

Rattle of Musketry

Von Bock had pushed on in the last of the moonlight and walked straight into the firing line of the 11th SAI who had hastily dug in to meet an assault believed to be the opening of von Lettow's big attack on Kondoa-Irangi.

All round the perimeter of the town men were on the alert, wondering whether the single shell had been a ranging shot, a random shot or even an accidental firing of the sixty-pounder. Meinertzhagen recounts the events:

We were sitting having supper when quite suddenly the loud rattle of musketry electrified us. The camp blazed, and we could see

An askari company on the march. These units were splendidly disciplined and resisted the British for four years of fighting.

the spiteful little flashes of rifles and hear the cheering of troops on the ridge to the south-east. By 9 p.m. it was clear that the main attack had developed on our eastern face. The night was clear but without moon, and the flashes of the rifles and machine guns was a beautiful sight. When I reached Camp Ridge I found the German firing line held up two hundred yards distant. Two determined assaults were driven back, the second with the bayonet, a fine sight in the glare of star shells and flares. By 10 p.m. the crisis approached. I advised Callendar, commanding a battalion [unnamed], to counter-attack as the enemy was clearly spent, but he wouldn't. I was just bursting for a bayonet charge.

By that time the fearless askaris had charged and charged again up the slopes at the South Africans, cheering and blowing bugles, urged on by their white officers and NCOs. But they had no cover; and in the bright starlight they were perfectly visible in the glare of starshells and soaring flares. When a German machine gun was worked forward to within thirty yards of the line the order went out to silence it.

Meinertzhagen joined in the rush of bayonets. It became a mêlée of men fighting hand-to-hand with clubbed rifles. Gunners were bayoneted. Meinertzhagen was seen using his rifle as a club until he smashed the butt.

By that time von Bock had been severely wounded and Kornatsky had taken command. The South Africans lay in their slit trenches, listening to the exhortations to the askaris rallying for a final charge.

'The South Africans behaved splendidly,' Meinertzhagen noted. 'Quiet, steady and collected. Their fire discipline was perfect' as they responded to orders for 'five rounds rapid . . . reload. Fire!'

At midnight the charge came, pressed forward against the steady rifle and machine gun fire. In the close fighting that ended in the shallow entrenchments Meinertzhagen found himself armed 'with nothing but my fists and boots'.

Killed with a Knobkerrie

Captain Kornatsky came for him brandishing a knobkerrie. Meinertzhagen grappled with him, and they rolled together in the trench. 'I wrenched the kerrie out of his hand, got my knee well into his stomach and then set to on his head until he was silent.'

This charge spent the attackers' fury. There were no more shouts of *'Deutschland über alles'*, only the cries and groans of the wounded as the surviving officer, Captain Lincke, tried to establish a line to hold off a counter-attack. He got out his wounded and waited. At 3 a.m. all was still. Quietly he began to vacate the position, hoping to be clear before daylight.

Dawn came. The South Africans tensely watched their front, waiting for the next attack. The dead lay where they had fallen. Light returned to the rocks and bush and now, curious, they emerged to examine the night's work, turn over the dead and search for identifications and papers.

Meinertzhagen returned to the forward trench 'to examine my victim, and was surprised to find he was a German officer called Kornatsky, a company commander. His head was well battered in,' says Meinertzhagen with casual brutality. 'I kept his knobkerrie.* My God! I should have liked to catch old von Lettow instead of poor Kornatsky. Lumme, I'm tired.'

When his berserker bloodlust was exhausted Meinertzhagen mused over the map taken from the dead company commander. 'Why the enemy attacked our strongest position is a mystery . . . However, all credit to old Van Deventer and his South Africans. The infantry fought like tigers. Our guns too did splendid work firing star-shell and shrapnel with fuses set at zero.'

In the space between the two opponents there were seven dead Germans and forty-six askaris who failed to reach the trenches. He

----

* He carried this knobkerrie until the end of the war, and on the day an armistice was called for he took part in a foray against bivouacking German soldiers in which he chased them through a cornfield with it, and he was furious when a bullet killed an officer whom he was chasing and about to brain.

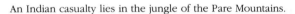

An Indian casualty lies in the jungle of the Pare Mountains.

could not know that von Lettow himself had come forward as shrapnel was showering the bush and tongue-lashed a medical officer who was slow in giving help to wounded askaris.

Unaware that the attack had been a costly blunder and not a calculated encounter, Van Deventer's staff were baffled by what they took to be the 'poor generalship of von Lettow'.

'We had to assume that if the attack had gone better he would have thrown in everything he had.'

Van Deventer believed that that was still a possibility, and with an energy and directness that amazed Meinertzhagen he ordered the improvement of defences everywhere. 'Wire is going up in all directions. Patrols are out and sentries alert. I told Van Deventer he is a very lucky man. If the Germans had made a feint attack against his front and a strong attack on his left flank, which was completely in the air, the whole defence could have collapsed. We should all now be prisoners of war.'

This assessment, of course, was made in ignorance of the accidental nature of the encounter by a subordinate commander who had pushed on a ridge too many in the darkness. What had happened was encouraging. South African marksmanship and courage at close quarters had been the stuff of veterans. They had stood up to fierce bayonet charges and fought hand-to-hand without giving ground. Sick and half-starved as they were, they were not found wanting.

Von Lettow Admits Heavy Losses

Von Lettow admitted: 'The 11th South African Infantry fought well, and repeatedly brought effective machine gun fire to bear on our companies.' He admitted casualties of 147 killed and wounded out of a force of four hundred.

Would he try again, this time in an attempt to set the matter right? Collyer, mulling it over, concluded that he would be very reluctant to do so. He called it 'a severe defeat'. Von Lettow had missed his chance. Indeed, his fatal mistake had been in not leaving an adequate garrison in the district. 'Had he done so, Van Deventer would have arrived there in no state to take the place with his depleted mounted force. It seems that he simply did not believe that Smuts would be so foolish as to attempt the march from Lol Kissale.'

It was a victory for Smuts. 'He had outwitted and forestalled von Lettow.' Victory or no, Van Deventer's 2nd Division was destined to remain immobile for the next two months. He was going to be besieged at Kondoa-Irangi and count the cost in men, horses, and mules struck down by disease. It was a victory that would have to be paid for. In terms of the Boer soldiers' acceptance of hardship, hunger

German askaris in action firing with black powder.

and the need to endure as part of their fighting tradition, it was not too high a price for a commander who had gone through it all himself.

When Van Deventer signalled to Smuts that he sat with his horses unshod, his men bootless and his reinforcements exhausted, and appealed for five thousand more men to meet the expected attack, Smuts told him in no uncertain terms that he could have no more. His Chief of Staff had pointed out that von Lettow could easily switch his force westward to meet any attack by Smuts there.

'He can do it in ten days and without opposition.'

When Van Deventer pressed his need, urging 'an excellent opportunity to surround the enemy here,' the answer was still no. Smuts needed his strength for the planned offensive in the east.

Collyer summed up. 'Van Deventer can't think except in terms of mounted men . . . a failing shared by several of his countrymen's best leaders.' At that point the ever-critical Meinertzhagen found himself praising the Boer system of command and contrasting it with the formal and rigid British system.

'Van Deventer's staff is not a staff as we know it. Each officer does that particular work which comes to hand. Being all good friends and with no records kept, there is neither friction nor confusion. The work gets done. Such a thing as red tape or precedents (the bugbear of the hierarchical British staff system) does not exist. They are distinctly efficient at this kind of rough and ready sort of warfare . . . doing what a normal British staff would find impossible.'

His summing up at that point in the campaign was that the troops were fine material, mobile, self-reliant, good scouts, good shots, loyal and keen to finish the business. 'They suffer from lack of discipline and lack of training, and the weakness of all South African regiments is bad officer material, untrained to lead or to take quick decisions.'

Ungrudgingly he admitted, 'For all that, Berrange's brigade gave the enemy a nasty knock last night, the first bad knock that von Lettow has had.'

Two-month Siege Begins

What was now beginning was a new phase. Siege was to test moral fibre in the two months to come with daily bombardment.

The troops called the *Königsberg*'s 4.1 inch gun 'Coughing Clara'. It woke them every morning at first light. 'A little way from the town,' wrote Private Reid of the 9th SAI, 'stood a large building that had been a mission church. The patients would watch the shells dropping into town . . . One morning a shell landed only forty yards away from the tents of the Mounted Brigade's hospital. A shell splinter killed one of the hospital cooks. We wondered why Clara was so wide of her target, but as shell after shell came at regular intervals and splinters rattled on the roof it became clear that we in hospital were the target. Those who could walk were told to get out. No sooner had this order been given than – crash! came the shell through the roof. Then a second and a third. The first shell landed just in front of the altar, right among the eight or ten worst cases, causing tremendous showers of dust, pieces of brick and splinters of wood, and tilting the altar forward.'

Evacuated Sick by Night

The shelling wiped out the medical supplies. As the more able carried out those who were helpless they were seen to emerge half-smothered in brick dust and choking in lyddite fumes. Yet not a man was injured. From then on patients were taken out during the night by ox-carts two miles away 'and from there we watched Clara dropping her shells round the empty mission church.'

Reid exonerated the enemy from blame. 'Two days before this a considerable number of troops were camped with their guns right next to the hospital with its prominent Red Cross flag.'

As he rode into town a few days after the battle Captain Deneys Reitz arrived in time for a bombardment of sixty-pounder shells.

> It was surprising in the heart of the wilds. Luckily the river bank was near and we were able to hustle our horses and men under cover. When it ceased after half an hour we emerged from the river bed to look round us. Some distance away stood a large church surrounded by tents, and there we found Colonel Fairweather of the Cyclist Corps, with his men. A shell had exploded inside the church, killing two men whose bodies were being extricated from the fallen masonry as we came up.
>
> We got directions for finding Van Deventer's headquarters, and recrossing the river, discovered him and his staff in one of the houses facing the square.

Van Deventer* told Reitz that he was immobilised and could not press on to his objective, the Central Railway. 'The enemy lay in an entrenched position across our front . . . Our men were strung out for miles to right and left, facing the German positions.'

It was stalemate in a country of ravines and gorges where it was difficult to know where the enemy lay or where his guns were firing from or from what quarter he might launch sudden audacious raids and disappear.

---

* There is little material extant to describe Van Deventer. Private Frank Reid of the 9th SA Infantry, a barrister in civilian life, wrote: 'He is a huge, dark man who never speaks, but just looks at you . . . he looks *stom* [dull].' Reid saw him at Kondoa, as a battle casualty. 'He said nothing, but just looked . . . and passed on without moving a muscle of his face.' The troops spoke of him as 'VDV.'

A BIG PUSH (in the rainy season)

"When do we get a rest, mate ?"
"Won't be long. Only 15 more miles to do."

(*East African Experiences 1916,* C W Shackleton, 1940)

8

Marching Down the Pangani River

Smuts and his staff had been quartered at Old Moshi since 21 March. The German civil administration had moved out of the fort. It was built of stone and clay and loopholed all round for action against rebellious natives, and its twelve-foot walls enclosed a guardroom and stores. On the second storey were the offices and the officers' mess. From its verandah there was a splendid view of the country.

Smuts and his officers could stand there and study the steep slopes of the Lossongoi Plateau and, to the south and east, the Pare Mountains. Between these barriers the valley of the Pangani River stretched away towards the Indian Ocean as far as the eye could see.

At 4 800 feet it was healthy, well above the anopheline mosquitoes and 'the fly'. The German hospital and a block of hotel buildings had quickly filled with men down with fever after weeks on outpost duty in the low ground among the rivers that ran into the Pangani. There were some charming bungalows occupied by staff, who exclaimed that the vistas of native cultivation and fruitful plantations in orderly terraces reminded them of life in the Indian hill stations. 'Instead of the Himalayas we have Kilimanjaro!'

Old Moshi had a bloody history. It was there that the former chief of the Wajagga people, who now supplied the porters, had defended their land. The Germans had besieged their boma and destroyed it with gunfire; and having massacred the chief and all his family, they built a new fort. From its verandah the staff officers could see the distant landscape that they were planning to invade. Below them on the plain at New Moshi was the rail terminus of the Usambara Railway that ran through the mountains to Kahe station and on down the valley to the port of Tanga.

Toiling in the Monsoon

Down there Smuts's engineers were toiling in monsoon heat to join their own tracks to this railway so that supplies coming through Kenya could be moved forward for the offensive as soon as the weather cleared. They were setting up their depots for motor transport and workshops in the former German rail terminus. They had made great efforts to push the track across the low-lying country before the monsoon rains came and every river and tributary became a torrent and the plains turned to swamps.

Fortunately the rains were nearly a month late; but they broke in tropical fury on 12 April. From his eyrie at Old Moshi Smuts had followed the march south of Van Deventer and seen the casualties straggle back. Now rain fell in such torrents that 27 inches were measured by the end of the month at his headquarters at Moshi.

What had been dry nullahs became roaring red torrents that swept away the temporary bridges on which all road transport depended. But by the end of April the railway was nearing the Kahe line. 'Any other form of wheeled transport was out of the question,' wrote Brigadier-General Crowe, 'and supplies could only be carried by porters. The mud and the greasy, slippery surface of the roads was such that they could move only slowly and with the lightest of the loads.' The mule waggons were bogged to their axles and motor transport, gun limbers and guns were totally immobilised. Along the railway track between Taveta and Kahe over twenty miles had turned to swamp. The rails vanished under water for long stretches. It took a train ten hours to cover twenty miles, and then only by the efforts of thousands of labouring blacks pushing bundles of reeds and brushwood under the tracks.

Troops *en route* to the battle wait as the driver attends to an engine failure.

'This Hellish Country'

White engineers, many of them sick with fever, laboured night and day to keep the trains moving. There was a fury among them 'to complete this vital link before the rains stopped, so come what might we struggled. We knew this could be the final phase of the campaign, and then we could all get out of this hellish country. Smuts came often to encourage us and hasten us on.'

Smuts had informed the War Office of his strategy and asked that a further thousand horses a month should be sent from better, more reliable sources than the Union. In discussions with his staff, most officers believed that this was the decisive drive, and that von Lettow would be brought to a final engagement.

His Intelligence Chief, the indefatigable Meinertzhagen was also at the table. His opinion was that with von Lettow's main force round Kondoa, and there himself in person, there was not likely to be any serious opposition to Smuts's advance.

'Tanga should be in our hands by the end of June,' he said. But he did not agree that there would be a decisive engagement. He predicted that the 'wily man' would avoid a decisive engagement and retire from the Central Railway with his force undefeated.

Meinertzhagen knew Smuts. He knew that the Commander listened respectfully to his opinions – but then went about things in his own way. Between the Chief of Intelligence and the General there had grown a bond of mutual admiration – at least on Meinertzhagen's side. Would he listen now? Not likely!

So, even before Smuts embarked on his big push down the Pangani River for Tanga, Meinertzhagen had shrugged his shoulders. If only the South Africans could be allowed to fight, and were not restricted to manoeuvre, it could be all over that year – 1916! Alas, no one listened to this Cassandra. He concluded, reluctantly, that it would be a fight to the finish – on von Lettow's terms.

Smuts Reveals Plan of Attack

On 22 May, 'the weather being fine,' as Collyer records, General Smuts left Old Moshi and at noon reached Kahe by train. He took with him his completed plans for the operation, to be discussed with his chosen commander, Major-General Reginald Hoskins of the 1st Division and his Brigadiers, Hannyngton, Sheppard and Beves. Collyer, as his Chief of Staff, was well aware of what Smuts was taking on in terms of logistics.

His eastern army was split into three main columns, an extraordinary mixture of races, regiments and nationalities: Rhodesians, Pun-

General Smuts and his inseparable companion, Brigadier-General Collyer, watching the operations in the Pangani River valley.

jabis, Baluchis, Pathans, Kashmiris, King's African Riflemen, and the ragbag regiment of British volunteers, the 25th Royal Fusiliers, better known as the 'Old and Bold'. There was the South African Cape Corps, much valued for their skill with horses, mules and oxen in their own carefree fashion.

The whole force amounted to about ten thousand, with field ambulances, ammunition trains, sappers and miners, engineers, mechanical transport drivers, ox train and mule drivers, and thousands of blacks recruited into the carrier corps to carry headloads. All these were to be funnelled down a narrow strip between mountains that ranged in height from 4 000 to 7 500 feet and a huge river bordered with virgin forest and raffia palm, nearly impenetrable. Dense thorn obstructed the flat waterless country that lay between the mountain and the river. This bush varied in width from a few hundred yards to a mile. This was the pathway to be taken by Smuts's army.

Deadly Machine-gun Nests

No one was in any doubt that wherever there was an empty space that could be raked with machine gun fire, von Lettow would have prepared his deadly nests, and that he would fight with great tenacity. And where could he be outflanked here?

Still, Smuts was sanguine, or made a fair show of it as he gave his orders to the commanders of the three columns. Had any of them any inkling of what lay ahead in human effort against Africa? Months later Smuts wrote:

> Their work has been done under tropical conditions which not only produce bodily weakness, weariness and unfitness, but which create mental languor and depression, and finally appal the stoutest hearts. To march day by day, week by week, through the African jungle or high grass, in which vision is limited to a few yards, in which danger always lurks near but seldom becomes visible, even when experienced, supplies a test to human nature often, in the long run, beyond the limits of human endurance.

As they prepared to leave, some of Smuts's officers were remembering a prediction made by German missionaries at Moshi. 'It will take you two years to push our troops out of the Pare and Usambara Mountains . . . By that time, we shall have won the war in Europe.' *Gott mit uns.* They had not been twenty-five years in the territory, nor had they built hospitals, missions and schools and brought some of the benefits of European civilisation to peoples who had long been at the mercy of disease and slavery to see their good work handed over to the British.

Here the war was indeed about the clash of rival empires. The rank and file of British soldiery were convinced that it would be a fine acquisition for the Empire.

Call of the Empire

In a foreword to the campaign journals of Captain Angus Buchanan, 25th Fusiliers, the writer gave the general opinion. 'While Germany held East Africa she was a potential menace to the whole continent.' This regiment, now about to push down the eastern sector, had come from the outer edges of empire. He wrote with pride that 'men of British blood had come to fight for their native land from Honolulu, Hong Kong, China, Ceylon, the Malay states, India, New Zealand, Australia, South and East Africa, America and Canada.'

They believed not only that their cause was just but that a divine providence would surely grant them a new slice of empire somewhat larger than Germany. 'How many brave souls,' wrote Buchanan, 'laughingly departed, never to return – their one great love their Home, their Empire's Honour.'

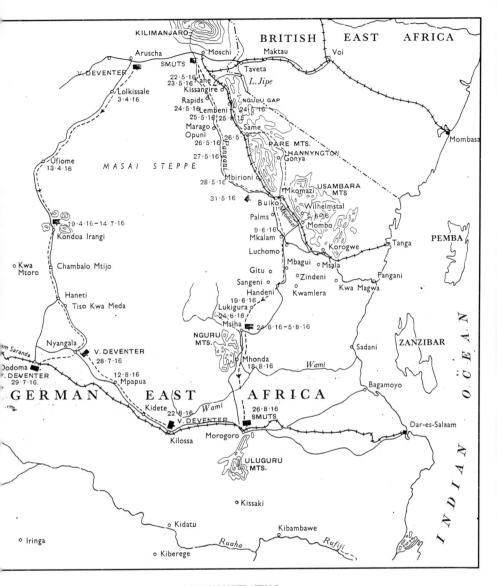

MAP ILLUSTRATING

ADVANCE of GENERAL SMUTS and GENERAL VAN DEVENTER
to CENTRAL RAILWAY via PANGANI RIVER and KONDOA IRANGI respectively

(*The South Africans with General Smuts in German East Africa 1916*,
Brig-Gen Collyer, 1939)

It was their destiny and their right, and the fortunate natives would rejoice in a rule infinitely more just than that of the Germans whom they would replace. Many of them regarded this campaign as no more than an African adventure that was distracting them from the real war.

Francis Brett Young, as a doctor with the Rhodesians, says that 'many were anxious to be done with this sideshow, to have it finished once and for all, so that we might help to get at the root of the whole tragedy, at home in Europe.'

There was a quaintly chivalrous idea that the jungle was no place for a gentleman to die for his country. Premature death in the trenches was preferable. In truth, this kind of Rupert Brooke-ish thinking was already discredited in France. Men there would have given much to change places and to march through what Brett Young called 'a lovely and most deadly land'.

The staff of the 2nd Rhodesian Regiment, he wrote, were certain of a quick outcome. Colonel Essex Capell was confident: 'Two months will do it.' Round the campfire where the odds were discussed, an old one-armed elephant hunter cautioned them about over-optimism. 'I wish I could agree with you,' he said, gazing into the flames. 'Still, we can only do our duty.' The hunter who knew Africa knew that the Germans, settlers and soldiers, were not at all likely to roll over belly-up.

They believed they were winning in Europe and soon Britain, gorged to excess with imperial spoils would have to disgorge some of her ill-gotten gains to the victors.

Smuts was in a hurry. By 18 May he was at last able to get through to Kahe as the rains moderated and the rivers subsided. There he met his old friend Pretorius, the scout. They clasped hands affectionately, for this was another comrade of the Boer War. Pretorius had been reluctant to live on in British-occupied South Africa and had betaken himself to German East Africa, where he settled in the Rufiji River district as an elephant hunter. No white man knew East Africa as well as he did. The Germans knew that. When war broke out they wanted to make use of his great knowledge of the uncharted jungle.

When he refused and disappeared into the wilds they set out to capture him. He was severely wounded but escaped with his faithful blacks who carried him. They eluded patrols and capture, crossed the Rovuma River and reached Portuguese territory. Weeks later he turned up in Pretoria to offer his services to Smuts.

With his black scouts he lived all but invisible in the jungle, often practically alongside the Germans. He rarely came in with messages himself but sent them by messenger. If he came in at all, it was generally because he was ill with malaria. To the Germans he was a most dangerous adversary, and they were forever trying to catch him. One

German scout who vowed never to return without his wily adversary did precisely that.

Pretorius trapped him and his entire safari within a day's march of his setting out and captured them all. Now he sat down with Smuts with a new tale to tell.

Scouting along the railway line near Kahe, he had come on an enemy company with a machine gun. He was forty miles inside enemy territory with his men, and he got away with the loss of two Europeans, a native tracker and seven horses and mules. They had walked into an ambush; but once again the elusive Pretorius had got away. No one could claim the price on his head. What the encounter did tell the Germans was that they were being closely watched. Curiously, von Lettow never even mentions this thorn in his flesh in his reminiscences of the campaign.

Deep into Deadly Valley

Now Smuts was asking Pretorius directly: what are my chances of advancing down the Pangani River valley with an army? Pretorius considered that it could be done. Smuts believed him, perhaps too readily. He was determined to drive down that deadly valley at whatever cost. He gave himself a fortnight to reach his first objective, the end of the Usambara Mountains; a march of a hundred miles.

Pretorius calculated that Major Kraut's detachment was something less than two thousand rifles. They would be in carefully prepared positions in the passes and on the bends of the river. But yes, he thought it could be done.

Smuts organised his 1st Division under Major-General A R Hoskins in three columns. The main body, under Brigadier-General S H Sheppard, was to move down the banks of the Pangani with his 1st East African Infantry Brigade.

Brigadier-General J A Hannyngton's 2nd East African Infantry Brigade was to push south along the railway line with the great ranges of the Pare and Usambara Mountains towering on his left, their slopes almost impenetrable with dense bush and virgin forest. Between the two brigades there would be a waterless tract of bush so thick that it would be almost impossible to hack through it, where elephant grass stood twice as high as a man and visibility was the length of a rifle.

A third force under Colonel T A Fitzgerald would go round the eastern side of the mountains, also through heavily wooded country. If the plan came off as he hoped, Smuts would emerge from the mountains with a noose round Major Kraut and holding every mile of the railway.

If this was ever a realistic plan, Major Pieter Pretorius's judgment would soon be cursed by the thousands in the marching battalions

South Africans threading the jungle of the Pangani River.

with their mules and oxen, supply lorries, motor ambulances, armoured cars, artillery caissons laden with gun ammunition, mule-drawn guns and mule-team field hospitals; all funnelling into this choking inferno where the men pushed on with a panga in one hand, a rifle in the other, fever in the blood and mostly with an empty belly.

Collyer's Considerable Understatement

It was a terrain where the advancing brigades would have to hack every step of the way, fired on by an all but invisible enemy and making forced marches at the killing pace that their commander demanded. 'A difficult terrain', Collyer, Smuts's Chief of Staff, described it with generous understatement.

No great battles were to be fought on the 'Pangani Trek'; but if it had been contrived by von Lettow to destroy the 1st Division he could hardly have done better. The men of the 5th and 6th South African Infantry, the 2nd Rhodesians, the 'Old and Bold' and the Indians never forgot it.

Mere descriptions of what became a fortnight of hell for those who took part can hardly convey the reality. The commander glossed over the details in his report, calling it 'a steady advance along the Pangani, the advanced guards and mounted troops keeping in touch with the enemy's rearguard.'

Von Lettow knew what Smuts's men were in for; but he did not underestimate his adversary. 'He seemed to me to be the most dangerous and important of our opponents.'

As a doctor with the 2nd Rhodesians, Francis Brett Young left the most vivid record in his *The March to Tanga*, written in 1917 while he was convalescent after they had 'jolted my poor body up the Tanga Line in one of their damned cattle trucks . . . '

Masterful Eyes

It was on the march to Tanga that the writer saw Smuts in the flesh for the first time. He had seen his face on a recruiting poster in Cape Town; and now he encountered him in the bush.

'We heard rapid hoofs ascending the track and three horsemen pushed by. The first I saw was a staff officer with a brown pointed beard, who looked like a Dutchman. The second wore a cord tunic . . . his features rather hard and coarse with most masterful eyes. The face of a man who is determined on success . . . one realised the driving force behind all this.'

The country they were hacking their way through was virgin bush, trackless, unfrequented even by tribesmen. As Regimental Surgeon Brett Young knew, even before they set out, that the valley of the Pangani had already 'acquired a most sinister reputation for disease'.

'We might lose a great number of men through sickness; we might lose a great part of the transport on which the existence of the force depended through horse-sickness and tsetse fly.' To succeed, 'our column, fighting its way with bullock transport through a savage land, would have to move rather faster than the enemy, who had the use of a railway system.'

That was what Smuts had reckoned with. If he pressed hard enough the enemy must either withdraw rather faster than he chose to, or stand and fight.

None of that meant anything to the sweat-blinded men, staggering under 60-lb packs, 150 rounds of rifle ammunition and in new boots that once taken off could hardly be got back on to swollen feet. As on the trek to Kondoa-Irangi, men were soon marching with puttees wound round their feet and their boots slung round their necks.

Nothing but Praise

Brett Young had nothing but praise for them. 'I do not think,' he wrote 'that so great a military movement had ever been made before through the heart of tropical Africa. They endured with wonderful patience hardships unequalled in any other campaign, lacking in food and water, marching day after day without respite beneath a vertical sun, ravaged by diseases from which there was no escape in a country which even the natives of Africa had found incompatible with human life.'

The Masai herdsmen knew better than to feed their cattle in the lush grasslands of the Pangani. In all this pestilential region never a reed hut or habitation was seen. Brett Young saw it as a place of rare and deadly beauty, of golden grasses and butterflies; and in the night, in the soft darkness 'one might have imagined oneself in England'.

As the columns plodded forward talking was forbidden. The only sound was the 'intolerably slow drag of many feet, the creaking of harness . . . '

Buchanan too, wrote of the night marches: 'How difficult it was to stay awake, either marching or on horseback. You will see a man dozing on his feet, but marching unsteadily on, and if the man in front should halt, the sleeping man behind will walk into him.'

A kind of slurring rhythm of march emerged, dragged out painfully by hundreds of heavy feet . . . all in suffocating silence broken by the hammering and shrilling of insects. After a twelve-hour march there was hardly time to eat. Orders were to make no fires. Then they were on their feet again, standing guard on outpost duty or out on patrol, while others went back with shovels to repair the track for transport coming on behind.

Pioneers Hacked a Path

On one such trek Brett Young observed that the pioneers, hacking ahead of the column, had been on the march for sixteen hours, and the advance guard was reporting ever-thicker bush, swarming with tsetse fly.

'Keep your mules in the open, also your oxen, and the men must put up mosquito nets after dark.' The order was repeated by officers

The advance guard along the Pangani River.

riding the miles of column. But there was no open space, the trees and the fly were everywhere and would soon show their lethal effect.

Behind the marchers came the struggling transport, straining beasts being lashed through sandy nullahs, over boulders that smashed axles and wheels and snapped the legs of horses and mules. Brett Young noted: 'The wretched bullocks worked until they dropped.' A veterinary surgeon's report recorded that 'a shot from the .45 was the best veterinary surgery we knew in that march.'

Three hours' sleep was a luxury. They were drugged with quinine when it was available. The men from kindlier climates were harassed by voracious insects. 'After an eighteen-mile march,' wrote Private Cooper, 'those not on guard lay down to snatch what sleep they could between watches only to be attacked by swarms of red ants.' There was also the black soldier ant, the *siafu,* which travelled in armies and stung the flesh like white-hot skewers.

'The red ants,' wrote a medical sergeant, J H Brown of the RAMC, 'stop at nothing, man or beast or any living creature; anything alive that is tied up or enclosed, or cannot get away, will die a living death . . . until at last you can only see the shape of the body covered with red ants as it heaves and twists in the throes of a horrible death.' Small wonder that the convalescents at Dar es Salaam sang:

A shocking land is German East
Accursed alike by man and beast;
A land of rains till comes a break
With days and nights so hot you bake!
From base to base in quest of foe,
We wretched fed-ups come and go.
With scrubby chins and dirty knees,
And toenails mined by jigger-fleas!

A Fortnum and Mason Warrior

Somewhere behind the advance guard – indeed, very far back, according to Captain Piet van der Bijl on Smuts's staff, came a British officer of the Indian empire breed. He was travelling in great style 'with a gang of bearers carrying boxes from Fortnum and Mason, Piccadilly, filled with such things as pâté de foie gras and caviare, half bottles of champagne, tinned cheese, butter, biscuits and other delicacies.'

When Smuts encountered this exquisite phenomenon at ease in his staff car he asked caustically how long it would take to build a bridge across the Pangani. 'Pangani? Where is that?' asked the Piccadilly warrior. Smuts exploded. 'Heavens, General, we've been walking down it for a week.'

The pursuit down the Pangani where the enemy destroyed the bridges. Here General Smuts makes the risky crossing and gets over safely.

After the advance of the River Column had been in progress for a few days without encountering anything, some Germans were captured. They were a patrol of one German and five askaris with porters, hiding at the end of a footpath cut through the high grass from a place called Same. Their orders were to lie in wait for the invaders, estimate their strength and retire to Buiko. From this information Collyer deduced that Major Kraut would be waiting at the confluence of the river and the railway.

Next day Smuts came forward to see for himself. Along with Captain van der Bijl and two others of his staff he climbed a steep wooded ridge and left one of his staff to hold the horses. 'We climbed to the top on all fours and a few yards down the face, so as not to show ourselves on the skyline. Through field glasses we saw, some miles away to our left and behind us, a wisp of dust . . . an enemy column moving down the road.'

They were suddenly startled to see two groups of enemy patrols coming towards the ridge, and vesting just below them. Then two more parties joined them, twenty or more askaris with white officers. They were so near to Smuts that, as Van der Bijl put it, 'If I had been able to lip-read and speak German I could easily have understood what they were saying.'

They were exchanging information that they had gathered. In this extraordinary situation an army commander and some of his staff were

166

dangerously exposed. But Smuts, the old Africa campaigner, merely sat tight without moving for half an hour. Then he gestured: 'time to move'.

Other accounts of the incident vary. Collyer says that Smuts first encountered two 'very diminutive natives with bows and arrows. These were Wandorobbo, slaves of the Masai, who wandered about the steppes following herds of game, hunting with poisoned arrows and throwing spears.'

When Smuts had seen the country ahead from the height of the mountain Old Le Sara his party slipped down to the cars under cover through the bush and 'fortunately met a patrol of Belfield's scouts at the foot of the hill.'

Smuts rejoined the headquarters convoy of motor cars and took his place in the grey Vauxhall, with its pointed, shining radiator, beside his Chief of Staff. 'The advance went on steadily,' wrote Collyer, 'without any incident of importance . . . '

The infantry ahead trudged hard on the heels of the pioneers. They were being hard driven to reach the end of the valley. 'A large percentage of us were cavalry and horse artillery, now on foot,' wrote Private Cooper, recalling that one day his unit marched from 3 a.m. till 1 a.m. the following night, far out-marching the bullock transport. A brush with the enemy was imminent.

Major Kraut Lay in Wait

It was 29 May 1916 at the place where road, railway and river came together as they squeezed through the bottleneck at the end of the Pare Mountains where the Usambara range began. There was no other way but through; and Major Kraut was waiting, with his artillery observers on the slopes and his big gun from the *Königsberg* ready to fire from its mobile platform on the railway line, facing aggressively north, indeed the only direction possible.

Brett Young was pushing on with his fifty African stretcher-bearers, 'untrained and ready to disappear into the bush on the approach of danger, led by their headman carrying a furled Red Cross flag.' The writer noted that 'the lower air was full of dragonflies . . . the soft tremor of grasses . . . many beetles, brilliant creatures with wing-cases barred with crimson.' Then into the bottleneck. Surely they would never have been allowed to reach it if the enemy were there. 'We were so near the Pare range, very soft and summery it looked, except for one place where a slab of rock rose perpendicularly for several hundred feet. Watching these mountains, enchanted by their beauty, I suddenly saw a little puff of smoke drifting away from the lower part of this sheer face . . . We heard a distant boom.'

'We're not too late after all,' said Brett Young.

'No, I suppose that's the bridge at Mikocheni.' His companion had hardly finished speaking when a great explosion on their right cut him short.

It was the *Königsberg*'s 4.1-inch high explosive shell ranging on the mass of transport spotted by the observer on the mountain. It went on all afternoon. From the front came the call for stretchers, and Brett Young came to the first casualty, a Sowar of the 17th Indian Cavalry. He had ridden with reckless bravery alongside the last train leaving Tanga station and fired at the engine-driver. A shot was returned. Hasmali, mortally wounded in the belly, clung to his horse and galloped back. As Brett Young did what he could for him his chestnut horse, beautifully groomed, stood by its rider with 'all its barbarous caparisons.' The trappings of war and death; carbine and sabre and regimental finery.

Sheppard's brigade took up a position in the loop of the Pangani while the mass of transport accumulated on the open grassy plain as they straggled in.

It was, as Collyer put it, 'a target rarely accorded to the artillery of either side in this country of dense bush.'

Too Exhausted to Care

All afternoon, until dusk, the great shells went over with the sound of tearing canvas. When darkness fell only one man had been killed. By sunset the force was much dispersed and its units had camped where they stopped. No one attempted to make a show of defence; not a trench was dug.

What if von Lettow made one of his swift attacks now? His askaris coming in with fixed bayonet in the darkness, yelling their warcries? No one seemed to have learned the lesson, or seemed to care. They were all too exhausted to care.

The rumour was that the Germans were withdrawing and that trains had been seen steaming south. That was a good enough excuse for exhausted men to flop down. The *Königsberg*'s firing had been regarded with derision. In any case the high-explosive shells meant for armour plate were ineffective in that terrain; they merely broke into large fragments. The poor gunnery might have been due to the death of the master gunner of the *Königsberg*.

Two days later, when Private Cooper reached the place where Rhodesians and Punjabis had attacked on 30 May he found, in a well-entrenched position served by machine guns and two pieces of light artillery, 'a rude piece of boxboard nailed to a tree trunk . . . the best our men could do at the moment to honour the spot where a master gunner of the *Königsberg* fell by the side of the gun he was defending' against the charge of the enemy.

In pursuit of the Germans down the Pangani the trucks were segregated by 'caste', e.g. Indians and natives on top, whites inside.

The gun itself was still intact on the railway line, and Major Kraut, after making a night attack on the Rhodesians and Punjabis in his own abandoned trenches, won time to withdraw his main body. By the time Sheppard sent for a section of mountain guns and ordered two companies up the mountain it was too late. Kraut was already on his way south down the railway to Tanga.

The Germans had not been brought to a decisive action. Collyer noted with dour accuracy from his place at Smuts's side that every mile Kraut put between them 'meant casualties in every unit and among all ranks from disease.'

Smuts's Achievement

Could Smuts be said to have failed? He had driven his force like a man possessed, he had taken a handful of prisoners and cleared the Pare Mountains. 'The rapidity of our advance had exceeded my best expectations. We had reached the Usambara in ten days, covering a distance of 130 miles over trackless country and through the mountains.'

No small achievement. But at what cost? His report to the War Office does not give figures of casualties, but Brett Young minces no words. In the costly attack by the Rhodesians their bayonet charge had reached the railway line before the heliograph message winked out the instruction: 'Break off the action'. To the men it was inexplicable.

In the evening light I took back the Rhodesian wounded . . . It was a slow return, but by dark we had them all under canvas. And now arose more urgently than ever the question of evacuating these wounded men, and those sick with malaria and dysentery who were pouring into our tents each day.

We had come down the Pangani too fast for our communications.

169

Rations were already diminished by half and likely to be scarcer. The railway was so well destroyed that our trains ran no farther than Kahe, our starting point.

The only way in which our sick men could return was on empty supply lorries, unsheltered from the sun, jolted without mercy in the deep nullahs, sleeping under the cold stars along the fever swamps of the Pangani. Already our tents were overflowing, and we might be moving on and so, in the end, they all performed that ghastly lorry journey of eighty miles at an average pace of four miles an hour.

The Sowar Hasmal who was wounded in the belly died. 'Such was the purgatory with which our wounded men were faced; and later on, when the line had been lengthened again, their case was harder still.'

Among the smell of blood and iodine Brett Young never lost his sense of beauty and wonder. Standing alone on the trampled earth round battle HQ of the Rhodesian regiment, he mused: Who in after years would visit the Pangani fields of purgatory? Perhaps some hunter would stumble on the place.

'No man, unless he wanders there in search of game, will seek to look upon her sinister smile in the lovely winter weather of that deadly land. Why, even if he sought for traces of our fighting, the rains of another year will have hidden them in drifted sand . . . '

Above the clouds on Pare Mountains. The district of Kilimanjaro as seen from an aeroplane flying over Ngulu Pass. In the immediate foreground are the formidable Pare Mountains.

The big German 4.7 gun (from the *Königsberg*) destroyed at Kahe to prevent its falling into enemy hands. Note the improvised gun carriage for this naval weapon.

Smuts established his headquarters at Buiko on 31 May. He had marched the length of the Pare valley and in ten days reached the railway station at the foot of the Usambara range to find a scene of devastation. The Germans had wrecked the station and blown up the offices, the system of points and the water tower. The natives had been driven off as carriers.

Collyer Urges Caution

Smuts was impatient to be off, but he could not move. His ox-waggon supply columns were moving down the valley at three miles an hour, his lorries were stalled in sandy nullahs, his mule teams much depleted. He had no choice but to pause while a reserve was built up to carry him forward again. He urged his supply officers to get a move on. Collyer advised caution. Ahead lay broken bridges and torn-up railway tracks. Build up a reserve. Without it an advance would be not only premature but something far more serious. An exhausted army would be over-extended with a capable, well-armed and well-fed enemy ready to strike.

'Wait now,' he urged Smuts. 'To be held up later, after a few marches at most, could find us in a place and a situation far less satisfactory.'

Together they examined the best place for the Pangani to be bridged. The river was like a canal, a hundred feet wide and fourteen feet deep. In the slow, dark four-knot current crocodiles abounded, and thirsty beasts going down to drink were seized and dragged under. There was no choice but to bridge it with a footbridge strong enough for troops in single file and to ferry the animals across.

He ordered Major-General Hoskins to hurry on the work of repairs to road, rail and the demolished bridge and to move on as soon as he was able. 'I am going to confer with Van Deventer at Kondoa-Irangi.' It meant a drive of three hundred miles.

'Waiting at Buiko to cross was beyond his patience,' noted an officer in the engineers.

Remarkable case of Protective Mimicry on the part of a British Observation Officer.

(*'Jambo' or with Jannie in the Jungle*, AW Lloyd, undated)

9

Smuts Finds Van Deventer Besieged

The journey back north to Old Moshi showed Smuts the extent of the difficulties in his communications; but already his engineers were busy restoring the torn-up railway, even using wooden fishplates to secure the rails. At his old headquarters he learned from Meinertzhagen that the Portuguese had declared war on Germany.

The news came by way of Zanzibar, and it was totally unexpected. In their attempt to invade German East Africa they had 'made a hopeless mess of it'.

As the details of the fiasco emerged the question arose: what had possessed the Portuguese? So far they had contributed nothing to the war in East Africa. Now, without warning, they had sent out an amphibious expedition to cross the broad Rovuma River that separated Portuguese and German territories.

Meinertzhagen told Smuts the details: 'Their boats ran aground, they forgot to bring with them any food. They landed in a spot where there was no fresh water and in full view of the enemy where they spent the day making up their minds where to attack. Finally they were cut to pieces by machine guns, of which I had warned them.

'The whole force is killed or captured. I understand,' said Meinertzhagen ironically, 'that they have wired to Portugal for a new expeditionary force.' No doubt they hoped for territorial gain; 'but those who know the Portuguese expected no more or no less . . . Their colonies are a scandal.'

Collyer took a cooler view of the disaster. In his account the Portuguese landed their troops under fire, with their boats grounded in the shallows. Although British warships were standing by to assist, the attackers soon lost three hundred men dead or missing for no gain.

The facts of the invasion were that when news reached Major da Silveira in Mozambique that his country was at war with Germany he determined to seize a small enclave on the south bank of the Rovuma, which the Germans had occupied in 1894. Without waiting for reinforcements promised from Portugal he assembled some four hundred European and African soldiers and attempted to cross the estuary with the support of the guns of the Royal Navy cruiser *Adamastor* and the gunboat *Chaimite*.

The four groups of lighters full of native infantry were towed across the mouth of the estuary. A force of three Germans and forty-six askari led by Lt Sprockhoff, a Naval Officer opened fire to such effect that the Portuguese force was nearly wiped out. It was the first of a series of Portuguese fiascos; but now Smuts was set on bringing von Lettow to decisive battle before he could unite his divided forces.

On 3 June he took the road to Lol Kissale at 7.30 a.m. and next day he rose before dawn eager to press on. All day he was beset with engine trouble. The Vauxhall had got water in the engine from crossing a ford the day before. By nightfall he was still twenty-four miles from Kondoa-Irangi. He had had plenty of time to see what the troops called 'Van Deventer's milestones': the broken waggons and stinking corpses of oxen and mules. There was more traffic struggling north with casualties than supply waggons getting through to Van Deventer.

'The Inspector General of Lines of Communication must take over here and get this situation in hand.' Collyer agreed. The transport position of the 2nd Division was parlous indeed. They camped again, and about midnight there was an alert. The sound of mounted men. There was a move to take up arms. There were German patrols all round. It turned out to be eight Boers on the look-out for them.

Smuts lay down with his usual sang-froid and slept undisturbed by the gibbering of hyenas and the roars of lions disputing carcases. He had the rare gift of tranquillity, the ability to turn his mind to ideas far removed from the hardships and squalor of the battlefield.

Louis Botha's Optimistic Letter

A letter was on its way to him from his loyal friend Louis Botha, congratulating him on his progress so far. 'For my part,' wrote the Prime Minister from his office in Cape Town, 'I can already see signs of the end. If only you remain well everything will be all right. We get a fair number of horses, especially now that we have lowered the height for horses. Our greater difficulty is ships . . .' And he urged a faster off-loading at Mombasa, where the habitual confusion delayed horses urgently needed at the front.

'Things in Europe look seriously like stalemate,' Botha said. 'The Germans are fighting excellently, and slowly but surely taking trench after trench at Verdun.' At home in the Cape there had been drought followed by unprecedented floods.

Smuts's concern was to wake early and press on before daylight. At Kondoa-Irangi he found Van Deventer in a state of siege. He had nearly eleven hundred men down with fever, and the Germans were shelling him every day. They were on quarter rations and what could be foraged from the fields and plantations. But both commanders were inured to hardship and hunger as part of their military tradition.

It was a cordial meeting of old comrades, the portly Van Deventer greeting his slim commander, whose reddish beard showed streaks of grey. Both were dressed in cord in the cut of standard British staff khaki with sun-helmet, red tabs, jodhpurs, and knee-length riding boots. Except for their beards, they were identical in every way to the men whom they had fought with such determination in the Boer War; but in their appreciation of the situation they were anything but British. It might have been a meeting of commando leaders to consider strategy. Van Deventer's GSOI had served on De Wet's staff. He was a former postmaster from Bloemfontein in the Free State, and he was regarded by many as a rough, ill-spoken townsman with little military knowledge – in marked contrast with the immaculate and literate Collyer. Leipold, Van Deventer's Intelligence Officer, was a shrewd and capable man with the brain and diligence of a scholar. He was a surveyor by profession, and he had handled a machine gun against the British. He was steady and cool in action, if slow in making decisions. Louis Botha's son, young Louis, had been at Colenso with his father and had captured a British general single-handed. At the outbreak of war he was already a professional staff officer who had served in the rebellion against the government in 1914 and in German South West Africa.

A Sign of Withdrawal?

Seldom were men so closely knit as these now contemplating the German positions.

'Where is Manie Botha?' Smuts asked. Botha commanded the 1st Mounted Brigade.

'I sent him out to cover the Handeni road. Von Lettow's placed a company there to stop my use of it.'

While they were talking, sounds of firing came from that direction. 'It could be von Lettow bringing up reinforcements and hitting Botha's outposts,' said Van Deventer.

'It might possibly be the start of his retirement from here,' suggested Collyer. 'If so, it might indicate that the drive down the Pangani has forced von Lettow to slacken his grip on Van Deventer.'

'If he pulls out of Kondoa to join Kraut we have a chance to trap his whole force at Handeni,' said Smuts. Indeed, the main reason for his visit was to urge on Van Deventer the need to co-ordinate with him in the combined drive to the Central Railway.

'If Van Deventer can cut the railway at Morogoro and Dodoma, between us we could press his two forces together on the railway and bring him to battle or surrender.' As they pored over the maps Smuts added another crucial reason. 'We would be able to operate against Dar es Salaam. That would give us a new sea base and . . .' he nodded at Collyer.

'It would mean that we could dispense with the lines of communication from the north,' said his Chief of Staff.

'Handeni's the place,' said Smuts.

It was there that the narrow-gauge link with the Central Railway had its terminus. Handeni was strategically vital as a jumping-off place for the Central Railway. The urgent need was to push the eastern force hard for Handeni and prevent von Lettow's force at Kondoa-Irangi from joining up with Major Kraut in the east.

When the sound of distant battle continued Smuts turned to Van Deventer: 'I want to go out and see for myself.'

This flare-up of machine guns and seven-pounders was nothing new. Manie Botha's men were often in touch with patrols. But this time Deneys Reitz was out on a reconnaissance patrol down a rocky gorge and he saw the skirmish. 'The Germans rushed up two companies of askaris, who came at us as eagerly as hounds on the scent. Young Lt Bowden (the machine-gun officer) stood up on a rock to get a better view and almost immediately fell dead, and we had four other men killed and a number wounded before the attack was staved off.'

Von Lettow himself recorded the incident. 'They had evidently no idea of our presence. They were allowed to approach quite near, and at short range they lost about half their number.'

Did Not Herald Attack

Smuts rode back from the scene assured that the enemy had not intended any further action. The guns in the South African perimeter opened fire and continued most of the day.

In the church building, now a hospital, Private Thompson lay with severe burns. He noted the gunfire and the sound of machine guns and saw two wounded officers of the 8th admitted.

Smuts heard of the frequent brushes with askaris and of a little six-pounder gun that was audaciously handled by a German officer who hurried it into a firing position on a wooden frame carried by four askaris and got off a few rounds before he had to move.

Reitz and comrades of his squadron set out to stalk the gun. 'All we found for our pains was a piece of paper bearing the derisive message: "15 Rupees for the bluddy Englisch," a joke at which we were not amused after our long crawl in the heat.'

On the morning of 8 June Smuts left Kondoa-Irangi. There is no record of what he thought of conditions there. 'His visit,' wrote Collyer, 'had been productive of good results. Personal discussion between the Commander-in-Chief and his lieutenant had helped in a decision as how best to co-operate in their future movements.'

Life at Kondoa-Irangi at the time of his visit is worth recording from the point of view of the men. The diary of Private Thompson describes aspects of the siege not in commanders' reports. Food, or rather the lack of it, was the main obsession. Thompson describes every meal of every day. The *malaise* and lethargy of the defenders is manifest in every entry.

25 May
Slept late. Had coffee and three spoonfuls of kaffircorn porridge, which was very nice but too little.
26 May
When rations had been issued Alf made some bread and scones, which were baked in the oven we made. I cut up the meat . . . a bit of a job as everybody wanted a bit of bone. At teatime the Germans began shelling the 10th Regiment's trenches.
27 May
Woke up at daylight and lit the fire and cut the steaks for breakfast.
28 May
The boys brought the water for the stew a bit late, so the meat could not be boiled much, but I managed to finish my share.

While they waited for the stalemate to break the men played cards, read books, longed for mail, watched the artillery duelling that took place every day, dug shelters, went to church services, visited friends in hospital, went to funerals, and swopped rumours; the most persistent being that an armistice was likely.

Rumours of Armistice

One splendid lie filtered through. Von Lettow had been killed 'by one of our shells and some six hundred askaris and some Germans had surrendered. Only rumours,' supposed the writer, a little wistfully. But he perked up to add: 'Further rumours to the effect that betting at headquarters was twenty to one on peace being declared before the 28th of this month [June]'.

Then there were lice. Thompson and his friends kept a tally of the 'greybacks' that now appeared even among hospital patients. 'Mac's score was twelve, mine seven and Bob's five.'

177

So it was to go on for two months, while the cemetery grew daily fuller as men were killed by shelling and in small fights in the hills.

Thompson noted one death that indicated stress. 'A man of the 8th Regiment by the name of Walker died from eating cordite.' Chewing cordite was an old soldier's dodge for simulating high fever. Walker had eaten too much. Thompson was put in hospital with severe burns, shockingly neglected by his regimental medical officer, who had treated an oil burn with vaseline until the third degree burn was almost beyond treatment and the leg in danger of amputation.

'Florence Nightingale,' wrote an officer, 'would have recognised the scene and the stench of the hospital in the old mission church.' Dozens of sick men lay on cement floors on groundsheets without blankets, groaning and retching amid the stench of dysentery discharges of mucus and blood; others shook with fever.

Diarist Shackleton recorded: 'The overworked orderly asked me to go and sit for a few minutes with a serious case lying on a stretcher outside. I got up weakly, "I'm half dead myself," to find the poor fellow already gone.'

The only food they got in the early days of the siege was a cup of arrowroot water three times a day, augmented with a little soup. Dysentery cases staggered out to the pit latrines, stumbling over cursing men.

Crimean Hygiene: Vermin and Flies

As one recorder of camp hygiene in this campaign, Brian Godbold, recalls it:

> The latrine was a long open trench, with a bush pole supported on forked poles at either end for a seat, and sick men, weak and dizzy from malaria or dysentery, or both, were in real danger of falling in. Flies swarmed there, and must have carried infection everywhere.
>
> Hearing agonised groans one day, I investigated and found a man sitting on the pole with about twelve inches of his intestines hanging out and running blood, a prolapsed bowel from dysentery.

Shades of the Crimea!

When Shackleton was stronger he went out with his bayonet to dig for sweet potatoes that might have been overlooked. Once he found some dirty rice abandoned in a burnt-out hut. He carried off the prize in a piece of sacking and boiled it in an oil tin. 'I shared it with no one.' At night he lay planning further excursions to the sweet potato field near the river.

'I dodged sentries at night and dug with my bayonet . . . fed myself and tramped off to rejoin my regiment entrenched at the top of a ridge, and before long I was shivering violently in the throes of another fever attack. No one would lend me a blanket. At daylight I crawled out of my groundsheet to cook my ration of food. Then the shells flew overhead . . . we all dived for our dugouts. I came out to find my fire, food and mess tin all gone, blown away.'

Yet there were times when 'comforts' came in. 'As the men lined up to receive their parcels, there was a hush of eager expectancy. We were handed two cigarettes each. I traded mine for a little extra ration of flour.'

In the town of Kondoa the men were billeted in the backyards of a row of old thatched houses, the main askari barracks having been burned down when the Germans abandoned the place. 'We ate outside, as they were vermin-ridden.'

With so many cooking fires made every day, firewood soon became scarce. The billet houses were quickly stripped bare of rafters, thatch and any possible fuel. 'Eventually, we had to climb the trees lining the street to gather dry twigs.'

Some nights Shackleton and his mate would go out with bayonets and search the hillside covered with weeds and scrub for arrowroot. They were now experts at the native art of stripping and cooking it.

Every day the shells came whistling in, doing little damage but fraying the nerves. The men waited tensely for the screech to pass on 'and some other poor bastard [to] catch it.' Private Thompson wrote daily of the excruciating pain of his septic leg and the agony of clumsy orderlies changing dressings. Yet he was always able to write: 'Lovely morning! Had a wash!' And describe his breakfast, however poor.

Smuts returned to the boma at Moshi, climbed the bald hill where the two German sentry boxes still flanked the pillars supporting an ornamental lamp. He found, with intense irritation, that British political officers were already claiming the territory for the Crown. They were treating German civilians as in enemy-occupied territory and officiously removing missionaries and their families.

Smuts Complains to War Office

Smuts telegraphed the War Office. He deprecated the removal, not only because it was 'an odious task which would be resented by Christians everywhere', but worse still, because 'the removal of white civilising influence would mean the break-up of these small centres of civilisation and the reversion of the population to complete barbarism.' That, he said, would be as much against the interests of the State as of the Church.

The General with his sleeping tent and camp bed.

In the middle of a campaign that would be famous chiefly for the suffering of man and beast Smuts the warrior-philosopher was showing concern over a matter of religion. This was the man that the Bishop of Pretoria* had described as fearing neither God nor man, 'especially God'. Smuts was no orthodox Christian believer, and few in England in 1916 would have much concern for the plight of German missionaries. Was it perhaps a lurking sympathy for people whom he now saw being uprooted, chased from the work of education and medical help, their homes and the civilisation they had created here? Was there an echo here of what had happened to his own people at the hands of the English? The high-handedness that had burned his heart with hatred and resentment?

Collyer relates the incident in matter-of-fact military prose and takes it no further. Nor do we know how the War Office responded to what must have seemed a strange request, for, after all, the future of the territory was already under discussion as a new colonial possession.

Meanwhile, Smuts's army in the east had gained a week in which to recover its strength. 'Each day,' wrote Brett Young, 'we wondered how long our blessed rest would last. We knew it could not be for long. I doubt if such a thruster as Smuts could have got more out of the men, who thankfully rested, or the beasts who now began to die in great numbers.'

---

* A senior chaplain in the campaign.

Smuts returned to the scene of action and to the stench of charred flesh as the carcases of dead beasts were burned on pyres*; and, when that failed to be efficient, were dragged into the bush a mile from the camps to be dealt with by the hyenas and vultures.

'All day we could see clouds of these obscene birds hanging in the sky . . . and in the dead of night, we heard lions, which had stolen down from the hills.'

Trolley Line to Mombo

Mombo was the railway station for Wilhelmstal, named after the Emperor. From it von Lettow had built a trolley line to Handeni, linking up the Tanga line with the military roads that ran down to the Central Railway. Along this trolley line the Germans would be taking out their men, supplies and guns. No one knew exactly how it ran, which was surprising perhaps when Meinertzhagen boasted of so many channels of information.

But it appeared from the inadequate maps as certain to cross the swelling floods of the Pangani at Mkalama, the only point where it could be bridged, for on one side were swamps and on the other the sheer rock of the Usambara. The only way forward was to follow the river down its valley, hacking paths through the bush all the way.

It was known that the valley was infested with tsetse fly with all that that entailed in loss of transport animals. Smuts wrote to his wife (14 June):

> We have now followed the Pangani for 140 miles and it has been an outstanding success. Books and doctors have told us that the Pangani is a deadly region as regards fever and fly. On the contrary, our health is still very good and no fly has been seen . . . We started on 22 May, and I expect that by 22 June we shall have marched about 200 miles, which is an outstanding feat in country where there is no road, about which we had no information . . .

Smuts's plan was to isolate the German force under Major Kraut and cut him off from all hope of further retirement; the familiar old tactics. The only way to achieve that was to press on with the utmost speed and endure the losses in men and beasts.

Mombo was the place where it seemed most likely that a stand would be made and where the plan would succeed or fail. Airmen were already flying down the river as far south as Mombo and returning to makeshift landing-grounds, where every take-off was a reckless adventure and forced landings in the bush a constant possibility.

---

* An officer described one such pyre as containing 500 carcases.

British officers watching the fight for Mombo, on the Tanga-Moshi Railway, in East Africa.

Hazards of Flying Over the Jungle

No 26 Squadron, with its mixed South African and British flying officers and ground crews, were now living almost as hard as the infantry. 'Man after man sickened and went down with malaria. We had no doctor with us, medicines were scarce and of comforts there were none.' Private stocks of aspirin to relieve the high temperatures and rigours of malaria were soon finished.

Then there were deaths in flying accidents. How many of these were due to unfit fevered pilots is unknown, but those on duty flew from dawn till dusk every day. One who went missing and returned was Captain A T O'Brien, who got back to his base after a fifty-mile march, a severe test of endurance. His aircraft was hit by ground fire and crashed into a tree, and O'Brien was thrown out on to the ground. How long he lay unconscious he had no idea. 'When I came round Germans were approaching. I set fire to my machine and started to run through the bush. I was two and a half days on foot, I swam across six streams and rivers and I was followed at one stage by a lion, which treed me, despite my three broken ribs.'

Von Lettow recorded: 'Several aeroplanes were brought down, or came to grief, and the passengers were captured and the machine destroyed.'

Ripping up Trolley Lines

Airmen now flying down the river, watching the German retirement reported that they were ripping up the lines to Handeni and destroying bridges. 'Every day as we flew along we could see them at work, and several times we saw the actual explosion when they dynamited a watertank or some other erection likely to be of use to us.'

Some time later Walmsley met the German officer in charge of demolitions. 'He told me that one of our bombs had actually hit the engine of a train, blowing it to atoms, and killing the driver and several military passengers.'

Walmsley noted how close the railway ran to the foot of the Usambara Mountains, 'whose precipitous granite cliffs, glowing red in the sun's lowering rays, towered well overhead in spite of our great altitude.'

To the west he saw the Pangani meandering like a great silver snake, its banks fringed with tall sycamore and mahogany trees, the river still turbulent and muddy.

Walmsley's flight reported to General Sheppard that the Germans were preparing to make a fight of it at Mombo. 'We were the first to discover this position, and a detailed map of it was handed in to the staff some days before our infantry attacked, showing the bridge.' Not that the staff took much notice of the maps given to

A BE2C biplane with 70 hp engine; top speed 60 mph. Throw-outs from the Western Front with small bombs rigged for dropping and streamers for guidance they harried the German retreat. Some were shot down by rifle fire.

them or had much confidence in the accuracy of hand-drawn sketches of defences. Walmsley himself admitted that 'puzzling out my notes for the Chief Intelligence Officer was usually more than I could do myself'.

While Smuts was away Sheppard had planned for both Mkalama and Mombo to be cleared. It was on the banks of the Pangani while the troops were fording it waist-deep, that Brett Young saw Sheppard. 'He was sitting in his car reading a play of Shakespeare and well content with the progress of his brigade across the river.'

Now he gave orders to intercept the enemy at the bridgehead at Mkalama. Colonel Dyke was to lead a flying column of the 2nd Rhodesians, the 130th Baluchis, the 29th Punjabis, the 61st Pioneers and the 27th Mountain Battery. It was routed over twenty miles through appalling country with a fight at the end. Men were to carry rations for two days but no other kit. Even the medical team under Brett Young would have no wheeled transport.

Battle for Bridgehead

On the evening of 8 June Brett Young found Colonel Dyke 'sweating under an awning with a bundle of maps and airmen's sketches and reports. It was a pity that neither were very reliable. That night we made a cold meal of bully beef and biscuit.'

As the Germans retreated they destroyed their locomotives and tore up the railway lines.

For officers and men it was the last food that they would eat for forty hours. The pace soon told on some Rhodesians, old campaigners though they were. 'We could not stop to pick them up . . . The poor devils had to shift for themselves.' The medical officer and his bearers followed as best they could. Hour after hour it went on, the heat suffocating in bush so dense that it seemed to be airless. Soon they had to halt frequently and keep on the alert for the sudden burst of fire.

Then came swamps. A narrow track was found through them and the brigade moved forward in single file in a panting silence of expectation, the mules' feet making no sound in the soft earth. It was quiet enough to hear the whirr of birds' wings and the jingle of equipment, and the hacking and slashing of the pioneers.

Then without warning an 80mm quick-firer opened up. Its shells screamed by in succession, bursting and tearing the trees. 'Push on!' went the order, but it was impossible to make a path through dense thornbush. Like a column of marching ants the brigade tried to move round the obstruction.

The air was stinking with trampled rank jungle vegetation and the reek of explosive, but fortunately the German gunners could see little more than their enemy. Sun and exhaustion and empty bellies were telling now, and the tense expectation of hearing the deadly chatter of the maxim too late to take cover.

Stretchers sent Forward

Suddenly the Baluchis bumped into them. Their leading men fell. Wounded began to dribble back to Brett Young's dressing station and stretchers went out for those lying in the bush. 'They lost heavily in that first minute,' he wrote.

No caution in approach could have prevented it. 'I threw off my tunic and belt, haversack and waterbottle and worked in my shirt sleeves. Two Baluchi subalterns were brought in on the point of death with shattering head wounds. A bloody business; strong and fair young bodies both of them.' Brett Young's assistant, his teeth chattering with fever, scraped a shallow pit in the ground to give the seriously wounded the illusion of safety.

As the surgeon worked on, bloody to the elbows, he saw the striped brown flashes of Rhodesian helmets moving past, hastening up from five miles back, and behind them came the rest of the brigade. The firing never abated. Soon the leaking water containers were empty, and the wounded were desperately thirsty. Four stretcher bearers, sent to the river, returned to report that the enemy were working round the rear of the brigade. Then came the sound of scattered rifle fire.

The revolving gun (World War I – 1914) opens fire with multiple barrels.

Brett Young's Account

'My God!' cried a wounded Baluchi officer, helpless on a stretcher with his thigh shattered by a gunshot wounds. 'If they find me like this . . .' The rifle fire was nearer now. 'We all knew very well what would happen if the Germans' savages found him like that . . .' Another bloody stretcher came in, a man with a chest wound. Already dead. Gurkhas hurried to Brett Young, urging him to make haste . . . get away.

At that moment the whole area was swept by maxim fire, 'hellishly loud in the bush, and bullets singing everywhere'. They dragged the wounded deeper into the bush as another burst of murderous fire raked the area, fortunately high. In that moment of terror the surgeon found himself sheltering behind the body of the dead Indian on the stretcher. When the firing slackened, he organised his bearers to pick up the wounded. They got some distance, then stopped to listen, panting like hunted men, knowing that the askaris were everywhere though still unseen.

'For a moment the firing had stopped. Then they came with a rush, sweeping through the dressing station, now occupied only by the dead; and then, having found it empty, hot on our track . . . we could hear them crashing through the bush. The machine gun started again . . . our pace was the pace of the slowest of the wounded, a ghastly Baluchi with a bullet through his chest. Whenever we paused for breath the askaris gained on us and bullets droned through the woods.'

186

First Water in Thirty-six Hours

Then the light failed and they came to a muddy creek. All his company scooped up the water in their cupped hands. The swamp gave the illusion of safety, and indeed it saved their lives. Not till late next day did they hear the creak of a waggon's wheels and the crack of a whip. They came out on the track . . . 'a queer spectacle with our bloody bandages and our clothes in tatters,' and accosted a South African transport officer, begging for water. It was the first that he had drunk for thirty-six hours.

Already the order for the advance had been given. 'I rode on in my rags at the head of the ambulance, on through the bush where the Baluchis had been swept by the German machine guns, past the German emplacements and trenches to Mkalama itself.'

So this fine writer and poet, later a South African citizen, described what General Collyer's book gave only two lines to. The enemy had escaped along the trolley line and was making for Handeni and the Central Railway. Once more it had all been too late. The chance of getting behind the enemy had been lost by Sheppard ordering his brigade to press in support of Colonel Dyke's column. In doing so they failed to turn the position.

The only German captured at Mkalama was an elderly man found sleeping in the bush, who could give no coherent account of himself or anything else.

But they had not failed alone. General Hannyngton's central column with orders to cut the trolley line from Mombo to Handeni also arrived too late or just in time to see the last Germans and the big gun from the *Königsberg* hurrying away down the line as the sappers destroyed it.

Tactful Handling of German Civilians

Smuts was left with Wilhelmstal and its five hundred civilians to be fed and protected. With his personal memories of France and the ravaging of Belgian towns and villages Brett Young reflected: 'Their abandonment implied an appreciation of our methods of warfare. I do not think we would have dared the same.'

In the cool summer bungalows and official residences of Wilhelmstal there were now crowded five hundred women and children, families of men with von Lettow, and missionaries driven from their stations. What was to be done with these people?

Five thousand feet above sea level in the Usambara range it was somewhat like Switzerland; but its apparent healthiness was illusory. 'The pallor of the children there was remarkable,' wrote Collyer. It seemed that the Usambara country was regarded by the settlers as something apart from the war. They believed that the presence of their own soldiers was threatening them. They had actually appealed to Dr Schnee, their Governor, to keep them out of it and to use his authority over von Lettow to do so.

In fact, Wilhelmstal was so far from the course of hostilities that it was in no danger, and there was no evidence of troops there when it was occupied. Smuts gave orders for a 'firm and tactful officer' to be appointed political officer to maintain the peace with a subaltern and twenty-five mounted men.

Smuts Rediscovers Hegel

Smuts was once more reading with pleasure Hegel's philosophy and had rediscovered what he called 'some of my dear old German philosophers I have found in this country and can therefore reread them at odd times.'

He did not, apparently, share the violent antipathy of so many of his British officers, to whom Germans were Huns. Somehow he seemed to have distanced himself from the brutality. They were finding photographs and newspaper articles that recorded harsh treatment.

Photographs taken at the turn of the century showed women in chains linked to each other with rings round their necks stamping the surface of roads and on the plantations, and overseers with sjamboks marching villagers to the cottonfields. A sportsman, posing with trophies of the chase, had a human skull as his centrepiece among the horns of buck. In bachelor quarters photographs of naked women embarrassed the sensitive with captions such as *'Eine schwarze Schöne'*, and suggestions of concubinage.

Captain R V Dolby, a doctor of the Royal Army Medical Corps, was most outspoken in his dislike of the Germans. He called them brutal in power, servile in captivity, and expressed his disgust at finding photographs of gallows with rows of hanged rebels 'while German officers and men stood by with self-satisfied expressions'.

Smuts's officers found the German civilians deeply depressed by the retreat of their army and the news that they were now cut off by the fall of the port of Tanga at the end of the line. All those who were not in the pleasant little green town in the hills with its cool bungalows and the seat of government in summers before the war were getting away to the south on the Central Railway to Morogoro. They believed that they would be safe there until the war ended in their favour.

However, there were Germans who feared that the tribesmen would attempt another rising; and without their protectors, what then? A terrible revenge.

188

Rhodesians at Pangani crossing.

'German nursing sisters told me,' wrote Captain Dolby, 'of the terror of the women who fled to Morogoro and how all the women were supplied with tablets of prussic acid to swallow if the dreaded end looked possible.' But what appeared to rankle most with German civilians was that they appeared to be losing their colony to the Boers.

'Did not German girls knit stockings for the women of that nation that was so akin to the Germans in blood, as presents for the poor Boers beneath the feet of England!'

THE VICTOR

THE VANQUISHED

(*'Jambo' or with Jannie in the Jungle*, AW Lloyd, undated)

10

March to Handeni
– A Thirsty Trek

Abruptly, after a surfeit of water, of rushing rivers, swollen tributaries, swamps and heavy morning mists that drenched and chilled to the bone there came a more familiar trial: thirst. Smuts's eastern force was about to march on territory where the lack of water for man, mule, horse and ox was to make the march on Handeni another test of endurance. But Smuts was confident that his engineer could quickly repair the destroyed trolley line.

'You can understand that when transport has to be provided so many hundreds of miles from base, our difficulties become enormous. Motors break down, animals die, everything goes wrong, and thousands of mouths have to be fed. If, however, we have the same success that we have had so far, there will be nothing serious to complain of.' The letter was in his usual affectionate vein to his wife and as always signed 'Pappa'.

Writing of the Pangani trek he told his son Jannie: 'Last week three mules tethered together went for a drink; a crocodile seized one by the nose and was strong enough to drag all three under the water and drown them. What a feast for him and his friends!'

It was a striking, if unintentional parable of the struggle between Smuts and von Lettow – with the German as the hidden enemy.

Smuts's army now girded up its loins for the ten-day march on Handeni. It was no great distance: thirty miles as the crow flies and the vulture's shadow followed along the trolley track.

Smuts was well aware of the risks of this move. There would be German ambushes set on the motor road, so he ordered flanking marches. The water waggons were to follow as best they could. Already it was known that such water as existed in the wells they would pass was not only almost undrinkable but highly purgative.

'Nothing,' wrote an infantry officer, 'is less conducive to an attacking spirit than loose bowels and cramps in the belly.'

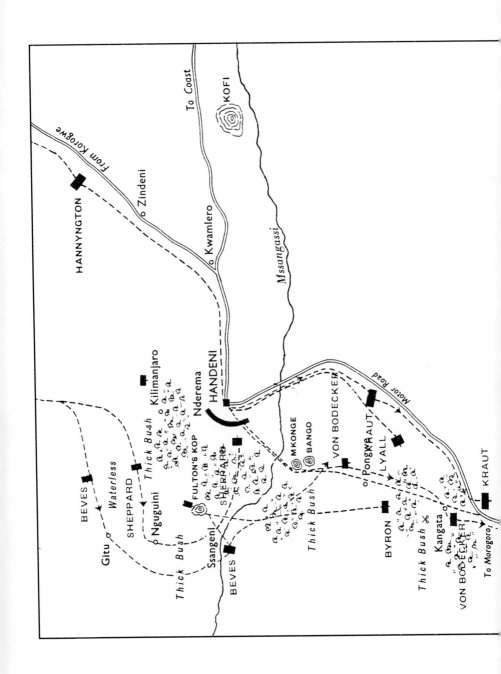

ADVANCE on HANDENI and MOVEMENT on KANGATA

(*The South Africans with General Smuts in German East Africa 1916*,
Brig-Gen Collyer, 1939)

So waterless was the stretch of country that from the day he set out, Sheppard's western column had to send back water carts and thirsty animals to the last available water at Luchomo. It was a preposterous waste of manpower and energy. The entire force depended on this cumbersome method, all too familiar to old hands from the desert of German South West in 1914.

Ahead lay the waters of Nderema. The airmen were ordered to bomb wherever there was an opportunity and to pay special attention to the defences at this paradise with ample water. There the enemy would resist, well knowing the plight that Smuts's men would be in after ten waterless days on the march.

Brett Young described his last glimpse of the island village of Luchomo before the march began. 'A beautiful spot, but one as treacherous to man as to the luckless animals.' A constant stream of sick men were awaiting evacuation to base hospitals. There was an illusion of tranquillity in those last hours beneath the spreading trees by the Pangani.

Then came the order to advance. Smuts had decided that he could not wait any longer for the repairing of the railway line. Ahead lay a hundred miles on foot under a burning sky, always in contact

A water supply column on trek to Nderema.

with an elusive enemy, yet never having the satisfaction of coming to grips. It meant thirst, fatigue and endless marching.

What did it feel like, a war of this kind in which mechanisation was primitive and the endurance of the individual meant everything? The experience was described by Lieutenant J H (Jack) Lowden of the 7th SAI. He had been a Rhodes scholar, had graduated at Balliol College and taken honours in classics before returning to South Africa to join the staff of Pretoria High School.

'The Sky is a Burning Glass'

Shortly before he was killed in action he wrote to his parents praising the remarkable fortitude of his platoon.

> My marching became a trudge. I ceased to think. There was merely a dwindled self that vaguely coincided with the idea that there was a goal to be reached by placing one foot before the other for an infinite time – a goal with water that could be drunk without robbing oneself of a drink.
>
> An hour later I took to sipping at my bottle and each time was refreshed for a few minutes, and each time saw there would be a moment, if I was not careful, when there would be no more. The sky became a burning glass, and the earth an unburnished mirror of flint . . .

Marching with the 2nd Rhodesians, Brett Young 'saw black pits which those who had passed before us had digged there' and left dry for those who followed.

German maps showed that somewhere ahead there was a permanent stream named M'zungu-wazara; but so far the brigade had found only a few rock pools of water trampled to frothy mud. The abundant waters still lay thirty miles away. 'Two of my mules fell down and died on the road,' wrote the patient surgeon, who was himself ill.

That night no one had water or food of any kind. The Germans had stripped the land as they passed, leaving not so much as a mealie-cob. Far ahead they could see smoke rising from cultivated fields and villages where they would find nothing but blackened stubble and smouldering huts. And there were still twenty miles to go to Handeni.

Nothing of this personal anguish is mentioned in official reports or in Collyer's careful study of the campaign. It was the stuff of a foot-slogger's war, marching in sand and dust, the long columns trudging in choking clouds, sweat running in rivulets down grimy faces; behind them, lorries were sunk to their axles in sand under the load of supplies that could not be got forward.

The High Price Paid for Pangani

Every day the fever cases were left behind. 'Ninety sick men in a single day from a brigade of less than four thousand,' Brett Young recorded of Sheppard's column. 'This was the price we paid for our nights by the Pangani.'

Smuts and his staff were often miles ahead of the men, and at Ssangeni he stopped. He was only ten miles from Handeni, where there was good water. His men were closing in on the objective and would be refreshed. Ahead lay the great conical hill with its castellated boma of stone and round it the long-established barracks of the askaris. It was a region of enormous cultivated fields of sisal hemp and endless plantations of young rubber trees. At Handeni three good new military roads had only recently been completed by thousands of labouring blacks impressed for the task.

The German flag flew from the tower. Smuts in habitual fashion rode through the bush to where a high kopje at Ssangeni reared out of the wilderness round it. He and his staff, apprehensive for his safety, were miles from their troops as he impetuously climbed the hill, ignoring suggestions that there might well be lurking askaris so near the main German force.

'There was only one Mauser between us,' one wrote. 'Half a dozen could have captured the Commander-in-Chief.' Smuts made a long survey of the landscape and then, to the relief of his staff, came back down.

'Send two companies to occupy the hill,' he ordered. Later he spoke to two Boer women, living alone on a nearby farm. They told him that there were only two companies at Handeni. 'A big stand,' they said, 'will be made at Tabora.'

But What Holds Up Brits?

Information now reached him that Coen Brits with his mounted brigade had reached Same by a gap in the mountains and was only about a hundred miles behind. 'If Brits can keep going,' Smuts told his staff, 'we should have him here in time to make a wide outflanking movement on this open country.' It looked promising.

There was great expectation among the marching men. The brigade of fresh troopers would round up the Germans at Handeni and it would be all over. A few days later the question was being asked: 'Where the hell is Brits . . . what's keeping him?'

Brits had ridden into the tsetse fly belt of the Pangani. His horses were dying at the rate of thirty to forty a day. There was no chance of his reaching Smuts in time to carry out the manoeuvre. In fact he was stuck there for a month.

Nevertheless Smuts insisted on repeating his outflanking tactics and brushed aside the difficulties. So far the outflanking manoeuvres had failed every time. Von Lettow was well aware that 'their effectiveness was greatly reduced by the difficulty of the country' and that he could exploit it to the full.

In the event, the manoeuvre and the forced march were to no avail as a means of bringing the Germans to a conclusive action. Handeni was found abandoned on 18 June. The unexpected came in a counter-attack against the companies that Smuts had posted on the hill at Ssangeni. Taken by surprise by the 5th and 6th South Africans, in occupation, the Germans twice attacked and retired, leaving fifteen dead in the bush. This was a rearguard action fought by Captain Freiherr von Bodecker, who twice that day brought his pom-poms and machine guns into action to delay the advance and allow Major Kraut to get away.

Through Seventy Miles of Forest

Smuts was right up in front with his battalions. RSM Molloy of the 5th SAI saw him when he 'took our colonel to one side after searching the country through his telescope, and gave him instructions to march on the village of Pongwe, some three miles off. We marched off in single file, taking a forest path, as we had done for the last seventy miles.' Ahead of the 5th went the Indian Pioneers 'hacking a way through the dense forests . . . invaluable work, very often in the face of severe maxim and rifle fire when the enemy could not be seen ten yards off.

'About 5.30 p.m. our local native guides returned with information that the village was still occupied by the enemy and heavily trenched. Our gallant old Colonel [Byron] formed his regiment up in a fold of ground near the village.' They were just in time to see the main group of the enemy marching away to Kangata, seven miles off.

'With some of my scouts and a platoon of C Company I could see the rearguard through the long grass and trees about sixty yards off. I let some of them pass, but on espying a group of about five Germans could resist the temptation no longer and fired, knocking over a sergeant-major. Taken utterly by surprise, they fled, leaving two wounded and some dead askaris. For a long distance ahead the road was littered with abandoned baggage, which our fellows helped themselves to . . .'

So much for Major Kraut's baggage guard. But 'once more,' wrote Collyer, 'General Smuts's objective had eluded him.' The dense bush country and the enemy's knowledge of its tracks and skilful tactics had been too good for the blundering advance of Smuts's three columns.

Handeni was found to have a number of European houses and the fort with its official quarters where a considerable number of sick men had been left behind in the barracks.

Collyer's Scorn of Rumour

If Smuts had to admit that he had missed another chance, some of his staff were heartened by intelligence reports that there was 'considerable demoralisation in Kraut's retirement.' Collyer dismissed the rumour. 'We had heard it all before; and if it were true, the effect must have been fleeting, as the events of the next twenty-four hours were to show.'

Indeed, he thought it possible that this so-called 'intelligence' had been deliberately planted, and he viewed with suspicion the 'astonishing amount' of locally distilled whisky left behind. 'Handeni "witski" mixed with Nderema water,' he wrote dryly, 'was calculated to reduce the strongest man to impotence.' And already they were falling out at a rate that alarmed the Chief of Staff. They were 'much diminished by disease aggravated by privation,' he noted, watching the division encamp above the trolley station.

Suffering though they were, the men were shocked by the sight of groups of 'miserable African porters, horribly emaciated'. The water was bad and dysentery was rife.

Some time before the place fell, Lieutenant Christopher Thornhill, one of Smuts's advance scouts with Intelligence, got into the place, which was already being abandoned.

> Among several large grass buildings we found two crowded with living skeletons – poor unfortunate blacks who could barely move from weakness because of overwork and dysentery. They had been left behind without any medical attention . . . They had not even anyone to bury their dead or collect or cook their food – a patch of hard dry maize.
>
> Most of the sick had no blankets to protect them from the cold damp night air, and some of their naked bodies lay still in death while masses of them lay huddled together outside, trying to get some warmth from the morning sun. Others crawled feebly towards the maize field and chewed at the hard grain . . . The sight of so many naked moving skeletons gave us the creeps, and we turned our backs and moved off, the sickly smell of the place haunting us . . .

Notice of Typhus

In a long shed lay two hundred Africans, left there to die. A notice warned 'Typhus'. These were some of the labourers whom the Ger-

197

mans had worked under great pressure building the trolley line on which they moved back their supplies. 'That appalling hospital,' wrote Brett Young, sickened by the sight and stench, 'had been left in the charge of a fat farmer with a great red cross on his arm.'

Within hours of the division marching past the smouldering ruins of the trolley station, the natives of the district began to come in with eggs and vegetables. It was the first fresh food for weeks, and just in time to stop the scurvy that had begun to manifest itself in some of the patients with malaria.

The 2nd Rhodesians were down to less than half-strength. Like the others they hoped for rest and fresh food as the rumour went about that there would be a fortnight's pause in the gruelling advance. It was no compassionate gesture. It would take that time for supplies to catch up. Mails might come forward and, with luck, reinforcements, and there would be time for the sweet oblivion of sleep without the order to fall in and march at 3 a.m.

New Hope of Decisive Action

There was to be no rest. At Smuts's headquarters the opinion was that although the enemy had escaped being enveloped there was still a chance to bring him to decisive battle before long.

'We have hustled them,' said Smuts. 'Now we have to press hard after them, never lose touch. We have to get as many men as possible into the field.'

Urgent arrangements were made to bring convalescent men forward from base hospitals and men on guard duties far behind the front were ordered to rejoin their units.

On 20 June Smuts was at Pongwe, and he sent for Colonel Byron. It was 2 p.m. when Byron got his orders to march the 5th on Kangata, and not to wait for the rest of the brigade to catch up. At the same time the force under Colonel Lyall was to march out within the hour and make good the Morogoro road.

No orders were given to Lyall to keep in touch with Byron's battalion, although they were on converging courses and Lyall, on the good road, could move faster. Byron was told that he was not likely to meet more than a patrol of the enemy at Kangata.

As he waited for Lyall's column to move off from Handeni, Brett Young spent the last moments of waiting in exploring the residence of the German Governor, Weiss. He found a complete set of Goethe in forty volumes; evidently a cultural necessity, but too cumbersome to take with him on his flight. In the flower garden he contemplated the pleasant view of the surrounding plantations and the evidence of civilised life. Now the family was on its way to Morogoro 'leaving these pathetic little evidences of their culture'.

Then, with a shock, he picked up a medicine bottle with a skull and crossbones label. To him, it seemed hideously eloquent of the German military philosophy of *Schrecklichkeit*. Dreadfulness. An hour later he was marching on the firm red-earth road, straight as a drawn line. By nightfall, he noted, the mules were already showing signs of tsetse. Soon they would be dying wholesale.

Fatal March of the 5th

Meanwhile, Byron's 5th was ready to march. RSM Molloy formed up his men.

> We marched out 342 strong, reduced considerably by sickness and fever. A good portion of this number were non-combatant – transport, stretcher-bearers, water men, medicals and officers' servants. Within a mile of the village we exchanged shots with a few of the enemy, driving them before us through the bush as we advanced. After advancing some twelve hundred yards the bush on our left became impassable, forcing our left flank to take to the road until we could clear it.
>
> I gave the order to the regimental scouts to deploy quickly to the left as we emerged into an open vale four hundred yards in breadth and fifteen hundred in length, through which a sluggish stream flowed. I had hardly given this order to deploy when we were met with maxim and rifle fire at point-blank range. That was about 4.45 p.m.

Colonel Byron's leading men had run into what seemed to be a screen of Kraut's skirmishers. These retreated skilfully, firing, keeping in touch, but always drawing the eager South Africans after them and towards their prepared positions covering the *Autoweg*.

In the past few days Byron's men had seemed to win in every skirmish, and they were eager as hounds on the scent. The sun was already low in the sky, the shadows were lengthening, and the glare was in the eyes of the South Africans, who saw only the darkened bush ahead while they were bathed in the golden glow.

A Well-prepared Trap

This then was the scene as Molloy led his company across a depression towards the slope of a hill on the other side of the clearing. The men scouting ahead did not see any significance in the cleared brush and felled trees. In the forest fringe ahead von Bodecker's company had dug their machine guns into log bunkers. Brushwood concealed rifle pits dug for about four hundred crouching askaris, eagerly awaiting the command to fire.

The South Africans advancing were dead meat. Only the over-eagerness of an askari who fired a shot without orders gave warning of the trap. At once the machine guns, carefully positioned on the flanks, opened fire. In the first few seconds the sun-dazzled South Africans were scythed down.

'Spread out . . . lie down and return fire!' RSM Molloy shouted, and beckoned his leading maxim team to set up and return the machine-gun fire. He had spotted the nearest German team only seventy yards away on his left. 'Stick to your ground!' he ordered.

Byron himself came forward and, seeing the situation, sent off a message to headquarters by a dispatch rider on a motorcycle saying that he was heavily engaged and needed reinforcements.

Back at Pongwe, some ten miles away, the sound of heavy firing had been noted: 'At 5.20 p.m. heavy and sustained firing to the south-west.' It was forty minutes later that the rider arrived.

At once Smuts ordered two companies of the 6th to move to Byron's assistance. The march would have to be made in growing darkness and would probably arrive too late.

Out in front with his company, RSM Molloy had marked the positions of more German machine guns, but any attempt to retire was impossible. His men raised their weapons in the thick grass and aimed at the puffs of smoke from the askaris' rifles.

Hardly had Molloy's maxim crew opened fire when they were cut down. As others sprang to take their places they too were killed or wounded and dragged away by the men who took their place. Every yard of ground was ranged by the Germans in this carefully prepared trap.

Molloy recorded his admiration of his youngsters.

Though inexperienced soldiers, to their credit, especially the wounded fellows, they stuck it like men and soldiers without a murmur. At times during the action one was almost blinded by the storm of flying bark and splinters caused by the maxims.

We hung on, firing the last shot about 6.45 p.m. A quarter of an hour afterwards, our fellows quickly dug themselves in in the darkness, after being exposed in the open with no better protection than some thick grass. About 8.30 the colonel gave me orders to go along the line and quietly withdraw every second man on to the road . . . and ten minutes later withdrew the balance. It was an anxious moment. All returned some couple of hundred yards to the crest of the hill.

A captured revolver gun (five barrels).

The Call for Medical Help

Meanwhile at Byron's headquarters a signals officer had connected a line to the fighting battalion. It was dark, the time 9 p.m. when his message got through calling for doctors, blankets, watercarts and medical necessities.

'How many casualties do you estimate, Captain?'

'So far about fifty wounded and more coming back.'

'Dead?'

'Unknown so far . . . it looks like being heavy.'

Molloy recorded in a letter: 'I had the unpleasant task of seeing to the dead being collected and carried back. All worked splendidly under the leadership of our gallant old CO who himself insisted on carrying on his back Company Sergeant Major Murray, badly wounded through the ankle.'

By this time Lyall's column had marched fourteen miles from Handeni and had still ten to go to reach Kangata. Orders were sent to him to push on and get in contact with Byron. When he got there in the early hours of the next morning he and Byron examined the position in front. 'It looked as if the enemy were still lying there with outposts forward, but as light grew we saw that they had vacated the entrenchments.' Lyall's move on the Morogoro road had persuaded them to escape before being cut off. But it was all too late.

Major Kraut was on his way to set up the next rearguard action. He had lost one man killed and eight wounded.

A Victory – but Costly

Next morning Molloy went forward to examine the enemy trenches that ran along the opposite slope of the valley the 5th had entered. 'It was two thousand yards long with four maxim emplacements and contained over four hundred rifle pits.' In these rifle pits astounded survivors counted between a hundred and three hundred odd rounds in each of 409 pits. This volume of fire had been directed at the 5th, whose front line did not exceed 250 yards, and was held by not more than two hundred men with four maxims. As the fight drew to a close the 5th had been firing blindly at the flashes of askari who ducked into their rifle pits. Only their habitual poor shooting saved the men of the 5th from worse.

If Smuts's main body, not merely a company, had blundered into this carefully prepared trap it would have been a massacre. 'I took thirty-one scouts into this action and lost a third of them,' Molloy wrote. 'Our casualties in all came to hundred, of whom twenty were killed. We claimed a victory, although a costly one.'

Collyer estimated that about a quarter of Byron's four hundred rifles had been lost. Others have put the casualties as high as two hundred killed and wounded. We may assume that if anyone knew the correct figure it was the sergeant major who called the roll of his men before battle and next day. He knew how many rifles he took in.

Smuts came forward with General Beves and their staffs and examined the positions. 'The dead were still unburied,' wrote Molloy. Colonel Byron sent for him, shook his hand and told him that General Beves had granted him a field commission.

In his summing-up of the encounter Collyer was not directly critical of Smuts. 'The pursuit of an enemy who is at once unbroken and enterprising, and the German force was both, is an operation calling for the nicest combination of boldness and caution. While no opportunity of scoring a success must be missed, no chance must be given your opponent, who will no doubt choose his place and occasion for his effort to inflict a heavy blow on an over-venturesome pursuer.'

A Rearguard's Hard Lesson

And such was his commander. 'Rearguards,' Collyer reflected, 'have given many lessons to their enemies, and Freiherr von Bodecker proceeded to add another to the list.' The demoralisation that his staff had over-sanguinely attributed to the Germans had 'clearly evaporated'.

Would Smuts act more cautiously from now on? Had he learned to curb his impatience with this evidence that recklessness and the difficulty of co-ordinating the movements of forces separated by difficult

Smashed radiator of a Ford car replaced with a petrol drum. A typical improvisation made at Njambe.

country, led to deathtraps? Would he add the lesson of Kangata to that of Salaita Hill?

Not bloody likely! Intelligence scouts brought news that several German companies were camped only four miles ahead and others beyond them. Another chance was being offered. There was not a moment to lose. The 5th and 6th battalions were on the march at once, with a collection of other units under Major-General Hoskins of the Divisional Reserve.

The objective was the Lukiguru River.

It had been estimated that Kraut's northern army would be massed in front of the river crossing with heavy artillery in support. At his rear the blue massifs of the Nguru Mountains towered over the well-made military road to Morogoro and the Central Railway. If Kraut got his army away into those well-watered and fertile hills, twelve hundred square miles in extent, it would be the devil's work to dislodge him.

Could Kraut be Trapped?

Smuts's plan was to cut off the forces still north of the Lukiguru River by crossing the river behind them while the 1st Brigade marched down the road to start a holding action and divert attention from the left hook. Hard marching and hard fighting lay ahead, but perhaps this time, if the outflanking troops could stand the pace, it would succeed and the nimble and resourceful Kraut would be trapped.

Could it be done? Until now the enemy had had the best of every rearguard action. At the crossing of the Buiko he had evaded envelopment; at Mkalama he had resisted the attackers and got away unmolested; at Handeni there had been only skirmishes; at Katanga he had held up the pursuit and inflicted a heavy price for trifling loss to himself.

In these actions Smuts's troops had been fitter and in greater numbers; and now he was asking them to give their best in what he hoped would be a last prodigious effort. On paper it looked unlikely. Commanders took the roll-call. The 25th Royal Fusiliers were down to two hundred men, the Rhodesians to 170 and the two Indian battalions to about 350 each. The Kashmir Rifles were still 450 strong and the 5th and 6th South Africans about 450 each.

In the dark hours of 23-24 June the 5th and 6th South Africans, the Kashmiris, the Lancs* and the Fusiliers took to the hills to the west on their secret march. Twenty-four hours' hard slogging lay ahead as they trudged off into the night. Everything depended on their getting

---

* A machine-gun company of the 2nd Lancs and the 27th Mountain Battery of the Royal Artillery.

behind Kraut before the force under Sheppard pushed him too hard on the river front.

Timing was vital; and in a war fought with poor communications, unlikely to succeed. Smuts had learned that lesson. He had ordered Sheppard to engage the enemy just seriously enough to hold him on the river: 'On no account are you to drive him into retreat before the outflanking movement is complete.'

A Thirty-mile Night March

The pressure on the outflanking column was to reach its objective at dawn and storm the village. 'All night we trekked,' wrote Captain Angus Buchanan, who described the column of Fusiliers (and others) stretched back for miles in single file on a narrow bush path with a native guide leading. They paused to rest only once during what became an agonising march of thirty miles, a stumbling night-mare. They had set off with empty bellies. Transport and Supply had issued each man with a pound of flour and a hunk of raw bacon, and they were ordered to make no fires.

'This caused ironical amusement,' wrote C T Stoneham, a Fusilier rifleman. 'It was the worst night march I ever endured. The winding bush path plunged us straight into a welter of wooded hills, divided by sudden rocky ridges. There was no moon.

'We kept going to sleep on our feet. The man in front of me fell headlong into a donga, and I and two others landed on top of him.'

Daylight saw Sheppard's column marching briskly along the motor road fringed with bush and forest. As the sky lightened the tramp of marching feet, the creak of wheels and clatter of hooves had ominous echoes to those with memories of the Boer War. Stormberg! There the entrenched Boers caught Gatacre's* column in just such a situation.

The silence across the river seemed to deepen where the road took a right-angled turn to the left. A shot rang out. Among the leading horsemen scouting ahead a trooper of the 17th Indian Cavalry tumbled from his mount. At once the hidden machine guns began their deadly chatter. A quick firer pumped over a stream of shells.

Armoured Cars in Action

Major Sir John Willoughby waved forward his three armoured cars, their engines roaring and backfiring as noisily as the pom-poms' fire.

---

* Lt-Gen Sir William Gatacre, commanding the 3rd Infantry Division, lost 696 men missing and captured after a night march to recapture a strategic railway junction. Dawn found him at the mercy of the hidden Boers. (10 December 1899.)

The fifty horse-power Rolls-Royce cars moved ponderously down the road and as abruptly pulled up. Willoughby looked from his car to see a four-foot trench.

'Back!' he ordered and as the car ground into reverse a pom-pom shell hit it exactly in the space between the opened louvres of the radiator. The other cars gave covering fire as Willoughby's crew worked with shovels to fill in the trench. From the turret their maxim engaged a machine gun across the river, and the car was got away.

Now the 29th Punjabis came trotting past, bent low, with bayonets fixed as they deployed and made for a tall hill rising from the luxuriant tropical growth. Orders were to seize it. The Germans had just realised its value and were scrambling up the rear side. There was a brisk fight, and the German force fell back, leaving its dead and wounded.

A message now came from Hoskins. The vital outflanking movement was held up. No one had foreseen the difficulties of the manoeuvre. 'Fairly easy going' had been the intelligence report.

When the sun rose they were still far from the river. 'All through the day we marched,' wrote Buchanan.

At mid-afternoon they heard the sound of distant battle.

Meanwhile, far to the rear, snipers had filtered through and attacked Sheppard's transport. Most of the native drivers took to the bush and the cry went up for stretcher-bearers.

Gunners' Frustration

The SA Field Artillery unlimbered its guns. In every action so far its men had toiled to fell trees and make a clearing to place their guns, only to find their targets impossible to hit. Like other units, its strength was severely depleted, and seven more gunners and three drivers had fallen out that morning. Their marching orders for the battle zone were to reach 'the river by the road'. Now as prisoners and wounded began coming back they were ordered into action. Once again the only battery position possible was masked by forest.

'Damned frustrating to come all this way and never fire a shot,' fumed their commander.

By now the flanking column had been marching for twenty-four hours, continually held up by dongas and the native guide's uncertainty. Some time in the morning the Indian advance guard was fired on in a maize field outside a village. With their officers knocked out, it fell back, leaving the Fusiliers in the lead.

Behind them on the path all was confusion. General Hoskins was afraid that his guns would be captured, and he ordered them to be retired until the nature of the ambush could be ascertained. By some misunderstanding the infantry went with them.

An armoured motor battery with Rolls Royce engines was of little use in East Africa's jungle and swamp.

Hours passed while the confusion in the ant-like procession through forest, bush and field was sorted out and machine guns were brought forward.

'In With the Bayonet!'

Ahead there was a steady rattle of small-arms fire. Stoneham heard his colonel give the order for the attack 'in his loud, hearty voice. "All right, go forward then. As soon as you see them get into them with the bayonet and drive them off the hill." He waved them on impatiently.'

The Fusiliers came out of the trees and into a denuded area cleared for fire and just in front of a double line of trenches. 'Directly we appeared the enemy opened up on us . . . The air seemed thick with lead, the din stunned the mind. We dropped on our knees and poured in a volley, emptying our magazines. Then the Major's whistle shrilled and he waved us forward.'

Charge of 'The Old and Bold'

'It was not a charge because no one had the energy to run; we shambled forward, yelling, fixing bayonets as we went . . . The sight of those grim, tattered figures steadily advancing unnerved the askaris.' Then the 25th were into the trenches with the bayonet.

Stoneham saw 'a tall, powerful fellow making straight for the pom-pom gun. A German officer rested his elbow on the gun barrel and presented a large Mauser pistol at him. I saw it jerk again and again as the recoil shook the German's hand, but the Fusilier kept walking ahead. Then he made a sudden rush, leapt into the trench, and drove his bayonet through the officer's chest. He killed four askaris round the gun and was himself unhurt.'

German quick-firing gun destroyed at Lukiguru.

Stoneham himself was facing an askari five yards from the trench. The askari fired, but hit Stoneham's waterbottle. 'I was deluged with a shower of tepid water, which I thought was blood. I went for that askari as hard as I could run. He turned and tried to scramble out of the trench, and I flung myself at him so that the bayonet went right through his back between the shoulders. I remember standing over the body in the trench struggling to withdraw my bayonet. When I looked round the trench was full of our men and dead bodies, and the remnants of the defenders were running for the huts in the background.'

Of the exhausted Fusiliers Buchanan wrote: 'I have never seen men so utterly tired and woebegone . . . yet when they went into battle all fatigue was forgotten. They fought like madmen – like heroes.' The sort, sharp engagement stormed the hill and carried the village of Kwa-Direma.

'And now to the southward,' wrote Brett Young, 'heavy firing began, and we knew the flanking column had got in touch with the enemy.' He saw Smuts sitting in his big grey Vauxhall, talking animatedly to General Collyer. 'I had never seen him so obviously pleased with himself.'

As the Germans tried to break away to the north-east the Baluchis and Punjabis were catching them in the open with very deadly maxim fire. By late afternoon all firing had stopped. Prisoners were still coming in, 'many of them scared to death by the terrifying amplification of the maxims in the echoing bush'. Some were so shaken by the din of battle that a single unarmed officer took the surrender of two Germans and eight askaris, all fully armed.

Admiration for the Indians

The 5th and 6th SAI were generous in their praise. 'In this action,' wrote Molloy, now a Lieutenant, 'the enemy lost thirty killed and about a hundred wounded and [taken] prisoner. Also a pom-pom, four maxims and a number of rifles. We knocked the stuffing out of them here!' He singled out the Fusiliers and the Gurkhas for 'the most gallant manner' in which they had stormed the enemy 'at the point of the bayonet'.

Significantly he added: 'The Indian troops are the admiration of all. Our fellows have already learned that the Indian has the true spirit of the soldier in him as much as any white man.'

At 64, F C Selous, the famous hunter joined the Legion of Frontiersmen – the 25th Royal Fusiliers. As a Captain he won the DSO for conspicuous gallantry, resource, and endurance. He was killed on 4 January 1917.

Smuts's weary men began to carry out the tasks that follow a battle and felt the reaction. 'It is remarkable,' wrote Fusilier Stoneham, 'that after an incident of this kind everyone has the desire to "knock off for lunch!" While the wounded were being carried into a hut the major in charge, a big pistol in hand, was holding a sandwich in the other. Suddenly an old woman sprang forward, quite crazy, seized the sandwich and squatted down to eat it.'

'Well, I'm damned!' exclaimed the officer. Nobody laughed.

Others had found the German officers' kit and food boxes. 'We found them well-stocked with champagne, tins of vegetables and fruit and sausage, presumably from a supply ship that had run the blockade. None of the champagne came my way, but I had some tinned cheese and vegetables.'

As soon as Kraut's artillerymen knew that the village had been lost they opened fire from the adjacent mountain twelve thousand yards away.

Huge 8.8cm shells were landing on the forest slopes with great flashes. Their stunning reports reverberated for three hours and drove the attackers into the abandoned trenches. The mules were hastily driven to a safer area with the wounded of both sides.

'They knew the range to a yard, and shells began to burst in our midst. The improvised hospital was hit, and we had to carry the surviving wounded men into the bush.' Stoneham himself was flung into the air by a bursting shell. 'Twice in an hour I had suffered the abominable torment of believing myself mortally wounded.'

With nightfall came reinforcements and rain. 'We lay out in the deluge without covering, and slept like the dead. In about forty hours we had marched fifty-seven miles and fought a battle; and this night of rain and mud was the climax.

'A Very Good Battle' – Smuts

Smuts has lost thirteen dead and fifty-seven wounded.

Writing home, he told his wife: 'We had a very good battle with the enemy in which he lost three maxims and one pom-pom. It had been a very warm day.' For the first time he felt the onset of fever. 'I shall use quinine for a week or two to drive all the poison out of me. I am amazed that I have not had fever sooner. Now that I am so far forward we do not get news, and I know little of what goes on in the great world or in other theatres of war. And I do not really worry about other things, for my hands are more than full. It is a hard task not only to fight and press forward but to keep these great masses of men and animals alive in this forest country . . .'

The 1st Division had fought the most successful action yet with a spirit that no physical exhaustion could quell. They had at last tasted the elation of victory. 'The enemy had been outwitted and defeated. The outflanking movement so often attempted had succeeded. For once,' concluded the official British account, 'the assault got home with the bayonet – the rarest of occurrences in this campaign. The whole force had gathered new confidence in itself and its commander.'

That then, was the outcome of the battle of Lukiguru.*

The army now had water in abundance and fields in which to forage. However, it was an army at the end of its tether.

---

* The German units under *Hauptmann* Doring numbered about five hundred in all. Their casualties were four Germans and thirty askaris found killed; twenty Germans and thirty-two askaris taken prisoner.

"Picking off the enemy"
(*East African Experiences 1916*, C W Shackleton, 1940)

CHAPTER

11

Smuts's Impressions of his Task

Richard Meinertzhagen was ever critical of his Commander-in-Chief. He accused him of creating an entirely false impression of the progress of the campaign in the 'fantastic' cables that he sent to the War Office.

> From these one would gather that Van Deventer, Brits, Enslin and Crowe were budding Napoleons. That fierce engagements were fought against overwhelming odds, our camps subjected to intense bombardments and that South Africans have shown themselves to be stubborn and determined fighters.
> But what are the facts? Van Deventer, Brits, Enslin and Crowe are incompetent gasbags, their official reports amounting to mere flatulence. Discipline does not exist, bush warfare is not understood, looting is rife, hospitals are full to overflowing with strong healthy men suffering from cold feet.

This was an extravagant outburst from a brilliant man who, at the time of this angry tirade was on the verge of a breakdown from overwork, an over-active imagination and the frustration of never being taken seriously by the generals. 'Smuts,' he complained, 'would not listen to the matured advice of his British staff, although he gulps down and digests any disconnected trash from a Boer scout.'

Presumably Pretorius!

How right was Meinertzhagen? How did Smuts see his campaign?

In a preface to a book on the campaign by General Crowe, Smuts recorded his own impression of the war, and of how well he had conducted it.

> When I arrived in February 1916 with South African reinforcements to take the offensive, I found opposed to me a very large army, in effective strength not much smaller than my own, well

trained and ably commanded, formidably equipped with artillery and machine guns, immune to most tropical diseases and able to live on the country, largely untroubled by transport difficulties and with a morale in some respects higher than that of our troops, who, in inferior strength, had borne the heat and the burden of the defence for the last eighteen months.

He described how he advanced the bulk of his force by night against the enemy's left flank, took from him the foothills of Kilimanjaro by surprise and 'without any effort on the morning of 8 March and within twenty-four hours' compelled him to vacate his 'practically impregnable' positions at Taveta.

Within twelve days he had complete possession of the entire Moshi-Arusha area, and finally drove the enemy army, after repeated defeats, over the Ruwu into the Pare Mountains and down the Tanga Railway towards the Usambara Mountains.

'Dauntless *élan*'

Never had I seen such a transformation in the spirits of opposing forces; our men who had retreated before the enemy in confusion at Salaita Hill now advanced with dauntless *élan*. The enemy, on whom fortune had hitherto smiled, now found himself suddenly and repeatedly manoeuvred out of his carefully prepared entrenchments . . .

Our object was not merely the defeat of the enemy but the effective occupation of his huge territory in the shortest possible time. Merely to follow the enemy in his very mobile retreat might prove an endless game, with the additional danger that the enemy forces might split into guerrilla bands doubling back in all directions and rendering effective occupation of the country impossible.

In view of the size of the country it was therefore necessary to invade it from various points with columns strong enough to deal with any combination that could be brought against them, and for these columns as they advanced to clear the country also laterally.

General Northey was operating eastwards and north-eastwards from Lake Nyasa; a Belgian column was launched eastwards from Lake Kivu [to the north of Lake Tanganyika]; in April another Belgian column and a British column were set in motion in a southerly direction from the Uganda border west of Lake Victoria Nyanza; a mounted brigade under Van Deventer was launched southwards from Arusha to Kondoa-Irangi, which is the most important strategic point on the interior plateau of the enemy territory.

And finally, towards the end of May, three columns advanced south-eastward from the Moshi area against the Pare Mountains and towards the Usambara Mountains.

His Gallant Boys

Here I will leave his summary for the moment at the place where his armies now stood and examine the cost of the campaign so far, details that apparently did not concern Smuts in his assessment of his achievement. True, he credited his men, describing how 'the gallant boys, marching far ahead under a pitiless African sun, with fever raging in their blood, pressed ever on after the retreating enemy, often on much reduced rations and without any of the small comforts which in this climate are real necessities.

'In the story of human endurance this campaign deserves a very special place, and the heroes who went through it uncomplainingly, doggedly, are entitled to all recognition and reverence.'*

In Smuts's view, he was fighting it in the only way in which it could be brought to successful conclusion, and that was by the conquest of the entire territory. But at that moment, in June 1916, with the battle of Lukiguru over, it was time to make a realistic assessment of the logistics and the future of the campaign.

Collyer, never a man to overstate a case, hit it exactly:

'Nature, flouted by this time to her limit, here took command. That it had been possible to keep on the move so long was due solely to the indomitable spirit and courage of the fighting soldiers of all units and to the splendid work of the personnel of the administrative units, transport, supply, and medical . . . along the difficult and drawn-out lines of communication.'

The gain, he considered, was worth the hardships; and Smuts could not be criticised for his hard driving. Once he had reached the bad water at Handeni he had had no choice but to go on. 'Hardship,' he wrote, 'is inseparable from war.' In the meantime, radical reorganisation was needed to keep the troops in action. Since 22 May the eastern force had marched and hacked its way for 250 miles. Only a month, but in that time it had been reduced by thirty per cent of its strength.

The difficulties in evacuating the sick were as great as those in bringing forward supplies. 'At Handeni,' wrote an officer of the Royal Army Service Corps, 'it seemed desperate. Rations were short for many

---

* Brett Young wrote of Smuts – 'This man's personality, remote, unsympathetic, cold, well-nigh inhuman as it seemed – impressed itself on the whole force as an incarnation of the will to conquer.'

Radio communications were chronically unreliable. Compounded with the almost total absence of reliable maps and information, this made communications nearly impossible between commanders.

days. No white flour had been issued for some time; hard biscuit eked out when mealie flour was provided . . . The only meat was the fly-blown trek ox, which had to be eaten at once as it would not keep.'

More Men than he Could Feed

Smuts had begun with fifteen thousand men . . . now, ironically, he had twenty thousand to provide for, the great mass of these additional mouths being the result of reinforcements coming forward and casualties going back. It was confusion all along the valley of the Pangani. The problem of motor transport was extreme. Everywhere trucks, lorries and cars were stranded for lack of spares for the variety of models. Nothing was standardised in this mixture of vehicles. Technical and supply services were no less vulnerable to climate and disease than the fighting men themselves.

Even more serious was the wastage of men sent back with lesser ailments and slight wounds. These disappeared into the maw of the system, languishing for weeks and months in unknown hospitals somewhere along the chain as far back as Mombasa and Nairobi.

Casualties other than those of battle in German East Africa were as high as thirty to one, which made it the worst front for sickness of any in the Kaiser's war. Mesopotamia came next, with twenty to one. Now as the force rested and recuperated as best as it could, Smuts had a fighting force reduced to half, as the Royal Army Service Corps (RASC) reported.

New Plans for Medical Cases

To stop the wastage it was now planned for hospitals to be closed behind the fighting troops, simple grass huts put up in an hour or two with the native type of bed made from available wood and fibre. That was exactly what the Germans had been doing. In such hospitals men would be treated with necessary drugs, simple medical care, those with fever kept warm with blankets instead of lying exposed on the ground in the delirium of malaria. Farther back more elaborate hospitals would be equipped to handle more serious cases.

It looked good on paper. No more loss of men for months at a time with huge wastage in base camps and transit camps and men lost to their own units for ever. There was only one snag: the transport to handle even so simple a method was not available. The RASC had suffered such casualties in men and transport that already it could not cope with existing needs, even though every vehicle available was being worked without cease.

Smuts, with his huge sprawling army spread back into the mountains, his supplies coming forward through fever-ridden areas, was dangerously extended. Von Lettow gave him no rest. The German tactics turned to sniping, ambush and the mining of roads. Soon every vehicle was running the gauntlet of German patrols far behind the lines.

Von Lettow noted: 'Even a staff car was effectively fired on.' General Hoskins was on the road between Korogwe and Handeni and almost in his own camp when a burst of firing from bush killed Captain Mullins, his aide-de-camp,* at his side. Other patrols hid in the high grass and bush alongside every route. They made daring night incursions behind Smuts's lines, where they lay in wait for the long columns of porters, and sent them in panicky flight into the undergrowth, throwing down their loads.

Guerrilla Tactics

Cutting and tapping telegraph lines was another enemy practice. Captain Dolby records moving towards Handeni with a small body of South Africans, Rhodesians and Fusiliers, returning from hospital. They were thirty miles behind the division when, at a turn in the road, they came on a number of askaris and several white men; one of whom was up the post, tapping the line.

---

* Molloy's version of this – or similar – incident tells of General Hannyngton ambushed between Kwa di Rema and Mshia. Two of his staff were killed. The General reached camp by escaping on foot.

Portable observation posts. These handy observation ladders, made at the Union Defence Force Ordnance Workshops, Pretoria, were used in the German-East campaign and proved exceedingly useful in a country of high grass and bush. The ladder is hinged and folded and then swung back on to the cart.

They all took to the bush when fire was opened, leaving their chop-boxes and a wounded German officer, who fired back furiously with his revolver at the bayoneting Fusiliers and killed one. 'We dressed his wound and gave him an injection of morphia, a cigarette and a good drink of brandy,' wrote Dolby. Meanwhile the men sat down to dispatch the contents of the chop-boxes – new bread, chocolates, sardines and many little delicacies.'

Private F H Cooper wrote of the danger to convoys. 'We were warned to be ready for snipers at any moment, and passed a big hole in the road beside which lay the remains of a Red Cross car, the work of a mining gang who had been there less than two days before'.*

If the Germans had been able to use disruptive tactics during the advance it might have been crippling; but with the army static it was more an annoyance than a hindrance. Von Lettow could not spare more men, but it did create the impression with Smuts's men that von Lettow was 'a master of bush tactics while we were all but incapable of retaliation, living on our nerves against this death that came from nowhere. You would be going about your camp task when suddenly there would be a shot, and a man would stumble and fall. By the time you reached for your rifle the bush had swallowed up the sniper.'

Secure in their tactics, the Germans had their tails up. It was a very different story for Smuts.

Severe Psychological Stress

Battle casualties had severely reduced the strength of the 5th and 6th South African regiments. The 2nd Rhodesians were down to a quarter of the brave force that had set out. Of the original eleven hundred Fusiliers, only two hundred were fit to answer roll-call. The East Lancs were no more than a single machine-gun company. The Indian regiments were reduced by two-thirds; even worse, these men, so brave in battle, were showing signs of psychological stress.

'They had no more interest in life,' wrote the surgeon Brett Young. 'Their souls were as sick as their bodies. It mattered nothing to them whether this detestable country, the scene of their exile and purgatory, were ruled by German or British.'

The striking edge of Smuts's weapon at the front was blunted. What did it avail that he had fifteen thousand useless mouths between them and Mombasa? The Germans were now on interior lines. While every step Smuts took drew him farther away from his main supply

---

* The diary of Captain E H Richardson, 8th SAI noted: 'The explosion I heard last night turned out to be a mine blowing up the leading car in a string of motor ambulances, car and man blown to smithereens.' (21 July 1916.)

bases, the Germans were getting nearer to the carefully stocked depots all along the Central Railway and to the fruitful country round Morogoro. They had stripped the country behind them of every bean and every stalk of millet and every wretched man who could carry a load.

Private Cooper has recorded how South African gunners coming forward to fill the gaps in units found themselves on a trail now trodden to a fine powdery dust so deep that eventually it had to be closed to traffic. Private Cooper and his companion were travelling with a supply column, so they lived well. 'We had more than ten days' rations with us, and our transport conductor was good for any more that we might require.' On this trek Cooper had his first experience of 'that truly misery-making parasite, the human louse. Although I frequently boiled my clothes and soaked them in petrol I was never rid of this scourge.'

Lions on Trail to the Front

At night the transport company kept big fires burning to keep predators from the mules; and the lions made the night hideous with their roarings.

There was also beauty on that road for anyone with eyes to see; but 'never for a moment could we forget there was war. The road grew ever more noisome with the rotting carcases of stricken animals. Oxen at first predominated. Then as we entered tsetse-fly areas, horses and mules lay along the path in daily increasing numbers. Nature's scavengers seemed rare, perhaps already surfeited with the putrid flesh of those tens of thousands fallen by the wayside.'

So they trudged on, covered with dust, in constant touch with the reality of death, frequently at the scene of recent battles. 'The corpses of askaris added to the general stench. The Germans never seemed to leave any white dead exposed, and almost invariably hid any trace of their losses. Frequently they buried them in shallow pits and then lit wood fires on the spot, the burnt ash concealing every sign of newly turned earth. Sometimes in haste they merely shovelled earth over a body.

'On one occasion,' confessed this sensitive recorder of his experiences, 'I was moved to cut the water-bottle from a dusky and dead warrior who had lain for two days in the tropical heat by the roadside. I felt only a sense of elation at securing a good German flask.' But in the end, the bloated face of the askari was too much for him. 'I gave it to a messmate who knew not its history.'

The new men came forward, marching from one camp to the next in the clouds of dust raised by as many as fifty waggons in a convoy with five hundred mules driven by shouting, whip-cracking Cape Corps muleteers.

Horse-Sickness Plays Havoc

Lt E H Richardson's diary records the march of the 8th SA Horse: 'Trekking through bush country on a very dusty road, everybody smothered in dust and unrecognisable . . . Transport in difficulty; one or two overturned.' Then into the jungles of the Pangani, on half-rations. 'Horses beginning to die from horse-sickness, also mules. Found two of my horses sick and dying. Can hear lions about at night-time.'

And next day: 'Both my horses dead. Horse-sickness playing havoc with regimental horses.' And three days later on the march: 'Trekked away at 4 a.m. from the Pangani. Passed innumerable dead horses.' At that point the 8th had to form a dismounted troop of men whose horses had died.

Such was the scene all the way back through the fever-ridden Pangani valley and farther north to the Pare Mountains and back to the railway line from the coast, where the overburdened tracks were carrying an equal volume of traffic moving away from the battle zone for fresh supplies. Huge dumps were growing along the route where men who could have been in battle were stationed to guard supplies and see to all the other duties that keep nine men out of battle for every one at the fighting front. And even farther back were the service depots and workshops and railwaymen and harbour experts and base hospitals and base headquarters staffs of redtab officers who would never hear a shot fired. The whole cumbersome, unbalanced proliferation of the needs of an army of invasion and the farther back you went the less understanding of what was happening. The gaunt, yellow-faced men in tattered clothing coming back were regarded as shirkers from the front.

But so it is in every army, and always has been so that the man at the sharp end asks for no more than food in his belly, sound boots on his feet and enough ammunition; and if he is lucky, the arrival of a few comforts such as cigarettes and letters from home. If he has confidence in his commander, his morale stays high.

Von Lettow Turns Back East

Von Lettow was also assessing his own situation at that time. He concluded that of the two forces penetrating his territory Smuts's was the more dangerous. He decided to leave Van Deventer to stew in his own juice. He would march his main body back to Dodoma and leave only a small detachment to face the 2nd Division. From Dodoma he would take his men by train to Morogoro and, from there, march east in support of Major Kraut.

Drawing of a German machine-gun post by von Lettow-Vorbeck's adjutant.

The redoubtable major was busily digging in his maxims and rifles on Kanga Mountain, north-east of Turiani. Von Lettow found him and his askaris 'in excellent spirits and full of confidence'. There was no sign of a demoralised and beaten army falling back before a better force. He noted: 'They have cleared the foreground for fifty to a hundred yards and are ready to beat off any attack.'

Meanwhile Smuts endeavoured to gather as much information as possible about developments in front of him. Meinertzhagen's intelligence men were sent out on dangerous duties far behind enemy lines. On one such expedition Lieutenant Arnold Weinholdt and two others set out with four black soldiers and five mules to reconnoitre German activity on the Nguru Mountains.

They were actually near von Lettow's headquarters when they intercepted a supply column. Pretending to be a German officer, Weinholdt ordered the startled porters to set down their loads and burn them. More than six tons of goods, including large quantities of sausages and cases of schnapps, went up in smoke.

Von Lettow recorded with amusement that what aroused 'painful interest' in the ragged *Schutztruppe* was the burning of a large consignment of much-needed trousers sent out from Germany in a blockade-running cargo boat. Before Weinholdt could extricate his men, who were making the most of the fare, he was ambushed and slightly wounded. He was taken to von Lettow, who appeared to enjoy the meeting and questioned him only about personal matters:

'I'm an Australian, Sir.'

'But your name is German.'

'Originally, I believe from Bremen, though not for the last three centuries.'

Since he was slightly wounded in the hip his guards were slack, and Weinholdt got away, hoping to join his two companions and make his way back to base; but only to be recaptured.

'None of us,' wrote von Lettow, 'could help honestly admiring the excellent work of his patrol, whose route was accurately marked on the map in his possession.'

The German patrols were also active in the Nguru Mountains and were being watched by the tireless Major Pieter Pretorius who, with his natives, reported all German activity; and from time to time he recounted hair-raising encounters and almost casual killings of Germans taken unaware. He cared nothing for the fact that he now had a price on his head.

Smuts Down with Malaria

To the west at Kondoa-Irangi Van Deventer was also patrolling and intercepting German messages. From them he learned that von Lettow was withdrawing his main force to Mahenge and Iringa, where Governor Schnee had set up his civil authority. He decided to see Smuts, and arrived at Luchimo to find Smuts down with malaria contracted on the Pangani.

The fever, which persisted on and off for the rest of his life as a legacy of the campaign, did not spare Smuts the work of co-ordinating the advance of the Belgians and Portuguese armies and that of General Northey from Nyasaland.

Van Deventer poured out his problems. He had over seven hundred men in hospital and over three hundred in convalescent camps where the food shortage was so acute that there was little chance for men to recover strength enough for active service. Most of his sick were lying on the ground. They were out of clothing, boots and soap.

Smuts told him that his own force was no better off. 'In the past month I've lost fifteen hundred men from Hoskin's division of 5 500.' There was simply nothing he could offer Van Deventer except to confirm the news that von Lettow was likely to relinquish his hold on Kondoa-Irangi.

Of his own situation he said:

'I expect fighting all the way from Lukiguru. Every man not fighting will be bridge-building, road-making and bush-cutting. After that we must drive south another hundred miles through the Uluguru Mountains to Kissaki and the Mgeta River . . . The hope is that one supreme effort will finish it there.'

Van Deventer's Marching Orders

Van Deventer was given his orders. 'You are to march south from Kondoa-Irangi to Kilimatinde and the Central Railway and from there east to Kilossa, and then southward to the Great Ruaha River . . . all in one continuous advance.'

It would be fighting all the way in awful country, in an appalling climate for white soldiers; altogether about eight hundred miles. It is possible that only a commander with Van Deventer's background and temperament could have tackled it. The taciturn Boer welcomed the challenge. 'Just give me fresh men, horses and supplies, I'll get there . . . to Morogoro, by the last week in August.'

Smuts knew what losses he was heading for. 'Efforts like these,' he wrote, 'cannot be made without inflicting the greatest hardship on all, but it is equally true to say that the commander who shrinks from such efforts should stay at home.'

With his knowledge and memory of Boer tactics in the Boer War Smuts was well aware that the occupation of a huge territory was meaningless as long as the enemy had freedom to rove behind him with highly mobile guerrilla bands. And never was there a country better suited to that. Von Lettow had left pockets of men in the east already, and these bands were now harrying Smuts's lines of communication. Ruthless tactics were necessary to stop these depredations.

'All bridges in the area bounded by the Pangani, the Indian Ocean and the road from Korogwe and Lukiguru are to be destroyed. Native chiefs are to be told that no new bridges may be built and that those destroyed are not to be repaired.'

Satisfied that he had done all that he could, Smuts prepared for the next phase of the campaign: the drive on the Central Railway running from Mombasa across the country to Lake Tanganyika.

Low Morale at Kondoa-Irangi

Van Deventer had certainly not exaggerated the situation at Kondoa-Irangi to his Commander. The morale of soldiers under constant enemy vigilance with little prospect of action was low, as it always is. When Van Deventer returned from his visit to Smuts the mood of his men was typified by an entry in Private Thompson's diary that rumours of an armistice had been in the wind. His return now started the new and dismaying rumour 'that there is more fighting and trekking ahead, which makes us feel rather gloomy'.

Life had become a monotonous routine. Dudley Phipson of the 4th Battery wrote that about 2 a.m. each morning 'a section of two guns was sent out to a nek outside the town to engage the enemy, who had firmly entrenched themselves on a hill four or five miles away, on which they had planted their 4.1-inch naval guns.' The South African thirteen-pounders were far outranged and were often under fire.

'Conditions during this period were extremely trying. All transport had been left behind . . . Not only was our clothing worn out, but what rations were issued consisted only of dirty rice, a quantity of which had been found in the old burnt-out fort and taken over by the

South African 13-pounder gunners at Mtama near Lindi.

commissariat for issue to the troops. It was full of grit and stones, and only the alternative of starving made it possible for us to eat it. The only other issue was meat, usually pretty high and flyblown by the time we got it. We scraped off the blow-fly eggs before putting it into the pot . . .'

But with the return of Van Deventer there was a stiffening of training to bring new gunners up to scratch. Thompson recorded the daily programme:

'The routine was saddle-up at 5 a.m. Gun drill at 6 a.m. Stables at 7.30 a.m. Breakfast at 8.30 a.m. Horses out to graze at 10 a.m. Clean-up camp till 11.30 a.m. Gun-laying at 12 p.m. Lunch at 1 p.m. Gun-laying at 2 p.m. Horses at 4 p.m. Stables at 5 p.m. Dinner at 6 p.m.'

The 'Daily Hate!'

During these activities the 'daily hate' went on as the German naval shells from the guns salvaged from the *Königsberg* came whistling in. They burst with loud detonations but little damage, as they were designed to penetrate heavy armour plate. Buried deep in the soil, they exploded harmlessly.

Jackson, a gunner arriving to reinforce the 2nd Battery, had just turned out the mules to graze after their long trek when: 'Boom!' went the big gun, and a shell came whizzing overhead and landed about fifty yards from our men marching in. Eight shells came over, then our howitzers opened up and they quietened down a bit.' Later that afternoon when they were rounding up the animals they had to gallop bareback as the guns opened up again. 'We were trapped in the river bank till after dark. The shells were bursting just over the bank, so we had to keep low and hang on to the horses.'

Thompson's apprehensive forecast of pending action was correct. Ahead of them lay another hard march towards the Central Railway across a waterless, boulder-strewn territory crossed by dried riverbeds. It was a place where even the wild animals were short of water, and patrolling horsemen rode for miles every night in search of pans that might not be dry.

Van Deventer's 2nd Division now had the 1st, 2nd 3rd, 4th and 9th SA Horse in its 1st SA Mounted Brigade. On their feet were the 9th, 10th, 11th and 12th SA Infantry with the East African Volunteer Machine-gun Company, in addition to their own maxims. He had four batteries of artillery, the 1st, 2nd and 4th Permanent SA Field Batteries and the 28th Mounted (Indian) Battery. At division were the SA Motor Cycle Corps and a light armoured-car battery.

Visit by Louis Botha

As if to give the army the rise in morale that it needed, General Louis Botha arrived at Smuts's headquarters on 20 July. The news went round like wildfire. This was the man who had driven the Germans from the deserts of South West Africa, a man who knew warfare in Africa from the Boer War days onwards. Now, as Prime Minister of the Union, he came despite much hostility from the parliamentary opposition, which constantly threw up the ruinous cost of supporting the

With General Botha in German East. On the road from Mombo to Wilhelmstal (on the Tanga-Moshi Railway). The figures are (left to right): General Deely, General Botha, and Captain Louis Botha.

British Empire. But here in Nderema he was with old comrades. 'Nearly every man with Smuts at this time had been in South West,' wrote Collyer, 'and now the sight of their former commander produced the extraordinary effect of encouragement and confidence which his presence never failed to arouse.'

In the short time with Smuts Botha discussed the campaign and affairs at home in an atmosphere of mutual esteem. He went with Smuts to inspect the forward position. As a soldier he had a deep appreciation of the obstacles, the hardships and the success so far. He left Smuts with the intention of visiting his old comrade Van Deventer.

General Collyer's history says that Botha visited Van Deventer at Kondoa-Irangi; but in fact he never reached there. When he got to Moshi he fell ill. In a letter to Smuts written from Kilindini, where he was waiting for a ship to go home, he wrote:

'We Pray for Your Success'

'I am deeply disappointed that I was not able to visit Van Deventer and his commando . . . Now quite better, had a severe attack of dysentery in the end.' In the same letter he wrote: 'Now that I have seen all your operations here and understand your difficulties, I admire more than ever your having done so much in the time. I am proud of your work, old chap, and on leaving can only say that all my influence is at your disposal, and be assured Jannie, we pray for your success and safe return.'

Botha was hardly gone when Van Deventer sent out a flying column to reach Dodoma as the first important objective of the new plan. At once the atmosphere of gloom evaporated. Thompson watched the 'howitzers and the *Pegasus*'s* naval guns going forward as well as the SA Horse. General van Deventer passed us in his motor.'

The hills above the town were abandoned by the enemy. Thompson went to look at the empty German trenches, 'mostly dugouts and bombproof shelters. Bandas were very well made, especially the hut used as an officers' mess.'

Below him stretched the jingling panoply of a dusty army moving forward, its advance troops ready to clash with the enemy rearguard. Gunner Jackson noted: 'We headed across the front of the German positions to a kopje behind which we got ready for action. The position we were to have shelled was taken by the infantry without opposition.'

---

* The cruiser *Pegasus* had shelled the wireless mast at Dar es Salaam on 6 August 1914, two days after war was declared. She was later sunk by the *Königsberg*, and her guns were salvaged for the land war, served by her own gunners.

Next day his battery followed up the retiring Germans along the road to Kilimatindi.

> We were forced to halt at sundown. They had burnt a wooden bridge, and a drift had to be made. We saw one of their hospitals, everything arranged with thoroughness and attention to detail. Though only grass huts, yet beds had been made, whereas our men, even so far back as Lol Kissale, had to lie on the ground.
> There was also a cemetery by the roadside with the remains of about eight Germans, very neatly arranged with a fence round it and a cross on each grave. One of our men had been buried there, evidently a prisoner who had died.

A patrol of the SA Horse galloped in with one of their men dead.

> They had sewn him up in a blanket and lashed a pole down each side, and he passed us slung over his horse's back. At 3 p.m. our right section came into action just alongside the road, the Germans were reported to be about eleven hundred yards away on the other bank of a dry riverbed. Deep holes had to be dug in the sand to yield even one bucket per animal.

Another Long, Thirsty Trek

So Van Deventer's new trek set out. Nearly a hundred miles of arid country, rich in game but little else, lay ahead. It was a country where men had fought for the waterholes from time immemorial, which the slave caravans had crossed from central Africa at their last gasp to the bountiful springs. Van Deventer's men knew where they were, but they would have to fight for every one. Captain Klinghardt's eight companies of seasoned askaris were ready to dispute their ownership.

Von Lettow wrote that the retirement was a difficult manoeuvre. The trick was to know the right moment to fall back, halt again, make the counter-attack then break off to the next point of defence.

As the division creaked and clattered its way out of Kondoa-Irangi it was well aware of what lay ahead. Instead of pelting rains and swollen rivers it would be dry dongas and endless vistas of grey bush. Records of that march have been left by official reports and by men who endured it. The transport was still in a miserable state but Van Deventer's brigade had been given new mounts. Almost as soon as they set out, it became a thirstland trek. Another test of endurance for man and beast. The mounted men rode ahead to seize the known watering places; the marching infantry came on behind, and behind them lumbered the guns and heavy equipment.

From the first days of the march it was a severe ordeal. According to Shackleton they marched all day, and as soon as packs were off the men got down on all fours and dug through the sand with their hands for water – 'like a crowd of children building sandcastles'. Scratching at arm's length, his comrade Somers still reached no water.

'My arm's longer than yours,' said Shackleton. A few inches lower down he brought up a fistful of wet sand. 'Eagerly picking up our tin mugs, we had a maddening wait of many minutes before enough water seeped through. Then half an hour's wait to fill our bottles.'

Next day the regiment stopped at a second dry riverbed and again they filled their bottles in the same way. They were busy at this when 'suddenly there came a deep rumbling sound from up river'. They had hardly scrambled onto the bank when a wall of water bearing trees and debris rushed past. A cloudburst up river! Next day the regiment tramped on till 9 p.m.

At 8 a.m. they were on the march again. Towards midday dense clouds of smoke could be seen ahead. 'The enemy had set fire to a wide stretch of grassland and bush over a front a few miles wide.' The march continued among smouldering trees with fire still raging on either side. The heat was too much to bear and the regiment fell back, covered with ash from head to foot. The joke went about: 'So you've joined the black brigade.'

The Fight for Waterholes

Meanwhile the mounted brigade moved fast. Van Deventer had divided his division into five columns, and there was sharp fighting at

10,5 cm gun of the *Königsberg,* mounted on a mobile gun carriage in action on the Lukiguru bridge.

the sparse watering places. The Germans held off the thirsty men and frantic horses at Tissa-Kwameda and at Naju and Membe, where they commanded the only waterholes for scores of miles.

Deneys Reitz was with one such column that had to fight for its water. He was sent out with a patrol to find a reputed pan where animals drank, and arrived there to find it trampled to mud by a herd of elephant. 'I sent back a man to report the water and went on.' That night lions roared all round the camp; and next day at Hanetti, a desolate village with a few muddy waterholes, he was told that the Germans had a strong rearguard at the next water, at Chenene.

Towards evening he relates, a weary horseman rode in from the 1st and 3rd mounted regiments. They had made a flank attack march of twenty-four hours without water, and when they approached Chenene they found the enemy holding the watering place in force. The 1st and 3rd were in poor condition. There was no possibility of their riding to any other source of water.

Into Van Deventer's headquarters rode a dusty horseman. Lurching from the saddle, he reported that they needed reinforcements to attack and seize the water. Van Deventer's men were too done in to make a forced march in support. 'Take the wells at all costs,' was his order to the messenger.

'Charge for the Wells!'

Deneys Reitz volunteered to take the order and so witnessed a rare spectacle, the kind of mounted charge that had not been seen since Churchill's ride with the British cavalry at Omdurman.

> Soon after daybreak we heard the crackle of rifle fire, and pushing forward, were just in time to see our mounted men gallop across a wide clearing at the far end of which lay the enemy around the wells. Desperate with thirst they had anticipated Van Deventer's instructions, and were riding full tilt upon the rifle pits. The enemy had opened up a ragged fire, but as we hurried up we saw several hundred askaris rise to their feet and make for the bush behind. Their German officers seemed to be trying to stop them, then they followed their men and the fight was over. Three or four men had been wounded in the charge.
> It was now a pleasure to see horses and men drinking their fill from the cool, clear waters, for these are famous wells, known for their excellent and abundant supply.

The way ahead lay through dense bush, and next day at a kloof flanked by rugged hills a fierce little battle began. Into this action there

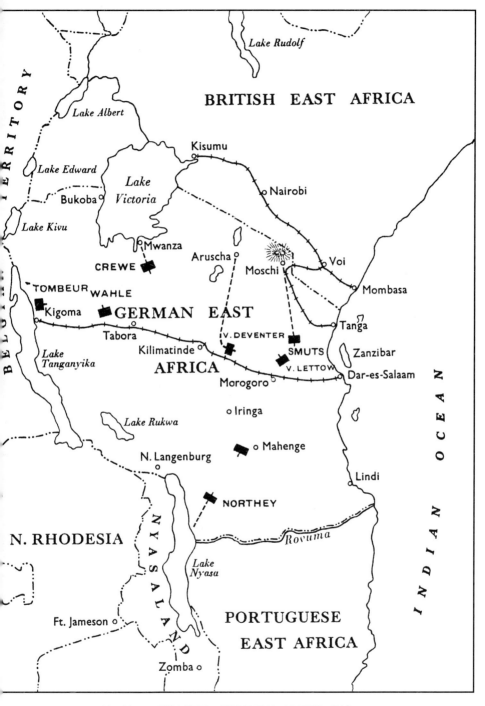

STRATEGIC SITUATION AT THE END OF JULY, 1916.

(*The South Africans with General Smuts in German East Africa 1916,*
Brig-Gen Collyer, 1939)

drove two Rolls-Royce armoured cars, just arrived from base and sent immediately into action. Captain Goldberg charged the enemy position, with machine-gun bullets rattling like hail off the armour, firing his maxims as they roared forward.

Hilgaard de Jager, Van Deventer's chief scout, had never seen anything like it. He clapped Reitz on the back, crying: 'My God, man, those things look for all the world like two rhino bulls charging upwind!'

The enemy broke, leaving their dead on the road and under the trees. After a night's rest the advance continued to Mei-Mei, another waterhole. There De Jager and his motley band of irregulars captured a detachment of the 9th Field Company, all Europeans, mounted on little Somali mules.

Distributing the Loot

'I did not see this fight,' wrote Reitz, 'but I arrived in time to see the old major distributing the loot among his followers.' Among the prisoners were two surly young Transvaal Boers. A few days later he saw De Jager again. The old major was lying, dangerously wounded, at the waterhole at Njamgalo. He had been shot below the heart but was in good spirits, begging Reitz not to make him laugh or it would kill him.

By 30 July 1st Mounted Brigade was on the railway line at Kikombo Station and eager to ride into Dodoma next day. But between them and the town lay Dodoma Nek, a narrow defile strongly held with machine guns. Behind the mounted men marched the infantry. They had been going hard for five days and a day of hard fighting lay ahead of them and the illusory comforts of Dodoma . . . if the Germans had left anything.

The fight went on all day, with the Indian Mounted Battery in action and at sunset the Germans withdrew. When skirmishers entered the village next morning it was empty.

Shackleton's regiment camped in a field of sweet potatoes that night, and it rained incessantly. The men with fever lay under groundsheets, burning and shivering in their tattered clothing. But at first light they were on the march again. Ahead the crackle of rifle fire could be heard, and the first wounded were coming back to the cement floor of the hastily contrived hospital at Dodoma.

Shackleton and a companion collapsed with malaria. They were only two of the fifty thousand cases of malaria in Smuts's army in 1916 out of 58 000 troops in East Africa. In 1917 the figure rose to 72 000 cases, of which 499 were fatal.

Shackleton, oblivious of figures, survived this attack, and three days later: 'My fellow sufferer was brought out in a blanket and consigned to the care of the cold earth.' Dodoma was the final resting place of many.

But the objective was reached. Reitz's first glimpse of Dodoma was a gleam of white buildings on the plain, the railway station and the hard glitter of the railway line. 'It was a great moment. We were astride the Central Railway at last.'

It was 29 July; five days before Smuts's offensive in the east began on 4 August 1916.

GERMAN DISGUISES

It was stated in Brigade Orders that the enemy were in the habit of disguising themselves, sometimes as Indians and sometimes as Natives.

(*'Jambo' or with Jannie in the Jungle*, AW Lloyd, undated)

12

Smuts's Drive in the Eastern Mountains

4 August 1916. The war had been in progress for two years. Those who had joined up in the expectation of quick victory – 'all over by Christmas!' had twice had to shift the year forward. While Smuts had been rapidly advancing his army, the French, German and British on the Western Front were suffering losses by hundreds of thousands for no gain in ground. Smuts had written that he had no idea what was going on in the greater war zone.* But one officer, coming out of the mincing machine of the Somme, where British sacrifices made possible the relief of the French fortress of Verdun, wrote: 'We have just come out of a place so terrible that . . . a raving lunatic could never imagine the horror of the last thirteen days.'

It was a year that saw the German chance of outright victory vanish; and by the end of it Britain would have to take up the main burden on the Western Front.

In Smuts's army British-born men chaffed to be done with this sideshow in the bush and shed their blood in Europe. In South Africa, the call was persistent for more men. The Union had already raised a brigade for Europe under Brigadier-General Tim Lukin, and it had found itself in Egypt, fighting a Senussi rising armed by the Turks.

In a swift engagement near Sidi Barrani – so well-known to the sons of these men in a later war – Lukin's brigade smashed through the Senussi defences in a brilliant charge of cavalry and infantry and caught the enemy on the retreat. The Dorset yeomanry galloped into action in two lines, while the 3rd SA Infantry broke into the enemy line and captured many prisoners, including the Commander-in-Chief, Gaafer Pasha.

---

* How little they were told is evident from an entry in the diary of Captain Richardson, 8th SA Horse, of 20 July 1916: 'Good news from Flanders today. British capture second line enemy trenches.' No mention of the cost.

Delville Wood's Grim Toll

Two months later the brigade was in France at the most critical month in the Western Front campaign. On 15 July the South Africans were assigned the attack on Delville Wood, where for six days and five nights they fought off repeated German attacks and endless bombardment in which 'the darkness of night was turned by shells and liquid fire into a feverish and blazing noon'.

In this month of July, when Smuts was claiming success in East Africa, the South Africans in France suffered 2 815 casualties. Yet in South Africa, as the casualty figures were published with the appalling lists of dead, wounded and missing, there was a cry for more men for France. Civic leaders and the clergy spouted a great deal of patriotic wind, and the hunt was on for shirkers, those wretches who shrank from their duty to the Motherland.

How it was that Smuts had no word of this can only be explained by the state of communications and his own presence at the forefront of his army. That such a holocaust should have passed him by without mention and even by Louis Botha, who was still in East Africa in the first days of August, is significant, showing how this war in isolation was totally absorbed in itself.

Even before the new offensive began prisoners had assured Meinertzhagen's Intelligence staff that they could count on von Lettow hanging on till the bitter end and cheerfully assured them that the worst was still to come: 'After the Nguru Mountains you will not be able to use cavalry . . . the tsetse fly will finish them all.'

A Surprise Offer to von Lettow

Already it appeared to Smuts's Chief of Staff that those prisoners were right; that von Lettow would not stand and fight on the Central Railway. It was more likely that he would abandon the main port of Dar es Salaam and withdraw his force intact south of the railway towards Mahenge and Iringa. There was still an immense space to be fought over.

'Smuts knew all too well that when he hit the railway his cavalry would cease to exist . . . or die faster than he could replace mounts. He knew, too, that if the immediate operation did not complete the campaign he would be entering a territory where white troops could not exist, only native soldiers.'

So thought Collyer; and Smuts agreed.

By then Meinertzhagen had come to a conclusion about Smuts as a man and a soldier: 'His knowledge of human nature, his exceptional power of imposing his will on others, his remarkable personality, reckless disregard of difficulties and his very remarkable brain, compel one

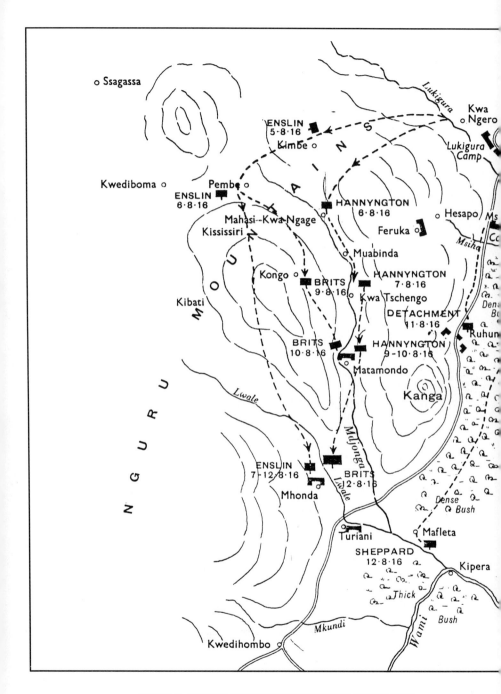

GENERAL SMUTS'S OPERATIONS IN NGURU MOUNTAINS

(*The South Africans with General Smuts in German East Africa 1916,*
Brig-Gen Collyer, 1939)

to respect and admire him. He is a bad tactician and strategist, an indifferent general, but in many ways a remarkable soldier.'

But he was always an amateur to the professionals.

With all these preoccupations Smuts had to make a commander's decision: to press on relentlessly or find a less costly solution. With immense waste behind and the prospects of worse ahead, was there perhaps some other way?

Quite unexpectedly he decided to treat with the enemy.

For one so implacable in the execution of his decisions this was astounding to his staff. Already it was recognised that white troops were unsuited to this country. Indeed, by that time Smuts had the 2nd and 3rd King's African Rifles under his command, and these were soon to show the superior stamina and swiftness of the black soldier on African ground.

Had the idea of treating been raised during Botha's visit? Would the kind of generous treatment that Botha's government had given the Germans in South West Africa the year before sway British opinion towards something similar? The idea was tentatively put before Sir Henry Fielding, the Governor of British East Africa.

If the German general would agree to some generous proposal it 'would save millions on expenditure involved in prolonging the campaign in the far south'. There is no doubt that Smuts looked south, far south, with trepidation, and in fact with little hope that von Lettow would agree. In the event, the British governor quietly shelved the proposal and nothing was said although it was no doubt the origin of a rich crop of rumours of armistice.

Nothing is worse for the morale of troops than the notion that it is all over. In Collyer's opinion 'General Smuts's suggestions were largely misunderstood by those to whom he addressed them.' Perhaps they were astonished that he should have made them at all; after all, he was in their eyes a hero and a victorious general. The British press was full of his triumphs so far. The illustrated papers showed him in the field as an antidote to the grim news from France, surveying 'an East African battlefield from his armoured car as motorcycle dispatch riders stand by to carry his orders'.

Men Rested and Ready

His men were rested, and with new boots and a replenishment of supplies they were as ready as they would ever be for the challenge of the Nguru Mountain defences. Scouts had brought back news that the roads through were heavily mined. At Ruhungu the defence positions were across the motor road, with sheer mountain on one side and dense bush on the other.

Here the Germans had cleared a 150 yard field of fire; and if the attackers got through the machine guns they would fall into pits filled with sharpened stakes. On the overhanging hills, caves and rifle pits were dug, with command-posts hewn out of solid rock. It had all the marks of a deathtrap. The mountain mass covered thirty miles in length by twenty miles at its widest. One single road ran through it. The foothills were defended by machine-gun ambushes and by snipers in tree platforms.

However, scouts had reported that there was a 'practicable route' for transport by following the valleys of two rivers.

General Sheppard's 1st Brigade was to hold the Germans in their main position barely four miles south of his camp at Ruhungu. The 2nd Brigade under General Hannyngton would drive through the middle, only ten miles to the west. Meanwhile General Coen Brits of the 3rd Brigade – another ten miles west – would be going hell for leather round the mass to emerge from the southern foothills and cut the road behind von Lettow. Brits had the 5th, 6th, 7th and 8th South African Horse in his 2nd Brigade under General Enslin and two battalions of infantry, the 5th and 6th Infantry under General Beves.

Battalions at Half Strength

Smuts had altogether eleven infantry battalions at half strength, seven thousand rifles against von Lettow's three thousand in twenty companies with heavy and light artillery. Smuts's advantage of two to one in men was more than outweighed by the fact that he was the attacker.

Even before the push began Smuts had made it clear that if the movement did not succeed the enemy must be pursued and encircled on the Central Railway. Van Deventer was to make for Kilossa as fast as possible and capture the enemy units not mobile enough to escape farther south. That was the plan.

'What no one had reckoned on,' wrote a transport officer, 'was that there was not a chance in hell of getting the transport through. Whoever said it was practicable, to scouts maybe, was crazy.'

But Smuts was committed to his strategy of out-manoeuvring the enemy from his positions, and the advance began on 3 August. It was eventually to bring him to Morogoro and result in the occupation of the Central Railway from Dodoma to Dar es Salaam, a distance of three hundred miles.

Within a day of marching off, the flanking columns had to abandon their transport. The main body under Sheppard was hacking its way through elephant grass so thick that it had to abandon its route and find another along the right bank of the Lukiguru. The troops, already without water, were felling trees to make corduroy strips across

A German observation post.

swamps or dragging waggons over slopes where the oxen had failed and cutting paths where none had existed. Within this jungle nightmare the marksmen of the *Schutztruppe* were picking them off from platforms in trees.

Transport Could Not Follow

The 7th SA Horse had vanished into the forest and at last joined the central column after a night march, dragging their horses through dark mountain passes where a stumble meant a broken leg and a yawning chasm precipitated horse and rider onto the rocks below. At intervals the night was lit by the flash of machine guns as the lurking askaris opened fire. Everyone was cursing the scouts for their idea of a practicable route, and at headquarters, as news of their slow progress came back, they were saying it had been a mistake to depend on the assessment of bushwhackers.

'Competent administrative staff officers should have gone with them,' fumed Collyer. It was now too late for that.

The 8th SA Horse were also marching on the flank. Colonel Murray Smith gave the order to advance on 5 August. They drove off an enemy patrol that day and camped about 10 p.m. 'It rained hard during the night, everybody drenched,' wrote Captain Richardson. 'Moved at 6 a.m. till 9 a.m., camped and dried blankets. No food for horses except grazing. Soon afterwards we captured about two thousand head of stock in the charge of some askaris, who fled.'

Richardson's squadron was rearguard to the regiment. It was slow work following the captured sheep and cattle through very difficult country; 'just kaffir paths along mountainsides. Regiment lost several pack mules and horses over precipices.' Still they did not abandon this valuable acquisition of meat on the hoof. Some were lost in bogs, and the sheep refused to go through the river. In pitch dark they made camp at 10 p.m. 'Horses and men dead beat. Put out picquets 10.30.'

Next day they passed through beautiful forests in the mountains where trees stood a hundred and fifty feet high and ten feet in diameter. Everywhere there were orchids, huge ferns and bracken.

> Caught up with the regiment . . . had terrible time getting through drifts blocked by cattle and smothered in mud from whipping horses through bogs. It appears the regiment got only just in time to Rhonda Mission Station. Colonel Murray Smith went out to arrange about picquets and walked right into the enemy. Heavy fighting for about an hour; enemy with three machine guns. Our two maxims under Lieutenant Strickland did good work.

Driven Off in Confusion

> Enemy driven off in confusion, leaving tripods of maxims, also other parts and kit. Colonel Murray Smith wounded in the back. Major Wilson shot through the helmet but not wounded. One maxim gunner, two men of the 8th and one of the 6th killed.*

At the mission Richardson's company found German Sisters of Mercy, some women and children, and some sick. His men were dead beat, but they had to stand to about 4 a.m. and the horses remained saddled all night.

Wednesday 9 August: 'At 10.30 a.m. we heard heavy firing. Our squadron ordered to saddle up and connect with the troops engaged under Lieutenant Sandy Malcolmson. On arriving at a bridge [suspension rope bridge] we dismounted, linked horses and walked across. Firing had ceased.'

On the other side they encountered men of two troops retiring in disorder. 'No officers with them. Captain Bodley took command and

---

* And six men of SAH wounded.

sent me to the left with orders to link up with Malcolmson. He took the right.

> After going about five hundred yards my front file reported seeing about thirty of the enemy in front. Country very thick bush and long grass with here and there a field of kaffir corn twelve to eighteen feet high. No hope of getting off the paths.
>
> I spread the men out as well as possible. We advanced again and came to a position that I thought might be held to advantage. Heavy firing then came from the direction Captain Bodley had taken. Bullets coming over us. I changed my front to face the direction of the fire. Lieutenant Essery came up and considered it necessary to get back to the bridge. But I held position and advised him to take position to command approaches to the bridge.

Now, to add to the confusion, Captain Bodley turned up with Malcolmson's troop. They reported that they had walked to within five yards of the hidden enemy, about two hundred strong.

> Malcolmson was in front as he topped the ridge. They opened fire point blank. Malcolmson sank down and never moved or spoke. The firing was so hot that the men tumbled down the hill, one man had his helmet shot off, one his shirt torn off and another his boot shot off. Trooper Hawkins reported that Malcolmson's tunic had a large hole through the side above the belt and he could see blood through the tunic.
>
> The enemy being too strong for us, we retired across the bridge and returned to camp, dismounted, off-saddled and took up a defensive position. At 5.30 we returned to our horses and had something to eat. Later we got into our trenches for the night.

Next day Richardson saw enemy shells falling round the mission station. 'The monks and nuns were very nervous.' Then the sound of aircraft was heard, and bombing, and the shelling ceased.

> They did no great damage; one officer of the SA Horse was killed. They shelled the hospital and damaged the building containing our wounded and the women. The enemy are retiring from their positions in front of our old camp at Lukiguru, and I suppose the shelling is to try and keep us from heckling their retreat to Morogoro.

Richardson spent a wakeful night.

No word of poor old Malcolmson. We miss him very much indeed. I do hope his wound has not proved mortal and that the enemy have been humane enough to save his life. I don't think the Germans would neglect him, but these askaris are savages, and if all the yarns are true, very cruel to the wounded.

Friday 11 August. 5.30 p.m. Have been busy entrenching and strengthening the position that we hold. The enemy shelled the hospital this morning and put three shells through the church, also killed Lieutenant Pole of the 5th SA Horse and two or three men of that regiment.

Aeroplanes passed over regularly bombing the Germans, but as soon as they had returned the shelling began again and Richardson recorded:

They are still at it at 5.30 p.m. Warned that the enemy were advancing . . . Nothing occurred. Spent anxious night as the position was undermanned.

Saturday 12 August: Stood to arms at 4.30 a.m. At 6.30 allowed some men to go down the valley and cook some food for the troops. Startled by rifle fire on Captain Bodley's position. Messenger stated that the scouts of the infantry brigade had fired on his picquet by mistake. All greatly relieved by the arrival of the column.

Sunday 13 August: Had breakfast and formed search party to seek for Lieutenant Malcolmson. It took us (dismounted) an hour and a half to climb to the position that Sandy was sent to. After searching for some time we found his grave, only about twelve inches deep, with a note on a split stick reading: 'Lieutenant Malcolmson 9.VIII.16'

South African gunners manhandle a field gun into position.

We dug a deep grave with our bayonets and buried him decently. Carved a deep cross on a big tree and wrote his name. Captain Bodley was too affected to say much, but what he did say was very dignified and solemn. Sandy had been shot through the chest and out the right side of the spine. We returned to camp sadly and found the regiment gone. After having some food we saddled up and trekked on, and caught up with the regiment at Turiani.* The enemy were in full retreat towards Morogoro.

Coen Brits's brigade was to be thoroughly cursed for not managing to link up with the central column; but from Richardson's description of their difficulties there was little chance of their going any faster. It was on 14 August that he recorded: 'Crossed a river and through long grass. Saw an ebony tree. Came in touch with General Sheppard's column.' As will be seen, it was too late, and Sheppard's column had also been in sharp fighting. It had marched for six days before it fought a fierce action, scaling the heights at Matomondo and surprising the detachment under Captain Stemmermann.

Contesting Every Inch at Matomondo

Lieutenant Molloy described that action as he saw it with the 5th battalion:

> Unfortunately our artillery had to be left behind three days before owing to the utter impassability of the roads. The scene of the fight took place, as usual, in dense forest and elephant grass six to ten feet in height . . . The ground rose in a series of conical kopjes three hundred feet high, their bases touching one another, but the angle of ascent for the struggling infantry was about sixty degrees. Although the grass sapped our last reserves of energy in pushing forward, it was something to cling on to on the precipitous slopes. The Germans fiercely contested every inch of the ground with a perfect hurricane of rifle and maxim fire . . . We had some fifteen killed and wounded. Our Captain Burke was shot through the head. The 57th Pathans fought splendidly and captured three maxims at the point of the bayonet.

The Germans kept firing from their overhanging emplacements in rock so that they had to be bayoneted to stop the firing. 'The Indians gave them scant mercy,' wrote Molloy, 'as they fired till the last second.'

---

* On 30 August Richardson noted that he was writing to Sandy Malcolmson's widow. Next day he wrote: 'Took over Sandy's boots.'

243

This fight went on all day, the embattled troops cursing the failure of Brits's horsemen to arrive. They knew that Enslin's troopers were eight miles in the enemy's rear. 'Had they simultaneously attacked in his rear, there is no knowing what effect it would have had on the campaign . . . Perhaps we would not have been in the field today.'

That was the feeling of the man who fought there; and at head-quarters there was chagrin and gritted teeth. This was no modern battlefield where a commander had control. He was at the mercy of the men on the spot, waiting for information that came back garbled or not at all.

Romantic Tale of Love in War

Von Lettow left an interesting account of this battle. His 21st Company made the counter-attack. It was a close-quarters fight. 'Major Buller, a son of the well-known general of the South African War, put a bullet through the hat of the company commander, Lieutenant von Ruck-teschell, but was then severely wounded by the latter. Major Buller was got away to the German hospital in Dar es Salaam and nursed back to health by the wife of his opponent, who was working there as a nurse.'

There is a tender story here, as Frau von Ruckteschell cared for the man who had narrowly missed killing her husband. What feelings blossomed between them can be imagined in those tropic nights as Buller recovered. Then came the news that Lieutenant von Ruck-teschell had been killed in action. The nurse and her patient were mar-ried, a sequel that von Lettow noted with some amusement.

About noon of the battle in question, Brits turned up with his horsemen. He had worked his way through one of the mountain passes and now threw in the 5th and 7th Infantry. His horsemen suf-fered heavy casualties.

By nightfall the positions were still unstormed, but morning found the heights deserted. Captain Schulz was falling back into the thick bush on the Wami River on the road from Turiani to Morogoro. About sixty men were lying dead or wounded on the fatal slopes as witness to the deadly closeness of the encounter. Smuts drew consolation from the thought that the German casualties must have been high; but von Lettow made no mention of that in his account.

Five days to Turiani! Says much for the men's tenacity. They had accomplished astonishing feats of endurance and courage. They had gained thirty miles, and the three columns had linked up. They were too late, however, to fulfil their commander's hopes. 'We are thor-oughly disgusted,' wrote Molloy. Every effort had been made to bottle up the German companies. There was bitter comment.

244

'If the terrain had permitted of the original scheme being carried out, and the whole 3rd Division (Brits) had proceeded to Mahondo as planned, the retreat of the enemy from these mountains would probably have been impossible.'

The terrain again; always the terrain, and the enemy who knew how to make the best use of it. But what alternative was there? The fact is that there was none, and speed was essential if the entire force were not to be seriously reduced by tropical diseases. Ruthless driving was paying or so it seemed.

Smuts did not pause to lick his wounds.

Battle of Wami River

He believed that the enemy had been driven south with great loss and must now be pursued at all speed down the Morogoro road towards Dakawa on the Wami River.

There was a fresh opportunity, this time to catch the enemy from both sides of the river. Sheppard marched his Indians and Enslin's mounted men arrived on opposite sides of the Wami on 16 August. 'It was as we expected: the bridge was blown and the river was wide. It was a strong defensive position. The attack was ordered for next morning, and we had to make a recce so that both our forces could achieve a combined attack, the cavalry to cross the river, our force to hold the front.'

At dawn on 17 August the enemy fired on patrols and the battle of the Wami River had begun. It was soon apparent that little was known about the ground, with the fast-flowing river in its surrounding jungle. Three intelligence officers had been sent to reconnoitre it while Smuts was still at Handeni and the plans for the advance on the Nguru Mountains were still on the table.

South African Field Artillery's 5th Battery constructs a raft on the Wami River.

The three officers were well accustomed to operating behind the enemy lines and sending back information by their native runners. They were often away for weeks at a time, even when desperately ill with malaria and living off the land. Lurking outside villages at sunset, they would rush in and seize cooking food and drink the calabashes of water. The alternative was to drink putrid green water from stagnant pools. Always there were brushes with tribesmen armed with flintlocks and spears as they dodged German patrols on the look-out for them while they were driving off native cattle.

'We marched by night and lay up by day and hoped that we would not be betrayed by the villagers.'

Lieutenant Christopher Thornhill and his band had hardly returned from a nineteen-day patrol, carrying a man on a stretcher, when they were summoned to general headquarters and given their next scouting mission.

We had only had two days' rest; now we were shown the Wami River, seventy miles away, as Smuts's next objective. Our job was to scout out any German force that might make a flank attack and cut Smuts's lines of communication and return with the news.

As we heard these words from a staff officer and watched him draw an imaginary line on the map I knew we were being given a pretty tall order. In fact, we were ambushed and had to scatter in the bush, where the Germans knew every watering place and had men on every jungle track. We got back guided by the booming of guns. But were they British or German?

Challenged by a rifleman of the 29th Punjabis and armed only with a Mauser rifle that they had found in the bush, they were marched to the Punjabi colonel. Bearded, with their uniforms in tatters, they were taken for German spies and only saved by the arrival of an intelligence officer.

'We were received as men from the dead. But a fresh intelligence officer, not the one who had instructed us, who was very much trying to show his authority, would not accept our information about crossing the Wami River.' In any case it was too late. They had been given up for lost and the offensive was on.

No one received the intimate knowledge that Thornhill had brought in.

The Impenetrable Wami River

What lay ahead of the columns was a wide and meandering river with many fast-flowing tributaries, choked with swamps and reeds, head-high grass and thick bush and crocodile-infested streams. Great plains stretched on either side of the river, dotted here and there with tall palms but mostly covered with impenetrable grass. So Thornhill described it in his report.

By that time the attackers had found out the hard way. As von Lettow saw the action, 'A force of at least one brigade of infantry, and General Brits's mounted brigade, attacked Captain Schulz's position while simultaneously another brigade which had marched up the right bank of the Wami attacked him from the east.' The total German force amounted to twelve hundred rifles.

It was small wonder that Enslin's mounted men could find no way of crossing to attack the Germans in the rear. The bridge was blown and Captain Schulz's company was well entrenched in the river village of Dakawa. At once Sheppard sent in the Gurkhas of the 2nd Kashmir Rifles and attempted to take the village in a bloody rush with the kukri; but he failed, and he lost about seventy casualties.

Infantry Anger Against Brits

'We had expected great things of Brits's horses,' wrote Molloy. They lay pinned down near the river, but unable to reach it to drink, and filled their bottles from stagnant water in a pool. They waited in vain for the horsemen to take the Germans in the rear. Next morning the 5th were joined by Sheppard and Hannyngton to make an attack on the enemy's rear.

'That same evening the mounted brigade were ordered to cross the river to the enemy left flank and close their only route of escape. This order they flatly ignored,' wrote Molloy, 'and they remained where they were, that is to say, out of the firing line. The enemy took full advantage by retreating on the night of 17 August.'

Captain Richardson's diary confirms the withdrawal of the enemy, but records that the 8th actually crossed the river that day. 'Heavy firing with big guns. After trekking about twelve miles, got behind the firing line, and found Lieutenant Reid with packs. Bullets whizzing around. About 4.30 (three hours after arriving) I saddled up and pushed on with the packs. After a good deal of wandering about we crossed the river and found the regiment about 4.30 p.m. Off-saddled, made the troop entrench. Slept.'

Next day Richardson noted: 'Friday 18 August. Found enemy had retired all along the line during the night.' But Molloy expressed his regiment's disgust. 'We learned later that they had been given orders to surrender when they had fired their last rounds. I cannot express our feelings strongly enough. This miserable failure by Brits's brigade has certainly prolonged the campaign.'

Another Failure of Communications

Again it was a failure of communication and of the terrain that had defeated Smuts. Richardson's diary noted on 16 August that he sent out a patrol in search of the river, 'but could not find it. The patrol took us through tambooti grass fourteen feet high, very hard on the horses, which gave bad signs of exhaustion. Outspanned for half an hour and then went four miles south. Horses getting very bad, so returned to starting point . . . Got a message through to General Enslin reporting result of patrol . . . Horses completely knocked up.'

What use Enslin made of the patrol's negative message we cannot know but, as we have seen, the 8th did cross the river at another point. And no doubt that put pressure on Schulz to withdraw.

Smuts was able to console himself with the reflection that 'the enemy had been very severely handled . . . our losses in this action coming to a hundred and twenty.' Eager though he was to push on, it would take two days to bridge the river for supplies.

Richardson recorded the rest with relief. 'Hearing we were to remain here for a day or two, proceeded to make ourselves comfortable. Enjoyed bathe and shave and change of undergarments. Men and horses very cheerful and much fresher. Managed to get some washing done. Scenery very nice and peaceful. Read and dozed all day.'

Meanwhile the other brigades marched on without pause and forded the river. They were soon unable to use the direct route to Morogoro for lack of water, which could not reach them across the unbridged river. They had to march across the parched plains, a long circuit of forty-five miles along the Ngere-Ngere River.

Molloy wrote of that march: 'The enemy set the surrounding country in flames, placing us on a couple of occasions in the greatest possible jeopardy.' Covered with ash and dust, half-choked with the acrid fumes of burning vegetation, the sky a pall of smoke, the long column marched, cursing Brits and his men, still unaware of their struggle and bitterly convinced that all their sufferings and effort had been thrown away and every opportunity lost.

In one of his weekly letters home Smuts told his wife of his frustration at the delays caused by the innumerable bridges that the enemy had burnt or destroyed. The day before the battle of the Wami River he confided: 'I am hopeful that many askaris will refuse to continue further and that von Lettow will be left with only a remnant.'

He clearly believed that once he had cut the Central Railway and Van Deventer had pushed von Lettow out of the enormous and prosperous western side of the colony, von Lettow would have no recourse other than to turn south towards Portuguese territory. Once he had been forced across the Rufiji River, how loyal would his askaris remain

ABOVE: On their retreat along the Central Railway, the Germans destroyed every bridge and culvert and ran their engines and rolling stock into the chasm thus formed.

RIGHT: Between Morogoro and Ngere Ngere, the Germans put a few trains on the bridges, then blew up the girders, and the weight of the trains caused the whole structure to collapse. Then they collected all the engines and rolling-stock on the systems, started the engines full steam from both ends, and had the most glorious smash-up in the history of railways.

as they found themselves living in jungle and swamp, totally cut off from supplies and from their tribal homes and with the entire plain of the Rufiji River one continuous sea of floodwater in the rainy season?

Limit of Smuts's Obligation

There was another inhibiting factor. Smuts's undertaking to the British Government was to go as far as the Rufiji River. Beyond that he was not morally obliged to advance in person. Suppose he were to be marooned with his men somewhere on this floodplain, at present an arid desert? What would become of them, cut off from the world? These were problems that never even entered the minds of his troops.

In the meantime Smuts had to follow hard on an enemy whose direction of withdrawal was still unknown. Would it be to Morogoro or

249

to Kilossa? At Kwedihombo, twenty miles ahead, the road forked in both directions. He had to know quickly. The Air Force was called on.

Lieutenant Observer Walmsley wrote: 'We were told that an aerodrome had been selected for us at Dakawa near the Wami River and that we were to get there as fast as the transport on the road would permit.' They set off in 'a filthy cloud of red dust thrown up by the plodding mule waggons crowding every yard of space and reached Dakawa next morning to the sound of continuous gunfire.

'The Huns were contesting the crossing and, judging by the large number of wounded coming back, the fighting was very intense. The aerodrome was not quite ready to receive the machines, and it was very depressing to sit listening to the fight and being absolutely impotent.'

The Road to Morogoro

Early next morning Walmsley took off with his pilot, the South African veteran airman Captain Carey-Thomas. For about ten miles they followed the straight, narrow red road to Morogoro without seeing any sign of the enemy or fortifications.

'When we did come across him at last he was engaged in fording the Ngere-Ngere River. It was thrilling to see the enemy run about like a flock of scared sheep, but exasperating, for we had strict instructions not to bomb or attack them. Once again a glorious chance of inflicting heavy casualties was lost . . . My pilot's fingers were simply itching to pull those innocent-looking little bomb levers but he contented himself by diving down, adding to the demoralisation on the ground.'

When they protested at this lost opportunity they were told the reason. The enemy were not to be harried. This was to encourage him 'to dally on his journey, giving our flanking column time to get round his rear'.

Thus the tortuous reasoning that followed the perpetual mirage of the grand climacteric flanking movement! This outflanking column was marching fast as it made a wide detour to the east of Morogoro. Sent to report on their progress, Walmsley wrote: 'There was no mistaking their whereabouts. Dense clouds of smoke were rising from the numerous bush fires that they had carelessly started. The air was filled with wisps of burnt grass, the ground almost invisible.' Then beyond the burning area he saw 'the column, winding like an immense black snake across the veldt'. They flew on with orders to describe the country between the column and the railway line, and soon came on a railway station. There were two long trains, each with steam up.

'The platforms on either side were littered with stores of every description, and hundreds of native porters took to the bush at our approach. Bullock waggons, hand-carts, trolleys, donkeys and transport filled the station . . . They were evidently evacuating their stores from Morogoro, and the fine broad road leading south towards the eastern flank of the Uluguru Mountains was to be their line of retreat.'

Diving the biplane at 100 mph, Carey-Thomas released his bombs. The second burst in the centre of the track ten yards behind the guard's van of the second train. 'The fourth and last made a direct hit on a large station building used as a store. After the first flash of the explosion, the whole roof seemed to rise slowly up, until its rafters showed like the teeth of a comb . . . Feeling quite pleased with ourselves, we turned for home.'

Next day they were again in the air, flying west along the railway line to Kilossa on the look-out for Van Deventer's force.

At the foot of the Uluguru Mountains the airmen flew several times over the town of Morogoro. 'A cheerful sight to see brick houses again and laid-out streets and squares. All the larger buildings were decorated with enormous Red Crosses.' They flew about looking for signs of fortifications, but found none.

'I was busy completing my notes when suddenly there came a terrific explosion just behind the machine. Looking back, I saw a cloud of black smoke in the air . . . It was my first real Archy.'* The gun fired again, and they pinpointed an artillery piece, an 88mm field gun, ingeniously mounted in the middle of the railway turntable.

Three-quarters of an hour farther on they came on Kilossa, a small settlement at the point where the railway line leaves the plain and enters the deep valley of the Mpapua Mountains. Six miles farther on Walmsley's field glasses picked out a line of about fifty gunpits overlooking the road. Each was occupied. They were waiting for Van Deventer's column, now a mile away down the road.

'Scribbling a short note with a sketch of the position, I tied it in my handkerchief and for want of a better weight placed a couple of cartridges inside and dropped it as near as possible to the road. Whether it was ever found or not I never knew.' Their fuel was getting low, and they had to turn for the smokefires of their own camp. It was so near that their comrades there had sat in the shade of the mess watching the black puffs of smoke rocking Carey-Thomas's plane. In the next few days pilots begged for a chance to bomb the military camp on the outskirts of the town and dodge the gunfire.

'Over by End of the Month'

There is no doubt that at that point Smuts had hoped to finish the war at Morogoro. Here would be concentrated the main army and the Gov-

---

* Archy: slang of the period for anti-aircraft fire.

251

BE2C biplanes dropped improvised bombs made from artillery shells with tail fins cut from tins.

ernor of German East Africa and senior civil servants; in fact, the official and military heart of the diminished colony.

In a diary entry of Sunday, 13 August a clerk of the political officer's department stationed at Arusha noted: 'I hear that Dar es Salaam was captured five days ago and that GHQ is being removed thither shortly. General Smuts, who says the campaign *will be over by the end of the month,** is believed to have warned the Germans still in the field that if they go in for guerrilla warfare he will confiscate all their property. So they are expected to surrender soon.

'Many officers in the field are writing home to South Africa requesting their wives and other relatives and friends to cease writing

---

* Author's emphasis.

252

to them up here, and men from the Old Country are already talking about eating their Christmas pudding in England this year.'

So confident were the political officers, apparently, that the writer, G C Aubrey, discussed decorations for the campaign. 'We expect a general African medal, with GEA, GSWA, Cameroons or Togoland inscribed on it and bars for general engagements.'

Can there be any doubt that Smuts believed that he would finish it now? After all, with Morogoro fallen and with it von Lettow's surrender there would be nothing further to engage his energies here.

The cry was 'forward to Morogoro and the Central Railway!' Who would be first to reach it? Smuts's eastern force or Van Deventer's, as both strove to close the hundred miles that separated them on the railway line? The great question was: Would von Lettow fight on with his back to the Uluguru Mountains, which lay behind Morogoro like a mighty rampart? Would it be possible to send a mounted column round the isolated bastion to shut off any further retreat to the south?

Indeed, it looked like being finished there.

Van Deventer Stalled Again

Then, to Smuts's chagrin, Van Deventer signalled that he was stuck at Nyangalo. 'My transport has been run to a standstill. Impossible to get supplies through to continue to Mpapua.' Van Deventer's main body had ground to a standstill, although his patrols were at Dodoma by 29 July.

It had been another epic feat of endurance but eleven critical days were to be lost waiting for fresh horses and supplies; ample time for von Lettow to get his men and supplies away from Morogoro and into the Uluguru fastnesses.

Smuts signalled Van Deventer daily, urging him to move, but the division was virtually immobile. The roughest terrain, thirst, short rations and stiff resistance by the *Schutztruppe* had not stopped the advance of twenty miles a day. Now, when his force was absolutely necessary to shut the jaws on the German Army, he could only curse the breakdown in supplies. He was on his last rations when Smuts signalled again to co-operate with him 'with the least possible delay'.

'The morning my quartermaster came to me to tell me that the last of our rations had been issued I gave the order to move. We could wait no longer but must take our chances on what we could forage and take from the enemy.' Van Deventer's men were already on the move forward and his horse patrols were out on his flanks when fresh supplies got through. The division marched in dusty silence all day.

In the late afternoon the red cloud above the column was sighted by the Germans waiting at Chunya. Attack! came the order. Tired

The *Schutztruppe* man a machine gun against a British reconnaissance plane.

though they were, Van Deventer's infantry went up the slope. 'A fine performance after a particularly trying march all day,' went the report. The enemy scattered.

Another Gruelling Waterless March

The advance pressed on. By 12 August Van Deventer had reached as far east towards Smuts as Mpapua. There he surrounded the German force and threatened to cut off further retreat. The men had been through thirty hours of hard marching and manoeuvring, without water or food. They were exhausted; some had marched thirty-two miles without stopping.

Van Deventer sent on his horsemen; but the footsloggers, far from resting, were sent out on foraging parties to find food of any kind. Behind them reinforcements were following, but these, the 9th and 10th Infantry, were no less exhausted by the relentless speed of their march.

Mpapua was an important German town among the rugged hills. As they followed the railway line the mounted men were spurred on by reports of a good waterhole ahead.

The 12th South African Infantry was already in the hills, pushing upwards at Chunya Nek, where the enemy held the crest in force. The only water was on the other side. The slopes were too steep and the scrub too dense for horsemen. 'We all climbed on foot,' wrote Deneys Reitz. 'Soon came the rattle of machine guns as the Germans searched the jungle.'

There was some fire from a six-pounder on the climbing men, but the gunners packed up when 'our quick-firer battery came up from the rear . . . they disappeared over the ridge, where it was impossible to follow, as it was nearly dark. Our men lost four killed and eleven wounded, so the waterhole was an expensive one, as most of them were in these days.'

Germans Still in Mpapua

Next morning the scene had changed. Native women of the densely populated district stood all along the road with baskets of beans and poultry as the men rode and marched towards Mpapua town twelve miles ahead, where the German fort with its machine guns and the six-pounder quickly opened fire.

'In the streets of the town were a few dead askari and two or three wounded men nursing their hurts, but the main force had doubled across the riverbed, and in a few minutes rifles were cracking at us from the slope beyond.'

From the parapet of the fort Reitz saw his comrades riding hard to cut off the retreat and almost succeeding.

Several field companies of askari with white officers were on the road beyond the river but 'as soon as our guns got the range the whole lot vanished . . . filtering away like water through a sieve though practically surrounded. And a moment later they were firing from the next bush-covered rise.'

Colonel Molyneux sent in the infantry. Reitz went with them. 'It was hot work with two or three hundred askari blazing away at us. But their shooting was bad, and we went steadily to the top, until we saw the askaris running for it. We lost three men killed, but we killed a considerable number of them and the ground was littered with abandoned rifles and equipment. The mounted men brought in ten Germans and about thirty askari. The rest got away.'

The pursuit was on again, supplies were far behind, the jaws of Smuts's pincers were being blunted by every day of resistance. Would they ever close in time against this enemy who fought from every vantage point, fell back only at the last moment, and even then exacted a high price as he slipped through the net to turn again and open fire? His morale was apparently as high as ever.

Trekking with the Meat Ration

How were supplies reaching the troops? Private Shackleton described how he and a fellow-sufferer from malaria were discharged from hospital with orders to drive two hundred oxen to Dodoma. With rations for twelve days and ten natives they set out on the hundred-and-sixty-mile trek through the bush, a column in single file a mile long.

On the first night fires kept the lions at bay, but by dawn several of the black drovers had deserted. By 8 o'clock the herd was on trek again, and approaching a tsetse-fly belt. It was fifteen miles wide, so they agreed to stop and move only after dark, when the flies were inactive. No sooner had they moved on than frantic yells told them that lions had stampeded the oxen into the dark jungle. Next morning, with the rations missing, the remaining drovers threatened to desert; so they slaughtered one of the oxen and feasted. That night lions came again, their eyes flashing on all sides of the barrier of fire round the terrified beasts.

It took the convalescents fifteen days to reach Kilossa, where a tribunal of officers demanded to know why they were seventy oxen short.

'That day,' wrote Shackleton, 'we were beating about Kilossa for what we could scrounge when we met two footsore individuals in tattered khaki. They had also been driving oxen on their return from convalescence and had managed to lose every one of the two hundred that they set out with.'

Small wonder that Van Deventer's men were obliged to shoot for the pot and loot the native fields they passed through. It was that kind of war, as brutal as jungle war had ever been. In logistics and dependence on the country for provisions nothing like it had been seen in Europe since the predatory troops of Napoleon and his generals.

Fighting for Every Mile

While the convalescents were struggling forward with their two hundred oxen Van Deventer's brigades were fighting every mile ahead. On 16 August he ordered an attack on Kidete. 'When we neared Kidete,' wrote Reitz, 'we had marched twenty-six miles without water, and again, on a line of rugged hills, lay the enemy barring us from the river behind. We were close to the railway line once more, and the Germans had a 4.1 naval gun on a truck pulled by an engine, which steamed up and down, shelling us as it went.'

The mounted men and some infantry went for the flanks while the remainder tried to force the hills. 'By dark they had suffered over fifty casualties, and were hung-up halfway up the slopes. Once more we were in a serious predicament, for the nearest water behind was many miles away and the only other water was in the hands of the enemy.' Fortunately the enemy retired after dark. Reitz described 'our whole army lining the river bank, drinking their fill from the swift-flowing stream.'

Morning brought news that Smuts's troops had forded the Wami, but Major Kraut had got his detachments free from Smuts's encirclement and speedily withdrawn along the railway to Kilossa, so fast and so hard-pressed that he was unable to blow the many bridges, points and water-tanks that his engineers had prepared for destruction. In such haste, in fact, that a train had been derailed.

Reitz's advance patrol came on the wreck. It was lying on its side halfway down an embankment. 'Part of the train was on fire, and a more complete smash I have never seen . . . Under the wreckage we found nine dead askari, and many more must have been injured, for there was an improvised dressing station under a tree with blood-stained bandages and uniforms scattered about.'

Smuts Closing in from the East

The enemy was fighting to enable von Lettow to organise his retreat from Morogoro. Smuts was closing in from the east, and the Germans by now had only twenty miles of railway line left for their use to send men out to delay the arrival of Van Deventer, who admitted that this was the hardest part of his long march from Kondoa-Irangi. 'The men's endurance and hardship through dry and waterless stretches on scanty rations were an achievement worthy of South African troops . . .' Meanwhile he had to drive them almost beyond the limits of endurance to close the gap between his force and Smuts.

Pressing on after the retreat Reitz's patrol came on a party of askaris laying mines; he caught them unawares, and they dropped five. The rest ran wildly to the rear, where they opened a hot fire.

This was at the mouth of the valley where the gorge narrowed to not more than two hundred yards wide. It was a formidable and forbidding entrance to the valley beyond. Back at Kidete Van Deventer received the report of his patrol. He wrote: 'The railway from Kidete to Kilossa for a distance of twenty-five miles follows a narrow defile cut through the Osagara Mountains by the Mkondokwa River, and every yard of the advance was contested by the enemy.'

Their method was to meet the South Africans' advance guard with ambushes, then fall back on well-prepared positions, fight again and fall back again. And now there was a new menace. 'In passing a timber thicket our horses began to kick and lash . . . One of the men identified the insects as the dreaded tsetse fly, a baleful omen for the future of a mounted force.'

The attackers were in the bad old situation that Smuts had been in on the Pangani: short visibility, no room to manoeuvre, men cut down by hidden machine guns and mines on the roads. 'Some of our men crossed the river to look at dead askari,' wrote Reitz. 'As we watched them there came a loud explosion, and a soldier was blown to pieces before our eyes.'

There was little chance of the horsemen being able to make out-flanking movements in thick bush and terrain obstructed by rocks and innumerable dry watercourses. Mounted men had to lead their horses in terrain so difficult that even men on foot could hardly penetrate it. Once a German officer jumped out at a patrol and fired a signal shot with his Mauser. At once a storm of artillery fire came down from the carefully ranged guns of the *Königsberg*.

'As always,' wrote Reitz, 'I removed my saddle to ease my animal's back, and just as I had done this, a shell burst on us like a thunderclap. When the smoke cleared there lay my poor chestnut dead . . . He had an easier death than was waiting for all our other horses, although we scarcely realised it as yet.'

Then on again, foraging where they could, often with only a mouthful of parched grain to chew. Reitz tells how he was picking millet in a field when a shell burst nearby. A youngster of the 9th was killed. 'I helped to bury the boy in his lonely grave under a tree in the foothills of the Ulugurus.' Reitz noted with some emotion that the boy's name was Allen.*

Held up again by a position in German hands, Van Deventer came forward to see for himself. As he came up the enemy sent over a storm of gunfire, and the advance halted until a quickfirer battery gal-loped up and dug in trails for a duel that lasted all day and cost more casualties. It was only at sunset that the 1st and 3rd Horse were able to take to the hills in an outflanking movement, with the troopers leading their horses and the infantry panting behind, manhandling machine guns, ammunition belts and water to cool the guns.

'The maxims always had to have water, even if we had none,' wrote a corporal in a machine-gun section. 'Sometimes we had to piss on them to keep them cool when the condenser tins ran dry. Some of the guns were not equipped with condensing tins, and when they boiled they gave away their position in clouds of steam.'

Suddenly the mounted men were out on the plain, ominously shimmering in the heat. The town of Kilossa had 'the usual fort and the usual official buildings, and a large native quarter. There were rail-way workshops, a rum distillery, and for miles around great rubber plantations.'

---

* A list of casualties published in 1917 gave his full name: John Henry Allen, 9th SA Horse.

Forces now Fifty Miles Apart

While they rested there for two days an aeroplane came over and dropped a message. General Smuts had reached Morogoro. The two forces were only fifty miles apart. The critical moment of the entire campaign was now approaching, and all commanders were aware of it. The heavy, moist tropical atmosphere was enervating, but perhaps it would be cooler up there in the Uluguru Mountains, the next bastion to be cleared. Smuts's army was reduced to a tatterdemalion remnant of what it had been, and both forces, meeting for the first time, were soon exchanging experiences. The real enemy, they agreed, had been the jungle, fever, tsetse and lack of supplies.

Two days' ride ahead of the main force Van Deventer's patrols had a first glimpse of the magnificent sweep of forest-clad heights running sixty miles from east to west and forty or fifty miles deep. How was von Lettow to be cleared from this fastness? To compound the fighting hazards, it was near the time of the 'small rains', with the prospect of supply columns getting bogged to the axles.

In fact, ahead of them rain was already falling.

Lieutenants von Schpueffer and von Kiddingheim, in order to penetrate the British lines unobserved, disguise themselves as a giraffe.

(*'Jambo' or with Jannie in the Jungle*, AW Lloyd, undated)

CHAPTER

13

No Rest at Morogoro –
Press On!

Smuts's hope of ending it all at Morogoro had left him with a vast conquest behind him and an unbeaten enemy in front. Any reasonable
enemy who had lost the whole of his inhabited, cultivated and developed country with all its infrastructure and all its ports – would have
wisely conceded victory.

The fall of the capital of the still unconquered area – Morogoro –
without bloodshed had a psychological effect. It also meant that when
the railway line from the now opened port of Dar es Salaam was in full
working order supplies could come across only a hundred miles. But
that time was not yet. The Germans had destroyed more than sixty
bridges and culverts along that stretch.

Meanwhile, Smuts had no intention of resting. In his report he
betrayed his consuming impatience: 'Owing to the exhaustion of man
and beast the next day [the 25th] was spent in reconnoitring the country, and on 26 August the advance was resumed.'

On that day he entered Morogoro, 'only to find that the enemy
had gone, the Commander-in-Chief von Lettow and Governor Schnee
with a force on the track due south of Morogoro through the mountains, and another force by the eastern or Kiroka route, while Enslin
engaged with a third force at Mlali.

'At Morogoro I found many proofs of the precipitate flight and
demoralised condition of the enemy forces, and I decided to continue
the pursuit in spite of the fact that my forces and animals were worn
out with the exertions of the last three weeks and that my transport
had reached its extreme radius of action.'

Press on regardless was the spirit of the new orders.

Even before they set out on the relentless pursuit Van Deventer's
2nd Division had a good idea of what lay ahead. Observers of
26 Squadron, now flying Henri Farman biplanes, had reported that the
western route would be tough hacking. The whole of the country
through which they would be marching was 'clothed in dense elephant

bush forest, impassable for wheeled transport . . . The maintenance of supplies [would be] an impossible task. Road there was none, water was scarce and the only things that really existed in abundance were German machine-gun nests, tsetse flies, mosquitoes, maggot-flies and malaria and dysentery.'

Writing with bitter hindsight in 1920, Leo Walmsley was eager to 'recommend that journey from Morogoro to Kissaki to any of those kind gentlemen who find it so easy to sit in an armchair and describe the East African Campaign as a joy-ride.' No doubt the portly ones were comparing it with the ghastly blood-letting of the Western Front.

'Thank heavens,' Walmsley wrote, 'I never had to march on that western route to Kissaki. Flying over it was enough. The elephant forest is continuous for nearly forty miles . . . the trees grow to immense height, the surface of the ground is hilly and abounds in deep ravines.'

It was no place to crash-land a Henri Farman biplane, this route to be taken by Van Deventer's men with every vantage point hotly contested by men still full of fight, despite Smuts's sanguine conjectures of desertions and disillusion.

'Striking Results'

Before following the struggle southwards it may be as well to review the situation and what General Smuts's strategy had achieved. General Collyer, his Chief of Staff, declared it 'sound, and its results striking'. In May 1916, German territory had been practically inviolate, and the German commander had held all his towns, ports and railways except a very small stretch of the Tanga line.

> In the space of three months [wrote Collyer] General von Lettow* had been deprived of all his railways, his capital town and main port at Dar es Salaam, with all the seaports to the north and, to quote General Smuts: 'every healthy or valuable part of the colony with the exception of the Mahenge plateau'.
> The force which moved under General Smuts's own direction from Moshi marched a distance of three hundred miles reckoned as the crow flies. It was actually considerably farther. Add to this bare statement of distance the tropical heat, the constant, serious and enervating lack of food, the steady forward movement, checked only when a total absence of sustenance compelled a halt, the daily experience of fighting and marching in dense bush where the nerves were constantly taut, with no prospect of respite till a wound or tropical disease should lay him low, then to be

---

* In 1916 von Lettow was still Lieutenant-Colonel.

transported back under exhausting conditions in rough transport to a distant base . . . and an idea may be formed of the lot of the soldier in the ranks in this extraordinary campaign.

28 000 Oxen Die

Until the occupation of Dar es Salaam on 4 September shortened his lines of communication, Smuts's small spearheads of fighting men were being dangled precariously at the end of supply lines that were breaking the backs of men, animals and motor transport in their endeavours to keep these lines open.

What had been accomplished had been at severe cost. Since 22 May, when the columns marched out of Kahe, twenty-eight thousand oxen had died on the three-month trek to Morogoro. Vast herds had been commandeered to keep pace with needs; and what was yet to come would defeat the imagination in its disregard for animal life.

It must not be forgotten, of course, that in this war, even in Europe, animals were still the principal means of transport. The guns were still galloped into the firing line; and even on the coast of Gallipoli, where the army was pinned down for months under withering

Demolished club house in Dar es Salaam after naval gunfire.

Turkish gunfire, the great gallant Shire horses of England were used to pull howitzers into position.

Animals of necessity were expendable, their only medication were injections of arsenic for tsetse fly, and the ultimate panacea, the .45 bullet in the brain. In the three months ahead, Smuts's army lost eleven thousand oxen, ten thousand horses, ten thousand mules and twenty-five hundred asses. So far they had perished from want of grain and from tsetse fly.

Meanwhile the RASC was performing extraordinary feats to get sufficient supplies forward before the rains set in. They were awaited with trepidation. As Collyer later wrote: 'The tracks along which supplies were forwarded became a mass of mud, bridges once more were swept away, all along the lines delay, congestion, and damage to vehicles. All these, and fresh attacks of disease, crippled the whole service of supply and medical work alike.'

Was There an Alternative?

Some argued that all this huge expenditure of animals could have been saved if there had been no advance down the Pangani. 'Why don't we make an amphibious landing at Dar es Salaam?' The trouble was that such a landing would have had to be made during the north-east monsoon.

Smuts decided that it was too difficult and too dangerous; and he had not forgotten Tanga. 'In any case it would expose a large number of men to the tropical diseases of the coastal area.' He was right. The Germans destroyed all the bridges on the Central Railway so that a shortcut via the sea would have solved nothing.

Now, until the port was working effectively in his hands, he had no choice but to press on in the old wasteful manner and at appalling cost in transport beasts. However, an ingenious solution to the destruction of the rolling stock of the Central Railway had been found.

Lieutenant-Colonel Dobson and his South African Pioneers devised a new species of locomotive. By narrowing the gauge of the heavy motor lorries and placing them on railway trolley wheels he could carry five tons in the lorry and ten more in its trailer. Pioneers dragged huge timbers from the forests and built temporary bridges from Dodoma to Kilossa. The big Rio trucks were such a success in hauling supplies by rail that Smuts at once saw their value. Within a month his engineers had the 'Rio train' running from his new sea base at Dar es Salaam to Dodoma.

Van Deventer also made use of it, and he was photographed beaming approval from a seat next to the driver. This was a good example of the resourcefulness of the South African Pioneers, recruited

Military motoring by road and railway through the luxuriant forests of tropical East Africa. On the left is a jigger train built from a lorry and mounted on flanged wheels.

as they were from railway workshops and the gold mines in a technically emergent South Africa in which they were masters of improvisation and inventive engineering.

Even the resourceful von Lettow's trolley line had been powered by his natives' sweat and muscle. Part of the newly opened line as far as Mingoya became known as the Ford Railway with lorries fitted with flanged wheels and carrying both goods and passengers at a steady twenty mph. Others called the diminutive power units the 'Jigger Fleet'.

Forest Fortress of Uluguru

However, to the infantrymen approaching the Ulugurus and horsemen on their staggering mounts dying from tsetse bites it meant little as they went forward to meet von Lettow's fourteen companies of between two and four thousand seasoned askaris with a small mounted detachment, adequate supplies, machine guns and artillery, all of them moving on tracks and over passes that their indefatigable commander had reconnoitred by bicycle and on foot; he knew every inch of his fortress in the Uluguru forest.

To the attackers it would be bewildering, unknown, and dangerous in the extreme. And there would be no pause for rest. General Hoskins's 1st Division did not even enter Morogoro. It was diverted south into the mountains to get behind the defences. Nussey's 1st Mounted Brigade had left Kilossa with over a thousand horsemen and two hundred and thirty dismounted men. By the time he joined Enslin a few days later his strength had wasted away to 850 rifles. 'I had no choice but to leave all my dismounted men and 249 horses at Mkata *en route* . . . and not a shot fired!'

Smuts had issued his orders from Morogoro. Reitz saw him at that time. 'He was thin and ill from malaria, but he spoke cheerfully and gave us the latest news from France.' It could not have been good. The Somme battles had begun on 26 June with an enormous bombardment. Since then, two offensives had failed and a third was in preparation. But Romania had joined the Allies!

Whatever cheer this brought to men about to assault the Uluguru massif there was at least comfort in the contrast of two fields of carnage. Yet letters of the time show that many officers and men regarded the Western Front as the prime place of duty, and were impatient for von Lettow's sideshow to be over.

The Toughest March Yet

On to Kissaki!

The 5th and 6th Infantry Battalions were part of the drive down the eastern side of the mountains, making for Tyaduma on the Mgeta River about eight miles from Kissaki. 'Here the main enemy army was entrenched,' wrote Molloy. 'This march of a hundred miles was the toughest to date. The infantry deserves nothing but praise for the manner in which they withstood the privations and hardships of this march through pathless mountains, on less than half rations, under a scorching sun by day and cold by night, with only the clothes they stood up in, the weight of their equipment being fifty pounds. Each man had to dig for his own water in the bed of some dry watercourse at the end of

On the march south towards Morogoro, squeezing von Lettow-Vorbeck into the south-eastern corner of German East Africa.

a most gruelling day, and wait patiently while enough moisture perco-
lated through to fill his waterbottle.'

Climax of Rail Destruction

Morogoro had been abandoned by the Germans a week before the
South Africans arrived. Smuts's advance detachments were only six
miles away when they heard the rending and tearing of metal, and the
night was lit by the flames of destruction as the Germans ran their
locomotives and rolling stock over the blown bridge into the narrow
gorge in what observers called the most astonishing heap of engines
and cars ever seen. From the air, observers described it as looking like
a child's game when the bored boy piles up his toys in a grand finale.
'They lay there like stricken monsters!'

This was the climax of destruction. While the town was under
orders to clear out; and porters were being called from their quarters to
pick up their loads, engineers were setting about blowing up a vast
quantity of artillery shells and small-arms ammunition.

On the night of 26 August the charges were fired, which killed
the demolition specialist responsible. When Smuts's men entered the
town next day explosions were still continuing. The area was scattered
far and wide with unexploded shells and there was a vast reeking
crater where the dumps had been. As they left Morogoro the askaris,
as a final gesture of hatred, fouled the rooms and the furniture of the
Bahnhof Hotel with excrement.

When the airmen of 26 Squadron moved in they found the hotel
'furnished with a chair, two beds, one table, a sausage machine and a
heller-in-the-slot automatic piano, which gave an accomplished rendering of the "Hymn of Hate" as we entered the room'. It was a pretty little town, with the inhabitants brightly dressed in festive robes, a place
of neat palm-shaded bungalows. The civilian population of women
and children was nowhere to be seen.

Marching into Morogoro

The German women were ready to expect the worst as the 2nd Rhodesian Regiment, then the 130th Baluchis entered, two double companies
strong as they marched to their bivouacs. Picquets were posted, and
the inhabitants waited for morning and the beginning of military rule
by their enemies.

It was to be far more benign than they had expected.

Within a few days the Post Commandant of Morogoro authorised
the publication of *The Morogoro News*. It printed the latest available
Reuters reports of the war in Europe and much soldierly humour:

'Obituary Notice: In Memoriam of the last polony sausage, which died of consumption on 26 August. RUHE SANFT: All the horses, dogs and kittens, were in fearful consternation when they heard of the death of this mutual relation.'

Printed notices of Church of England services announced that the chaplain could be seen in his banda at any time by request.

'The German occupation,' gushed one contributor E H, 'has now given place to star-studded British officialdom and the noise and bustle of motor traffic. War-worn details saunter with curious gaze . . . The native, perfectly satisfied with his new master, slips into the yoke with perfect contentment, and a thousand swarthy arms are now employed on the railway, shouldering the heavy rails while singing their monotonous native chants.'

Walmsley was surprised to see quite a number of German women, 'apparently not in the least perturbed by the presence of our troops. One of these, recognising that I was an airman by the badge on my tunic, looked me frankly in the face and elevated her nose in an aristocratic sneer. As I had not set eyes on a member of the fair sex for nearly six months, I blushed violently at the familiarity and turned my head.' So much for the brutal and licentious soldiery!

Sufferings of the Wounded

The German gaol was at once turned into a hospital. It had been like-wise fouled, and it was quickly whitewashed. Captain Robert Dolby RAMC made sure that the message the Germans left on the lime-washed wall was carefully preserved: *'Gott strafe England'*.

It was there that Dolby operated on the white table 'on all the human wreckage that marked the savage bush fighting . . . Its white cleanliness, our towels and surgical gloves and overalls filled them with a sense of comfort . . . Even that chamber of pain was a haven to these broken men after long jolting rides over execrable roads.'

As far back as Handeni Captain Dolby had scoured the country-side and looted the empty houses of planters of bedsteads and soft mattresses, down pillows, and eiderdown quilts for broken legs. 'It would have done your heart good to see their dirty, unwashed faces grinning at me from lace-edged pillows. Silk-covered cushions from Hun drawing rooms rested painful amputation stumps.'

Here at Morogoro he used the excellent, if surly, services of Sister Elizabeth, a German nurse who, with good enough reason, hated the English but showed tenderness to the wounded. 'When I told her of Portugal's entry into the war she snorted with rage and said that England forced all the little nations to fight against Germany.' But in her long white dress and with her blonde hair drawn under her cap she was an angel to the wounded and particularly skilful at changing dressings.

There were also German soldiers left behind for care. Dolby noted that there was no resentment between the German and his own men. Only, curiously, 'the Boers were different. They were never unkind, but they ignored them completely, for the Union of South Africa had too much to forgive in the Rebellion and in German South West Africa.'

It was to this hospital that the early casualties of Smuts's new drive would be coming, some of them after being carried on stretchers for two days. One aspect of medicine that Dolby found to his advantage was that the earth of Africa did not contain the deadly germs of gangrene and tetanus, such as he had found in France and Gallipoli.

'We did not need to inject the wounded with tetanus antitoxin.' That at least was a small mercy from a brutal land that spared no one. The worst of the deadly diseases that he fought to overcome was blackwater fever, the final result of many bouts of malaria.

'It was written on their faces as they were lifted from the ambulance or mule waggon . . . the blanched lips, the grey-green pallor of their faces, jaundiced eye, hurried breathing . . . and deadly, exhausting vomiting, lasting for days, resulting in great prostration and thirst.'

Ehrlich's Life-saving .606

By the time such men were brought in they were nearly finished. Dolby used the drug .606 devised by Ehrlich, who had worked with Robert Koch in the territory before the war on the problems of sleeping sickness and relapsing fever. Dolby used a set of fine injection needles left by German surgeons and praised the drug created by 'that excellent Hun bacteriologist, Ehrlich'. They were all Huns to Dolby, who could never forgive them for the brutal excesses that he had seen in Belgium.

Sufferers from cerebral malaria arrived in convulsions, sometimes already in a deep coma or in frantic struggling delirium, and they were only saved from death by huge injections of quinine. As a rule conscious life returned after a few hours.

'But not always,' wrote Dolby. 'Then it is the padre's turn and in the cool of the following afternoon the firing party toils to the graveyard on the sunlit slopes of Mount Uluguru.'

Bullet-shattered limbs for amputation were common, as the German machine guns were set to fire low, unlike the askari rifle fire, which was invariably high. Among the hundreds that Dolby worked with was Shelley, an Irish policeman from Johannesburg. He had been left behind by the retreating Germans, with wounds so severe that only amputation saved him.

269

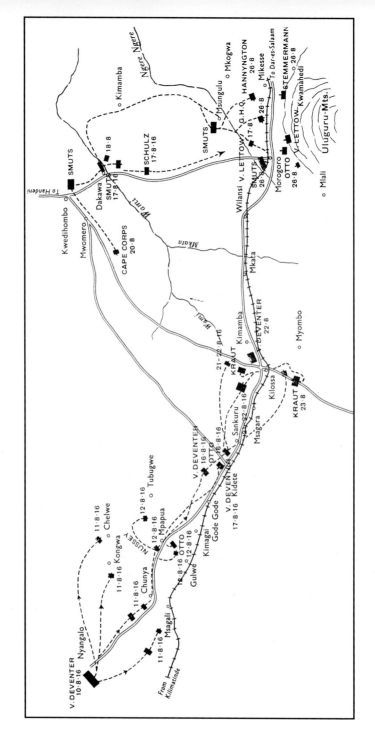

RATIONS of GENERAL SMUTS with GENERAL van DEVENTER IN SECURING
CENTRAL RAILWAY

(*The South Africans with General Smuts in German East Africa 1916*,
Brig-Gen Collyer, 1939)

Sister Elizabeth showed a special tenderness to him, and it touched the crusty surgeon. And there were Parson, a printer of the *Rand Daily Mail,* and Drury, a trooper of the SA Horse so badly shot through the shoulder that only the skill of a Cape Town surgeon, Moffat, had saved what was left of his shattered arm. Now in the delirium of malaria he screamed that the German prisoners in the ward were going to shoot him.*

Then there was Green, a Rhodesian sergeant laid low by blackwater, which was very common among the Rhodesians with their years in the bush. The ambulance conveying Green hit a mine, turned over and killed the driver. Murray, a Regimental Sergeant Major, lay there with a leg smashed by a lead slug from an askari's rifle.

For those who believed that round-nosed ball was a case of German frightfulness, the notes in the diary of a political officer's clerk are perhaps instructive: '*Ammunition* Service II mm ('71) – 500. Service II mm ('71) *softnosed* – 800.' This appeared in Aubrey's diary without comment among details of his work in the political section. The frightful wounds caused by soft-nosed bullets are well documented.

Pain was unending; but Dolby never lost his belief in the 'ultimate goodness' of the soldier. Captured German officers often said to him: 'How can your men stand it? It's incredible to us.' And they had a poor opinion of the medical services in Smuts's army compared with their own.

Superior German Equipment

Indeed, so far in the campaign the Germans had lived better than Smuts's men. In Dolby's account, 'Our men had to carry kit and heavy ammunition and sleep with only a groundsheet through tropic rains without the protection of mosquito nets.† The German soldier, even a private in a white or *Schutzen Kompanie,* as distinct from the *Unteroffizier* with an askari regiment or *Feldkompanie,* had at least eight porters to carry all his kit, his food, his bed, to have his food ready prepared at the halting places, his bed erected and mosquito curtains hung.'

'How can you ask your men to carry loads and then fight in equatorial Africa?' they asked Dolby.

Each German soldier had his own personal chop box with plentiful and varied food, eggs, chickens and the fruit of the country paid for

---

* One of the victims of cerebral malaria was Lieutenant Ian Bisset of the 8th SAI. Commissioned at nineteen for his efficiency and high morale, he shot and killed himself in hospital.
† These were issued at the beginning of the campaign, but proved useless under jungle and bush conditions.

by a special ration money at three rupees a day. Medically, his hospitals were better in every way, from surgical equipment to beds and trained nurses. And all this was still available as he fell back from one prepared position to the next.

Although von Lettow had been forced to abandon much in the retreat from Morogoro, he had never had any intention of standing there, as Smuts had hoped. To the German commander the idea was 'surely madness to wait at this place for the junction of the hostile columns . . . and then fight with our backs to the steep and rocky mountains'.

He had easily foreseen the manoeuvre that Smuts would use. 'Knowing that General Brits had a liking for wide turning movements, I felt sure that one column would move off from Dakawa or from Kilossa to reach our rear by working round the west side of the Uluguru Mountains. This possibility was so obvious that I rode out every day on a bicycle to the mountains, so as to get the reports from the patrols in good time.' Clouds of dust soon confirmed the correctness of his estimate. Observers reported similar signs of movement towards Mlali, a depot, and the South African horsemen riding against it were in for a stiff fight.

Brits's men had come up with Captain Otto's detachment and one of the *Königsberg's* four-inch guns. It had been von Lettow's plan to isolate this South African force, but the steep hills impeded the movement of his own force, and he gave orders for them to fall back. The South Africans blew up the stores of shells in the depot.

Captain Richardson of the 8th noted on 25 August: 'Evident that the enemy are making strenuous efforts to get away. Can hear them blasting a road. We hold the main road from Morogoro southwards and there is no other line of retreat, except over the mountains. We can't attack, because we are not strong enough, but expect to be joined by Van Deventer's mounted brigade tonight.'

Von Lettow himself became so entangled in the mountains that he was cut off from his carriers and supplies. He spent a cold night, but appeased his hunger with a fowl roasted on a spit, surmising, correctly, that the enemy was moving south-west to reach Kissaki before him. At Mlali the waggon road stopped. From there on it was native tracks through passes broken by many ravines and obstacles.

Only SA Victoria Cross of the Campaign

'We had no time to waste,' wrote von Lettow. Already there were rumours that the South Africans were ahead of him on the way to Kissaki. Riding with the scout corps of the 2nd Mounted Brigade, Captain W A Bloomfield's men commanded the only waggon road, making it dangerous for the Germans to get their guns away. The Germans

Another *Königsberg* gun destroyed by the Germans in retreat.

fought their way round his flanks. Bloomfield had to extricate his men, who were being wounded.

While the scouts fell back Bloomfield found that one of his wounded had been left behind. In full view of the enemy and across four hundred yards of bullet-swept ground he reached Corporal D P M Bowker and carried him back to safety. For this action Captain Bloomfield was awarded the only South African Victoria Cross* of the campaign. This rare distinction was gazetted on 20 December 1916.

At this distance in time we may speculate on why this brave deed by Captain Bloomfield was selected for so high an honour in a campaign that could cite many instances of great courage that went unrewarded.† A cynical assessment might be that the campaign needed a Victoria Cross at that stage and Smuts was notoriously stingy, as were his generals, in making awards. Perhaps it was a legacy of the Boers' attitude to warfare. It was not until January 1918, when the British War Office asked for a despatch on the German South West Africa Campaign in 1914-15, with recommendations for decorations, that something was done.

Piet van der Bijl wrote: 'Having done the officers, Collyer instructed me to prepare an honours list of NCOs and other ranks. This meant endless work studying reports both by general officers commanding divisions and by officers commanding regiments and units.

---

* At Maktau on 3 September 1916 Lt Wilbur Dartnell, Royal Fusiliers, was severely wounded and helpless but insisted on being left behind, hoping his presence might save the lives of seven other wounded men nearby. All were killed by askaris as they rushed the hill. He was awarded a posthumous Victoria Cross.
† See Appendix.

Collyer asked Botha not to put his name forward for any decorations as everyone knew of his work on the honours list.'

It is worth noting that in the period from January 1917 to the end of the campaign the Nigerian Brigade was given sixty Military Crosses, sixteen Distinguished Conduct Medals, twenty Military Medals and sixty-three mentions in despatches to its white officers and NCOs and eighty-three Distinguished Conduct Medals, thirty-one Military Medals and forty-seven mentions in despatches to its black soldiers.

South Africa's only VC in East Africa, Major W A Bloomfield VC, 2nd Mounted Brigade.

On 29 August, Smuts arrived with Brits, who took command of both mounted brigades. Meanwhile the Germans were compelled to blow up the 3,5-inch naval guns that had served them so well for so many months and abandon their five hundred remaining shells. While the South Africans pressed hard after them, von Lettow led Governor Schnee and ten companies deep into the mountains, and his personal party made its way along a mountain track to reach the Mgeta Mission.

Von Lettow was struck by the charm of the rural buildings set in a river glade that strikingly reminded him of home. Here we are given a rare glimpse of the enemy's sorrow at leaving their good works behind. A few European refugees from Morogoro were at the mission 'and bade farewell to the force for the last time'.

Writing of that night the German commander spent at Mgeta Mission, Frau Engelmann, wife of a German merchant at Morogoro, left this account: 'He was just recovering from a bout of blackwater fever and he was thin. He ate very little and only sipped at his wine. Halfway through the meal a message came for him to say that an English division was driving in towards us and that we were in danger of being cut off. "We must leave quickly," the staff officer said. He replied: "Not until we have finished our meal and made arrangements for these ladies." Some of us had husbands and sons attached to the *Schutztruppe,* and these he summoned to spend the last few hours with us. While we bade our farewells and embraced for the last time, he dispatched an envoy to the English [sic] . . . asking for protection for the women.'

Although he left the civilian women at Mgeta, von Lettow took with him about twenty young German women nurses, and at dawn they slipped away into the mountains.

Von Lettow Spared Smuts's Life

It was at that meal that von Lettow told the astonishing story of how only a few days before he had Smuts in the sights of his rifle.

> He was on a reconnaissance at the head of his troops, and he rode into a nullah overlooked by one of our machine-gun posts. I had him in my sights and was about to fire, when I recognised from his hat and red beard who he was. I decided that it would be unsportsmanlike to shoot an enemy commander in such circumstances, and I held my fire. One of our captured askaris who escaped from them told Smuts of this occurrence. Smuts said: Von Lettow is a fool – but a gentleman. There must be honour and chivalry even in war.

When Brits's troopers rode in next day they found a number of sick and wounded Germans and some nursing sisters. They heard that von Lettow had slept there the night before. Evidence that he was not far off came when a native messenger trotted in carrying a message in a cleft stick. Deneys Reitz relieved him of it. It was a note signed by von Lettow ordering the *Bahnschutz* (Railway Protection) Field Company to retire south to Kissaki.

The pursuit went on. Brits's weary horsemen spent two days of endless descents and ascents of endless parallel ridges, dragging their sick and exhausted beasts behind them. The horses were thin and sluggish, for the tsetse poison acts slowly. By the evening of the third day Reitz's troop came out on the skyline above the village of Kikeo. Two thousand feet below, in a deep valley companies of askari were forming up and marching away into the darkness. To follow was impossible.

At dawn a native messenger trotted out of the forest with a letter addressed to the 'Truppenkommando' at Kikeo. It was from *Hauptmann* Schulz, and it was an accurate report, to the very number of horses, of the company's strength. They had been given by askari Ali Hassan who, divesting himself of his uniform, obligingly offered to serve the South Africans by cutting grass for the horses – and then slipped off into the forest.

At Kikeo, several storehouses and pools of oil blazed fiercely; but the rivers were still bridged and the swamps were adequately crossed by corduroy roads of logs. Sonkomero lay ahead in the evening light, the forest round it lurid with the glare of burning storehouses and the stunning detonation of shells and the crackle of exploding cartridges. A German NCO had been killed setting the charges.

'We estimated the destruction at a million rounds,' wrote Reitz, 'and the men began to say that the campaign was over. We were soon to be disillusioned on that head.'

The End in Sight?

So was Smuts. On 16 August he had written to his wife from Turiani, to which he had returned to attend to belated official correspondence after directing the drive through the Nguru Mountains. Of the forward movement that would take him to Morogoro he wrote:

> I wonder whether the Germans are going to fight it out there so that we can go home soon, or whether they will retire southwards and prolong the war for months. My hope is that the askaris will refuse to go south and that von Lettow will therefore flee with only a small part of his force.

On 31 August he wrote from Morogoro:

> It is now four weeks that we have been advancing day and night to drive the enemy and give him no rest, and, of course, that we ourselves have had no rest or quiet . . . The enemy flees on, fighting all the time, to Kissaki south of this great block of mountains called the Uluguru Mountains, and only when we have taken this place and seen in what direction the enemy retires shall we know how to advance ourselves.
>
> Things are going fairly fast and I hope to see the beginning of the end in two months. You can see that my hands are shaking and my writing is bad; that is because of the quinine that I have to take twice a week.

He concludes with his usual expression of affection and obvious longing.

> Well mamma, many good wishes, many kisses to you and the little ones. I hope soon not to send kisses any more but to bring them in person. Oh, how joyful that would be, as the hymn says. Pappa thinks constantly of you in the midst of his most pressing difficulties.

Who among his men would have suspected that the man they thought ruthless and heartless could be so tender-hearted or long so much for it all to be over? They saw only the commander. Yet those close to him knew otherwise. He wrote often of his concern about the health of his driver, George Hodgson, who was suffering from chronic dysentery 'and now lives on Ideal milk and soup. He looks dreadful but still does his work. He won't go either to hospital or home.'

The enigma that was Smuts was never better illustrated than by Piet van der Bijl's anecdotes of their sojourn in Morogoro. The general and his small GHQ had quarters in a house for the first time for months. When Smuts announced that he was to make a five-day visit to Van Deventer the younger staff members decided to give a party.

'About a quarter way through we heard the roar of a car and, to my utter horror, in walked the chief, with a bright red sunburnt face, looking like a thunderstorm at sunset. As he stopped at the door there was a dead silence while he pierced each one in turn with those steely blue eyes.' The hilarity ended.

But an hour later, when he had washed and dressed he sat down with them and talked about science, evolution, philosophy, Greek and Roman classics and botany. 'His light, almost gossamer talk wove a spell round all present, as only he could do when in the mood.'

Signed a Death Warrant

It was during that time that Smuts signed a death warrant. It was not for the first time in his life as a soldier.*

'Shortly after we reached Morogoro, a native caught looting an empty German bungalow was tried by court martial and sentenced to be shot. My sympathies were with the offender, knowing that he had no doubt seen some of our men taking furniture out of empty houses. But such is the logic of war.'

It shocked Van der Bijl that the man had been sentenced to be shot publicly and that all the local inhabitants had been ordered to attend. The British officer in charge of the execution† revolted Van der Bijl by announcing that there was no hurry and that there was time for afternoon tea. 'I for one,' wrote Van der Bijl, 'would not feed a sadistic curiosity by being present at this spectacle. After about an hour I heard, some hundred yards away, the volley of the firing squad.

---

* In his raid into the Cape in the Anglo-Boer War he ordered the execution of Lemuel Colaine who had joined his commando only to betray it to the English cavalry. Smuts lost seventeen men killed and wounded as they lay asleep. Having captured Colaine Smuts ordered summary execution by firing party.
† Some time later this same officer was found trying to get a looted grand piano shipped to England and was only prevented by alert embarkation officials.

'This illiterate near-savage died with great dignity. After the charge had been read aloud in English, German and Swahili, he took out of his pocket some money and a few trashy personal effects, and handed them to the officer to give to his family. Then calmly he faced the execution, while a three-sided hollow square looked on.' A severe example had been set.

BAGGED !

THE HUN: "Donnerwetter! Dah goes my CAPITAL seat."
[Dar es Salaam surrendered to the British forces.]

(The *Cape Times*, 9 September 1916)

14

Von Lettow's Struggle to Evacuate Stores

When von Lettow's forces left Morogoro a thousand native labourers working in the forestry department were pressed into service by the insistence of the energetic Captain Feilke. Some persuasion was necessary, as the Africans saw that the German power was waning, and they refused to volunteer as porters, much 'to the despair of the sensible chiefs who would gladly have helped us', wrote von Lettow, perhaps with sly humour.

Many troubles lay ahead. Von Lettow had pinned his hopes on getting supplies away to the south. At Kissaki he found 'an abundance' and no means of getting them away. The local natives were terrified at the arrival of an army in retreat and askaris trying to round them up with the persuasive *kiboko* only sent them fleeing into the bush, abandoning their villages till the danger was past. The chiefs could not be coaxed even by gifts of clothing and gold sovereigns.

Worse still, the column of several hundred pack donkeys driven over the mountains from Morogoro had arrived completely exhausted, and his ox-waggons plodding round east of the mountains had not been seen. If the war were to be continued to the south as he planned, how were the stocks of food and ammunition to be carried? Fall back to the south he must! There was nothing for it but to hold off his enemy in the hills, rivers and bush before Kissaki, at the same time working energetically to get away what stores he could. For this he stripped the troops of their carriers, used all the natives he could muster in the district and gave up the last of his own waggons.

At Kissaki he waited with his main body, ready to make use of any favourable opportunity to attack and, he hoped, to destroy the enemy's separate columns one by one. He knew his Smuts and his Brits and his Enslin, and as always they obliged him by doing the expected. Gleefully he noted later that 'the enemy's beautiful plans completely collapsed.'

Smuts saw the retreat as his victory. He still believed that von Lettow had planned to turn the Ulugurus into a fortress. From the vast quantities of heavy artillery ammunition captured it seemed evident to Smuts that 'the enemy had intended a long and elaborate defence . . . and it was only the unexpected arrival of General Enslin at Mlali and the audacious and successful pursuit into the mountains, combined with the operations of General Hoskins on the other side, that had forced the enemy to abandon his plans.' Smuts never gave his opponent the benefit of the doubt when his own plans miscarried. Nor did he now.

On Foot Along Elephant Tracks

As always, it had been a matter of brigades groping forward without contact, each in a pathway miles from his support and without wireless or visual contact. Messengers on horseback seldom got through. It was a case of slowly working ahead without guns or waggons, following native or elephant tracks through jungle.

By 7 September Brits's main columns had emerged from the hills before Kissaki, but Hoskins's 1st Division still had at least a two-day march before it could link up with Brits. Nussey's brigade was still in the mountains with no idea where the others were. Nevertheless Brits determined to attack. It seemed fairly simple. Beves's 2nd SA Infantry Brigade was to follow the footpath south along the river Mgeta to Kissaki. Enslin's 2nd Mounted Brigade was to march round by the right to attack from the west and south-west.

Captain Richardson was riding with the 8th Horse in the same sweep southwards to Kissaki. On Thursday, 7 September, he recorded reaching a *poort* in the hills overlooking Kissaki. Next day the squadron extended in skirmishing order and advanced through long grass into bush so thick that by the time he was through it he had only a sergeant and five men with him.

But then they came in touch with the 5th, 6th and 7th Regiments and advanced again on foot through a rubber plantation. There they met the enemy in strength. 'Kept advancing slowly, then lay down and returned fire. The general [Beves] then removed 6th Regiment to strengthen left flank. Very heavy rifle and maxim fire from the enemy, evidently in great strength.'

In the event, Enslin's horsemen had emerged to find the bulk of the enemy on the right bank of the river in front of him. Dense bush on the other side of the river prevented Beves from going to his assistance. When von Lettow judged that Enslin had got round in the rear of Captain Otto near the fort at Kissaki he let loose his reserves.

'Evidently the enemy did not expect German reserves to be posted under cover still further back . . . The gallant 11th Field Company under Lt Volkwein worked through the dense bush close up to the outflanking enemy, and immediately attacked with the bayonet, cheering.'

'The Fire was Terrific!'

Those who had not heard it before now heard the bugles blaring and the bloodcurdling yells of 'Piga! Piga!' as the askaris came on with the bayonet. Richardson wrote:

> We held our own till about 4.30 p.m., when the enemy were suddenly reinforced opposite our right flank with three maxims and four hundred men, a hundred whites and three hundred askaris. We held them for some time when they advanced their maxims to within thirty yards of our extreme front . . . they then pushed round our right flank and started enfilading us with maxim and rifle fire at about fifty yards.
>
> We sent for reinforcements, but found that the troops on our left flank had retired . . . It was miraculous that the whole squadron was not annihilated. The fire was terrific. We were fortunate enough to get two troops away without further casualties, but we lost Mr Driver, who waited to help a wounded man and got shot in the head.

Horses were neighing and rearing as men tried to mount and get away. With nine dead, twelve wounded and seven taken prisoner Brits called off the action for the night. His men were scattered about in all directions in the darkness and the led horses and horse-keepers were captured.

Not till nearly midnight were the units of Enslin's brigade in touch with each other again. Next day Richardson listed his losses. 'The regiment had twenty-seven casualties and our squadron lost thirty-one horses killed and captured'.

'Even next day,' wrote von Lettow, 'a soldier arrived from quite another direction. He had lost himself with his led horses in the dense bush and had no idea where to go.' The man threw his rifle and ammunition across a small stream, observing philosophically: 'It's just luck. I might have taken the right road or the wrong one. I had the bad luck to take the wrong one. That's my fault.' The Germans admired his equanimity with good humour.

During the afternoon of 8 September eight of Richardson's missing men turned up. 'The Germans had captured them and allowed them to go on parole.'

Plains of the Rufiji

Once the horsemen had penetrated the Ulugurus and come out on the southern foothills they had their first view of the shimmering plain that stretched to the Rufiji River. Another day's march brought them within sight of Kissaki. Through field-glasses it was possible to see the white-washed fort, apparently empty, and red cross flags fluttered over the hospital.

'But between us and Kissaki was five miles of jungle in which, unknown to us, von Lettow was lying in wait.' So wrote Deneys Reitz, riding in front with the advanced patrol of Nussey's brigade. They were riding straight into von Lettow's trap.

'As we neared the end of the cotton field,' wrote Reitz, 'we spied a German seated on a platform in the fork of a tree. He fired a single shot, which killed a horse, and scrambled down. A few minutes later, as we rode into the jungle beyond the clearing, heavy fire broke out.' Nussey came forward and ordered them to dismount and deploy on foot on either side of the road. 'Immediately we were swallowed in jungle. Even the sky overhead was invisible . . . one could not see a man three feet away. Far from evacuating Kissaki, the enemy had dug rifle pits and trenches, and from the noise of their fire there were thousands of askaris shooting at us.'

The troopers dug themselves in with their bayonets and prepared to sweat out a violent day of battle in stifling heat, with no water and wounded men groaning and dying without help.

Only a few miles away Brits was unaware of Nussey's plight. The sound of rifle fire did not carry far in such forest country. Earlier in the day the Germans had kept half their force opposing him, but when he did not move, and the hours passed, they threw these men into the fight against Nussey.

Ugly Rushes by Askaris

Fire grew increasingly severe and they began to press us hard. They made several ugly rushes, and for the first time in the campaign I saw the askari in action in close quarters, and I even heard them shouting their 'Piga! Piga!' as they came. Only here and there could we make out their earthworks and barricades. We hung on. With repeated attacks threatening us we could not advance against the enemy works, and to retire under those conditions was impracticable, so we fought in the steaming heat. As darkness approached at last, the firing died down and the encounter came to an end. We had lost four officers and twenty-three men killed and as many wounded. Thirsty and hungry, our

The KAR reached the Rufiji River but once again von Lettow-Vorbeck had slipped away. Although the majority of German East Africa was in Smuts's hands, he still had not decisively defeated his enemy.

Schutztruppe askaris step out smartly on the march with drums and bugles.

men lay on their arms beyond the cotton clearing, but I was ordered to ride back to Sonkomero to hurry on the native carriers with water . . . I rode away in the dusk with the ugly memory of some of our men whom I had seen lying dead, their skulls smashed by the askari . . .

Next day the rest joined Brits's horsemen and one of his infantry regiments. They had heard the firing, but said they could make no headway to help. Smuts admitted that his plan had failed. If only Brits and Nussey could have been in contact. If only a joint attack had been possible!

Von Lettow had his tail up! Smuts's forces had been beaten piecemeal. It had been just as von Lettow had foreseen. 'A regrettable recovery of enemy morale,' explained Smuts; and he must have seen it as a portent of the future.

Von Lettow had only one regret. The dense bush and rugged country had robbed him of what he longed for: 'an energetic pursuit' that would have thrown General Brits into fatal confusion and total defeat.

Brits Furious at Failure

Brits himself was angry at his failure. 'He was as surly as a bear,' wrote Reitz. Brits's exasperation took the form of a letter of protest about the mutilation of his dead. He sent Reitz into Kissaki under a flag of truce to ask for information about some of their men who had been missing since the fight.

I cut a bamboo pole to which I tied a piece of cloth, and with an orderly as standard-bearer I rode away. I hoped to meet the redoubtable von Lettow himself, but that was not to be.

We were told to dismount, and, at a shout, half a dozen askari came running from the trees to guard us while the senior officer went into Kissaki with the message. The askari looked blood-thirsty ruffians who handled their bayonets as if they would have liked to spit us, but the officer was a decent young fellow. He proudly showed me his Mauser pistol, which he said was one of a number sent out in a blockade-runner by the people of Germany as gifts for the stand they were making.

On his way back to Brits Reitz came across a native lying mortally wounded in his millet field. He said he had been shot down by an askari the day before. 'I gave him my waterbottle. He clutched it with trembling hands and emptied its contents at a gulp, then with a low moan he fell back dead.'

The letter from von Lettow to Brits denied the murder of the wounded but gave news of several of his men lying in hospital. He said they were being well treated.

Resentment and Suspicion

The failure of the great end game to bag von Lettow once and for all was sourly commented on by the British troops in Sheppard's brigade. 'Their disappointment,' wrote Brett Young, 'found vent in murmurs of resentful suspicion. Why had Enslin retired? The Boers had funked it, betrayed them when the end lay within their grasp . . . It was a damnable piece of treachery.'

However, the *Official History* exonerated Enslin's brigade and actually blamed Brigadier-General Sheppard's laggard march for his failure to carry out his part of the operation in time. From the commanders down nerves were under strain and accusations were flying back and forth.

Had the Boers funked it at a crucial moment? Collyer puts the blame on Brits for his order to Beves to withdraw. 'Beves,' he wrote, 'had two seasoned infantry battalions with machine guns in a position of his own selection, which he had entrenched on the north bank of the Mgeta River, and he had two days' supplies on the hoof with him and an abundance of water. The only attack that had been made on him he had beaten off without machine guns.' Lt Molloy was in this night withdrawal.

The orders came to us at midnight, when we were quietly aroused and told that the enemy were in great force and were

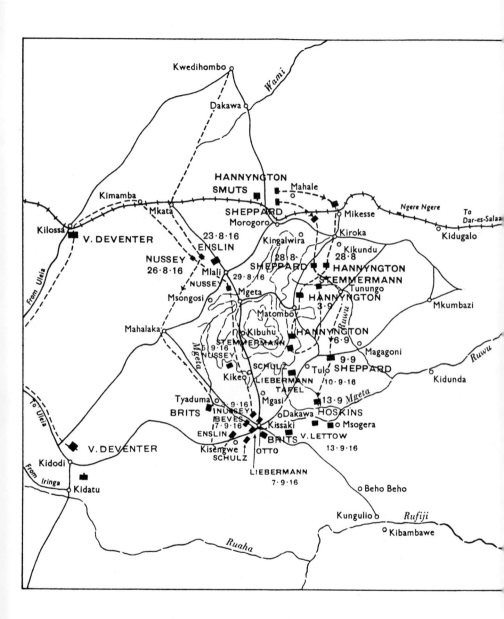

GENERAL SMUTS'S OPERATIONS SOUTH OF MOROGORO
TO 20 SEPTEMBER 1916.

(*The South Africans with General Smuts in German East Africa 1916*,
Brig-Gen Collyer, 1939)

endeavouring to encircle us. We knew that Enslin's brigade had retreated to Tyaduma at 5 a.m. We were given twenty minutes to prepare to withdraw. We expected hell. Our regiment led the way and the 6th acted as rearguard. The moon was on the wane.

We crossed the river. Everyone's nerves were strained to the breaking point in anticipation of a sudden and terrific burst of fire at point blank range in dense forest at dead of night.

They got through without casualties, but were bitter. They had been forced to abandon their positions without a shot being fired. Once again they had been let down by the mounted men.

'We are proud of them – I don't think!' wrote Lt Molloy.

The bitter fact was that both commanders of the infantry had urged Beves to reconsider his order to pull out. He wavered but eventually decided that General Brits must know the position better. Six hundred South African rifles were withdrawn from well entrenched positions. The enemy came as expected, to find only empty trenches.

The havoc that those six hundred rifles could have inflicted in the dawn light could have saved Nussey the casualties that he suffered the following morning. So raged the angry argument.

Brits Blamed for Failure

'Brits seems to have judged the situation wrongly,' Collyer admitted, and from Smuts there came no censure. In view of what had been achieved – the clearing of the Ulugurus in a week – it seemed more like a reverse than a disaster; except that once more the Germans successfully disengaged and began to withdraw south towards the Rufiji River.

The river was a great psychological barrier for both contestants. There was danger there for both. But for the Germans, once they were south of the flooded plain there was no place where they could be outflanked and forced to give battle. They would be swallowed up in swamp and jungle. Those who followed would do so at their peril.

'Meanwhile,' wrote Reitz, 'we were living under famine conditions. There was little or no game in the forest, nor any cattle in this tsetse-haunted region, and the millet fields lay mostly reaped.' The twelve hundred South Africans had to be supplied by the few native porters who could get through to them.

It was on the Mgeta River that the Germans prepared a new defence. The South Africans dug in in what was to become trench warfare, with the opposing forces varying from two to four hundred yards from one another. General Brits was now in command of two brigades, infantry and horseless cavalry.

We dug rifle pits and trenches and for the next three weeks lay in the jungle with the enemy about four hundred yards away, though we saw little enough of them in the high grass and dense forest. We could hear them felling trees, and sometimes, after dark, they sang 'Deutchland über alles' and other songs, which the men declared were on rum nights, for they were enviously convinced that the Germans received a rum ration twice a week.

The weather now changed and torrential rains came down. When it did not rain the heat was terrific, and day and night mosquitoes buzzed and persecuted. This lowland is one of the most unhealthy parts of Africa, and soon malaria and dysentery were rife. Further, there was the food problem. With the heavy rains the carriers failed, and where we had been on short commons before, we went on shorter now. During this dismal time we lay on the south bank of the Mgeta with rifle and machine-gun bullets swishing through the rain.

Jungle Trench Warfare

Nothing could reach them. All the streams were up and what artillery they had was ineffective in that dense country. The dismounted men hung on next to the 5th and 6th Infantry, who had no great faith in them, in what turned out to be a bizarre battle that could only have been fought in tropical Africa.

'For sixteen days,' wrote Lieutenant Molloy of the 5th, 'we strafed each other day and night. During two night attacks they made on us a herd of elephant crashed across the river towards us in the middle of one attack but changed their line of advance . . .'

South African Field Artillery's 5th Battery in action, Mgeta Valley where von Lettow still had 3 500 fighting men in action.

There were lions roaring just beyond their lines, but the meat shortage was solved by the shooting of hippopotamus 'within a mile of this paradise of a swamp'. Neither side could effectively penetrate the other's positions because of the river swamps and the density of the bush.

The African character of the struggle was even more marked when the Germans resorted to fire as a weapon. 'The devils tried to burn us out of our trenches, using a strong wind blowing towards us. Luckily it changed at the last moment and drove the fire across our front. Seeing this, the enemy lit a fresh fire on our right flank, and if it had not been for a hastily cut firebelt we would have had to get out, with disastrous results. Fortunately the grass was not quite ripe.'

The Germans pressed forward behind the screen of smoke. 'They hoped to catch us in the confusion of retirement, but we were ready in our trenches and with twenty maxims we gave them particular blazes. Next morning some enemy deserters came into our camp and reported that they had suffered about two hundred casualties.'

So the days of confrontation passed. 'Considering that our men have had to lie in sodden trenches every minute of the night and day for sixteen days, without any shelter, their spirit was splendid.'

Smuts Obsessed?

Was Smuts obsessed by his consuming passion to bring his adversary to bay? Did he see himself in some kind of kinship with the German who was now playing the part that Smuts had played against the British Empire? The skilful adversary, the man who knew the people and the ground against the commander with the huge, unwieldy polyglot army of empire troops? His biographer Hancock believed that he was obsessed.

If so, it would be in the manner of the perfectionist, a man who would not be baulked of his success, who had too great an investment in his own self-esteem to fail. And what of the 'gamesmanship' aspect in which his army, now nearly eighty thousand strong, were pieces in a game of match-wits? It was perhaps to him already like some mediaeval knightly ritual. We do not know what he thought as he lay at night under his mosquito net, listening to the shrilling of the deadly insects, reading his favourite works of philosophy.

Time for Reflection

A man in Smuts's situation, even in his most intimate writings, may never have expressed the ultimate truth. Did he think, perhaps, of what lay behind him, his totally self-absorbed career, his enemies waiting in the Union, the anger and the bitterness of the thousands who had already fallen victim to what – his ambition? What was German East Africa to him but another proving ground for his military prowess? His total belief in himself? For never did a man doubt less.

Did Smuts, as he lay with chattering teeth in the rigours of malaria, imagine his enemy in similar plight? Had some of his arrogant assumptions about the value of black soldiers fighting on their own soil been adjusted to the reality that on this ground they were better fitted for survival than his own?* The background, the legacy of his breeding was contrary to that; and yet here were his sturdy South Africans, even his brave Boers, his reckless, heedless and often contemptuous old comrades being bested.

Did he know that he was looked at askance by the 'foreign' commanders of his force?† Undoubtedly, but in his unwavering arrogance he took no heed of it. He had concentrated this campaign onto a personal duel with an adversary worthy of his steel, and a man of his mettle must have rejoiced at the challenge.

Smuts never fully recovered from his recurring malaria. Years later his son, Jan described him as 'a fever-stricken wreck'. Like so many of his men he paid a heavy price. For a long while the attacks were to leave him white, weak, but undaunted. He, the commander, was but one of seventy-two thousand men who succumbed – a ratio to battle casualties of thirty-one to one!

Did he ever consider the physical condition of his adversary? Von Lettow took good care never to appear in person when emissaries came under the white flag. But when he talked in 1936 to the British author Leonard Mosley he was frank about his condition. 'I had discovered that I was peculiarly vulnerable to the African mosquito, and he bit me right into my bones . . . so hard do they bite and so maddening are their stings that I have known my officers to sleep in the swamp waters, preferring leeches and crocodiles and water-snakes to their tortures.'

Von Lettow's Suffering

Now, as he fell back from his assured sources of supply and the ingenious improvisations of medical relief, von Lettow was reduced to drinking infusions of tree bark with his coffee. Lettow-schnapps they called the bitter brew. His body was in agony, but his spirit never faltered.

---

* When the KAR made a forty-four-mile march in twenty-four hours Smuts showed approval. 'They were even faster than my cavalry!' Which may have been an ironic commentary on the failure of his mounted brigades.
† To his staff, he often used to soliloquise, 'and it was always a joy to listen to this brilliant brain thinking out loud.' – Piet van der Bijl.

Von Lettow, a yellow, shrunken skeleton of a man by this time, was finding it difficult to walk. He had been bitten badly by jigger fleas too, but these his cook, Baba, cut out of his feet each evening, and they had inflamed his left foot so badly that it had become a pulpy mass of scabs and festering flesh over which he found it agony to strap even the light sandals that he had adopted instead of boots. The medical officer had extracted two of his toenails and enabled him to limp about in constant pain.

Did von Lettow think of Smuts as he lay at night under the mosquito netting tucked round him by devoted bearers who carried him by day in a blind loyalty that few men are capable of arousing? He never lost his sense of humour. There is little record of Smuts having any, and he positively loathed any horseplay or over-indulgence in the mess.

With Smuts, whose men were in too much awe of him to venture to jest with him, this harsh experience was something of a metaphysical exercise: the spirit prevailing over the weakness of the flesh.

Yet the letters he wrote home to wife and children are full of fun and tenderness and longing. Was it duty to a noble ideal that drove him, or duty to his conception of himself? Was this just another proving ground, perhaps the greatest so far? Smuts and von Lettow. The Colonel and the General. They were born adversaries. Yet there is little doubt that by now Smuts sensed that he had been bested by this German whom his men called 'general', although he was in fact still only a colonel. That was the measure of the German's stature in their eyes.

To Quit with Honour

There is no record available of Smuts knowing by now that only an armistice or some other way out would save his face. We do not know when he first thought of quitting the field and being able to do so with honour.

At this stage he believed in just one more battle, one more attempt to bring his respected adversary to an honourable defeat and of finishing what he had begun with such zeal and high hopes. Cross the Rufiji River. The final objective. After all, that was as far as he had undertaken to go. He had added a vast new territory to the British Empire. Who could call him a quitter?

Meanwhile his volunteer soldiers lay on the south banks of the Mgeta River and could make no further progress. Ahead were entrenched Germans, round them the evidence of their plight.

'Our horses began to die at such a rate,' wrote Reitz, 'that weakened as we were, we could not muster hands enough to bury the rotting carcases, so the stench of hundreds of dead animals was added to the miasma of the swamps. More than half the men were down with fever, and I doubt whether there were a dozen horses left, all told.'

So much for the mounted brigade! The Germans had warned them that this would be their fate. Everywhere there were heaps of saddles and bridles rotting in the humid tropical heat. 'The wastage was awful,' noted a mounted officer, 'and all we can do is look for relief to get away from this festering place.'

The naïve belief in quick victory and home by Christmas had withered away. Smuts was yet to face their resentment when they conceived him to be not only the architect of their misery but their betrayer. What was it to them that he had taken possession of 160 000 square miles of equatorial Africa? They would refuse him the triumph that he had earned through their pain. But that was still to come.

'What Am I To Do?'

On 26 September Smuts wrote to his wife from Morogoro.

> Dearest Mamma, I think there are a few letters to you that have not yet left this place, as there has been no transport for the last week because of the great rains and the roads washed away. But tomorrow there will be an opportunity for dispatch to the coast, and I again send a line to refresh your little heart.
>
> Everything here still well. I am back from Kissaki as there are more important matters elsewhere. Besides, there is an amazing amount of sickness at Kissaki, especially in these rains. Colonel Piet Botha of Brits's division tells me that 700 of Brits's men are down with fever at Kissaki! What am I to do? It is really amazing how people are getting fever. I am bringing Brits's division back here where conditions are better.
>
> You cannot imagine how dangerous the rains are in this country. An old missionary informs me that the forty-mile plain between Kissaki and the Rufiji River becomes one continuous sea of water in the rainy season. How am I to pursue the enemy thither? And if I do so and the rain comes, how do we get food and what will become of us cut off from the world on the Rufiji? This forty miles is now an arid desert, so there is not enough water for the troops should they now go forward. So it is a case of nothing or too much. We are having a terribly hard time. But how much harder a time the fleeing Germans and askaris are having! So let us be patient and persevere to the end.

It was in this letter that the question of repatriation to South Africa sur-faced in his intimate sharing of thoughts with his wife. 'I am going to send all the bad sick cases back to the Union; and am only afraid that their arrival will make a very bad and unpleasant impression there. But the sooner they return the better chance they will have of a quick recovery.'

His fresh hope was based on the belief that most of von Lettow's askaris would now desert him. For how could the Germans continue to hold out in a region of such appalling difficulty? Smuts's desire to be done with it all was only equalled by his admiration for his chivalrous enemy. But the signs that his own white troops were at the end of their tether were looming large. It looked more and more as if Africa were going to win this war.

Von Lettow's Tireless Energy

If Smuts was near the end of his patience and suffering recurrent bouts of fever, von Lettow was hardly in better shape physically.

'He has lost twelve kilos in the past two weeks,' wrote his adju-tant, 'and is yellow with fever, but he will not stop. He seems to live on coffee. But he steams with energy and never complains of the oppressive heat . . . He has climbed mountains, swum rivers, waded through swamps and been badly stung by bees, but he is indefatigable. He arrived here dragging his horse behind him, and I am not sure which one more resembled a skeleton.'

However, von Lettow still had five thousand men under his direct command and other units moving to join him amounted to a further forty-five hundred. These were the troops that had been holding off the Belgians and the Portuguese. With something like ten thousand still in the field, he was in fact not much short of the three thousand Euro-peans and eleven thousand askaris that he had started out with. His supply lines were still behind him, his men were fed, even if their uni-forms were tattered and patched.

An Audacious Offer

No doubt von Lettow smiled when an emissary from Smuts rode into his camp. Governor Schnee, who conceived it his duty to accompany von Lettow as far as the campaign would take him and thus maintain his authority as Commander-in-Chief, had sent Smuts a note. Schnee was expressing his indignation at reports that his nationals were being ill-treated in British-occupied Dar es Salaam.

Smuts had no knowledge of that and strongly doubted its truth; but he saw an opportunity, and with typical audacity he used it to turn to his advantage the opportunity of civilities exchanged between reasonable-minded enemies. He sent Schnee's emissary back with a message exhorting von Lettow to surrender. Smuts argued that:

> . . . a continuance of the campaign for even a short while longer at this season of the year and in deadly country to which your forces are now confined must mean untold suffering for them, and at the end there will be no alternative to an unconditional surrender . . . If any discussion with me could assist your Excellency and Colonel von Lettow in coming to a conclusion on this question I am prepared to meet you and him at a time and place to be agreed on. I have the honour to be, Sir, Your Excellency's obedient servant, J C Smuts, Commanding British East African Expeditionary Force.

Von Lettow did not reply to this letter of mock solicitude. Smuts's letter was patently a pretext for an honourable way out for himself. It only encouraged von Lettow to resist. 'General Smuts realised that his blow had failed,' he wrote. 'His letter calling on me to surrender showed that, as far as his force was concerned, he had reached the end of his resources.'

How right he was! It is worth noting that Smuts did not reproach his commanders for their repeated failures to carry through his strategies to success. He must have agreed in his heart with Meinertzhagen's caustic and all-too-prophetic comment earlier in the campaign: 'It will be difficult to say what will be the last phase of the campaign unless Smuts manoeuvres von Lettow into Portuguese East Africa and rounds him up somewhere near Pretoria. But von Lettow knows the country better than we do, his troops understand the last word in bush warfare and can live on the country. I think we are in for an expensive game of hide-and-seek, and von Lettow will be cuckooing somewhere in Africa when the cease-fire goes.'

If only, some said, Smuts had listened to the advice of his Intelligence Chief in February when Smuts, wary of casualties to frighten home opinion and excite criticism, hesitated to bring the Germans to decisive battle by the head-on confrontation urged on him.

Call for More Men

Could that decision, it was now being asked, have caused more deaths and suffering than the course that he had chosen to follow? Smuts, however, continued to believe that the Germans were suffering worse. He needed every man that he could raise for another attempt. Hospitals and detail camps were scoured for the remnants of regiments waiting to rejoin their units at Maktau, the big depot camp five hundred miles from the battlefront.

Private Reid of the 9th tells the story of the last effort to reinforce the front at Kissanga. 'One day the order came to send forward all available men. Would it mean the Kondoa Trek all over again? . . . How much of the five hundred miles would be on foot?' The journey began in large, iron-covered cattle trucks with forty-two men to a truck. 'Past Salaita Hill and down the Tanga line for two hundred miles. The men hoped to go by sea to Dar es Salaam and so up to the Central Railway. No such luck!'

The journey had to be made on foot. About eleven hundred details and reinforcements set out from Korogwe for Morogoro – two hundred miles along the narrow-gauge hand railway.

Poor rations and hard going soon told their tale. Fever took hold . . . At each camping stage some men would be dropped. The column, doing from ten to eighteen miles a day, marched by night. Reveille at 2.30, move off at 3. At Turiani the column was reduced to four hundred men (measles too had broken out).

On the eighteenth day of the trek's second stage we were 332 out of the original 1 100, and arrived at Morogoro just in time to see General Brits saying farewell to his men of the 2nd Mounted Brigade, horseless and decimated by disease, returning to the Union.

The roll-call at Morogoro counted 332, but by the time Reid's remnants of the 9th reached Kissanga they were down to eighteen out of the hundred who had set out. 'But mighty welcome to the worn-out, fever-stricken outpost party. We had trekked five hundred miles just to rejoin.'

'Our troops,' recorded Brigadier Sir Charles Crewe, 'are thoroughly exhausted . . . During the whole advance from Kilossa they had been on short rations . . . continuous trekking and over bad country, and the labours of road and drift-making had been very disastrous. Strongly worded reports went in from the medical officers to headquarters.'

The Moment of Crisis

The moment of crisis was upon them. Brutal questions had to be asked and answered without delay. Smuts called a meeting of his medical chiefs. They must decide.

Could his white troops stand further operations? Thousands of men were already sick with malaria, with recurrent bouts that made them incapable of action. Thousands more would go down, including fresh men from the Union, if he sent them marching to the Rufiji River.

Part of the huge Uluguru range where the Germans made a stubborn defence.

Rains were already falling in this pestilential region, heralding weeks of deluge and fever.

'It was now clear,' wrote Smuts's Chief of Staff, 'that the enemy was determined to hang on unless compelled to retire.' Even the fresh 3rd KAR could make no dent on the new line that ran for fifty miles. 'The Commander-in-Chief decided to abandon any further action against the enemy's strong position in difficult country.' He made this decision with great reluctance only on being informed that once again supply and transport problems made a new offensive impossible.

Smuts told his commanders that he would attempt no further advance towards the Rufiji 'until he could review the situation with a view to fresh plans'. The time had come, in fact, when he had to admit 'that disease had played havoc amongst the troops, of whom large numbers were totally unfit without medical attention, prolonged rest, change of climate and nourishment to make any sustained effort.'

The wastage had been enormous. As Collyer put it: 'The strain upon all ranks of all units and services due to the steadily increasing effect of disease had reached the limit endurable.'

It was no longer possible to evade the truth. This was the end of a great endeavour as far as the South Africans were concerned. Smuts knew at this moment of truth that, barring a miracle, he would never see the end.* Von Lettow could rightly conclude that Smuts was at the end of his tether. True, he had lost a territory, but he had not lost the

---

* Meanwhile a press, so far docile, was recording: '. . . complete success has crowned General Smuts's efforts . . . in herding the remnants among the swamps of the Mahenge . . . a guarantee that the campaign will be brought to a speedy conclusion that the sound strategy at HQ and the indomitable determination on the part of the troops can give'. (*Cape Times*, 8 November 1916)

battle. His askaris were almost immune to disease, his white officers were hardened like himself.

Facing Facts and Figures

Smuts knew that the attempt to reinforce his front substantially had been a disaster. Of those still holding on, the 3rd Infantry Brigade was down to 460 rifles. The 1st Mounted Brigade was down to nine hundred, and among the Rhodesians fewer than two hundred could answer roll-call. The figures of wastage were unparalleled in this, or indeed in any other comparable war of men against climate.

Was this wastage only among the Europeans? Consider the plight of the African carriers, those nameless faceless creatures on both sides on whose load-bearing strength so much depended. They too were susceptible to disease and no less vulnerable to wounds. They were bombed, shelled, often ambushed and sniped at. Von Lettow lost between six and seven thousand men, women and children (many carriers were accompanied by their families) from wounds or sickness.

Smuts's East Africa Force suffered enormous losses. Forty-five thousand carriers and 'boys' died from disease, 376 were killed and 1 645 wounded. These figures include those who marched with the Portuguese and Belgian forces, and they are a shocking indictment of the methods used. The Allies took the high moral ground when it came to their treatment of carriers and accused the Germans of kidnapping and manacling carriers to their guns and abandoning and even shooting those too ill to march further. It is possible that, included in this ghastly roll-call, there were numbers of German carriers picked up on their last legs.

But forty-five thousand dead compared with the total of 6 558 who died* of disease or accident among the British, South African, Indian, and East and West African troops!

In his autobiography William Plomer wrote that as a captain in the South African native corps his father was in charge of the enrolment and transport of large numbers of South African drivers and carriers for the campaign in German East Africa. Captain Plomer attached great importance to the status and welfare of each individual and kept records of the men of tribal origins in the Union.

Expendable Men

'This was not done in East Africa, where the men were no doubt regarded as expendable. Many were lost there and never heard of

---

* Leonard Mosley supplied the statistics of losses in the Allied forces. A J Barker puts the total British casualties in this campaign in East Africa at 62 220, minus carriers.

again. Many others, returning to Durban in the last stages of dysentery and fever, died at sea, into which not only their bodies but their identity discs were dropped.'

Nowhere in Smuts's report to their Lordships in London or in Brigadier-General Collyer's account of the campaign is any mention made of these victims of a white colonial war. Small wonder, then, that von Lettow could not find willing carriers. Smuts's supply was inexhaustible from the neighbouring colonial territories with district officers and pliable chiefs to keep the army going.

Little has been recorded of these men. Private Frank Reid of the 9th, a maxim gunner, recalled that they were called 'bom-bom boys'. The word is Swahili for a machine gun. The bom-bom boy carried either the gun, the ammunition, the spare-parts box, the tripod or the water-can for cooling the barrel.

'There were about a dozen to each gun and a few more to carry the groundsheets and blankets of the carriers. They carried their loads on their heads on a circular pad of twisted grass. Their necks were strong, but they could not get the loads on to their heads without help.'

The soldiers could not get their tongues round the carriers' names, so they were given nicknames. In Reid's No 1 Gun Section they were called into action by the shout: 'Number One Bom-Bom Boys!' If the firing was fierce the porters 'threw themselves into the grass in a paroxysm of terror and could not be expected to carry their loads. Poor brutes! Who will blame them, defenceless as they were against missiles of death invented by their civilised overlords?'

Reid's Native Machine-gun Porters (their official title) were named Gertie, Piano, Wall Eye and Magoo. Others were nameless. What became of this group? According to Reid, 'most of them have carried their last load'. In an ambush that wiped out most of his gun team 'their black and battered bodies were found in the grass near the spot.'

At least these men were remembered, however inadequately. Is there a memorial anywhere to these men? TO THE UNKNOWN CARRIER! Their bones were no doubt scattered by the scavengers of the bush. In Kenyatta Avenue in Nairobi a bronze group has been erected, representing three heroic African figures, and inscribed in English and Swahili:

This is to the memory of the native African troops who fought; to the carriers who were the hands and feet of the army; and to all the other men who served for their king and country in Eastern Africa in the Great War of 1914-1918.

'If you fight for your country even if you die, your sons will remember your name.'

FIRST GERMAN EAST CAMPAIGNER: "They don't seem to think it's up to them to do their bit."

SECOND DITTO: "No. They're relying on us getting fit and doing another bit."

(The *Cape Times*, 13 March 1917)

"ALLIES"

DISEASE TO STARVATION: "My best friend ! You're doing wonders."

(The *Rand Daily Mail*, 14 November 1916)

15

South African Press Attack on the Campaign

On 21 November 1916 Lord Buxton, the Governor General of the Union, sat down at Government House in Pretoria to write a distressing letter to Smuts.

> My dear Smuts, I am very sorry that the *Rand Daily Mail* and the *Sunday Times* have been running amuck over the question of discomforts endured by the troops during the campaign. The cartoon in the *Daily Mail* was really disgraceful, and will have harrowed the hearts of a very large number of parents and others. They probably did not think of this when they thought they would make a scoop. However, your message published today will, I am sure, do a lot of good, and the General [Botha] has been giving the complainers a piece of his mind . . .

The cartoon that Buxton alluded to was certainly striking. It appeared in the *Rand Daily Mail* of 14 November. In the background South African soldiers are carrying stretchers. In the foreground two grim apocalyptic figures with skeleton visages clasp hands. The caption reads: (DISEASE TO STARVATION): 'My best friend. You're doing wonders!'

The fusillade against Smuts's conduct of the war in East Africa was opened by the *Sunday Times* on 12 November on its leader page under the caption: 'Half-Starved Soldiers'.*

> We indulge in no hasty criticism. What we are going to say has troubled us for many weeks, and now that we speak we do so deliberately . . . based upon numberless letters from the front and from personal information volunteered by reliable men of

---

* At the same time it campaigned against maladministration in the Army, the *Sunday Times* was waging war on South Africa's flies. It recorded that 'more than 12 000 000 flies have been received up to date' in its fourth campaign.

Tree palisades in the battle area of the highlands of Mahenge made formidable defences for German askaris.

every rank . . . bitter and emphatic about privations which many competent men consider could easily have been avoided.*

Our information leaves us in doubt whether the responsibility for this wretched state of affairs is due to the inefficiency of the transport officers or to the indifference and incompetence of a large proportion of regimental officers. In the opinion of the *Sunday Times* this thing wanted saying . . . the complaints are well founded . . . very drastic measures must be taken to remedy the evil.

In a subsequent leader on 19 November which appeared at the same time as an official reply by the Union Government, the newspaper rejected the explanation by the Defence Department with contempt: 'We cannot regard the official communiqué as convincing. Any planning worth the name would have taken into consideration the difficulties.' Indeed, the army order issued by the Commander-in-Chief and published in the press yesterday is from start to finish more an attempt to impugn the accuracy of their [the men's] statements than to deny the truth of them.'

Smuts's statement was issued from Morogoro when the planning for the Rufiji operation was still in progress and his letters make no

---

* On 14 November 1916, the *Cape Times* commented favourably on the visit by Miss Phyllis Buxton (the GG's daughter) to East African hospitals and her comments on the welfare of the men and 'the splendid work of the nursing sisters.'

reference to the attack. Perhaps he took it as merely another example of the stab in the back that his life in politics had accustomed him to endure with equanimity. But the problem would not go away. He could praise his men's endurance and drive them on, but sooner or later something would have to give.

Orders to Disengage

Gradually the news of the decision to send them home filtered down to the remnants of regiments. Orders came to disengage some units and withdraw to Dar es Salaam before the rains made it impossible to get them away.

The account by C W Shackleton of the 3rd Infantry Brigade is typical of their reaction and condition when the news reached them:

> The balance of our regiment when paraded was found to muster some two hundred men, all that remained of the original thousand. Worn out by hardship, exposure, fever and semi-starvation, we all underwent medical examination. Early next morning we departed for Kilossa to rest, accompanied by donkey-waggons carrying the men's rifles and kit.
> Some men were so weak that they could not have carried a rifle. Whenever a man collapsed he was lifted on to one of the waggons. We marched for three days back to Kilossa . . . a decrepit band of hollow-eyed men, with clothes hanging in rags on their skinny bodies, unkempt beards and drooping moustaches – which helped to age us.

And then the journey in open iron trucks to Dar es Salaam, where they were dumped without shelter or tents to await embarkation among 'thousands of other worn-out campaigners waiting their turn to embark for home'. New kit was issued from helmets to boots – 'leaving the old lice-infested garments in a heap, just as they had fallen from our bodies.'

As they marched to the docks for embarkation they saw a large camp of reinforcements; 'cleanly dressed men and officers busied themselves among rows of tents.' The contrast with their condition amazed Shackleton and his comrades now that the East African nightmare was over for them.

30 000 Dead Horses

Deneys Reitz had similar feelings as the remnants of his mounted unit began their withdrawal. 'It was pitiful to see the fever-racked men dragging themselves along on foot, for their animals were dead and we had ceased to be a mounted arm . . . More than thirty thousand of these gentle brutes had died.'

The vestiges of a mounted brigade marched eighty miles to the railway, stopping at a supply camp where a number of sick men were lying under trees. 'From among them,' wrote Reitz, 'a gaunt figure staggered to his feet and addressed me. Disease had so emaciated him that I did not recognise my own cousin, Bill Schreiner from Cape Town, and his condition was similar to hundreds of others.'

So the column staggered back from swamp and forest to reach Morogoro and the railway line to Dar es Salaam. The cool white Arab town by the blue Indian Ocean with its breezes, white coral sands and swishing palms was no longer a fevered dream.

At Dar es Salaam Captain Piet van der Bijl, of Smuts's staff, soon got a whiff of the ill-feeling that dogged the South Africans. The senior British officers enjoying the fleshpots of the port:

> . . . used to speak of us as 'that tribe', and, living in great com-fort, they had very little consideration for the thousands of men returning to base, completely unfit for further service. Shortly after my arrival there, two South African infantry privates asked to see me at my office. I found them dressed almost in rags and both looking so ill that, although they were friends, I failed to recognise them until they mentioned their names.
>
> One of them, Bill Schreiner, a barrister and son of my father's friend, the former Cape Prime Minister, W P Schreiner, had joined up at the outbreak of war as a private . . . Now he was to be discharged with 100% disability and wait in a filthy camp for transport . . . Hundreds there like him without proper medical attention were made to parade and drill at dawn each day.

Shake up GHQ!

Van der Bijl's anger came to a head when he overheard a senior British officer remark in the mess: 'The only battle honours the South Africans have are five towns looted.' White with rage, Van der Bijl excused himself from the GHQ mess and never went back. He sent a coded signal to Collyer asking him to 'come up to Dar and give the whole base GHQ a good shake-up'.

General Collyer was so incensed by the insult that he refused to accept an invitation to live in the mess, and chose to live with Van der Bijl.

Soon afterwards General Smuts arrived and boarded a cruiser. His intention was to reconnoitre the harbours south of Dar es Salam for possible landings that would outflank the Germans on the Rufiji and prevent reinforcement or supplies from Germany.

Wanted in London

No one on his staff knew then that Smuts was wanted in London. For him the East African adventure was about to end. But there was much to be done before he consented to hand over to another commander who would lead the new initiative inland from the coast.

The new plan of attack was still Smuts's. He was still Commander-in-Chief, but the campaign report that he was writing from his headquarters dated 27 October 1916 was hurried and incomplete. He no longer wrote of objectives achieved but of things unfinished; of operations 'which I proposed to conduct'. But no longer would they be under his own driving hand.

The news of the offer from London was still secret. Van der Bijl wrote of his astonishment in January 1917 when he 'found out, through secret documents I was seeing, that Lloyd George wanted him to come to London'. Was Smuts in any agony of spirit about abandoning the task unfinished? He was leaving a small South African force to take part in the last throes of the struggle on what Deneys Reitz called 'the last safari'. Most of the force would be British and colonial.

Capt F C Selous in camp, Christmas 1916. Captain Selous was killed in action on 4 January 1917.

But he could only go with honour when the Rufiji had been crossed. To that end he now bent his furious and undiminished energies while his enormous casualties* sailed south from the huge embarkation camps around Dar es Salaam.

How did the officers and men feel about this man who had driven them with whips of scorpions under conditions that he himself acknowledged would 'appal the stoutest hearts'? Was it three cheers for 'good old Jannie' now that they were being sent home for discharge? An extraordinary incident would soon take place.

In the meantime he had to reorganise his forces to reach the Rufiji River, where in the north-east and about thirty miles to the north they were still dug in.

Flooded for Miles

On 21 December Smuts wrote to his wife on the occasion of:

> . . . your dear birthday . . . Time is now flying fast. Tomorrow I leave for the Mgeta front to make preparations for the continuation of the campaign, and if the rain does not bother us too much I shall probably be over the Rufiji when this reaches you. Once we are over the Rufiji, which is the greatest obstacle in our way, I think things will speed up a great deal. But it has already rained much and between Kissaki and Rufiji the country is flooded for miles; yes, the aeroplanes say it looks more like lakes than solid earth. And we have to traverse that with our motor cars and heavy guns!

In the west von Lettow still had detachments along the Great Ruaha and Ulanga Rivers. As Smuts described them to his wife: 'You must remember the rivers here are among the biggest in Africa. The great Ruaha south of Dodoma, when full, is twelve miles broad! And the other big rivers run into the Rufiji which we must cross . . . a series of morasses in the rainy season. And fever, and the impossibility of transport, and hunger, etc., etc.' So he had written on 24 November; he well knew what he was asking of his men.

However, on the positive side he was able to tell London:

'With the exception of the Mahenge Plateau they have lost every healthy and valuable part of their colony. In the east they are cut off from the coast, and in the south the Portuguese army has appeared north of the Rovuma River.' It looked good in the report to their Lord-

---

* Smuts himself was vague about the total. He wrote: 'I believe between October and December we evacuated between 12 000 and 15 000 patients, mostly malaria cases.'

ships. No one, probably not even Smuts, imagined that two more years of fighting were still to come.

The immediate need was to push, and push hard with a reorganised army. Although thousands of South Africans had been sent home, Van Deventer could still muster fifteen hundred rifles of the now dismounted 1st SA Mounted Brigade, and with the 17th Indian Infantry and the I/4 KAR, he had thirty-five hundred rifles altogether, with twenty-four machine guns and two field guns.

With British and Nigerian forces augmenting this force Smuts could still command sixty-two hundred rifles and fifty-one machine guns and twenty-odd field guns. Once again Smuts was looking for a final conclusive encircling movement that would close its ring round von Lettow near Kibata.

Christmas Eve Offensive

The offensive was to begin on Christmas Eve*. While his forces were moving into favourable positions, fresh horses arrived from South Africa, enough to mount the 4th South African Horse, now commanded by Colonel Deneys Reitz.

'On paper I was given a fully-mounted regiment,' wrote Reitz, 'but I knew that every one of these poor exiled animals was doomed and that we would soon be on foot again.' Indeed, by the time he had said goodbye to Smuts and other friends at Morogoro and reached Kilossa the horses were already falling out. 'There came the merciful fusillade of a firing party left behind to put an end to animals that could travel no more.' These simple, heart-felt lines underline the gross inhumanity of the campaign, the indifference to suffering that we now find appalling. At that time it was taken for granted.

From Kilossa Reitz's regiment was following the 3rd and 9th Regiments of the mounted brigade. Every mile of the way was marked with dead horses as the march brought them to where the Great Ruaha River flowed in a swollen brown stream miles wide through its endless swamps, jungle and elephant country.

The brigade crossed the river and marched on, losing dozens of horses every day. 'By the time we approached Iringa there were ten horses left. These we used to carry the sick, men with fever, and for the rest, the entire regiment marched on foot.'

At Iringa General van Deventer came by car to direct the next phase himself. Reitz's regiment was ordered south to where *Haupt-*

---

* A few days before Smuts had written to his wife: 'I have given flour, sugar, honey, jam, etc. for the German children here [at Morogoro] for cake-baking for Christmas; they are most grateful; they have rather a hard time.'

mann Lincke was holding an entrenched camp at Mount Erica in dense forest country. The 4th set off on foot, with two hundred carriers – for by now there was not a horse left – and driving oxen for slaughter. Up there at five thousand feet the air was cool, and even the fever-stricken men stepped out with a will.

On 16 December the day was celebrated, or commemorated, by the struggling remnants of this South African army, as Dingaan's Day, a memory of the Boer nation's triumph against the Zulu Army, when a waggon-train laager of Voortrekkers beat back the thousands of charging Zulus and broke the power of their chief Dingaan. Now these men, for the most part of the same blood, were fighting in a part of Africa where the black soldier, for all his primitive background, had been turned by German efficiency into a formidable wielder of modern weapons, including the machine gun.

Van Deventer's Plan

On that day Van Deventer was busy with map and indelible pencil, outlining his plan to surround Lincke. Like all moves planned by staff, it looked possible on paper. It took little account of the struggle of men against a terrain where forest, deep gorges and torrential rains made the chance of progress almost impossible.

Reitz with his horseless cavalry was to get behind Lincke; the usual move, with even less hope of success than before. But Smuts was pressing for finality before he disappeared from the scene. Reitz's men had a march of thirty-six hours before them.

'Christmas Day found us in primaeval forest, without a morsel of food. Hungry and tired we pushed on in the rain and got astride the Muhanga Road next morning. Here we discovered a herd of goats . . .'

But although the plan nearly worked, the separate units had no contact with one another. The cordon round Lincke was full of gaps. They got a glimpse of him withdrawing from his fortified camp, slipping away into the mist with his five hundred men and as many porters. Even though the 9th Regiment was across their path in that terrain there was no hope of bringing them to action. They simply melted away.

But it was a success of a kind. 'We had now cleared the uplands, for the enemy was forced down the escarpment into the unhealthy swamps of Mahenge.' The drive being over, the South African troops who had taken part were ordered to return to the Central Railway line at Dodoma, two hundred miles away, leaving Indian soldiers to garrison the district.

'We marched to Boma Himbu in three days. On top of Mount Kyalu we passed Lincke's fortified camp, with trenches and dugouts that would have cost us many men in frontal attack.'

The South Africans saw the old year out camped by a river at the bottom of a rugged gorge, and on 1 January 1917, they were back at Iringa once more. From there they marched to Dodoma in six days, across level bush country that carried more giraffe and other big game than Reitz had seen in all the rest of East Africa. At Dodoma the fort had been turned into a hospital, 'and most of the other buildings were soon filled to overflowing with fever patients, for the long marches and the rains had laid low a great many of our men.'

Orders for Home

Then came the orders to return to South Africa.

> We were glad to go. The campaign had degenerated into something like searching for a needle in a haystack, with a handful of Germans hidden in thousands of square miles of bush. They had made a splendid stand, but they were not the real enemy. The real enemies were the deadly climate, the wild regions, and the swamps and forests and scrub.

It was arguable, wrote Reitz (and he was echoing what many intelligent men were saying) that the campaign should never have been fought at all. The fate of German East Africa depended on the outcome in France. Indeed, some said that Smuts's fatal mistake was to have driven his army into Tanganyika. He should have contained the Germans on the borders of British East Africa, at a fraction of the cost.

Time has not solved this question. Others have seen it as a triumph of generalship.

'At Dar es Salaam,' wrote Reitz, 'We marched over the causeway of the lagoon to a lovely palm-fringed beach and lay camped for a week or two, awaiting transport to South Africa.' So, for him and thousands of others, it was over. Except that it was still far from over.

Smuts was in a hurry to get it finished. His own men were on the ocean and arriving home after the five-day voyage, some eager for discharge. To others still keen to serve again the duty to King and Empire still called. The world had still to be delivered from the imperial ambitions of Kaiser Wilhelm.

But with the war in its fourth year, the morale of the European nations was low. England, exhausted and weakened by the enormous haemorrhage of the trenches and led by a weak Prime Minister, Asquith, needed a transfusion of vital energy and renewed faith in itself. There was even talk in some quarters of a negotiated peace.

Over a Million Dead

The two most frightful battles of the war so far had been concluded within a few days of each other in late 1916 – and just before Christmas: The French defence of Verdun and the British massacre on the Somme. None of the idealistic soldiers of the first years of the war or the flag-wagging public could have foreseen such atrocious slaughter. The total of British, French and German dead, wounded and missing came to well over a million and a half. After that, French and German commanders, and British and French prime ministers were dismissed as incompetent failures. Lord Kitchener was dead, drowned in the North Sea on a secret mission to Russia. The Irish had rebelled against British rule. For the first time married men had been called up for compulsory military service. David Lloyd George, the fiery Welsh critic of the misconduct of the war, became Secretary of State for War. Having forced the issue he pushed Asquith from power and formed a War Cabinet early in December 1916.

One of Lloyd George's first actions was to invite the Dominions to send their prime ministers to an Imperial War Conference. He asked Louis Botha to attend. Botha did not want to go. He had his hands full watching the interests of the Union. Besides, by that time the tide of casualties from East Africa was already arriving in South Africa and there was much criticism and anger. Suppose he sent Smuts? That would be one way of forestalling the outcry that was sure to come. His handling of the war in East Africa was being severely attacked.

Smuts's last camp in East Africa before he was called to London in January 1917. It was here that he decided that the South African forces had shot their bolt and had to be repatriated on medical grounds.

Is there any evidence that Smuts seized the chance to dodge out of what looked like being a long drawn-out affair? None. Indeed, he was writing to his wife on 21 December that he hoped to be back with her before March 1917 in time for the parliamentary session; but he doubted it, because he had 'that very moment' received a telegram from Botha asking him to represent the Union in London.

Hancock's Question

He did not say that he had agreed to go, but his biographer, Hancock, questions his sincerity when he encouraged his wife to expect him home soon. Certainly his letter, as he wrote it, was full of longing to fill the gaps of years of separations in their married life caused by wars, past and present.

Perhaps he truly believed that he could finish off the Germans with one last effort and be back in the Union in time to take charge of the next session. 'Smuts showed no eagerness to go to London,' wrote Hancock; he only gave in to Botha's insistence that it was the unanimous wish of the Cabinet that he should represent the Union at the meeting.

Smuts was being urged to sit in conference with a new British government which he disliked, especially with Lloyd George's advent to power. He would be sitting at the same table as his old enemy Lord Milner, the architect of so much misery for the Boer people. Was it ambition that made him accept? The desire to take the stage in a larger theatre? The need to be acclaimed as the hero of a successful campaign – indeed, the first successful campaign of imperial arms in the war – though he must have known it was far from over? Was it a search for the honours that his own people would deny him and the chance to be heard on a stage where he would not be pelted with the hateful taunts of his enemies at home?

One thing was certain: the war in East Africa had to be pushed to a decisive conclusion before he left for England in March 1917. To that end he now devoted all his formidable energies.

The South Africans were replaced by reinforcements from England, by the Loyal North Lancs, already so reduced by fever that they had been sent to South Africa to recuperate, fresh regiments from India and Nigeria and notably, several newly raised battalions of the once-underestimated King's African Rifles.

Calls for Volunteers

Meanwhile the casualties were beginning to arrive in South African ports with as little fuss as possible. The officials wanted no emotional scenes; indeed, relatives were not even informed of their arrival. There was public anger over the fact that the wounded from Delville Wood had not been met on their arrival and given an official welcome. Censorship had been tight, and few of the public expected such an avalanche of men from East Africa.

At the same time that these men were disembarking, newspapers were printing long columns detailing dead and wounded in France alongside impassioned appeals for fresh recruits. Calls for volunteers came from the mayors of towns and clergymen,* the former calling on the sons of the Motherland to hasten to her aid, the latter assuring recruits at patriotic meetings that the soldier who fell as a Christian believer was assured of life eternal.

The recruits, sometimes only a handful at a hysterical meeting, were supplied with gifts and comforts by ladies' committees and marched off behind a military band. Yet recruitment was not going well. Nothing was so abhorrent to the patriotic citizen who would never hear a shot fired as the thought of 'slackers'.

Even Smuts joined the chorus of condemnation.

At the same time that his cautiously worded statement was giving advance notice of the 'return to South Africa of a considerable number of Union forces' (as the *Cape Times* put it) he took the opportunity to castigate those who had shirked death on the Somme battlefields, referring to them contemptuously as 'those who have been content to remain in safety and comfort while their patriotic fellow-countrymen were offering their lives and health for the common cause'. Incredible though it may seem now, he urged those returning from East Africa 'unfit for further duty to induce eligible men to save themselves at the last moment from the ignominy which will attach to them for the rest of their lives if they still hesitate'.

There was no hint in the press that the Commander-in-Chief would be abandoning his mission in East Africa; nothing but congratulations on his success so far and confident assertions that 'we may now reasonably expect to hear within a few weeks that the final stage of the operation has been opened'.

Optimistic Editorial

So said the *Cape Times* in an editorial, noting its satisfaction that the former German colony north of the Central Railway would be opened to trade under military restrictions. That was a triumph indeed, and when it was supported by an enthusiastic report from Dar es Salaam

---

* At a meeting in Cape Town on 9 November which netted only seventeen young men, the mayor said he had done his best to get away and The Rev Caradoc Davies Rector of Maitland orated: 'Our Motherland calls to her sons to go to her help . . . No man is a dutiful son who does not respond at once.'

by the daughter of the Governor General, Lord Buxton, that all was well with our brave boys in hospital there, satisfaction was complete.

On the same page the newspaper printed verses so redolent of the glory-in-death spirit of the time that the writer, T A A, was supposed to have heard the voices of the dead raised in 'A Call to Slackers':

> From town and veld, from desk and farm
> Came we. Stern duty made us go
> 'Gainst brutal might ourselves to arm
> Pro Rege, pro Imperio.
> We came, we fought. Some count it loss
> that we have died and suffered so.
> We rest content. Our meed* a cross
> Pro Rege, pro Imperio.
> And you, will you not heed our call
> from lonely grave where we lie low?
> Come! Carry on, while comrades fall,
> Pro Reg et Imperio.

It was at this time that Smuts performed an action that was typical of the ambivalent feeling he had for his tenacious adversary. He had picked up a wireless signal for von Lettow-Vorbeck telling him that the Kaiser had awarded him the *Pour le Mérite*, the highest German military award.

Von Lettow Declines

At once Smuts sent an emissary under a white flag to tell his enemy the news. Perhaps this was an act of reciprocal chivalry; after all, he knew that von Lettow had spared his life that day when his head appeared in the sights of his adversary's rifle. Now he stopped the war for twenty-four hours and sent Captain van der Bijl under a flag of truce. Van der Bijl, a man noted for his charm and courtesy, had been an emissary more than once, and he was cordially received. 'I always took a bottle of whisky with me,' he wrote.

Whether Smuts sincerely wished to congratulate the man who had led him such a dance for a year or whether he wished to use the occasion to his advantage is an open question. He certainly used the moment of felicitation to suggest to von Lettow that it might be a good time to surrender with honour.

Von Lettow received the emissary with courtesy, and in his reply to Smuts he suggested that his good wishes were mistaken. Was Smuts

---

* meed: reward.

not possibly referring to the Second Class Order of the Crown with Swords 'which I received a.short time ago?'

In his memoirs von Lettow referred to Smuts's personal letter as 'a· proof of the mutual personal esteem and chivalry that existed throughout in spite of the exhausting warfare carried on by both sides . . . On many other occasions the enemy intimated his great appreciation of the achievements of the German forces.'

In fact, von Lettow took the gesture as a fillip to morale. He had only recently been awarded an unexpected gift of arms in the beaching of a gun-runner that broke the British naval blockade. Not only was he completely rearmed with the latest weapons, guns, machine guns, rifles and large reserves of ammunition, but he now had shrapnel and high explosive shells for his naval guns from the *Königsberg*.

Still got New Arms

Smuts wanted to know all about that. He was incensed that once again the Royal Navy had failed to stop a blockade-runner. Van der Bijl was told to look out for evidence of new weapons while he was entertaining Major Kraut's Chief of Staff, von Brandis, with whisky and cigarettes. Van der Bijl, always the gentleman, excused himself from the drinking to relieve himself discreetly on one side. 'I turned over a rifle with my foot and read the date: Karlsruhe 1915.' It was one of the latest, firing smokeless ammunition. A bad omen. The invitation to surrender was declined.

Smuts's new offensive began after careful planning and under his personal direction in the central and eastern regions with his general headquarters at Dutumi on the Mgeta River front. It was timed to begin on 26 December, but the opening movement on the Mgeta front had to be postponed because of the torrential rains.

Smuts's object was to secure the crossing of the Rufiji and capture the German force directly opposite to him. Crossing the great river barrier was the more important.

'Our chief problem,' he told Collyer, 'is to find a way to seize the river crossing without the enemy being aware. I am most anxious that they do not escape a heavy blow by retirement. This movement, if successfully combined with General Hoskins's north-west march from the Matumbi Mountains, would cut all connection between von Lettow's main forces. We must not fail this time either to envelop them on the Rufiji, or at worst, deal them a tremendous blow as they escape southwards.' Smuts had great confidence in Beves's 2nd South African Brigade.

You will have to make a wide detour and capture and hold a bridgehead on the river at Kwa Mkalomzo [Makalinso] . . . near the junction of the stream with the Ruaha. It will be hard going. We must prevent the enemy retiring from Mgeta [from] making a crossing there. It will be a seventy-mile march. Meanwhile, I will make a holding attack on this front with Cunliffe's Nigerians supported by the army artillery, the east flanking column of 2nd Kashmiris and a battalion of Nigerians under Lt-Col Lyall and the west flanking column of Sheppard's brigade will take the right flank. We hope, of course, to surround the force engaged by Cunliffe.

It was obvious from his enthusiasm that nothing could quench his belief in this strategy; indeed, what other was possible? Accordingly, the engineers and pioneers moved out to put the road in order for light transport and get the collapsible Berthon boats brought forward for the crossing.

To Cross the Rufiji

To cross the Rufiji, the great psychological barrier, was everything; and to reach it Beves's 5th and 6th South Africans made a march of twenty-eight hours over dry and roadless country. It was yet another feat of endurance for his fourteen hundred men who made a supreme effort to reach the Rufiji.

Meanwhile Sheppard's force had reached the village of Bohibeho on the same day as Beves crossed the river higher up. He was only halfway to the Rufiji and partly round the German forward lines. There was a brisk fight as a company of the Fusiliers encountered Otto's rearguard falling back. It was there that the famous old hunter and scout Selous was leading his men, in his safari clothes and battered felt hat, when a sniper got him. The sixty-four-year-old hero of many an engagement died instantly, with his old African servant and gun-bearer by his side. It is told that Ramazan went berserk and charged into the Germans and killed several, including the sniper who had killed his master.

The Fusiliers were enraged by his death, and within hours they had driven off the Germans and were astride the road leading to the Rufiji. But they were still three days' march short of their objective, and Otto was trapped . . . or would have been, if he had stood and fought. But within a few hours he had scattered his forces, which melted away to meet again at some prearranged rendezvous across the river.

There was no dismay among his men. As the German gunnery specialist Nils Kock wrote after watching them cross the river: 'They came marching over the long bridge, in their torn and faded uniforms. They looked rather the worse for wear, but they stepped out well and sang.' Even the bearers still sang.

No Hope of Success

Smuts's strategy of preventing the German crossing of the river had failed; and although his forces had made great efforts they came nowhere near to pulling off the coup. Von Lettow later commented ironically: 'The unity of General Smuts's well-planned strategy did not succeed.' Worse than that, Beves had failed to move down the river from upstream and cut off Otto's attempt to cross the river. True, they had crossed as ordered, only to find no one there, and they were too exhausted to march the further thirty miles that could have decided the business. Otto was free, and von Lettow's main force was still intact.

The hope of destroying him on the Mgeta front was gone; but there was still a chance that Smuts could finish the campaign before the end of January – three weeks from then. He had achieved a strong force on the south bank of the Rufiji and he was determined to continue. There had been some hard fighting, and the men dug in across the river were harassed by gunfire and sniping.

One can sense Smuts's impatience to put an end to it. In fact, he had less than two weeks left to see it through. His orders to hand over to General Hoskins were already awaiting him; and the rains were less than two weeks away. When they came, they were the heaviest for years. Smuts himself had feared those rains and foresaw that they would cut off his army from all supplies.

On 14 January he arrived at Kimbabawe on the Rufiji to urge forward movement. He had three brigades on the Rufiji now, but the old enemy was once more upon him. His staff had warned him that there was no hope of pushing on further.

'The maintenance of three brigades is impossible,' Collyer warned him, 'and unless a large reinforcement of drivers and Ford cars can be guaranteed, rations will begin to go down, and by the end of the month the forces will be on half-rations. Perhaps even sooner if the rains begin.'

Major Kraut leads his troops across the 'pori'.

Why was that? The transport drivers were falling sick in droves and there were not enough reserve drivers to meet the continual loss. Animals, of course, were out of the question. The Quartermaster-General warned Smuts: 'I cannot honestly see how we are going to feed the troops.' His advice was to bring all men who could be spared back to the Central Railway.

New Deadly Phase

It was at that point that the Rufiji campaign was abandoned. But while Smuts pulled out his South African white troops he left the Cape Corps to fight alongside the Nigerians and the Indians and other black troops. These were to continue the struggle in the most prolonged and deadly phase of the fighting, but for both armies hostilities were stalemated. So far the fighting had been during dry weather and water was scarce. That would soon be forgotten in the weeks of African rain and flood that were to come.

Von Lettow still regarded the situation as favourable to him. 'We could continue calmly to contemplate the continuation of the war for a considerable time.' He did not know then that the South Africans had been replaced by strong reinforcements, among them black askaris: a brigade of Nigerians. But when he did learn of that he regarded them as new troops with little or no battle experience. And indeed, in their first action on 24 January they were beaten off with heavy losses in officers and chased through the bush by Captain Otto's detachment.

The German counter-attack came after an hour of battle in which the Nigerians had captured two machine guns and counted about thirty enemy dead between the two gun positions. But Major Gardner, Second-in-Command of the 3rd Nigerians was wounded when the Germans charged and two captains and two lieutenants were also killed.

The Nigerian askaris fell back in disorder, losing three of their own machine guns. When reinforcements came up in support they were immediately counter-attacked. The carriers for two battalions stampeded while enemy snipers took their toll.

There were acts of great bravery amid the confusion. A gun-carrier, Awudu Katsena, was with his officer, Captain Barclay, who was organising the retreat when Barclay was shot in the back. Katsena and his mortally wounded master were alone and the Germans were advancing very rapidly on each side of the path where Captain Barclay was lying.

'Awudu Katsena picked up a rifle that was lying beside a dead soldier, and while kneeling over his mortally wounded master, opened rapid fire so effectively that the enemy were checked long enough to get Barclay away.'

A Crucial Battle

This battle of Mawa was more crucial than anyone in it realised. A sergeant who lay out in the bush all night saw wounded men 'being carried away in a continuous stream.' German casualties were heavy, and Captain Otto himself was wounded. The German position was such that British wounded prisoners sent back reports that Otto's men were in deadly fear of being attacked again on 25 January. 'If we had done so they would certainly have broken,' wrote Captain W D Downes of the Nigerian Regiment. 'At this crisis of the campaign it is quite possible that if the British had got through to Mawa the whole campaign might have taken very different lines . . . but for some reason or another the battle was not continued on the 25th.'

Once again it was a question of what might have been. For want of a horseshoe nail the battle was lost, as the old jingle goes.

16

War Enters its Most Deadly Phase

The dreaded rains began on 25 January. 'It was as if the floodgates of the heavens had burst,' wrote a supply officer. 'Not since Noah's flood had there been anything to compare.' The Nigerians and the Cape Corps were at once cut off. Every ounce of food (for rations were soon measured in ounces) had to be carried nearly a hundred miles by carriers waist-deep in water. By the end of the month the situation on the Rufiji was such that there were neither reserves of food nor enough carriers. Pack animals died after a single journey, and there were so few transport drivers that hundreds of Fords stood for days with no one capable of driving them. Soon the real nightmare began. Captain Downes records:

> Men driven by hunger started to dig up roots, or picked herbs, with disastrous results. Crime became common as men raided supply dumps for rice and biscuits. Many died from eating poisoned roots. So acute became the need that some resorted to digging up the rotting bodies of pack animals. A temporary bridge was brought down when famished men cut the rawhide strips binding the spars.
> The hides were cooked down into soup, and so disposed of by the starving men.*

Meanwhile Smuts had returned to South Africa to a hero's welcome, and by the end of January he was restored to his family at Doornkloof.

It would only be for a week, he told his wife. He had, he said, 'consented to step into the breach'. He was going to England at once, but he hoped to be home for good 'next May at the latest'. He hoped,

---

* Back on the Rufiji a bottle of brandy from a dead officer's effects was sold for £10 and an NCO's toothbrush for £1.13s.4d. Officers were eating roasted jungle rats and monkey brains.

fervently, that there would not be many more separations; perhaps this would be the last.

He was about to be hailed as the man who had wiped out German imperial ambitions in South West and East Africa, the destroyer of German hopes, ambitions and power in Africa. Indeed, he himself took it further. He believed that his campaigns had denied Africa to the Germans as part of their global strategy. What had been achieved had important implications for the future history of the world. A Germany astride Africa was a Germany astride the globe. Now, fortunately, that ambition had been destroyed.

Rejection by his Officers

Did he tell his wife of the extraordinary incident in Dar es Salaam shortly before he embarked for home? As the conquering general on his way to every honour that King and Empire could bestow on him he was suddenly brought face to face with what his army thought of him. Surely he had no inkling of what was coming when he expressed a whim to shake the hand of all his officers awaiting transport home.

Captain Rupert Pilkington-Jordan, Acting Adjutant of the South African Field Artillery, received Smuts's signal at the depot camp where four hundred officers and seven thousand other ranks were awaiting repatriation on medical grounds with recurrent malaria.

In his 1967 memoir of the incident Pilkington-Jordan wrote:

> I told Major Prins of the signal that he was to put the officers on parade and tell them of the Commander-in-Chief's wish. I suggested he take the parade, but he said it was the adjutant's job. An hour later a lieutenant-colonel and a major came to the orderly room and told me that an order to shake hands with the C-in-C was not a lawful order and that the officers refused to do so.
> I reported this to Major Prins and asked if he would meet and tell the general. Major Prins replied, 'Ach, no man! I think it's the adjutant's job.'
> I went to the station to meet the general. I had never spoken to him before and did not relish the task ahead of me. However, I asked if I could have a minute alone with him. He looked a bit surprised but took me aside. I then told him the position. For a second or so he gave me an impression of being hurt, but his steel self-control asserted itself, and he gave me the order to put the camp on parade and said that he would speak to the officers and men. In it he dwelt on the hardships of the campaign.

'A Reckless Campaign'

But as Pilkington-Jordan (later a Smuts MP and Senator) pointed out: 'He had only himself to blame for the reception. Unlike his brilliant raid into the Cape during the Boer War, when he could count on supplies from friends, he had embarked on a reckless campaign far beyond the limits of his supply and transport to support him. What angered his officers and men in East Africa was that he was well aware of the hardships he was creating . . . yet he never sought to alleviate them.'*

In East Africa the war had entered its most deadly phase. There were almost two more years of fighting ahead and the most costly battles of the war. This was the war that was supposed to be 'all over in a month or two'. On the very day when the rains began and Smuts was on the water homeward the War Office issued an official statement. Smuts had assured them that the enemy was in general withdrawal.

'In these circumstances it has been possible to accede to the request of the Union Government and arrange for the release of General Smuts from the East African command.'

Was he aware that he was leaving the British and Imperial troops and the remnants of his own to fight a war of attrition in the tropical forest against a man who would never surrender? Did he believe that the call to higher duty was an absolvement of his duty to his army?

In his report to the War Office on 'the behaviour of the troops' he said that the facts of the campaign as stated were sufficient . . . 'Eulogy seems unnecessary and misplaced. The plain tale of their achievements bears the most convincing testimony to the spirit, determination and prodigious efforts of all ranks.' He praised his staff, his divisional and brigade commanders and every branch of the service and sent his recommendations for awards and decorations. 'May the end soon crown their labours,' he concluded.

By this time the army that he had created in East Africa was nearly a hundred thousand strong. Deaths in battle were 3 443 and other casualties 6 558. Of these, just under two thousand were South Africans.

'Ill-timed Declaration'

But there was a further act; those still serving in East Africa saw it as betrayal. Smuts had decided that the campaign must be ended under

---

* 'On one occasion he said to the Commanding Officer of the Brigade of Artillery, Lt-Col D D Taylor: "Toby, I think I have disproved Napoleon's maxim that an army marches on its stomach".
"By God you have, sir!" was the reply. "You have made yours crawl on its stomach."'
– R Pilkington-Jordan.

the command of a South African: none other than his faithful comrade Jaap van Deventer.

The news that the War Office had given the command in East Africa to Van Deventer came as a shock. It came after what General Fendall called 'Smuts's ill-timed declaration that the campaign was over' and the man who had to take up the slack, Lieutenant-General A R Hoskins, had spent months trying to put the 'blunted and useless instrument for any offensive action' back into fighting shape. Hoskins had done that for a force, worn out in body and mind and without transport, that had absolutely no value left as an offensive instrument. It had reached the Rufiji on its last legs.

Lieutenant-General A R Hoskins, CMG succeeded General Smuts in the command of the British forces in German East Africa in 1917 but was superseded by General van Deventer.

Suddenly Hoskins was ordered to hand over. 'Needless to say he had the fullest sympathy of the whole force in this bitter disappointment'. Why had it happened? Rumour had it that the War Office was dissatisfied because more could have been done. That was a manifest impossibility. It must be for political reasons, Fendall argued. Obviously the military authorities in Britain had had no say in the matter.

Smuts, who else? Making his old comrade his proxy in East Africa and, as it were, keeping his own hand on the campaign that he had abandoned unfinished. It would be a South African victory, even if he were not there in person. Perhaps the advice of Louis Botha was still in his mind: 'Let Van Deventer always keep a captaincy with you!'

Fendall did not blame Smuts directly, but his view that it was the work of politicians makes sense. The War Office was merely the conveyer of the order.

'Surely it can only have been so, for such an action might well seem as nothing to the politician *when out to please one of their own kind*[*], though a grave injustice to a regular soldier.'

---

[*] Emphasis by the author.

Kaiser's Compliments

Meanwhile the German commander, von Lettow, was reading a special message from the Kaiser that had come to him through a British emissary under a white flag.

> I cannot allow the opening of a new year of war to go by without again expressing to you, my dear Colonel, and your gallant troops my thanks and boundless admiration for your heroic conduct. Your many victories have shown me that in a fateful hour the right man is in the right place . . . Today, on the threshold of a new year of war, the grateful Fatherland is mindful with me of its distant heroes and their victorious leader, whose quiet performance of his duty will ever be a brilliant example of the history of war. May God further bless your arms.

No doubt it was a comfort to von Lettow to know that his emperor still trusted in God to bless his bayonets in the bush. He still held the rank of colonel. Later he calculated that he had been faced at one time or another with no fewer than a hundred and thirty-seven generals, British, South African, Belgian, Portuguese and Indian.

He was far from finished when the year 1917 began. While his lauded adversary was being fêted in England (much against the grain, as he protested) and showered with academic honours and the freedom of ancient cities, the German prepared to face two more years of privation and suffering more intense than anything that Smuts's men had endured.

Soon he would be without drugs or anaesthetics. For bandages his surgeons would be using tree bark and strips of uniform boiled and disinfected. It is a measure of this extraordinary commander's will to endure that, despite feet festering with jiggers, he marched for three weeks without boots to test whether it were possible for Europeans to go barefoot like the askaris. He concluded that it was possible when the feet were hardened enough to move easily over rocks and well-trodden paths, but not through the spines and spikes of the bush. These caused 'grievously painful sores'.

His white soldiers wore shoes made of buckskin with soles cut from the leather of captured saddles. With no organised sources of supplies every man became responsible for his own rations. Some moved with their own flocks of poultry. Von Lettow's order was typical of his unquenchable humour: 'Any cock found crowing before 9 a.m. is to be shot for giving information to the enemy and its carcase forfeited to Headquarters.'

For him the war of endless bush, swamp, river and mountain, of ambush and raiding for survival, of living eternally as a fugitive from powerful armies, ever pursuing but never closing the trap, was to continue until Germany surrendered in Europe. Who was in whose trap was a question often asked.

At the waterholes of Narungombe, about forty miles south-west of Kilwa, Captain Eberhard von Lieberman lay waiting for a force led by Colonel G M Orr. Eberhard's thousand askaris were behind solid earthworks stretching nearly three miles on high ground. He had forty-eight machine guns and two field guns, and his flanks were protected by thorn and swamp. The bush was cleared in front of cleverly concealed positions.

Bloodiest Battle So Far

One of the two columns in the attack on 19 July 1917 was led by Captain J H A Payne, a South African in command of 170 men of the 8th SAI heavily armed with four maxims, three Lewis guns and two Stokes mortars; there were also 177 men of the 40th Pathans with two maxims and a hundred men of the 3/3 KAR with him.

They were going into the bloodiest confrontation of the war so far, with the Gold Coast Regiment spearheading the attack. The Stokes mortar, developed for lobbing shells into trenches in France, was a new weapon here and excellent for bush warfare. It was easily portable and quickly set up, and it could lob over a barrage of missiles that dropped out of the sky almost without sound. But it was badly used. The inexperienced mortarmen dropped their rounds short among their own men and set fire to the dry grass, driving the Gold Coast men out of cover. Most of their officers were killed as the *Schutztruppe* maxims scythed into the confusion.

Captain Payne ordered the newly recruited 3/3 KAR to attack with two companies of the 8th SAI on his flanks. 'We came into action and occupied a low ridge said to be facing water . . . The enemy were reinforced and fire became fairly severe. With their officers and NCOs killed or wounded, the raw KAR men wavered. I received orders to push in on the left and ordered the whole line to advance. Casualties were heavy, including the OC of the KAR, Colonel Dickinson.' With their Colonel down the KAR broke in disorder. 'The 8th SAI held the enemy for a time on the right flank, but finally they also broke.'

Captain Payne's bare narrative in his journal does not tell of the confusion as the German askaris charged with terrifying howls. The centre broke, and the Pathans panicked and fled.

'The officers with the troops retiring did everything to check the rout and rallied the Pathans, who steadied and opened a heavy fire on the advancing enemy. The KAR made two charges through the smoke of burning grass, and the askaris were driven back.'

Men of the Cape Corps entrenched in training for the fierce jungle battles they took part in during the latter months of the campaign in 1917-1918. The German askaris learned to respect their tenacity and courage.

Night fell. 'A line was formed and we dug in at once,' wrote Captain Payne. 'I had with me approximately 150 rifles of different units . . . After daylight I was ordered to withdraw.' The enemy had abandoned the wells. The price had been high. The attackers lost about six hundred men killed, wounded or missing, nearly a quarter of the force.

Captain Payne's column suffered 210 casualties out of the 350 men whom he led into action. Strangely enough, von Lettow was angered by the result. As a master tactician he had ordered von Lieberman to defend the place at any cost until he arrived with fresh troops. Somehow he conceived that he had been robbed of an even greater victory.

When Captain Payne was killed later in 1917, Jeppe High School in Johannesburg published a moving tribute:

The hand of Death has lain heavily on us. The dread grimness of war has been brought home to us with a ruthlessness that even the youngest will not easily forget . . . Work and play have been overshadowed by one awful event – the death of our beloved Headmaster, Captain James Humphrey Allan Payne . . . Nine other and younger lives we also mourn.

And in the patriotic logic of the time: 'Jeppe is to be counted fortunate to have given such a man and such boys to the Empire in the cause of freedom and righteousness.'

The Climactic Battle

Months later, in October 1917, occurred the battle that was the true climax of the war in German East Africa. It was the battle that at last compelled von Lettow to cross the Rovuma River into Portuguese territory. He still had with him a force of 278 white soldiers and officials, about sixteen hundred askaris and two thousand porters.

The place was Mahiwa (Nyanga) in the remote eastern corner of the German colony. It was a place of swamp and river and mountains that became the scene of a four-day battle of the utmost ferocity on both sides. Here, by the fortunes of war, von Lettow was to inflict the most fearsome losses of the entire war on his old adversary General Beves, Van Deventer's chosen leader in the battle. Von Lettow based his tactics on his knowledge of the way in which Beves handled men.

'I had learned that General Beves threw his men into action in the engagement at Reata [11 March 1916] regardless of loss of life and did not hesitate to try for a success, not by skilful handling and small losses, but rather by repeated frontal attacks.'

The four-day battle was one that could not be won by outflanking. It had to be a head-on clash of men meeting one another with the bayonet in the ferocious storming of trenches and by guns firing on zero fuses as battle-crazed men flung themselves across this jungle no man's land.

Beves had been informed by Pretorius, now scouting for the Nigerians, that the Germans were in strength at Mahiwa. When von Lettow crossed the Linkangara Mountains with five companies to join nine companies already there he found the opposing forces dug in at a distance of less than a hundred yards.

Charge after Charge

'After we had eaten our midday meal undisturbed', he sent in a determined attack to turn Beves's flank. At the same time Beves made his first frontal assault. It was made with such determination and indifference to losses that von Lettow feared that his outflanking movement would be too late to be effective: 'In that case the battle would be lost.'

He reinforced his strength so that the enemy 'by the increasing fierceness of his frontal attacks was bleeding himself to death. For four days wave after wave of the attack broke on our front . . . on the evening of 18 October we had, with about fifteen hundred men, completely defeated a whole enemy detachment probably not less than six thousand strong.'

The British force of KAR, British troops, Indian and South Africans amounted to about five thousand men and suffered nearly three thousand casualties. It was as if there were a new element in this battle: a last frenzy; not so much uncaring generals as a desperate wish to get it finished. For both sides it was climacteric. The campaign that Smuts had abandoned with the light assurance that it was all over had blown up into a thing of horror.

Captain A J Molloy MC. His diaries of the campaign in German East Africa left a vivid picture of the ferocity of the jungle war in 1916. Molloy was in it to the end in 1918.

From the diary of a veteran campaigner, Captain A J Molloy, comes a comment in those last days: 'Although General Smuts said it was over last Christmas, even the greatest generals sometimes make mistakes. Subalterns and even lance-corporals never . . . especially if amateurs. It's a great war, this is!' However: 'From the latest intelligence the end of the campaign does not seem far off.'

His Worst Losses

Von Lettow had suffered his worst losses, about five hundred casualties. It was more than he could bear. But before he retired into Portuguese territory for the last month of the war he made a surprise attack on the camp of the 25th Indian Cavalry Regiment. He found them 'with transport harnessed and standing ready to march, the camp was stormed and lost almost 350 horses'.

In these actions von Lettow's oldest and bravest company commanders, men who had been with him since the beginning, fell at the head of their men.

The end came in a message to General van Deventer, now, at forty-one, Commander-in-Chief of the British Force in East Africa: in Europe an armistice had been arranged. The date was 11 November 1918.

Van Deventer had been von Lettow's adversary since February 1915, and for the past two years he had directed the last phase of the struggle against him. The full story of Van Deventer's generalship still has to be told. So far it has been seen only in glimpses in the regimental histories of the Nigerians, the KAR and the Indian regiments. The man, a giant in his own time and a general uniquely equipped for combat in Africa, has never emerged as the personality by which he deserves to be known. Inarticulate, not given to dramatic utterances or theatrical gestures, he has been undeservedly consigned to oblivion. Indeed, the bitter and gruelling campaign that he fought with a limited force of South Africans* and an army of empire troops deserves a volume to itself, for Collyer's history of the campaign and the official British account of the war by Lieutenant-Colonel Charles Holdern ended with the departure of Smuts. Indeed, the official British account concluded in September 1916.

Smuts, now in the War Cabinet, had been at the table in the drafting of the terms of the armistice and the British proposals for the peace conference to come. Did he ever think of the plight of his chiefest adversary, there in the bush, during those weeks of meetings?

Now his old comrade in the wars of Africa would summon von Lettow to lay down his arms.

An Armistice

Von Lettow was on his bicycle, riding to visit a detachment near the Chambeshi River in Northern Rhodesia, when he saw another cyclist pedalling towards him. This was Captain Müller, who had intercepted the British dispatch rider in the jungle and found a telegram in his dispatch case.

> 12.11.18:   To be forwarded via MB cable and dispatch rider. Send following to General von Lettow-Vorbeck under white flag. The Prime Minister of England has announced that an armistice was signed at 5 hours on Nov 11th and that hostilities cease on all fronts on Nov 11th.

Von Lettow read the message with mixed feelings. It was already 13 November. For several days he had been pressing forward to attack and loot the well-stocked depot at Chambeshi. There had been fighting on the 12th. He was still trying to get food for his men, and he was convinced that if hostilities had ended they could not be unfavourable to Germany. They had just sacked a food depot at Kasama, and his mind was as much on food as on the ill news. He was tasting jam 'and other good things which had been unknown to me hitherto'.

---

* In this period the Cape Corps under Lieutenant-Colonel G A Morris fought in a number of notable actions. They took the surrender of Lt Zingel and *Oberleutnant* Naumann's companies and were in action until 18 November. The Cape Corps suffered thirty-eight officers and men killed in 1917, and 121 died of tropical diseases. The War Office commended the unit for its zeal and valuable service and recommended it for service in another theatre.

A native artist's representation of the surrender of General von Lettow-Vorbeck after news of Germany's defeat in Europe reached him from General van Deventer. It took place at Abercorn, Northern Rhodesia on 25 November 1918 and was accepted by Lt-Colonel E B B Hawkins of the KAR.

Then at midnight came a message directed to him from Salisbury, to the effect that Germany had accepted the unconditional handing-over of all troops operating in East Africa and setting forth Van Deventer's terms of surrender.

'This was news enough if it were confirmed,' wrote von Lettow. But he would not give in until he had, in his loyalty to his Emperor, 'drafted a telegram to His Majesty, in which I reported what had happened and added that I would act accordingly.'

There was no reply. The emperor had fled to neutral Holland. No doubt von Lettow saw his telegram as a last gesture of honour. With him at that moment were Governor von Schnee, twenty officers, five medical officers, a doctor of the Volunteer Medical Detachment, a senior veterinary officer, a senior chemist, a field telegraph officer and 125 European soldiers. He still had the loyal remnant of over a thousand askaris and about two thousand bearers.*

'My men were well armed, equipped and fed and the strategic position was more favourable than it had been for a long time. It was doubtful whether our resources would last out if the war lasted several years more.' But he was quite confident about the prospect of another year. Indeed, he was prepared to argue about the terms of the surren-

---

* At the highest figure he commanded 3 007 whites and 12 100 askaris in March 1916.

329

der, pointing out that Van Deventer's documents had stipulated 'unconditional evacuation'.

Honour Satisfied

He even protested to the British War Office, the governments of the
Allied countries and the German Government. No one took any notice
of this obstinate character in the wilds. 'In the end I decided to go to
Dar es Salaam as General van Deventer required.' His honour was satisfied only when he was informed that the surrender of his arms would
'not have the character of a laying-down of arms'.

In other words, that it was recognised that he had never been
beaten. And there were officers with him who begged him not to surrender. Even after his arms had been dumped they were for storming
an enemy camp and continuing their private war.

Von Lettow had in fact been honoured in a unique manner. A
special clause had been written into the armistice permitting his surrender to take place within a month after 11 November, and Van
Deventer allowed him and his officers to keep their weapons 'in consideration of the gallant fight you have made'. He and his officers now
had to take ship across Lake Tanganyika to reach the railhead for Dar
es Salaam. Once on the Central Railway his progress east was more of
a triumph* than a defeat. At every station German settlers and officials
greeted him with cheers.

At Morogoro station German women had arranged tables and
offered them 'tea and coffee, with plenty of rolls and cake and fruit.'
Von Lettow was amused by being buttonholed by a tipsy soldier, 'a tall,
lanky corporal who had apparently drunk a whole series of glasses to
our health before the train arrived. I managed to slip away from him at
last'.

At Dar es Salaam, Van Deventer's Chief of Staff, General Sheppard, personally conducted his famous opponent to the handsome
white house allocated to him and his personal staff. A car and a driver
were put at his disposal, and Van Deventer invited him to lunch. What
was said at that meal is not recorded; but Brigadier-General Fendall of
Van Deventer's staff wrote: 'He had the bearing of a Prussian guards-
man, but none of the bluster and swagger . . . His manner was just
what it should have been, courteous and polite. He talked extremely
good English.'

---

* In the mood of general adulation one British officer wrote that he had 'gained more
esteem and affection than our own leaders'. There was similar admiration in the Western Desert in 1941 for Erwin Rommel by soldiers who held the British generals in
derision.

330

Between the Wars

It was March 1919 before von Lettow returned to Germany. Mounted on a black charger, he rode through Berlin at the head of the remnant of his men, still in their sun-bleached khaki and battered sun-helmets. He had been invited to a mayoral banquet, but it was cancelled for fear of a violent anti-*Junker* reaction among the mobs of revolutionary soldiers of the defeated army. But no one could take from him the honour of being the only German who had never accepted defeat.

In 1920 he went into politics and served ten years in the *Reichstag* before resigning when the Nazis appeared. In the meantime he had been received with honour in England, when he was seated next to Smuts at an anniversary dinner in London in 1929, commemorating the campaign of the British East African Expeditionary Force. The two generals stayed afterwards as guests of Colonel Richard Meinertzhagen, now retired after a military career of soldierly 'brinkmanship' and much influence in high places. He was a man who everywhere found an ear to listen to his sound – but sometimes bizarre – schemes.

It was Meinertzhagen, strange to relate, who when he went to Berlin on behalf of German Jews in 1935 suggested to Hitler that von

General von Lettow-Vorbeck was accorded a hero's welcome by the crowds in Berlin when he entered the city with his officers and surviving men on his return from East Africa – undefeated.

Lettow would make an excellent ambassador to England. Hitler, well aware of von Lettow's prestige with his former enemies, sent for the old campaigner and offered him the appointment. Von Lettow rejected it with scorn. From then on he was on Hitler's black list, slandered, harassed and under surveillance.

'When peace came after the Second World War, the 75-year-old general was destitute, subsisting for a time on the food parcels sent to him by Meinertzhagen and Smuts,' according to Charles Miller. Piet van der Bijl wrote that 'thirty-six years after the campaign, in the early 1950s and shortly after General Smuts's death, General von Lettow-Vorbeck with his daughter visited South Africa.

'A large number of ex-servicemen clubbed together to give them a great banquet. General Kenneth van der Spuy was in the chair. Kenneth made a witty speech proposing von Lettow's health, and the General followed with a brilliant and delightful reply in which he reminded Van der Bijl of the surrender message Smuts had sent with him:'

> I remember Captain van der Bijl bringing me that kindly and generous letter from my great opponent. But that was not all. He brought me something else that showed the general's great hospitality. It was an invitation asking not only me but all my officers to become his guests for the rest of the war. But I felt this would be too much, especially with the great shortage of food that his country was experiencing. To prevent myself imposing on him and his country, I was in honour bound to decline the kind invitation.

In the hilarious mood that reigned, it was difficult for Van der Bijl to propose the toast of the evening: 'To the memory of General Smuts

and those who lost their lives in the German East African campaign'.

Nevertheless the toast was proposed and honoured.

For von Lettow the only sour note struck in the name of Smuts came in the biography by Smuts's son, the little Jannie to whom his father wrote such charming and amusing letters from East Africa. Very politely

This photograph of General von Lettow-Vorbeck taken after the war shows the ravages of the campaign on his features. Like his men he suffered from malaria, dysentery and the other debilitating effects of the tropics on European soldiers.

332

and with typical control, von Lettow wrote to *The Times* of London on 10 December 1952, politely correcting him for his errors, in particular for his harsh words about German colonial methods.

The natives themselves used to say, 'The Germans use rough words but they have good hearts.' Of course there were native rebellions, as there have been in every colony in the world, and is now, for instance, with the Mau Mau movement in Kenya. Does Mr Smuts think it convenient to suppress rebellions only with kid gloves? Was it so in South Africa with the Zulus or the Kaffirs?

Van Deventer Honoured

What of Van Deventer? He ended the campaign having gained the admiration of his British officers and the imperial force that he commanded. 'It was with real regret that everyone said goodbye to the last Commander-in-Chief . . . He undoubtedly made good and left respected, trusted and liked by all. He was a big man morally as well as physically . . . He was a great optimist, and never disheartened by the failure to bring the enemy to book.'

In the last months of his campaign Van Deventer at last had cleared the Germans from their most prized colonial possession, conquering nearly fifty thousand square miles of hostile territory. He had taken 1 410 Germans and other Europeans, 4 149 native soldiers, eleven guns and 56 machine guns, most of these captured in the last month of the war.

In the fulsome manner of the war news magazines of the day *The Standard History of the World Wide Conflict*, edited by H W Wilson, noted: 'Satisfaction was universal throughout the Empire when King George conferred a Knight-Commandership of the Bath on Temporary Lieutenant-General Jacob Louis van Deventer, Commander-in-Chief in East Africa in recognition of distinguished services in the field.'

His name had been put forward by Smuts. The knighthood* embarrassed him. 'It's just a silly British thing,' he said with typical Boer contempt for such honours. And with that shrug of disdain he unconsciously made a pungent comment on all wars of empire.

It was not until nine months after the war ended that in July 1919 Smuts returned to his wife and family at Doornkloof. In Britain he had been described as the most romantic figure in the country in that hour when he arrived in 1917. 'Yes,' he told his wife, 'the story is romantic indeed – the lonely Cambridge graduate, the passionate Boer patriot, the enemy of England and her Empire returning to help them in their hour of need.'

---

* In 1920 he was made ADC to King George V, and on 22 August 1922 he died as Lieutenant-General Sir J L van Deventer KCB, CMG, DTD at the age of forty-eight.

A NOTABLE ENTRY

(The *Cape Times*, 8 April 1919)

Epilogue

Colonialism and the European attitude to the acquisition of subject peoples inhabiting huge undeveloped lands had been an important question in European politics in the last years of the 19th century, when Germany was a latecomer in the field. In 1919, as the powers sat down to redesign Europe and reapportion its colonies, there was a body of opinion that wanted to return German East Africa to the nation that had developed it so rapidly in its brief ten years of colonial occupation. Was that now to happen? After all, many Germans were still settled on the land, in the thriving plantations and in several hundred mission stations. Were these people to be dispossessed and driven out? It became a very heated matter of debate:

Von Lettow was still in East Africa when the Indian Office put up a claim to be mandatory power in German East Africa. Meinertzhagen, a member of the British delegation at the Peace Conference in Paris in 1919, noted that an official of the India Office 'claims that Indian troops rendered invaluable services in conquering the colony and Indian merchants were there three centuries before the white man'. Indian colonisation was the new incentive. The Indian would civilise the African, and Indian colonists would be 'economically a gain to humanity'.

Meinertzhagen poured ridicule on the idea. 'During the first phases of the campaign Indian soldiers proved useless and unable to stand up to the German askari. Every disaster we suffered during the first twelve months was attributable to the unreliable qualities of the Indian soldier.' He also said: 'India has introduced dishonesty and disease into East Africa – nothing more. God help the natives of German East if the Indian Government becomes its mandatory power.'

Already Decided

In fact, the victorious Allies had entered into reciprocal obligations long before the end of the war. The countries that had suffered most from the war, France and Belgium, would be compensated and that

335

included the empires in Africa. It was Smuts's monograph *League of Nations* that created the notion of mandates over conquered territory. He hoped that this compromise, as he called it, would 'prove to be only of a temporary nature' until the inhabitants of the former German colonies were able 'to stand by themselves under the strenuous conditions of the modern world'. A sacred trust of civilisation!

But Smuts, for all his skill in steering the future at Versailles, was disgusted by the peace treaty. He regarded it, he told Meinertzhagen, as an impossible document that was unjust and could not endure. In a dinner with Smuts and Botha, Meinertzhagen recorded their denunciation of its terms.

'They say,' he wrote in June 1919, 'that we had the most glorious opportunity to make a lasting and great peace; but we had frittered it away.'

Less distinguished mortals, especially those who had fought in the campaigns, wrote with enthusiasm about the new acquisition to empire. 'May the lives of those that have fallen in German East Africa not have been given in vain, but by their sacrifice shall yet another great tropical country be added to our vast empire.' So wrote a chronicler of the Nigerian army in the campaign.

A year before Smuts formulated his idea of mandates he had the future of the German colonies very much in mind. Nine months before the armistice he found enough time from his multifarious duties in Europe to sit down and write a preface to a history of the campaign by Brigadier-General J H V Crowe,* who had lost no time in finding a publisher for his account of Smuts's campaign of 1916. In February 1918 Smuts made himself clear on the subject:

German Ambition Foiled

The enemy's stubborn defence of his last colony is not only a great tribute to the military qualities of General von Lettow, but as proof of the supreme importance of the Imperial German Government to this African colony, both as an economic asset and as a strategic point of departure for the establishment of the future Central African Empire which is a cardinal feature in [the] Pan-Germanic dream.

With German East Africa restored to the Kaiser at the end of the war, and a large askari army recruited and trained from its eight million natives, the conquest or forced acquisition of the Congo Free State, Portuguese East and West Africa . . . may be only a matter of time. In this way this immense tropical territory, with

---

* Commander of the Royal Artillery in East Africa.

almost unlimited economic and military possibilities, and provided with excellent submarine bases on both the Atlantic and Indian seaboards, might yet become an important milestone on the road to World Empire.

The East African campaign, therefore, while apparently a minor sideshow in this great World War, may yet have important bearings on the future history of the world. It is to be hoped that our rulers will bear these wider and obscurer issues in mind when terms of peace come to be arranged at the end of this war.

On 7 May 1919 the Supreme War Council assigned German East Africa to Great Britain. On 10 January 1920 the British mandate over German East Africa was put into effect. The name of the territory was changed to Tanganyika. The German settlers were sent home and their estates sold. They left with bitter thoughts about what had been lost and what might have been achieved. Among them were some who saw von Lettow as the ultimate repository of German honour in the field and others who saw him at the end as leader of a band of outlaws, living by plunder and ambush. Governor von Schnee had ended as governor of nothing. For most, however, the legend of the unvanquished would live on.

The era of post-war colonialism began. No doubt it was more benevolent, more devoted to the ultimate amelioration of the native peoples than the crass colonialism of before 1914. But as Richard Meinertzhagen had shrewdly noted in Kenya before the war began (it was then the British East African Protectorate), it would be only a matter of time before the peoples that they had prodded out of a timeless Africanism would be ready to demand their freedom and assert their own tribal and national interests.

Some may say it had all been for the best. Others might quote the old tag: *tempus edax rerum*. All-devouring Time in the end restores what it destroys.

Appendix A

Hospitalisation of South African and Imperial forces from German East Africa from 20 March 1916 to 31 December 1917 Admissions to No 1 General Hospital, Wynberg, Cape Town

Imperial Forces	Officers	235
	NCOs and men	9 220
South African Expeditionary Forces	Officers	55
	NCOs and men	2 039
Belgian Officers		2
		12 551

Of these, 219 were for blackwater fever, 1 095 for dysentery, 8 313 for malaria, 289 for venereal diseases and 733 for gunshot wounds.

Wynberg Hospital was opened for the German South West Campaign on 27 August 1914. Total admissions for diseases and deaths up to 31 December 1917 amounted to 28 408.

Figures in report by Major A Dunbey-Owen, Adjutant and Registrar from South African Defence Force Archives.

Appendix B

The forces available to Lieutenant-General Smuts for the initial operations of the German East Africa campaign under his command at March 1916

Under his immediate command:

2nd Division
Major-General Tighe
Mounted Troops

4th SA Horse
Belfield's Scouts
MI Company (LN Lancs)
No 10 (RN) Armoured Car Battery

1st East African Brigade (Infantry)
Brigadier-General Malleson

2/L North Lancs Regiment
2/Rhodesia Regiment
130th Baluchis
3/KAR
Kashmir Rifles
Volunteer MG Company

Artillery

No 2 Group, RA
4th Indian Artillery Brigade
No 6 Field Battery
No 8 Field Battery
No 9 Field Battery
No 10 Heavy Battery
134th Howitzer Battery
2nd Div: Ammunition Column
Div Signal Company
1/2 Coy Faridkot Sappers and Miners
Section East African Pioneers
2nd Division approximate total rifles: 4 700
19 guns
34 machine guns

Detached Force:
Brigadier-General van Deventer
SA Mounted Brigade (Van Deventer's own brigade)
1st SA Horse
2nd SA Horse
3rd SA Horse
3rd SA Infantry Brigade:
Brigadier-General Berrange
9th SA Infantry
10th SA Infantry
11th SA Infantry
12th SA Infantry
Artillery
2nd SA Field Brigade (2 and 4 Batteries)
28th Mountain Battery
SA Div Ammunition Column
Detached Force approximate total rifles: 5 900
14 guns
28 machine guns
Force Reserve:
Brigadier-General Beves
2nd SA Infantry Brigade (Beves's Brigade)
5th SA Infantry
6th SA Infantry
7th SA Infantry
8th SA Infantry
Artillery
No 5 SA Field Battery
No 12 Howitzer Battery
Force Reserve approximate total rifles: 3 800
6 guns
16 machine guns
Under GHQ:
No 26 Squadron, RFC
61st Pioneers

The detached force which moved by the west of Kilimanjaro was the
1st Division and was composed as follows:
1st Division
Major-General Stewart
Mounted Troops
East African Mounted Rifles
1 Squadron 17th (Indian) Cavalry
KAR MI Company

Infantry

25/Royal Fusiliers
29th Punjabis
129th Baluchis
Cape Corps Battalion
1 KAR (four companies)
East African Machine Gun Company

Artillery

No 1 Group RA
1st SA Field Battery (1 and 3 Batteries)
No 7 Field Battery
27th Mountain Battery
1st Div Ammunition Column
Div Signal Company
1/2 Company Faridkot Sappers and Miners
No 1 Division approximate total rifles: 4 000
18 guns
22 machine guns

Appendix C

Forces under Lieutenant-General Smuts for the Rufiji River offensive which began in December–January 1916–1917

1st East Africa Brigade
(Sheppard)

25th Royal Fusiliers
30th Punjabis
130th Baluchis
3rd Kashmir Rifles
No 3 Field Battery (four guns)
No 6 Field Battery (two guns)
No 7 Field Battery (less one section) (two guns)
No 13 Howitzer Battery (one gun)
1/2 Double company, 61st Pioneers
One section, East African Pioneers
One section, Faridkot Sappers and Miners
No 1 Armoured Motor Battery
One section, No 5 Armoured Car Battery
1 300 rifles, nine guns, fourteen machine guns

Force Reserve
(Beves)

6th SA Infantry
Cape Corps (less 350 rifles)
Kashmir Mountain Battery (four guns)
1/2 Double Company, 61st Pioneers
Faridkot Sappers and Miners
1 400 rifles, four guns, ten machine guns

Duthumi Column
(Cunliffe)

1st Nigerian Regiment
4th Nigerian Regiment
Cape Corps (350 rifles)
One section, Nigerian Battery
1 250 rifles, two guns, 12 machine guns

Kiburu Column
(Lyall)
2nd Kashmir Rifles
2nd Nigerian Regiment
One section, Nigerian Battery
800 rifles, two guns, seven machine guns
GHQ Reserve
2nd Rhodesian Regiment
African Scouts (local natives under Major Pretorius)
3rd Nigerian Regiment
Detachment Cape Corps
One section, No 7 Field Battery (two guns)
15th Heavy Battery (two guns)
134th Howitzer Battery (4 guns)
One section, No 5 Armoured Car Battery
1 450 rifles, eight guns, eight machine guns

Appendix D

Casualty List of the German East Africa Campaign

Originally published in *The Nongqai* , the official South African Services Magazine in a special edition of 1 March 1917 by Philip J Sampson, Editor

THE CONQUEST OF GERMAN EAST

FOR KING AND COUNTRY.

" Greater love hath no man than this ; that he lay down his life for a friend."

The following is an approximately correct list of the men of the Union Forces who lost their lives, either by wounds or disease, in the operations in German East — and Nyasaland, up to the end of February, 1917. —

2ND S.A.I. BRIGADE.

C.Q.M.S. Slack, Douglas Lockhart (Veteran Reserve).

Sergts. Bent, Richard Augustine; Wilkins, George Proctor; Quinn, Peter.

Corpl. Jones, Clifford Basil.

Ptes. Oliver, Albert Edward; Kanes, Jacob; Basson, Wm. James; Nixon, Alex. Stephen; Keogh, Chas.; Leendertz, Fredk. Wm. August; Stapelburg, Henry Frank Peter; Hickey, Patrick Joseph; Lyne, Edward Augustus; Britz, Rudolph C.; Mountford, Wm.; Byres, Robert; Jansen, Fredk. Andries; Du Toit, Andries Francois.

2ND S.A.I. BRIGADE DEPOT.

Sergt. Benson, John.

Ptes. Venter, Jacobus Hermanus; Clennell, Gilbert; Moram, James Edmund; Yond, Thos.

3RD S.A.I. BRIGADE.

Ptes. Jacobs, Arthur Phipp; Gaynor, John Walfetone; Alt, Anthony; Skillicorn, George Wm.; Backstroom, John; Railton, Thomas W. M.; Reynders, Wm. James.

3RD S.A.I. BRIGADE DEPOT.

Ptes. Matthews, Howard Ward; Hann, Cyril Wilfred Arlow; Hunter, Robert; Swanson, George; Davey, Albert Edward; Durrant, George Fredk.

3RD S.A.I.

Pte. Burke, Stanley Dominico.

4TH S.A.I.

Sergt. Shaw, Matthew.

Ptes. Ashworth, Wm. Geo.; Garton, Edwin Chas.; Kennedy, Norman.

5TH S.A.I.

Capt. Lardner-Burke, Edmund Colpoys.

Lieut. Lardner-Burke, Henry Dyon.

C.Q.M.S. Elliott, Chas. Howe; Gaynor, Cecil.

Sergts. Donnelly, James Edmund; Ingle, Wm. Wright; Mallett, George; Hosken, Frank Francis; O'Meara, John.

'or King and Country—*continued.*

Corpls. Love, Leslie Terry; McRae, Malcolm.

Lance-Corpls. Wheeler, Eugene; Smith, Joseph enry.

Ptes. Fleming, George; Roos, Peter Barend; Coppard, ohn Robert; Pratt, John; McMullan, John Andrews; awlor, Patrick; Long, Samuel; Dixon, Henry Clark; 'homson, Gerald; Roux, Jacobus Marthinus; du Toit, arnard; Roos, Frederick Paul; Bester, Johannes Baden- orst; Hansen, George Wm.; Stock, John Owen Clarence; 'ish, William James Frederick; Milne, John amuel; McDonald, Francis Ernest; Harvey, Walter amuel; de Villiers, Esli; Fitzmaurice, Bartho- omew; Nielson, William Lewis; Hurley, John Edmond Sheffield, Wm. Henry; Watson, John Henry; Matson, Matthew Charles; Heyler, John acobs, Richard; Merckel, Richard; van Rhyn, Michael Christian Bester; Scarburgh, John James; Lancellas, Charles John; Nienaber, Geo. Henry; Foss, Geo. Henry Brinkman; Clough, Thos. Hindell; Cooper, Edwin Augustus; Beswetherich.

6TH S.A.I.

Capts. Rennie, James Gordon; McWilliam, Charles Norman.

Lieuts. Goodall, Arthur Morton; Anderson, Wm.

C.Q.M.S. Fitzgerald, Thomas.

Sergts. Gordon, Reginald Henry; Ramsay, Adam.

Corpls. Miles, Charles Reginald; O'Meara, James Justin; Mate, Herbert John Newton.

Lance-Corpls. Robertson, Duncan Cumming; Laidlaw, John; Brown, Robert; Swart, Diedrick Adrian.

Ptes. Thomas, Henry Cecil; Harbottle, Walter Lam- bourne; Blackie, Chas. Pearson; White, John; Williams, Harry Phillips; Thomas, Harold Rodwell; Early, John Henry Wylie, Robert Miller Chapham; Spencer, Frank; Kingsey, William Arnold Selkirk; Pate, William Edward; King, Paul Berry; Wade, Henry Joseph Patrick; Hardy, George; Pohlman, Fredk. William; Brown, Thomas

OUR WOUNDED HEROES AT WYNBERG.

A morning parade of the convalescents.

[*Photo: F. W. Baxter.*

For King and Country—*continued.*

William; Sanders, Edward Charles; Artz, James William Glen; French, Edward John; Rhodes, Sydney Richard; Marlev, William Bell; Gibdon, Thomas Blair; Hills, Norman Charles; Mundell, George Alexander; Shepperson, Robert Godlonton; Budge, Francis John; Taylor, Charles Ernest; Furniss, Alex.; Allen, Joseph Arthur; Kennedy, Patrick; Scholtz, Oscar; Graham, Cecil Lauder; Irving, Charles; McLean, David Moffat; Norman, Joseph; Lubbe, Jacobus Johannes; Herbert, Alfred James; Holmes, Walton Bruce.

7TH S.A.I.

Lieut. Lowden, John Howat.

Sergt. Thomas, Cecil.

Corpls. Adamson, David; Beabon, James; Collins, Douglas; Shepherd, James Henry; Stuart, Jack.

Lance-Corpls. Jones, George Edward; Wild, Stafford; Gallie, Allan; Hebbing, George; Spottiswoode, Robert James.

Ptes. Hogsett, Thomas; Folley, John Clark; Goodwill William Carlyle; Taggart, Henry; Gosch, John Henry Ingram, James Byers; Kannemeyer, Charles William Adams, Thomas; Cohen, Archibald V.; Dodd, Reube Francis; Neilson, Fredk. John; Cross, Roderick David Fhilpott, Robert Henry; Kent, William Hurling; White Willoughby; Moyle, William Henty; Ballantine, Eric John; Atkinson, Herbert; Gleesom, James Martin Heysen, Louis; Williams, George; Gordon-Palmer Harris; Eke, William James; Chittenden, Herbert Tennant, Lawrence Dennison; Mennie, Cornelius Reseirh, John Oats; Spencer, James; Hanrahan, Michael Wilson, Ade Theodore; McCann, Frederick; Bottger Albert Claud; Stegmann, Peter Ryk; Smith, Fred Ernest Lehmen, Max Victor; Nicholson, Joseph William Hooper, Albert; Rennie, Frank; Humphreys, Frederick Prince, John; Thompson, Edwin John; Lowe, Herber Melville; Walter, Douglas; Barnes, Robert Norman Jensen, Max Alfred; Gaul, John.

OUR WOUNDED HEROES AT WYNBERG.

A party of patients marching down the main road, Wynberg, where trams are in waiting to take them for an outing to Camps' Bay.

[*Photo: F. W. Baxter.*

For King and Country—*continued.*

8TH S.A.I.

Capt. Locke, John Henry Thomas.

Lieuts. Rodda, Mathias Aitken; Bowden, John Tom; Austin, Essex Percival Montgomery; Bridge, Fred. Wm.

Armour-Sergt. Smith, Andrew Alex.

Sergts. Wright, William; Williams, Maurice Griffith.

. Corpls. Anderson, Thomas Edward; Pfohl, Frederick Wiltse.

Lance-Corpls. Andrews, George Henry; Smith, Walter Aubrey; Morton, James Syme.

Ptes. Manuel, William Charles; Lyons, John Smart; Symons, William; Fourie, Frans Jacobus; Smith, Charles; Jones, Daniel; Meneely, James; Reed, Clement Cliff; Barker, Joseph; Terry, Henry Richard; Verbeek, Bernard Robert Louis; Fowler, George; Grant, Robert Godfrey; Olsen, Harold; Benecke, William; McCarthy, Herbert William; Lee, Thomas; Davies, George Edward; van Zyl, Marthinus Philipus; Southward, Norman Lamb; Barnes, James; McDonald, Alex.; Flitcroft, William; Topp, Robert Lamb; Neuhinick, Sydney; McVicar, Donald; Gough, Hilton; Walker, Thomas; Edwards, Herbert Frederick; Meiring, Christian Gabriel; Straiton, Robert; Low, Alex.; Pascoe, William James; Schmidt, William August; Earl, William Henry; Innes, James Robert; Leslie, Stephanus Johannes; Sey, William.

9TH S.A.I.

C.S.M. Rourke, James.

Sergts. Lockwood. Edmund Emilius; Hudson, Chas.

Ptes. Leatt, George; Rowan, Walter; Steele, William Henry; McGaw, Robert; McInnes. James; Griffin, Chas. James; Meyer, Antony; Holloway, Charles Edward; Pearson, Charles Bernard; Shires, John Edwin; Cole, Robert; Elder, Andrew; Castro, William; Best, Thomas

347

For King and Country—*continued.*

Edward; O'Donoghue, Patrick Roderick; Green, Joseph; Marriott, Roy Dudley; Campbell, James; Cottier, William; Rubin, Jack.

10TH S.A.I.

Cants. MacKenzie, Ulric Knut; Paine, Alfred; Gem, William (attached S.A.M.C.).

Lieut. Limerick, Ian St. Clear.

2nd Lieut. Wallace, Robert Cecil.

Sergts. Daws, George Edward; Norgard, Trygue; Baillie, Robert Henry; Seely, William; Harvey, Kenneth.

Corpls. Neveling, Peter Antonio; Paterson, Affleck; Duffus, John.

Lance-Corpls. Wehner, Albert Frederick Valentine; Withers, John.

Ptes. Jupe, Frederick; Austin, Walter; Stande Adam; Cloete, Michael Peter; Dickens, Stephen William Cruse, Henry Symington; Wilkinson, James; Whee wright, Walter Wilfred Dillon; van der Wat, Joh Johannes Jurgens; Rogerson, Thomas; de Klerk, Dav Frederick Nicholas; van der Westhuizen, Johann Jacobus; Swarts, William John; Theesen, Charl Andrew; Knowles, James Frederick; Hayward, Jam John; Lloyd, George Ellis; Barnes, Vyvyan; Connochi Peter; Kennedy, Martin; Martin, Henry; Pollac Frederick; Cloete, Jacobus Hendrik; Darling, George de Lange, John Adrian; Mossop, Clement; Williamso Barry; Hendricks, Stephanus Jacobus; Foster, Lione Bronhorst, Abraham Jacobus; Gardiner, David Coutts Baker, William Henry; Cleary, Raymond; Snyder Johannes Daniel; Pasques, Benjamin Albert; Kotz Frederick; Tate, Arthur; Bruce, William; Campbel Cyril; Harwin, Jasper William; Hynch, Alfred Ernest Swartz, Joseph Maquellie Antonie; Walsh, John George Goodchild, Ernest George; Spero, Leon; Watson, Joh George Petrie; Bailey, George Munford.

For King and Country—continued.

11TH S.A.I.

Major Humphrey, Humphrey Charles.

Capt. Layton, Edward Charles Maurice.

Lieuts. King, Cecil; van Niekerk, Henry Jacobus.

Sergts. Barry, Alfred Martin Harte; Prentice, Joseph; Calgey, Christopher Charles.

Lance-Corpls. Simpson, George Gilchrist; Dubery, William J.

Ptes. Greenhough, Leonard Rowney; McDonald, George; Dart, Leslie West; Graham, Vernon Montagu; Lawrence, Gordon William Massey; Ubsdell, William Talbot; Froude, Charles George; Macfarlane, Alex. Nelson; Blackbeard, Bernard Robert; Wood, Herbert Walter James; Madsen, Arnold; McLaren, William Errol; Serfontein, John Lodewijk; O'Brien, Dominie Joseph; de Lange, Barend Francois; Toomey, Herbert Charles; Saaiman, Joachim Petrus; Baker, Thomas Edwin; Grant, Birt Adriaan; Ahrens, Jacobus Petrus Daniel; Thompson, Charles William; Petrus, Richard

Stephen; Young, Benjamin; Wyles, Frank William; Reynolds, William Charles; Olsen, William Henry; Brandsma, Wylie Jacob; Mackie, Archibald; van der Watt, Hendrick.

12TH S.A.I.

Lieuts. Mackintosh, William Alex.; Anderson, George Lennox.

Sergts. Richardson, John Haviland Sperrin; Inglesby, Thomas Joseph; Ingram, Lewis.

Corpls. Crofton, Frederick Percival; Dom, Charles Peter; Anderson, Roderick J.; Lyon, William John Thompson.

Ptes. Herold, Henry Johannes; Nel, Stephanus Andries; Horne, Michael Christian; Clack, Hilton Albert; van der Spuy, Harold Ewart; van der Linden, Rijk; Kruger, Jacobus Johannes; Wagner, Henry; de Villiers, David Stephen; Prins, Peter Johannes Jacobus; Chevalier,

349

For King and Country—*continued.*

George; Francis, Joseph Worral; Carneson, John Thomas; de Kock, William Lebrech; Palmer, Sydney Herbert Victor; Hoffeldt, Johannes; Gaskell, Lawrence John; McHarrie, William; du Toit, Antonie Johannes; Wyman, Edward; Reid, Matthew; Donald, Bertram Smith; Channock, Edward; Franzsen, Duke Louis; Birnie, James; Coetzee, Diedrik Johannes; Ogston, William George; Brits, Jack; Adcock, Cecil John Wilson; Niemand, Petrus Johannes; Evans, Robert James; Bullard, Edwin William; Snell, Herbert Edward; Birks, Joseph Henry; Calitz, Jacobus Johannes; Day, Charles Henry.

1st S.A.H.

Sergt-Major Harris, Fred Vincent.

Sergts. Patmore, George Robert; de Beer, Martinus Christoffel; Fleet, Ernest James; Strang, John.

Corpl. Rand, Herbert Charles.

Ptes. Pero, Antonie; Quibell, Frederick William; Anderson, Henry Herbert; Kruger, Abraham Jacobus Johannes; Mundey, Edward Arthur; Weatherhead, Frederick John; Taylor, Henry William; Thompson, David John; Bruyn, Martinus Daniel; Cowley, Edward Robert John; Bester, Johannes Hendricks; v. d. Berg, Hans Jurgens; van Jaarsveld, Josias Hendrikus; Partridge, James Arnold; Neethling, Frederick; Ryk, Rudolph.

2nd S.A.H.

Capt. Heavingham, Ernest.

Sergts. Jones, William Abbott; Scheuble, Joseph Bell Napier; Tinsley, Robert.

Corpls. Johnstone, George Hugh Cameron; Smith, Harry Bedford; Le Roux, Johannes Hendrik; Denyssen, Henry T.

Trumpeter Curtis, Sydney Herbert.

Ptes. White, Maurice; Keeley, Charles Henry; Oosthuyse, Johan Bernard; Rautenbach, James Jackson; Acton, Albert Victor Emanuel de Lion; van Aaswegen, Gideon Petrus; Molyneux, Herbert Dennis; Graham, Joseph; Stephenson, Josias; Puzey, Charles Christopher; Marriott, Walter John; Green, Maynard; van Vuuren,

For King and Country—*continued*.

Willem Jansen; Roberts, Edward; Goss, Johannes Jacobus; Green, Leslie Charles.

Stuart; Montague, Kenneth Norman; Cleave, Aubrey Claude.

___

3RD S.A.H.

Major Cowie, W. W.

Lieuts. Smith, T. C.; Flynn, A. R.; Anderson, T.

Sergts. Flynn; Rabie, Jan Stephanus Voster; Thompson, Ernest Gordon; du Toit, Johannes Jack; Willis, John; Cottingham, George Wolfram.

Corpls. Baker, Harry; Miennie, Carel Johannes; Harris, Samuel Alex.; Glennon, Thomas.

Lance-Corpl. Reynolds, Isaac William.

Ptes. Fleming, Michael John; Cloete, Gideon Johannes; van Edan, Evert Phillipus; O'Brien, Thomas; van Dyk, Henry Wm.; Wiman, Eric; Morrison, Donald; du Toit, Benjamin Johannes; Shearer, Alfred; Classen, Daniel Jacobus; Aling, John; Petersen, Andrew; Venables, Albert; Muir, Andrew; Harmse, Bartlemus Thomas; Kruger, Johannes Willem; Gellatly, George

4TH S.A.H.

Lieuts. Basson, Christian Coenraad; Versfeld, Joshua Metcalfe.

Sergts. Kennedy, Kenneth Kyle; Swallow, James Stewart.

Corpls. Dunbar, James Morton; Ross, George Robert Wait, Charles; Lawrence, Charles Edgar; Friedlander Albert Herbert; McHardy, William Mann.

Lance-Corpl. Dayton, Archibald.

Ptes. Chadwick, Henry Slingsby Osler; Forbes William Samuel; Mackillican, Thomas Frederick Johnstone, Percy William; Tatlow, Reginald Dalgetty; Bennett, William Ernest; Turnbull, James Lindsay; Cooper, Sidney Sinclair; Burrows, John; Hutchinson, Frederick Boast; Wahl, John; Wilde, Alfred William; Maskew, Allen Wilson; Liebenberg, Johannes Matthys; Hobson, Alex. Carey; Watson, Alfred Somerville; Brown, Francis Mallock; Rex, Reginald Ruddock; Cowlin, Hugh

For King and Country—continued.

Houghton; Stevenson, James Kerr; Whitcher, Percy; Aldred, Anthony John; Johnston, John Buist; Hawe, Edward Francis; Magill, William David; Strapp, Henry Eric; King, Douglas Scott.

————

5TH S.A.H.

Major Pocock, Austin Alfred.

Lieuts. Pole, Thomas Reginald Montague; Fourie, Willem Hendrik.

Shoeing-Smith Meyer, Joseph Andries.

Corpls. Law, Christopher Bernard; Stoltz, Gabriel Gert Frederick.

Ptes. Duffy, Desmond Beresford; Wainwright, John Daniel; Behrens, William Jacobus; Lawrence, Cecil Gordon Cavanagh; Liebenberg, Stephen; Jacobs, Gert Christoffel; Greyling, Barend Johannes Pretorius; Jordaan, Pieter Willem; Mienie, Derck; Moolman, Johannes William; Brennen, Edward Danville; Taylor, William Edward; Strauss, Albertus Iohannes Francois.

6TH S.A.H.

Sergt.-Major Francis, Thomas Henry.

Sergt. Smithdorff, Andrew.

Corpls. Potgieter, Hendrik Nicolas; Newcombe, Leonard Norman; Orpen, Thomas Herbert.

Lance-Corpl. Troskie, Christian Jacob Lourens.

Ptes. Kruger, Martin Petrus; van Zijl, Theunis Lodewijk; Verreynne, Willem; Vermulen, Gert Jacobus; Akers, John Harold; Koetzie, Abel Jacobus; Taylor, Norman Bruce; van Wijk, Johannes Petrus Marais.

————

7TH S.A.H.

Lieuts. Winer, Paul; Murray, Andrew Haldene.

Sergt. Oberholzer, Nicolaas Tyaart.

Corpl. Baker, Edward.

Ptes. Ziefbein, Christian; Banks, Eric Blakeway; Bartram, Louis August; Reid, Arthur Ernest; Lombard,

For King and Country—*continued.*

Geoffrey Stephen; Abrahams, James Bernard; de Wet, Johannes Martinus; Baker, Eric Victor; Bell, John Francis Campbell; Reinscke, Charles Theodorus; Bruwer, James; McDonagh, Basil Terrance; Solomon, Louis Vintcent; Bisset, Hugh Matheson; Coetzer, William Johannes; Hay, Harry Carrack.

8TH S.A.H.

Lieuts. Malcolmson, George; Driver, Garnet Edwin.

Sergts. Jones, John Brown; Glover, Henry Herbert; Kemp, George Alex.; Houbert, Charles.

Ptes. Doorly, William George; Moore, Arthur John; Walker, Arthur; Daly, Edward Harold; Gifford, Leslie James; Slinger, Robert Willem; Bickley, Hubert Ernest; Cosadinos, George; Stephans, George; Harrison, Benjamin; Groom, Spensley Boyd; Lindsay, Arthur Nevison.

9TH S.A.H.

S.-Sergt. Radley, Robert James.

Corpl. McKenzie, Ronald.

Ptes. Welgemoed, F. G.; Greenwood, Arthur Herbert; Larkin, Harold John; Allen, John Henry; Sarry, Gernet Sidney; Arnott, William Charles; Williams, William; Jordaan, Pieter Johannes; v. d. Merwe, Andries Petrus; Brooks, Arthur James; Cowie, Rodney Charles Francis; Lombard, Hendrick Andries.

10TH S.A.H.

Pte. du Toit, Stephanus Christian.

1ST MOUNTED BRIGADE SCOUTS.

Sergt. King, Thomas.

Ptes. Burke, John Barton; Morkel, Jan William Hurler; Payne, Henry Robert; Ford, Eric Anthony

353

For King and Country—*continued.*

Stransham; Uys, Johannes Jacobus; Pulley, Frederick William; Farr, Walter Edward; Wallis, Thomas; Gunning, William Harold.

2ND MOUNTED BRIGADE SCOUTS.

Corpl. Liebenberg, Andries Petrus.

1ST MOUNTED BRIGADE.

Corpl. Oosthuizen, Thomas Phillipus.

Ptes. Grapentin, Arthur; Gilan, Cecil Carl Benjamin; Ellis, John Butt.

2ND MOUNTED BRIGADE.

Pte. Carse, John Abraham.

5TH HOWITZER BRIGADE.

Pte. Buffalo, Isaac.

ANIMAL TRANSPORT COY.

S.-Sergt. Brown, George Lennox.
Ptes. Raath, George; van Jaarsveld, Johannes; Freeman, Maurice; McNaughton, Alex.; McClung, William; Farr, Cyril Edward.

MOUNTAIN ENGINEERING COY.

Ptes. Heanan, John Rupert; Marchant, Henry Thos.

SCOUTS CORPS.

Corpls. Malraison, William Henry; Brotherton, Samuel Perrott.

S.A AVIATION CORPS

2nd Lieut. Steenekamp, P. A.
Sergt. Hutchings, Edward Morris.
Air Mechanics Firth, Thomas; Cowie, James Henry.

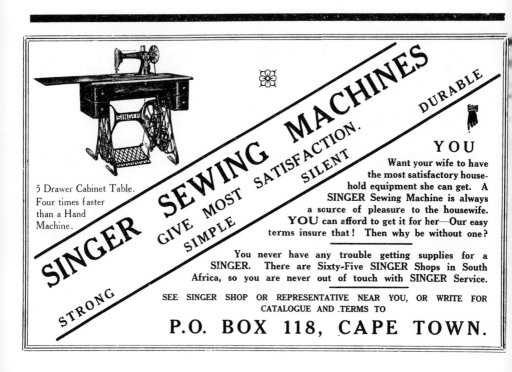

For King and Country—*continued.*

ROYAL FLYING CORPS.

Lieut. Bertram, C. Rld.

Sergt. Horne, Albert James.

Air Mechanic Thompson, Gordon.

S.A.F.A.

C.S.M. Tozer, Edward Alfred.

Ptes. van der Hoven, Oswald Henry; Dahse, Stephen Geoffrey; Badham, John Basil; Runnalls, William; Julius, Benjamin; Coetzee, Nicholas; McLean, Joseph; Blake, Charles Joseph; Phillipson, Cecil Vaughan; Ruiters, William; Gillies, George; van Wijk, Carl; Wrennall, Walter; van Blerck, William Sebastian; van Zijl, John; Smit, Rulf; Dean, Joseph; Abrams, John; McLeod, John; Robertson, Ernest; Slabbert, Daniel Jacobus; Bartels, John Henry; Williams, Arthur; Louw, Johannes; Morris, John; Oosthuizen, Johannes.

Drivers Plaatjes, John; Njandu, Mashek; Sotshani, Vani; Witbooi, Cobus; Russouw, Isaac; Mahlahlani; Links, Johannes; Mjune, Jack; Mamema, David; Charlie; Mgwensu, Martin; Molise, John; Hervel, Klass; Davies, John.

S.A.S.C.

Lieut. Hockly, Albert Chalmers.

Sergt.-Majors Feltong, Percival George; Doherty, Thomas.

Sergts. Wallace, William Walker; Richards, John.

Corpl. Munro, William John Campbell.

Lance-Corpls. Lorie, Soloman; Linnejar, John; Loynes, Frederick Stanley; Almond, Frederick; Butler, Joseph; Lake, Ernest William.

Ptes. Davies, Granville; Labuschagne, Stephanus Martinus; Hallett, Thomas Henry; Thompson, Thomas Vincent; Pearce, Henry Alford; Meyer, Jacobus Johannes Phillippus; Marsden, Edward William; Snijman, Barend Daniel Johannes; Grey, Reginald; Hewson, Thomas; Vine, Edgar; Glassock, Horace Henry; Hamilton, Benjamin; Senne, Thomas; Holmes, Arthur John.

For King and Country—*continued.*

DIVISIONAL SIGNALLING CO.

Corpl. Hartley, Herbert Clynton.

Ptes. Brown, Frederick; Coombes, Edward James; Gleeson, John; Bond, Arthur Edward (attached 5th S.A.H.); Cooper, Herbert Theophilus; Rorke, Charles Frederick; Fletcher, John William; Osborne, Harry; Rowlands, David Llewellyn; Norton, Albert Victor (attached 2nd Mounted Brigade); Jarvis, Reginald; Rand, Frederick William George; Taylor, Sam Holland; Cameron, Peter Cameron Black.

S.A. MOTOR CYCLE CORPS.

Lance-Corpl. Goodwin, Wilfred Cyril.

Ptes. Judd, Robert Charles; Munro, Graham Alexander; Visser, Jochim Jacobus; Paul, Cyril William.
S.A.M.R. (Attached 3rd Infantry Brigade).
Sergt.-Major Jones, S. G. (5th S.A.M.R.).

B.M.S. Kelly, Guy Wardman (attached to S.A.F.A.).

MECHANICAL TRANSPORT.

Ptes. Gurney, William Watson; Du Plessis, John Walter Lewis; Gardner, James; Small, Hermanus Christoffel; Snashall, Douglas Arthur; Shiers, Reuben; Fellowes, Herbert; Derby, Edgar Phillip; Bell, James Francis; Phelps, Godfrey; Smith, Thomas; Hull, Charles; Neish, George; Beaton, Alexander.

S.A. WIRELESS SECTION.

Corpl. Hutchings, Vivian Edward.

VETERAN RESERVE.

Sergts. Noakes, Frank (attached to 2nd Infantry Brigade); Jones, John Smithson.

S.A.V.C.

Ptes. Barrett, Charles Hugh; Walker, George; Wright, Warwick Edward; Aitken, John; Crowe, Albert Edward; de Villiers, Jacob; Doak, Chris Charles.

For King and Country—*continued.*

S.A.M.C.

Capts. Hofmeyer, N. J.; Groenewald, Albert.

Sergt.-Major Nisbet, John Fleming.

Staff-Sergt. Scully, Thomas C.

Sergts. Parsons, Sydney Davey; Carmichael, Peter Kenneth; Herrington, Frank; Ogilvie, Charles.

Corpls. Farrar, Bernard Eric; Fogarty, Cornelius.

Lance-Corpl. Murray, Samuel Holmes.

Ptes. Chilcott, Robt. Davis; Wilson, Wm. Alfred; Hinks, Walter; Lister, Thomas; Dunbar, Quinton; Langston, Darwin Howard; Miller, Harry Rudolph; van Oosten, Rudolph; Dalton, Stanley · McKenzie; Mills, Alfred; Meintjes, Harold Edwin Haffenden; Polkinghorne, Ernest; Stewart, William George Gordon; Wilson, George Cameron; Newman, Walter Francis; Sieviers, Jeremiah; Stirling, Norman William; Mardon, Alfred William; Morreira, Sydney; Richards, William Charles; Lucas, John Henry Thomas

CAPE CORPS.

Lieut. Hosack, Chas.

Q.M.S. Daniel, Arthur John

Sergts. de Jong, Francis Nicholas; Felton, A. C. L.; Jembe, Joseph P.; Adams, Thos. Clancy.

Corpls. Jozaffe, Gabriel; Thompson, John Joseph; Joseph, Cecil J.; de Villiers, Isaac J.

Lance-Corpls. Lombard, Boy Christian; Joseph, Gert.

Ptes. Basson, Andries; Ricketts, John; Thomas, Willie; Gordon, John; de Jong, George; Visago, Jacob; Sport, Tom; Cotton, R. J.; Vyver, Peter; Moody, John; Speelman, Baatjes; Antoni (John) Joseph; Gorep, Matthew; Francis, David; Slingers, John; Morris, Jacobus; McLean, Daniel; Julio, Daniel; Bowers, Henry; Royce, Francis; Pitt, Wm.; Brown, Samuel; Jefters, Sam; Jacobus, Isaac; Williams, J.; Felix, A. C.; Thrueben, J. T.; Ziedel, Johannes; Adams, Peter; Peterpen, Pete; Hendricks, Thos.; Kemp, Martin; Ories, Cornelius; Christians, David; du Plessis, Mikel; Hartz, Adam; van Haardt, Marthinus; Allison, Chas.; Zaccharias, Frans; Franks, Joseph; Geduld, James; May,

For King and Country—*continued*.

John; Osborne, John; Visagie, Abram; Prins, Wm.; Johnson, Samuel; Tarantal, Wm.; Hendricks, Abdulla; de Vrie, Fred; de Goede, Henry.

INDIAN BEARER COMPANIES.

Abdulrahiman, Kistna; Modaly, T. Munusamy; Chendriah, Muthlialaru; Maicken, Thima Marie.

S.A. PIONEER REGT.

Heard, Robert Alex; Rigg, Thos.

S.A. ENGINEER TROOPS.

Radwell, Philip Caleb; Wilson, Edward.

BASE DEPOT CO.

Sergt. Longden, Robert.
Pte. Markham, Wm.

PAY STAFF.

Staff-Sergts. Ramsay, John Greig; Sewell, Alfred George.

NATIVE LABOUR CORPS.

Sergt. Preis, Frants Johan.
Pte. Smart, Edgar.

2ND S.A. FIELD AMBULANCE.

Esson, Robert.

CENTRAL AFRICA.

1ST S.A.R.
Capt. and Adjt. Hearn.
Sinclair, Wm. Blair.

2ND S.A.R.

Lieuts. Bothamley, James Powell; Marshall, H. J. Corpls. Carswell, James Cook; King, Charles Edward; Keyser, Jacob Charles; McLean, Robert; Todd, Joseph.
Ptes. Venter, Rudolph Gideon; Daniel, Theophilus Charles; Rabie, Jacob Andries; McLean, Robert; Anger,

For King and Country—*continued.*

Samuel; Pretorius, Albert Erasmus Botha; Clover, George Martin; Goodrean, George Henry; Meyer, John Cloete.

5TH S.A.I.

Sergts. de Kock, Wm. Fredk.; Solomon, Sidney James.

Corpls. MacPhee, Edwin Cuthbert; Johnston, Alexander.

Ptes. Williams, John George; Miles, John Henry; McCann, Anthony; Dixon, Arthur Samuel; Whitcomb, Charles James; Hattingh, du Plessis Wilhelmus; Dixon, Bertram Elwin; Lally, Michael James; du Plessis, Barend Hermanus; Prosser, Ernest Samuel; Robinson, Victor Noel; Hoffman, John; Dalmane, Henry Alfred; Potgieter, John Andries.

S.A.M.C.C.

Col. Fairweather, James McIntyre.

S.A.M.R.

Capt. Clarke, Colpoys Brodie.
Lieut. Bones, Arthur Meyrick.
Lammas, Arnold.

S.A.M.C.

Tyacke, George Stanley.

5TH PERMANENT MOUNTAIN BATTERY.

Sergts. Bucholtz, John Andrew; Wray.
Pte. Pinnock, Edwin Victor.

RHODESIAN LOSSES.

2ND RHODESIAN REGIMENT.

Capt. McCarthy, W. O.
Lieut. Cartwright, S. (attached).
Sergts. Carter, R. A.; Bates, L.; Hurr, E. B.; Turner. F. G.; Faulkner, F. J.;
Corpls. Cox, V. M.; Morrison, R. S.
Lance-Corpls. Spencer, W. K.; Hamilton, J.
Ptes. Chave, J.; McRae, E.; Martin, L. A.; Vernon, E. H.; Wells, E. M.; Potts, G. C.; Townsend, C. S.; Nelson, W. A.; Puckle, O.; Jamieson, R. C.; Bolus, G. W.; Ely, T.; Kelly, P. D.; Partridge, G. A.; Schunck, G. B.; McLean, J. S.; Fraser, C. W.; Bennett, W. E.; Holmes, R. W.; Andreson, P.; Johnstone, R. H.; Seward, H.; Mellor, S.; Howe, H. J.; Doyle, A. T.; Alexander, V. C.; Seward, R. A.; Edwards, N.; Mandy, E. C.; Passmore, C. N.; Sutherland, J.; de Latour, C. A.; Blamey, W.; Moorhouse, W.; Green, A. G.; Becker, D.; Morris, D.; Taylor, H. G.; Richards, L. W. G.; Wilson,

For King and Country—continued.

J. H.; Liandee, C. E.; McDonald, J. A.; van der Walt, G.; Crossland, A.; Peacock, K. I.; Faber, O.; Taylor, J. C.

NORTHERN RHODESIAN POLICE.
Chaswenga.

S.R. COLUMN.
Major Baxendale, W.
Lieut. Ingpen, E. L. (N.R.P.)
Sergt. Simpson, J. F.
Corpls. Hou', F. G.; Taylor (B.S.A.P.)
Ptes. Stevens, W. (N.R. Rifles); Kemp, H. J.; Short, J.; Steele, H. M.; Hampson, F. J.; Curran, J.; Judson. J. W. (B.S.A.P.); Bradbury (B.S.A.P.); Williams, W. P.; Parrott, R. N.

·IST RHODESIAN NATIVE REGIMENT.
Lieuts. Piggin, P. L. (B.S.A.P.); Simpson, H. J.; Bridges, Eric Forster.
Sergt.-Major Jones, W. W. (B.S.A.P.).
Sergt. Selfe, E. C.
Ptes. Cumming, M. G.; Christopher, J.; Bullock, J. E. (B.S.A.P.); Hepburn, G. (N.R.R.); Wright, E. C.; Baines, E.; Selfe, G.; Coulthard, W. L.; Sinclair; Oliver, W. H.; Hughes, T. M.; Francis, V. N.

Postscript

One could ask why the war went as it did. One comment that has been made is that von Lettow fought like a Boer and Smuts like an Englishman. There is some truth in this assumption. Von Lettow, because he was able to travel light and live off the country to a large extent, was able to exploit the terrain and take advantage of the initiative. His strategies might not have worked in another country, but they certainly did in East Africa. Smuts could not have fought a guerrilla war: his mission and his forces would not allow that.

Von Lettow's soldiers were undoubtedly one of his greatest assets. East Africa breeds warlike men who responded well to the training and leadership provided, and they had the great advantage of being indigenous to the country.

Von Lettow's great organisational skill and general military expertise worked in his favour as well. It is not always appreciated that Germany produced the most scientific and highly-trained military officers in the world at that time. Provide a man of in-born military talent with these resources, then temper him in the heat of operations, and you have someone of the mettle of von Lettow.

There is another question which will remain forever unanswered: Should Smuts have contented himself with safeguarding the borders of British East Africa instead of driving into Tanganyika after von Lettow? After all, a German-held Tanganyika apparently would not have posed any great threat to the outcome of the war, which was being decided in Europe.

With a man like von Lettow at the helm nothing could be certain. Given his talents as a soldier and as a leader, it is not impossible that he might have raised a vast black army, overrun British East Africa and headed southwards, perhaps even threatening South Africa and its gold and diamond resources which were so important to the Allied cause.

It is often forgotten that in those days very small colonial armies held vast territories, and that control was always an uncertain and fragile thing. Von Lettow had proved to be more than a match for the Portuguese. Imagine a Mozambique partly or wholly occupied by his forces, poised to seize South Africa which was torn apart by its own internal divisions – to such an extent that the declaration of war in 1914 had sparked a rebellion. Smuts certainly believed that Tanganyika could have been the springboard of a fresh German war effort.

There is an even more fascinating bit of speculation. What if Governor von Schnee had somehow managed to keep Tanganyika out of the war, as he would have liked to? Could it, suitably fortified, have become a post-war German enclave, left alone by the war-weary British? It is a long shot, but it raises fascinating possibilities.

Then there is the question of Smuts's recall in early 1917. Why did Smuts leave then? Was it to extricate himself from a long and wearisome business, far from the centre of events, that showed no signs of an early resolution?

One can give Smuts the benefit of the doubt in this matter. He was not a quitter; moreover, to Botha it must have been quite obvious that Smuts was by far the most able man to speak for him in London. In fact, given his talents, it seemed a positive waste to keep him in East Africa.

Another mystery revolves around how much advance warning Smuts had of his recall. It seems likely that Smuts and Louis Botha were in constant contact by letters carried by reliable couriers. However, no trace of such correspondence remains. Circumstantial evidence would seem to indicate such an interchange existed, however, based on the closeness of the relationship between Smuts and Botha, the diamond-bright genius of the one softened by the warm-spirited nature and natural wisdom of the other.

And what of Smuts, the General? One can point to his deficiencies, and indeed he made mistakes which, in retrospect, seem obvious. But the fact remains that by the time he took ship for London he had conquered half of Tanganyika. The turning-point in the campaign had been reached and passed.

Willem Steenkamp

Bibliography

Books

Adler, F B, Lorch A E and Curson H H. *The South African Field Artillery, 1915-1919.* Pretoria, J J van Schaik 1958.

Armstrong, H C. *Grey Steel: J C Smuts: A study in arrogance.* London, Methuen 1945.

Beukes, P. *The Holistic Smuts – a Study in Personality.* Cape Town and Pretoria, Human & Rousseau 1989.

Birkby, C. *Uncle George.* Johannesburg, Jonathan Ball 1957

Brett Young, F. *Marching on Tanga.* London, Collins 1917.

Brown, J A. *A Gathering of Eagles.* Cape Town, Purnell 1970.

Brown, J H. *A Missionary in the Making.* Pinelands, Cape, J H Brown 1982.

Buchan, J. *Nelson's History of the War.* Vol. XXI, London, Thomas Nelson (no date).

Buchanan, A. *Three Years of War in East Africa.* London, John Murray 1919.

Campbell, W W. *East Africa by Motor Lorry.* London, John Murray 1928.

Cocker, M. *Richard Meinertzhagen.* London, Secker and Warburg 1989.

Collyer, J J. *The South Africans with General Smuts in German East Africa 1916.* Pretoria, Government Printer 1939.

Cooper, F H. *On Safari.* Juta 1917.

Crafford, F S. *Jan Smuts.* Cape Town, Howard Timmins 1945.

Crowe, J H V. *General Smuts' Campaign in East Africa.* London, John Murray 1918.

Dane, E. *British Campaigns in Africa and the Pacific 1914–1918.* London, Hodder and Stoughton 1919.

Deppe, L. *Mit Lettow-Vorbeck durch Africa*. Berlin, Verlag August Scherl G M B H, 1919.

Desmore, A J B. *With the 2nd Cape Corps thro' Central Africa*. Cape Town, Citadel Press 1920.

Dolby, R V. *Sketches of an East Africa Campaign*. London, John Murray 1918.

Downes, W D. *With the Nigerians in German East Africa*. London, Methuen 1919.

Fendall, C P. *The East African Force, 1915–1919*. London, H F and G Witherby 1921.

Gardner, B. *German East*. London, Cassell 1963.

Graudenz, K. *Die Deutschen Kolonien*. München, Wilhelm Heyne Verlag 1982.

Hancock, W K. *Smuts: The Sanguine Years*. Cambridge University Press 1962.

Hancock, W K and Van der Poel, J. *Selections from the Smuts Papers*. Vol 3, June 1910 – November 1918. Cambridge University Press 1966.

Haywood, A and Clarke, F A S. *History of the Royal West African Frontier Force*. Aldershot, Gale and Polden (Ltd) 1964.

Holdern, C. *Military Operations in East Africa, 1914–16*. Nashville, Battery Press 1990.

Huxley, E. *White Man's Country*. Vol II, 1914–1934. London, Macmillan 1935.

Lord, J. *Duty, Honour and Empire*. New York, Random House 1970.

Macfall, H. *Germany at Bay*. London, Cassell & Co 1918.

McCann, H. *Utmost Fish*. London, Heinemann 1966.

Miller, C. *Battle for the Bundu. The First World War in East Africa*. London, Macdonald and Jane's 1974.

Mosley, L. *Duel for Kilimanjaro, the East African Campaign 1914–1918*. London, Widenfeld and Nicholson, 1921.

Moyse-Bartlett, H. *The King's African Rifles*. Aldershot, Gale and Polden 1956.

Official History: SA and the Great War 1914–1918. Pretoria, Government Printer 1923.

Plomer, W. *A Passage to Africa*. London, Jonathan Cape 1957.

Reid, F. *Footslogging in East Africa*. Cape Town, Maskew Miller 1918.

Reitz, D. *Trekking On*. London, The Travel Book Club 1947.

Schindler, H M. *Die Deutschen Kolonien*.

Shackleton, C W. *East African Experiences 1916*. Durban, The Knox Publishing Company 1940.

Sibley, J R. *Tanganyika Guerilla, East African Campaign 1914–1918*. London, Pan Ballantine Illustrated History of the First World War. Book No 4 1973.

Smuts, J C. *Jan Christian Smuts*. London, Cassell 1952.

Spanton, E F. *In German Gaols*. London, University Mission to Central Africa 1918.

Steer, G L. *Judgement on German Africa*. London, Hodder and Stoughton 1939.

Stoneham, C T. *From Hobo to Hunter*. London, John Long 1956.

Thornhill, C J. *Taking Tanganyika*. London, Stanley Paul & Co 1937.

Timm, U. *Deutschen Kolonien*. Köln, Kiepenheuer & Witsch 1986.

Uys, I S. *For Valour: The History of Southern Africa's Victoria Cross Heroes*. Johannesburg, The Author 1973.

Van der Bijl, P. *From Playground to Battlefields*. Timmins 1971.

Van der Spuy, K R. *Chasing the Wind*. Books of Africa 1966.

Von Lettow-Vorbeck, P E. *My Reminiscences of East Africa*. London, Hurst and Blackett 1920.

Von Lettow-Vorbeck, P E. *Meine Erinnerungen aus Ostafrika*. Leipzig, Verlag von K F Koehler 1920.

Whittall, W. *With Botha and Smuts in Africa*. London, Green, Cassell & Co 1917.

Historical Magazines

Militaria, Vol 2/1, 1970. Ploeger, J. (Kol). *26-Eskader RFC*.

Militaria, Vol 7/1, 1977. Digby, E A. *Historical Records of the 8th SA Infantry*.

Military History Journal, Vol 4, No 1, June 1977. Maker, J G. *5th Mountain Battery SA Mounted Riflemen, narrative of the Right Section, Part 1*.

Military History Journal, Vol 4, No 2, December 1977. Maker, J G. *5th Mountain Battery SA Mounted Riflemen, narrative of the Right Section. Part 2.*

Military History Journal, Vol 6, No 6, December 1985. *The German East Africa Campaign 1914–1918.* Various Diary Extracts.

Military History Journal, Vol 7, No 3, June 1987. *German East Africa, the Diary of E S Thompson, January 1916 to February 1917.* Editor's Preface.

Military History Journal, Vol 7, No 4, December 1987. *Diary of E S Thompson, Part 1.*

Military History Journal, Vol 7, No 5, June 1988. *Diary of E S Thompson, Part 2, 25 May to 17 September 1917.*

Military History Journal, Vol 7, No 6, December 1988. *Diary of E S Thompson, Part 3, 18 September 1916 to 26 February 1917.*

Quarterly Bulletin of the SA Library, June 1973. *The East African War Diary of G E Lewis, 1916.*

Standard History of the All-Europe Conflict, Part 107. *The Conquest of German East Africa.* September 1916.

Standard History of the World Wide Conflict, Part 185. *The Conquest of German East Africa Completed.* March 1918.

Extracts from Newspapers, Letters, Diaries, Memoirs, Verse

Karonga Kronical (undated), Vol 1, No 1 (1916?)

Menkin, A A 'Incident with 9th SAI, 1916'. Cape *Argus* (undated).

Rand Daily Mail, 14 November and 18 November 1916. Cartoon.

SA War Museum, Johannesburg. Brochure on German East Africa. (undated).

Sunday Times, 12 November and 19 November 1916.

Sunday Times, 18 November 1916. Verse by T A A. 'Our Heroes Call to Slackers'.

The Morogoro News, No 1, September 1916.

Aubrey G C. *Diary, East African Mounted Rifles, 1916.*

Bisset, Chronicle of the Family. *In memoriam Ian Bisset, 8th SAI,* Private Publication, April 1917.

Bisset M. Scrapbook kept by schoolboy Maceian Bisset with article by A A Menkin on 'the creamy 9th' – the 9th SA Infantry in German East Africa.

Dowsett, S C. *Notes on East African Campaign 1915–1916.*

Dunman, (Ltd). *Note Book, East African Campaign 1916.*

Godbold, B. *Memoirs, Chapter 7, The Great Adventure.* Unpublished.

Guy, R T. *Scraps of Diary, East African Campaign, 1916.*

Hare, Charles. *Diary, East African Campaign 1915–1916.*

Jackson, J K. *Diary, 2nd SA Artillery, East African Campaign 1916.*

Molloy, A J (Major). *Letters to 'Middleman' 1916–1917.*

Notes on *South African crew in Royal Navy, 1915.*

Payne, J H A. *Notes on diary of Captain J H A Payne, 8th Batt SAI, 1916–1917.* Compiled by Julian Orford, 1986.

Pilkington-Jordan, Rupert. *Memoir on Smuts in 1916.* Written in 1967.

Richardson, E H. *Diary of Lieutenant E H Richardson, East African Campaign, June–October 1916.*

Simpson, Winnie. *Memoirs, Section 3, 1914–1919, the Benoni volunteers.*

Index

Germany:
Political ambitions in Africa: 1, 3-7, 20
Gibeon, German defeat at: 37
Gillett, M C: 136
Goldberg, Captain: 232
Godbold, Brian: 178
Gold Coast Regiment: 324
Gosch, Hans: 76, 77
Great Ruaha River: 223, 306, 315
Grenzboten, Die (political journal): 5
Guerrilla tactics:
Practised by Germans: 217-8, 224
Gusii people, revolt of: 15-16
Gwansawe Mission Station: 132

Handeni: 137, 175-6, 181-2, 187, 191-8,
215-7
Hannyngton, Brigadier-General J A: 156,
161, 187, 238, 247
Hassan, Ali: 275
Hemedi: 8
Henri Farman biplanes: 261-2
Herero people: 4, 12, 13
Heri, Bwana: 9
Himo River: 101-2
Hitler, Adolf: 331-2
Hodgson, George: 277
Holdern, Lt-Col Charles: 328
Horses, casualties during campaigns: 51,
132-3, 136, 221, 264, 292, 303-4, 307
Hoskins, Major-General Reginald: 156,
161, 204, 206, 217, 223, 265, 280, 314,
322
Hunter, G D, Surgeon-General: 117

Imperial War Conference: 310
Indian Mountain Battery: 76
Iringa: 223, 235, 307, 309

Jackson, Gunner J K: 116, 225-6, 227-8
Jasin, British defeat at: xv

Kahe: 103-9, 154-6, 160-1, 263
Kanga Mountain: 222
Kangata: 198, 202
Kasama: 328
Katsena, Awudu: 317
Kenya, subjugation of: 14-16
Kibara: 307
Kidete: 256, 257
Kikeo: 275
Kikombo station: 232
Kilimatinde: 223, 228
Kilossa: 223, 238, 251, 256-8, 265, 272,
295, 303, 307

Kilossa Hospital: 116
King, Norman: 25
King's African Rifles: 15-16, 19, 31, 89,
90, 93, 94, 237, 307, 311, 324
Kiroka: 261
Kissaki: 223, 262, 272, 275, 276, 279,
280-4, 292
Kissanga: 295
Kissangire: 108
Kitchener, Lord: xiii, xiv, xv, 80, 110, 310
Klinghardt, Captain: 139, 228
Kitovo, Battle of: 100
Kock, Nils: 315
Koehl, Captain, 97
Kondoa-Irangi: 121, 123, 126, 131, 134-9,
141-2, 144-9, 151-2, 174-5, 176-9, 223-
5, 227-8
Königsberg (naval guns): 107, 151,
167-8, 187, 225, 258, 314
Korogwe: 224, 295
Kraut, Major: 53, 66, 67, 72-4, 76, 82, 90,
99-100, 161, 166, 167, 169, 176, 181,
196, 199, 202, 204-5, 210,
221-2, 257, 314
Krige, Capt P S (Tottie): 56, 119
Kwa-Direma: 208
Kwa Mkalomzo: 314
Kwedihombo: 250

Laconia SS: 38
Latema Hill: 85, 89-91, 93-4, 97-9
Leipold (Intelligence Officer): 175
Leipzig (cruiser): 8
Lewis, Gunner G E: 78, 80, 102-3, 115,
116, 141
Lincke, Captain: 147, 308
Linkagara Mountains: 326
Lol Kissale, attack on: 123-4, 126, 131,
134, 174
Lossongoi Plateau: 154
Lowden, Lt J H (Jack): 194
Loyal North Lancashire Regiment: 311
Luchomo: 193
Lüderitz: 37
Lüderitz Bay-Keetmanshoop railway: 5
Lukin, Brigadier-General (Tim): 34
Lukiguru River, Battle of: 204-11
March from: 223-4, 238
Lusitania, sinking of: 42
Lyall, Colonel: 198, 202, 315

Machemba: 9
Mackenzie, General: 36, 37
Mahenge Plateau: 223, 235, 306, 308
Mahiwa: 326